HARDPRESS.NET
HOME OF HARD-TO-FIND BOOKS

Artis Logicae Rudimenta
by Henry Aldrich

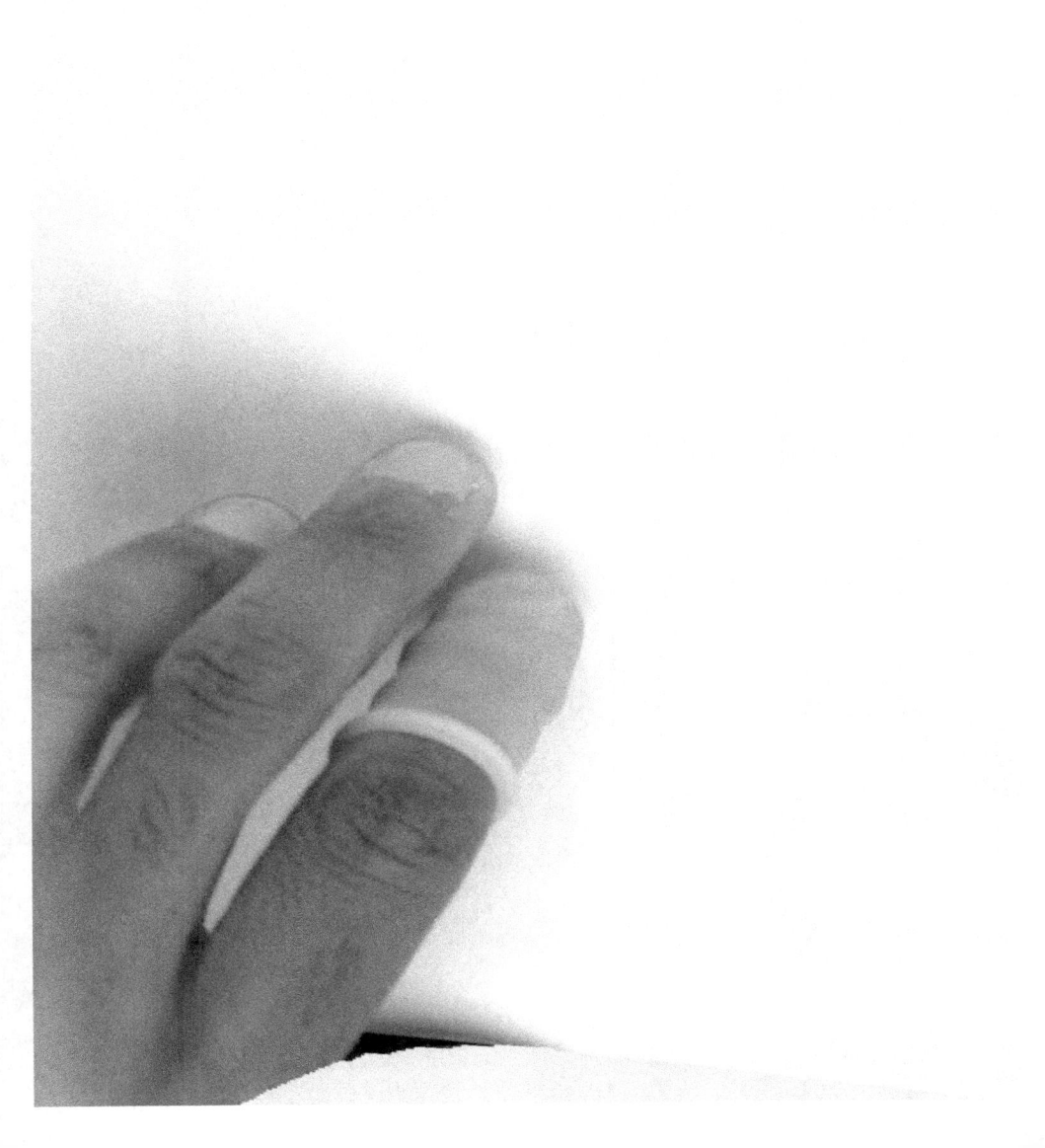

ARTIS LOGICÆ

RUDIMENTA.

ARTIS LOGICÆ

RUDIMENTA,

FROM

THE TEXT OF ALDRICH,

WITH NOTES AND MARGINAL REFERENCES.

———

BY THE

REV. H. L. MANSEL, B.D.

WAYNFLETE PROFESSOR OF MORAL AND METAPHYSICAL PHILOSOPHY,
TUTOR AND LATE FELLOW OF ST. JOHN'S COLLEGE.

———

FOURTH EDITION, CORRECTED AND ENLARGED.

———

OXFORD,
HENRY HAMMANS:
WHITTAKER AND CO. LONDON.
1862.

BAXTER, PRINTER, OXFORD.

PREFACE.

WHATEVER variety of opinion may exist as to the absolute merits of Aldrich's Logic, there are many considerations which recommend a new edition of that work, as by far the most convenient mode of supplying an acknowledged deficiency in the studies of the University. The majority of Teachers will probably agree with me in regarding the dry skeleton of a Latin Manual as better adapted to the discipline of beginners than any of the more elegant, but somewhat diluted Essays of the present day : to which must be added the consideration, that Latin is the original language of many of the technicalities of the subject, which cannot be so conveniently learned through the medium of a translation. But among the Latin Compendia, that of Aldrich has long reigned almost exclusively in Oxford; nor would it be easy to select any rival manual of such decided superiority as to counterbalance the evils necessarily attendant on all violent changes in a long-established system. Deficient as the work unde-

b

niably is in many of the prominent features of the
Scholastic Logic, its very deficiencies render it in
some respects preferable to a more faithful exponent.   The criticism of the present age has contributed much towards a more just appreciation of
the merits of the mediæval Philosophy ; but he
must be a bold champion of reaction who would
advocate the complete disinterment of the Logic
of the Schools.   Who would desire now to oppress
the Student with the heavy burden of modals, or
to bewilder him with the mysteries of *Suppositio,
Ampliatio, Restrictio,* and the whole farrago of the
Parva Logicalia ? Omissions of this character
may, with equal probability and more charity, be
attributed to the sound judgment of the University,
than to the decline of the Professorial System and
the incompetency of College Tutors[*].

On the other hand, it must be confessed that
there is much to be added to this or any other
Compendium, to enable it to meet the demands of
the existing University Examinations.   This will
at once be admitted by all who have had any
recent practice in tuition ; it may be easily ascertained by any who will take the trouble of comparing the contents of the book with those of
any of the present examination-papers.   To this
deficiency, the increasing study of the original
writings of Aristotle has not a little contributed.
But the transition from the bare text of Aldrich to

[*] See Edinburgh Review, No. 115. p. 195.

that of Aristotle is far too abrupt to be beneficial to the Student. Occasionally indeed he may recognise an old friend in a new dress; but the difference of language, order, and manner of treatment will conceal from the unpractised eye most of the passages in which his Latin successors have attempted any thing more than a bare translation of the words of the Stagirite.

In this respect, it is hoped that the numerous references to, and quotations from, the Organon, which will be found in the following pages, will contribute in some degree towards a most important object,—the clear discrimination between those portions of the system which belong to the original work of Aristotle, and those for which we are indebted to subsequent Logicians. For a like reason, in my references to the latter, I have occasionally endeavoured to furnish some information as to the author and the period of the innovation. Nothing is more strongly to be reprehended than the slovenly practice of referring in general terms to the Logic of the Schoolmen; as if every individual of that body had written a distinct treatise on the subject, or as if those who have were a race of harmonious commentators, whose labours exhibit a supernatural uniformity, such as tradition narrates of the translators of the Septuagint. What would be thought of a reference in general terms to the doctrine of the Greek Philosophers? Yet Aristotle scarcely departed more widely from Plato, than did Abelard from William of Champeaux, or Occam from Scotus. In some cases it is indispensable to the right understanding of doctrines and modes of expression, to know when and by whom they were first introduced into Logic. If, for example, as in the treatment of the Predicables and of Definition, we find language held neither by Aristotle nor by Porphyry, expressly insisted on by one sect of the Schoolmen, and as expressly repudiated by another, there can be no doubt what views, whether right or wrong in themselves, must be adopted as a necessary basis for the interpretation of that language.

Of my own very imperfect acquaintance with the post-Aristotelian Logicians, I am well aware. But when the alternative lies between the postponement of the present work to an almost indefinite period, and the attempting it from such resources as I can at present command, the necessity that has long been felt for something of the kind, will, I trust, be allowed as some apology for the deficiencies of the execution.

One other point remains to be noticed. In commenting, whether for explanation or correction, on the language of a manual so brief as that of Aldrich, there is no tutor but must have felt the difficulty of attaining the happy medium between dogmatic assumption on the one hand and prolix discussion on the other. It is possible so to bewilder a pupil with premises that he shall utterly lose sight of the conclusion : it is possible so to overwhelm him with assertion, as to leave him no choice but that of blind submission to the *ipse dixit* of his tutor or the *ipse scripsit* of his text-book. The same difficulty meets the editor. In controverting the positions of a work which for more than a century and a half has enjoyed the sanction of the University, somewhat more of the *verecunde dissentio* is becoming than can always be comprised within the necessary limits of a foot-note. The further discussion of such points in an Appendix has in some instances unavoidably produced a certain amount of repetition. This however, though injurious to the form of the work, will, it is hoped, not render it the less serviceable to that not inconsiderable class of students

οἷς οὐδὲ τρὶς λέγοντες ἐξικνούμεθα.

A few passages omitted in recent editions of the Compendium have been restored in the present. This, however, has been done but sparingly. An account of the *Arbor Porphyriana* has been transferred to the first chapter from its original place in the *Penus Logica*. The obvious utility of the insertion will, it is hoped, warrant the liberty in this single instance taken with the text.

The references to Aristotle have been adapted to the Oxford reprint of Bekker's text. In Germany, a custom seems to be gaining ground of referring to the pages of the Berlin edition, but that work has not been sufficiently circulated here to make the example convenient to follow. Of the Isagoge of Porphyry, Buhle's edition has been used. With the Greek Commentators, my chief acquaintance has been made through the medium of the Berlin Scholia collected by Brandis, to which, as the most accessible edition, reference has in general been made. Boethius is quoted from the Basel edition of 1570. The other quotations will in most instances speak for themselves.

To the present edition is prefixed an Introduction, containing a short historical account of logical writers, ancient and modern, which, though necessarily cursory and incomplete, will, it is hoped, be found more satisfactory than the notices which can be gathered from most English works of a similar character. In the compilation of this sketch I have derived considerable assistance from the valuable Essay of M. St. Hilaire; and in the revision of the earlier part, from the learned and able *Geschichte der Logik* of Prantl, the first volume of which appeared in 1855, and the second in 1861. Mr. Blakey's elaborate History of Logic has been occasionally consulted; but his principle of classification and examination is too different from mine to enable me to make much use of his labours. My critical views of Logic are briefly exhibited in the second part of the Introduction, and have been published at greater length in a separate work. Some apology is perhaps needed for the references to this work which will be found in the following pages, especially in the earlier portion. But I have long been of opinion that Logic, as generally taught, requires constant illustration from Psychology, and that the earlier part of Aldrich's text in particular is especially liable to be misunderstood without some such assistance as it was one principal aim of the *Prolegomena Logica* to supply. My obligations in the present work, as in that, to the writings of Kant, of M. Cousin, and of Sir William Hamilton, require special acknowledgment ; to these works must be added here the logical works of Professor Trendelenburg, Waitz's excellent edition of the Organon, and Biese's "Philosophie des Aristoteles." My thanks are also due to Professor De Morgan, and to Mr. Chandler, Fellow of Pembroke College, for valuable assistance in correcting the present edition.

INTRODUCTION.

PART I. HISTORICAL.

ALTHOUGH the writings of Aristotle are the source from which the science of Logic is principally derived, it is remarkable that there is no single name sanctioned by the Stagirite himself, under which can be comprehended either the whole collection of treatises known by the name of the Organon, or the whole subject of which they treat. Λογική, as the name of an art or science, is not to be found in his works, and the cognate terms λογικὸς and λογικῶς, are used in a very different sense from that which has subsequently been given to them[a]. The *logical syllogism* of Aristotle is opposed sometimes to the *analytical*, sometimes to the *physical*, sometimes to the *demonstrative* syllogism; and signifies a process of reasoning from general principles of probability, as distinguished from one of which the principles are elicited by special contemplation of a given object or notion[b]. It is therefore opposed, alike to the demonstrative reasoning, in which necessary truths are resolved into the axiomatic principles on which they depend, and to that by which physical phenomena are referred to general laws of nature.

The first use of the term *Logic*, as the name of a science, is probably later than Aristotle, and to be re-

---

[a] Cf. *Anal. Post.* i. 22. 16. i. 24. 11. ii. 8. 3. Top. i. 14. 4. *Phys.* iii. 3. 2.

[b] See Gassendi, *Logicæ Prœmium init.* Biese, *Philosophie des Aristoteles*, vol. i. p. 133. Waitz, *Organon*, vol. ii. p. 353. Trendelenburg, *Elementa*, p. 47.

ferred to Zeno the Stoic. The division of Philosophy into Logic, Physics, and Ethics, probably originated with this Philosopher[c], and the use of the name *Logic* in Cicero is principally in relation to the Stoical doctrines[d]. For the application of the term to the contents of the Aristotelian Organon, the Greek commentators upon Aristotle are our earliest extant authority. Alexander of Aphrodisias, the oldest of these whose works have come down to us[e], speaks of ἡ λογικὴ καὶ συλλογιστικὴ πραγματεία as containing under it ἀποδεικτική, διαλεκτική, πειραστική, and σοφιστική[f]. Here, while *Dialectic* retains its Aristotelian sense, *Logic* is extended so as to include the syllogistic theory in general, and its particular applications to necessary and probable matter. A similar extension of *Dialectic* is found in the commentaries of David the Armenian[g]; and Philoponus uses both terms as synonymous, and in the same extent[h].

[c] Laert. vii. 39. Pseudo-Plutarch, *De Plac. Phil.* i. 1. This division is sometimes attributed to Plato. (Cf. Cicero, *Quæst. Acad.* i. 19. *De Fin.* i. 22. Euseb. *Præp. Evan.* xi. 1. Augustin, *De Civ. Dei*, viii. 4.) But none of the three names occur in any of the extant Platonic writings; and a different division of sciences into *cognitive* and *practical* is intimated by Plato himself, *Polit.* p. 258. Indeed the state of philosophy in Plato's day would hardly allow of the Stoical division being made. Cf. Van Heusde, *Initia Phil. Platon.* p. 41. 117. Aristotle's supposed adoption of the same threefold classification is still more questionable; being founded on a misinterpretation of Topics, i. 14. 4. and at variance, as well with the earliest commentary on that passage, as with Aristotle's constant use of the word λογικός, and with his well-known division of theoretical Philosophy into Physics, Mathematics, and Theology.

[d] *Tusc. Quæst.* iv. 33. Cf. Trendelenburg, *Elementa*, p. 47.

[e] The Paraphrase on the Ethics, attributed to his predecessor Andronicus Rhodius, is spurious. Its real author is probably Heliodorus Prusensis. See Sainte-Croix, *Examen Critique des Anciens Histoires d'Alexandre le Grand*, p. 524.

[f] *Scholia*, p. 141. a. 19. The testimony of Boethius (*In Top. Cic.* p. 766.) would seem to refer this usage of the word to the elder Peripatetics, but we must reject his reference to Aristotle.

[g] *Scholia*, p. 18. a. 34. Waitz, vol. ii. p. 437.

[h] *Scholia*, p. 143. a. 4.

Two names sanctioned by Aristotle are applicable to parts, but to parts only, of the Organon. These are *Analytic* and *Dialectic*. The former term is applied by Aristotle to the four books which treat of the syllogism and of demonstration[i], and appears to denote the resolution of the reasoning process into its scientific forms. This word is the most nearly synonymous with the modern *Logic* of any used by Aristotle himself; but it embraces the process of Reasoning only, to the exclusion of Conception and Judgment[k]. *Dialectic* is a word pro- bably invented by Plato[l], though afterwards applied to the works of earlier philosophers, e. g. Zeno the Eleatic. In its Platonic sense it denoted the highest of all sciences; that which takes cognisance of the eternal and immutable, of being in general and its attributes, and thus has insight into the universal principles upon which all other knowledge is dependent[m]. It thus corresponds in matter, though different in form, with the first Philosophy or Theology of Aristotle, afterwards called Metaphysics. The name Dialectic had reference

---

[i] Galen (*de libris propriis*, ch. 11.) says that the title *Analytica* is not Aristotelian; the Prior Analytics being called by their author περὶ συλλογισμοῦ, and the Posterior, περὶ ἀποδείξεως. This testimony is accepted by M. St. Hilaire, *Memoire*, p. 42. But the name ἀναλυτικὰ occurs too frequently in Aristotle's own writings to warrant this view, unless we suppose (which is very improbable) that all the references have been interpolated by a later hand. Cf. Waitz, vol. i. p. 367. The distinction, however, between Prior and Posterior Analytics is not recognised by Aristotle, and we may perhaps conjecture that the name ἀναλυτικὰ was given by him to the entire four books, each division being also distinguished by its own title, as mentioned by Galen.

[k] Cf. *An. Pr.* i. 33. 2. Τοὺς γεγενημένους συλλογισμοὺς ἀναλύοιμεν εἰς τὰ προειρημένα σχήματα. Cf. Trendelenburg, *Elementa*, p. 47, Waitz. vol. i. p. 366. The *analytical method* of inquiry, attributed to Plato by Laertius, iii. 24. is his method of division, exemplified especially in the *Sophistes* and *Politicus*; though he does not give it the name of analysis.

[l] See *Phædrus*, p. 266. Laert. iii. 24. Cousin's Plato, vol. vi. p. 450.

[m] *Phædrus*, p. 276. *Sophist.* p. 253. *Repub.* vi. p. 510 sqq. vii. p. 521. 534. Cf. Van Heusde, *Initia*, p. 247.

to the colloquial form, which, whether in solitary meditation, or in conversation with others, Plato regarded as the true method of eliciting and communicating knowledge[n]; a view intimately connected with his doctrine of ideas, and with the theory which placed all knowledge in reminiscence. The Dialectic of Aristotle holds a far lower position, being merely the act of disputing by question; of attacking and defending a given thesis from principles of mere probability, such as the opinions of men in general, or of the majority, or of certain eminent authorities. The *Dialectical Syllogism* is thus the same as the *Logical;* and the names Logic and Dialectic, if used solely in conformity with Aristotle's authority, would correspond, not to the Organon as a whole, but only to the two last treatises, the Topics and Sophistic Refutations[o].

History of Logical Science.

Thus much may suffice, as regards the origin and use of the name Logic and the cognate terms. More important is the inquiry, to what extent the science itself, as exhibited in Aristotle, is indebted to the labours of previous philosophers. Dialectic, the thing though probably not the name, is regarded, on the authority of Aristotle, as the invention of Zeno the Eleatic[p]. By this

Zeno the Eleatic.

is probably only meant that Zeno was the first to employ dialogue as the medium of philosophical instruction; his predecessors of the same school, Xenophanes and Parmenides, having communicated their doctrines in verse. The dialectic method was afterwards extensively used by different schools, and for different pur-

[n] *Theæt.* p. 189. *Soph.* p. 263. *Phædrus*, p. 275. *Protag.* p. 329.

[o] *Top.* i. 1. 2.

[p] Laert. ix. 25. But in another passage (iii. 48.) he quotes Aristotle, as attributing the first written dialogues to Alexamenus of Styra. See also Athenæus, xi. 112. Cf. Tyrwhitt on Aristotle's *Poetics*, p. 3. l. 5. who conjectures that the dialogues of Alexamenus were written in metre.

poses, which ultimately obtained distinctive names. Aristotle enumerates four different kinds of reasoning, to which the colloquial form (τὸ διαλέγεσθαι) was applied, λόγοι διδασκαλικοί, διαλεκτικοί, πειραστικοί, and ἐριστικοί[q]. The first are demonstrative reasonings, from the proper and axiomatic principles of a given subject. The second, or dialectic reasonings in the Aristotelian sense of the term, are those derived from general principles of probability, such as the opinions of the majority of mankind, or of philosophers. The third are only a special application of probable reasonings to expose the ignorance of pretenders in science[r]. The fourth are fallacious reasonings, from apparent but not real probabilities. In a subsequent passage, he distinguishes between ἐριστικοί and σοφιστικοί; the former being such as employ fallacy merely for a display of skill; the latter, for pecuniary profit. Hence he defines σοφιστική as χρηματιστική τις ἀπὸ σοφίας φαινομένης[s]. These distinctions however will be of comparatively late origin; after the various applications of the original method of Zeno had rendered specific names necessary.

The eristic or sophistic was, as might naturally be expected, the earliest of these special developments of the dialectic method. The arguments of Zeno himself had no small affinity to sophistry; and the state of philosophy at that period was such as naturally to promote further advance in the same direction. The conflicting opinions of the pre-Socratic schools, the one-sided and exclusive character of their principles, The Sophists.

---

[q] Soph. Elench. 2. 1.

[r] *Kritik des dialektischen Scheins*, Kant, *Kritik der r. V.* p. 64. Kant is unjust to the ancient dialectic, when he describes it as a sophistical art of giving illusion the appearance of truth. The tentative use of dialectic very nearly corresponded with his own.

[s] Soph. Elench. 11. 1. 5.

combined with the universality of their aims, and the consequent failure of each in the attempt to resolve diffi-culties beyond their respective provinces—all this could hardly fail to produce a spirit of scepticism, which should end in denying the possibility of attaining to truth at all[t]. The decline of the philosophy of things was naturally accompanied by a corresponding rise of the method of words : the denial of all real truth stimulated the invention of verbal devices for producing the appear-ance of truth as occasion might require. Such was the origin of the eristic method of the Sophists. They employed it chiefly to enforce their leading dogma of the unreality of all knowledge, speculative or practical. Accordingly, they endeavoured, by ingenious applications of the dialectic mode of reasoning, to involve those with whom they disputed in self-contradictions and ab-surdities ; thus contributing at the same time to under-mine all fixed principles of knowledge, and to procure a temporary triumph for the disputant. With these practical applications of the dialectic method, seem to have been coupled corresponding speculations on the theory of thought, and of its exponent, language ; traces of which remain in the doctrine attributed to Protagoras, denying the possibility of falsehood in opinion or speech, from the absence of any objective reality in things[u]; and in the theory noticed by Plato in the *Cratylus*, which, almost anticipating the views of Hobbes and Condillac, declared the knowledge of things to be dependent on the right use of words[v]. At a later period, the eristic method was adopted and pursued to a con-siderable extent by Euclid of Megara, and his successors Eubulides, Diodorus Cronus, Alexinus, and Stilpo.

[t] See Plato, *Theæt.* p. 152. *Cratyl.* p. 386. 402. Van Heusde, *Initia*, p. 121.
[u] Plato, *Euthyd.* p. 286. Laert. ix. 53. See Prantl, *Geschichte der Logik*, p. 13. [v] *Crat.* p. 435. 437. Cf. Prantl, p. 18.

On the other hand, the method of Socrates partook largely of the πειραστική, or tentative, which Aristotle describes as follows, ἡ γὰρ πειραστική ἐστι διαλεκτική τις καὶ θεωρεῖ οὐ τὸν εἰδότα ἀλλὰ τὸν ἀγνοοῦντα καὶ προσποιούμενον. The opinion which Socrates entertained of the professions of his contemporaries, and his manner of exposing their ignorance, appears in his well-known explanation of the oracle which pronounced him the wisest of men[w]; and the same conviction and exposure of ignorance and pretension constantly appear in the Platonic dialogues, as well as in the *Memorabilia* of Xenophon[x]. For this purpose, he insists on the superior fitness of his own brief discourses to the longer mode of reasoning employed by some of the Sophists, and says that many orators can discourse ably at length, but that, if examined by searching questions, they are like written books, unable to reply[y]. In the same spirit, like Bacon and Descartes in modern times, he urges the necessity of a purification of the mind from prejudice and false opinions, as a necessary preliminary to the investigation of truth ; the principal means of purification being Dialectic[z].

In all this, as well as in the Dialectic of Plato, we find no anticipation of any important part of the Aristotelian Analytic; though the various modifications of the dialectic form may have contributed more or less to that systematized method of disputation exhibited in the two last treatises of the Organon. The antecedents of Aristotle's more strictly logical labours appear in other and more subordinate points of the philosophy of his predecessors. We may pass over, as unquestionably

[w] Plato, *Apol.* p. 21.
[x] Cf. Plato, *Sophist.* p. 230. Xenoph. *Mem.* iii. 6. §. 2—6.
[y] *Phædrus,* p. 275. *Protag.* p. 329.
[z] *Theæt.* p. 150. Cf. *Sophist.* p. 230. where the Socratic method is described, though Socrates is not the speaker.

forgeries of a later period, the Categories attributed to Archytas, and the other logical relics of the Pythagorean school[a]. There remain two important logical discoveries attributed by Aristotle to Socrates, Induction and Definition[b]. The Induction, however, of Socrates

Socratic Induction.

is not, like that of Aristotle, a strictly formal process of reasoning from the aggregate of particulars to the universal constituted by them. It rather resembles the Aristotelian Example or Parable[c], being a material inference from a selected number of similar or analogous cases to another individual instance under discussion. As a specimen, may be taken the following argument from the Gorgias. ΣΩ. Τί οὖν; ὁ τὰ τεκτονικὰ μεμαθηκὼς τεκτονικός, ἢ οὔ; ΓΟΡ. Ναί. ΣΩ. Οὐκοῦν καὶ ὁ τὰ μουσικὰ μουσικός; ΓΟΡ. Ναί. ΣΩ. Καὶ ὁ τὰ ἰατρικὰ ἰατρικός; καὶ τἄλλα οὕτω κατὰ τὸν αὐτὸν λόγον· ὁ μεμαθηκὼς ἕκαστα τοιοῦτός ἐστιν οἷον ἡ ἐπιστήμη ἕκαστον ἀπεργάζεται; ΓΟΡ. Πάνυ γε. ΣΩ. Οὐκοῦν κατὰ τοῦτον τὸν λόγον καὶ ὁ τὰ δίκαια μεμαθηκὼς δίκαιος; ΓΟΡ. Πάντως δήπου[d]. A reasoning of this kind has no place in a system of Formal Logic. That science recognises no inference that is not necessitated by the laws of thought; whereas in instances like the above, it is obvious that the premises may be true, and yet the conclusion false[e]. Or two specimens may be found, both complying with the above form, one of which shall carry conviction to every reasonable man, while the other is utterly worthless. Its *moral* force may thus vary " from the highest moral certainty to the very lowest presumption[f]." Its *logical* value is zero.

[a] See Hamilton's Reid, p. 686.

[b] *Metaph.* xii. 4, 5. Δύο γάρ ἐστιν ἅ τις ἂν ἀποδοίη Σωκράτει δικαίως, τούς τ᾿ ἐπακτικοὺς λόγους καὶ τὸ ὁρίζεσθαι καθόλου.

[c] Arist. *Rhet.* ii. 20. 4. Παραβολὴ δὲ τὰ Σωκρατικά.

[d] *Gorgias*, p. 460.

[e] Of which the above example is adduced as a specimen by Boethius, *Opera*, p. 600.

[f] Butler, Introduction to Analogy.

The Definition of Socrates has also more of a material than a logical character. He continually distinguishes between the essence and the qualities of a thing, and insists on determining what a thing *is*, rather than what it *resembles*[g]; a distinction afterwards repudiated by his disciple Antisthenes, who denied the possibility of real definition. But Definition, as treated by Socrates, is a contribution, not to Logic, but to Metaphysics. It does not analyse by the laws of pure thought the contents of a given notion; but endeavours to penetrate the real essence of things[h]. The same may in some degree be said of the Aristotelian treatment of Definition in the Posterior Analytics.

In the imperfect Socratic Schools, as they are sometimes called, Logic, so far as it was cultivated at all, appears to have gone back to the frivolities of the Sophists, instead of advancing from, or even retaining, the position gained by Socrates. To Antisthenes, the founder of the Cynics, are attributed two theories; the one a direct reversal of the teaching of Socrates; the other an apparent return to the sensational and verbal standard of Protagoras. The first of these denied the possibility of ascertaining the nature of any thing by definition[1]: the second denied the possibility of contradiction, and, by consequence, of falsehood[k]. The captious reasonings of the Sophists also appear again, as has been already observed, in the Megarian School, especially in its later development[1].

From the position constantly assigned to Socrates in

Socratic Definition.

Socratic Schools.

Plato.

---

[g] Cf. *Gorgias*, p. 448. *Theæt.* p. 146.

[h] Cf. Fries, *System der Logik*, §. 3. For specimens of the Socratic Definition and the Dialectic Method, see the inquiries into the nature of piety, justice, wisdom, &c. Xen. *Mem.* iv. 6.; of holiness, Plato, *Euthyphron*, p. 6.; of virtue, *Meno*, p. 72.

[1] Arist. *Metaph.* vii. 3. Cf. Prantl, vol. i. p. 31.

[k] Arist. *Metaph.* iv. 29. Cf. Prantl, vol. i. p. 31.

[1] Prantl, vol. i. p. 33.

the Platonic Dialogues, it is impossible to determine
with any accuracy how much of the doctrines and
methods advocated in those writings is due to the master,
and how much has been added by his disciple. From
the express testimony of Aristotle, however, we may
conclude that Socrates did not, like Plato, maintain the
existence of ideas separate from the sensible phenomena
of the world [m]; and consequently, that the exaltation of
Dialectic from its tentative use to the rank of the science
of absolute being, a view intimately connected with the
ideal theory, is due to Plato rather than to Socrates. To
Plato also probably belong in a great degree the methods
of συναγωγή and διαίρεσις, mentioned in the Phædrus as the
two principal parts of Dialectic, and illustrated at some
length in the Sophistes and the Politicus [n]. The former
consists in the collection of a number of scattered
objects, in reference to one idea, with a view to definition ;
the latter in a gradual dichotomy, by means of contrary
or contradictory members, so as to ascertain as accurately
as possible the number of subordinate species contained
under each genus. It is the careful performance of this
process, proceeding gradually through the intermediate
classes to the lowest, that especially distinguishes the
true dialectic method from the eristic [o]. These processes, for which Plato was perhaps in some degree indebted to the Eleatic and Megaric Philosophy [p], may be

---

[m] *Metaph.* xii. 4. 5. ’Αλλ’ ὁ μὲν Σωκράτης τὰ καθόλου οὐ χωριστὰ ἐποίει οὐδὲ
τοὺς ὁρισμούς· οἱ δ’ ἐχώρισαν, καὶ τὰ τοιαῦτα τῶν ὄντων ἰδέας προσηγόρευσαν.
  [n] *Phædrus,* p. 265. 277. *Soph.* p. 218. 253. *Polit.* p. 262. 286. *Phileb.*
p. 16.
  [o] *Phileb.* p. 17. With this may be compared Bacon's aphorism on the
importance of *axiomata media.* *Nov. Org.* l. i. aph. 19. Bacon indeed,
(aph. 105.) intimates that his own method was perhaps anticipated by
Plato, and this hint has been developed at greater length by Coleridge
in his *Treatise on Method.* But the accuracy of the parallel may be
questioned.
  [p] Cf. Stallbaum, *Prolegomena in Philebum,* p. 16.

regarded as the precursors of the Aristotelian doctrine of searching for definitions by the two opposite methods, afterwards known as those of Division and Induction[q].

In Plato we find also the analysis of the Proposition, with the noun and the verb as its constituent elements; the union of the two being necessary to every assertion. Διάνοια and λόγος correspond to each other as the ὁ ἴσω and ὁ ἔξω λόγος of Aristotle; the former being internal discourse without speech, the latter external, by the voice. Λόγος is divided into φάσις and ἀπόφασις[r]. In this passage, Plato has furnished the groundwork of the grammatical researches of the *De Interpretatione*.

The three highest laws of thought, the Principles of Identity, Contradiction, and Excluded Middle, are also indicated, though not explicitly enunciated, in Plato[s]. But neither he nor Aristotle has accurately distinguished between their very different positions in Logic and in Metaphysics. Indeed, this distinction cannot be considered as having been made with exactness by any philosopher before Kant.

Some few elements of the Logic of Aristotle thus Aristotle. appear in the philosophy of his predecessors; though the science was not accurately distinguished either from Grammar or from Metaphysics. A distinct treatment of logical questions was undeniably first undertaken by the Stagirite; though still, if we regard the Organon as a single work, with a considerable admixture of extraneous

---

[q] See *Anal. Post.* ii. 13. and Appendix, note C.

[r] *Sophist.* p. 262.

[s] The Principle of Identity may be gathered from the *Sophistes*, p. 254; those of Contradiction and Excluded Middle, from the *Republic*, iv. p. 436. the *Phædo*, p. 103. and the *Sophistes*, p. 252. 250. The two latter principles also appear in the *Second Alcibiades*, p. 139; but this dialogue is generally allowed to be spurious. Aristotle enunciates them more distinctly, *Anal. Pr.* ii. 2. *Anal. Post.* i. 11. i. 2. ii. 13. *Metaph.* iii. 3, x. 5. iii. 7. ix. 4.

matters, which a more accurate classification of the sciences would relegate to Metaphysics, to Psychology, to Rhetoric, or to Grammar.   But Aristotle must not be considered as responsible for the present composition of the Organon, but only for six distinct treatises, which his commentators have combined into one volume[1].   Of these, the latter part of the *De Interpretatione* and the *Prior Analytics* may be regarded as containing most of the essential parts of pure Logic; though, as regards the laws and forms of judgment in some degree, and of conception almost entirely, much must be added and much retrenched, before we can bring the entire products of pure thought into harmony with the elaborate development of the various forms of the syllogism.   The treatise on the *Categories,* with the early part of the *De Interpretatione,* is grammatical rather than logical, with a few trespasses on the domain of Metaphysics; while the *Posterior Analytics,* together with the *Topics* and *Sophistic Refutations,* contain applications of Logic to necessary and contingent matter in demonstration and dialectic disputation, and should be accurately classed rather as parts of the *Logica utens* than of the *Logica docens.*   But we are not justified in criticising the Organon of Aristotle as though it were a single work composed on a single subject.

Theophrastus and Eudemus.

Of the post-Aristotelian Logicians, my limits will only allow a very brief notice.   To Theophrastus is attributed the invention of the Hypothetical Syllogism, which was afterwards more fully developed by Eudemus and the

---

[1] On the composition of the Organon, some further remarks will be found, *Prolegomena Logica,* p. 261. (2nd ed. p. 280.)   The name *Organon,* according to M. St. Hilaire, was not habitually given to the collected works before the 15th century. *Mémoire,* vol. i. p. 19.   At an earlier date however this title seems to have been assigned to the Posterior Analytics, from which it was afterwards extended to the other works. Cf. Waitz, vol. ii. p. 293. Prantl, vol. i. p. 89.

Stoics. The Stoics have already been noticed as the
probable authors of the name *Logic,* and of the division
of philosophy into Logic, Physics, and Ethics. The
Stoical Logic, while it had less admixture of Metaphysics than the Aristotelian[u], embraced on the other
hand considerably more of Grammar and of Rhetoric.
It was divided into two parts, Dialectic and Rhetoric, to
which some added a third, the ὁρικὸν or doctrine of
Definition, employed as a criterion of truth[x]. Their
Dialectic, which also contained a considerable mixture
of Grammar, was defined as the science of rightly con-
versing in question and answer, as Rhetoric was that of
continuous speech, and was divided into two principal
parts; one of which treated of words, and the other of
the things signified by words[y]. It is criticised by Cicero,
as prolix in the treatment of judgment, deficient in that of
invention[z]. It also, particularly in the hands of Chrysippus, contained many of the same captious sophisms
which had occupied the Megaric School. Their Rhetoric
contained four parts, Invention, Elocution, Division, and
Action. Cicero appears to have entertained no very
high opinion of it[a]. But of the details of the Stoical
Logic very little is known[b].

The Epicureans, on the other hand, professed a contempt for Dialectic[c], and regarded Logic, which they

---

[u] See Trendelenburg, *Logische Untersuchungen*, vol. i. p. 21.

[x] Diog. Laert. vii. 41.

[y] Diog. Laert. vii. 43. 62. Seneca, Ep. 89.   Cf. Prantl, i. p. 414.

[z] *Top.* 6. *De Orat.* ii. 159.   With these passages may be compared the
following : Οἱ μὲν ἀπὸ τῆς στοᾶς ὁριζόμενοι τὴν διαλεκτικὴν ἐπιστήμην τοῦ εὖ
λέγειν ὁρίζονται, τὸ δὲ εὖ λέγειν ἐν τῷ τἀληθῆ καὶ προσήκοντα λέγειν εἶναι
τιθέμενοι, τοῦτο δὲ ἴδιον ἡγούμενοι τοῦ φιλοσόφου, κατὰ τῆς τελεωτάτης φιλο-
σοφίας φέρουσιν αὐτό, καὶ διὰ τοῦτο μόνος ὁ φιλόσοφος κατ᾽ αὐτοὺς διαλεκτικός.
Alexander in Topica, p. 3. (*Scholia,* p. 251. a. 22.)

[a] *De Fin.* iv. 7.

[b] St. Hilaire, *Mémoire*, vol. ii. p. 185.

[c] Laert. x. 31.   Cf. Seneca, Ep. 89.

called Canonic, merely as an adjunct to physical science. They paid no regard to Syllogism, Induction, or Definition, but confined their logical method to a set of rules for the investigation of physical truth[d]. A detailed account of these is given by Gassendi, *De Origine Logicæ*, c. 7.

The Greek Commentators.
To the Philosophers succeeded the Commentators. These contributed but little new material to logical science, but did a good deal for the explanation and illustration of the text of Aristotle, and assisted in some degree in fixing the language of the science[e]. The Greek Commentators on the Organon are principally valuable to a modern reader, from the interesting historical notices which they furnish of philosophers whose original contributions to the science have perished. Of the extant Greek Commentators, the earliest and

Alexander.
best is Alexander of Aphrodisias[f], whose eminence is testified by the title of *the Commentator* (ὁ ἐξηγητής), a title afterwards given to the Arabian Averroes. The school of Greek Commentators extends to the latter

Other Commentators.
part of the sixth century: the principal writers, after Alexander, are Themistius, Ammonius, David the Armenian, Simplicius, and Philoponus.

Porphyry.
The only important addition to the *matter* of logical science emanated from the Neo-Platonic school. The εἰσαγωγή or Introduction to the Categories, written by Porphyry in the third century, is the original source of

---

[d] Trendelenburg, *Kategorienlehre*. p. 232. Cf. Prantl, i. p. 402.

[e] St. Hilaire, *Mémoire*, vol. ii. p. 123, 145.

[f] Galen, in point of time, is a few years earlier than Alexander, but no important commentary of his is extant. Of the numerous logical writings attributed to him, there remains only a small treatise, περὶ τῶν παρὰ τὴν λέξιν σοφισμάτων, to which has recently been added the Εἰσαγωγὴ Διαλεκτικὴ discovered and published by M. Mynas. The genuineness of both is questionable, and neither is of any great logical value. Galen's invention of the fourth figure of Syllogism (attributed to him by Averroes) is doubtful. See below, p. 77, note x.

the fivefold classification of the Predicables, adopted by most subsequent Logicians. Whether this classification is an improvement on, or consistent with, the Aristotelian doctrine, admits of considerable question[g].

The Greek Abridgments of Aristotle, though in point of chronology they extend below the scholastic period, are in matter rather connected with the preceding series of Commentators. While the Scholastic Logic began in the extreme west of Europe, the Greek Logicians of this class belong entirely to the extreme east, or to Asia. John of Damascus, in the early part of the eighth century, made a brief analysis of the Isagoge of Porphyry and of the Categories, and is remarkable as one of the first who applied Logic to Theology. Photius, the learned and turbulent Patriarch of Constantinople in the ninth century, was the author of abridgments of the Categories and the De Interpretatione. Michael Psellus the younger, in the eleventh century, composed a Synopsis of the Categories and of Porphyry's Introduction. To Psellus has also been attributed a Synopsis of the Organon, published by Ehinger in 1597, the contents of which correspond almost to a word with those of the celebrated Latin text book of the thirteenth and following centuries, the *Summulæ Logicales* of Petrus Hispanus. The latter work has been by the majority of critics regarded as a translation of the former; but there are some difficulties connected with this view which have not as yet been satisfactorily disposed of[h]. The most remarkable work of this kind

Greek Abridgments.

Joannes Damascenus.

Photius.

Psellus.

---

[g] See below, p. 24, note q.

[h] That Hispanus is a mere translator of Psellus is maintained by Keckermann, by Buhle, and recently by Prantl. On the other hand, Sir W. Hamilton (*Discussions*, pp. 128, 673. 2nd ed.) is of opinion that the Greek is a translation from the Latin, and of course erroneously attributed to Psellus. The strongest argument in favour of the former opinion is the remarkable fact, recently discovered by Prantl, of the existence in manu-

Blemmi-
das.

is the *Epitome Logica* of Nicephorus Blemmidas, written
in the thirteenth century, which has been quoted as
containing the earliest instance of that system of logical
mnemonics which the schoolmen afterwards brought to
such perfection[1]. The list of Greek Logicians closes

script of other Latin compendia similar in contents to the *Summulæ*, and
having the appearance of distinct translations from the same original.
To this must be added the testimony of the Augsburg MS. used by
Ehinger, (now at Munich,) which is inscribed τοῦ σοφωτάτου Ψέλλου εἰς
τὴν Ἀριστοτέλους λογικὴν ἐπιστήμην σύνοψις.

On the other hand it should be observed,

1°. That there is in the Bodleian Library (Cod. Misc. cclxxv. f. 282. b.)
a MS. inscribed ἐκ τῆς διαλεκτικῆς τοῦ Μαΐστωρος Πέτρου τοῦ Ἰσπανοῦ
ἑρμηνεία τοῦ Σχολαρίου. This MS. I have examined in several places, and
find it to correspond exactly with the work published by Ehinger under
the name of Psellus. There are also extant four other MSS. having the
same title and the same beginning, (Διαλεκτική ἐστι τέχνη τεχνῶν καὶ
ἐπιστήμη ἐπιστημῶν,) viz. one at Florence, (Bandini, vol. iii. p. 19.) one
at Madrid, (Iriarte, vol. i. p. 276.) one at Vienna, (Lambec. vol. viii. p.
818.) and one at Milan, (Allatius apud Fabricium, Bibl. Græc. vol. xi. p.
392. Harles.) Of these the three last are expressly ascribed to Scholarius as the translator. A sixth MS. at Moscow with the same title
is mentioned by Fabricius, (vol. xi. p. 337. Harles,) but I have not been
able to ascertain any thing about its contents.

2°. It is evident that the Author of the Summulæ was very ignorant of
Greek. His derivation of *Dialectica*, " A *dia* quod est *duo*, et *logos* quod
est *sermo*, vel *lexis* quod est *ratio;* quasi duorum sermo vel ratio," could
hardly have been made by a translator from the Greek Synopsis, where
the derivation is given correctly.

3°. The only mnemonic which occurs in the body of the Greek Synopsis
is one for the opposition of modals, expressed by the words, δουλούμεναι
ἰλιάδες παρνασιὸυ ἐκτρέχουσι. The use of the diphthong would hardly have
occurred to an original writer, though naturally suggested by the *purpurea,
iliace, amabimus, edentuli* of the Latin logician.

On the whole, the weight of evidence seems decidedly in favour of the
opinion which considers the Greek Synopsis to be a translation of the
Summulæ of Hispanus, probably made by Georgius Scholarius, afterwards
known as Gennadius.

For some of the materials of this note I am indebted to a private
communication from the late Sir W. Hamilton, whose published opinion
has been referred to already.

[1] See St. Hilaire, *Mémoire*, vol. ii. p. 160. It may be questioned whether
the Latin Logicians are indebted to the Greek in this respect. See Sir
W. Hamilton's *Discussions*, p. 128, 671, and below, p. 84.

with the names of George Pachymeres of Constantinople, Pachy-
author of an abridgment of the Isagoge and the Cate-meres.
gories; and of Leo Magentinus, Metropolitan of Myti-Leo Ma-
lene, author of an Exegesis of the De Interpretatione, gentinus.
principally taken from Ammonius, and of Commentaries,
some of which are still unpublished. To this list, some
have added the name of George of Trebizond; but he, Georgius
though a Greek by birth, is better known as a resident Trape-
at Rome, and, as an author, by his Latin translations
and abridgments of Aristotle. His name is rather connected with a different phase of philosophy, with the
Platonic and Aristotelian controversies in the time of
Pope Nicholas V.

The progress of Logic among the Latins presents in Latin Lo-
one respect a contrast to that among the Greeks. With gicians.
the latter, the age of abridgments and distinct treatises
followed that of commentaries; with the former, it
preceded. The earliest work of a logical character in
Latin is the abridgment of Aristotle's Topics by Cicero; Cicero.
the object of which, however, is rather rhetorical than
dialectical. This treatise, which was written from
memory, differs in many respects considerably from the
original. After Cicero, we find nothing but a few
allusions to the subject in Quintilian and Aulus Gellius[k],
till we come to the short account of the doctrine of the
De Interpretatione and the Prior Analytics, written in
the second century by Apuleius. This occurs in the Apuleius.
third book of his treatise *De Dogmate Platonis*; and the
singular error of attributing the syllogistic theory to
Plato has caused the genuineness of this book to be
questioned[l]. The only other logical writings in Latin Augustine
before Boethius, are the two works attributed to St.
Augustine; the one, an abridgment of the Categories,

[k] See St. Hilaire, *Mémoire*, vol. ii. p. 165.
[l] Hildebrand, *De Apuleii Scriptis*, p. xliv.

now generally allowed to be spurious, but probably written about the same period; the other, an unfinished treatise called *Principia Dialectica*, the commencement of an essay on language with a view to disputation. To these must be added the singular allegory of Mar-

Capella. cianus Capella, on the Marriage of Mercury and Philology; a medley of prose and verse, composed probably towards the end of the fifth century. The Seven Liberal Arts, afterwards so celebrated as forming the Trivium, and Quadrivium, or Encyclopædia of the middle ages, appear in the following order, Grammar, Dialectic, Rhetoric, Geometry, Arithmetic, Astronomy, and Music[m]. Dialectic is represented as a female of a sour countenance, holding in her left hand a serpent, and in her right a hook baited with sundry formulæ. She discloses her wisdom by a brief abstract of the Isagoge of Porphyry and of the first three treatises of Aristotle. This is followed by an account of hypothetical syllogisms; and the lady is about to proceed to an exposition of sophisms, when she is interrupted and very summarily dismissed by Minerva.

Boethius. Boethius, in the sixth century, is the only commentator proper among the Latins. He has left a considerable number of valuable logical works, viz. two commentaries on the Isagoge of Porphyry, one on the Categories, two on the De Interpretatione, and translations of the other parts of the Organon; besides original treatises on the

---

[m] M. St. Hilaire has committed an oversight in citing the division of the Seven Liberal Arts from the Dialectic of Augustine. No such division occurs there; though one nearly the same is found in his second Book *De Ordine*, ch. 13. M. Hauréau (*de la Philosophie Scholastique*, vol. i. p. 21.) attributes the invention of this classification to Capella, which is hardly reconcileable with the above reference. The Seven Liberal Arts were afterwards exhibited in the following mnemonic:

" *Gram.* loquitur, *Dia.* vera docet, *Rhet.* verba colorat,
Mus. canit, *Ar.* numerat, *Geo.* ponderat, *Ast.* colit astra."

Categorical and Hypothetical Syllogism, on Division, on Definition, and on Topical Differences; together with a commentary on the Topics of Cicero. His works are of great importance in the history of Logic. They form the connecting link between the Greek and Scholastic writings, and were, with those of Augustine and Capella, the principal authority of subsequent generations, at a time when the Greek language was but little cultivated, and when the original fountains of logical science were consequently inaccessible.

Contemporary with Boethius was Cassiodorus the *Cassiodorus.* Senator, the author of a Treatise on the Seven Liberal Arts. His Dialectic contains a brief analysis of the Isagoge of Porphyry and the Organon of Aristotle, with additions, a considerable portion being borrowed from Apuleius and Boethius. His analysis of the Organon does not include the Sophistic Refutations, but contains a separate chapter *De Paralogismis,* which treats of purely logical fallacies. The arrangement of the work is by no means methodical, and extraneous matters are introduced which properly belong to Rhetoric.

The works attributed to Augustine, together with those *Early Mediæval Logicians.* of Capella, Cassiodorus, and a part of Boethius, formed the sole sources of the Latin mediæval Logic down to the twelfth century[n]. The materials furnished by these writings appear in the logical treatises of those authors who flourished previous to the rise of scholasticism proper, the principal of whom are Isidorus Hispalensis in the seventh century, Alcuin in the eighth, Rabanus Maurus and Scotus Erigena in the ninth, Gerbert, afterwards Pope Sylvester II, in the tenth, and the monks of St. Gall[o], especially Notker Labeo, in the early part of the

[n] Prantl, vol. ii. p. 2.
[o] For an account of these and other writers of the same period, see Prantl, vol. ii. sect. 13.

eleventh. From the middle of the eleventh century may be dated the rise of the Scholastic Philosophy properly so called.

The Arabian Commentators. The body of Arabian Commentators derive their appellation from the language in which they wrote: their places of residence were various, and none of them within the limits of Arabia. In fact, the Arabian literature did not arise till after the conquests of the successors of Mahomet had extended the Saracen empire far beyond the boundaries of their original country. Like the later Greek Logicians, the Arabians contributed little original matter to the science; their principal works being either translations, made sometimes from the Greek but more frequently from the earlier Syriac versions, or abridgments and commentaries. Of these the most important are the logical abridgments of Avicenna and Algazel, and especially the voluminous **Averroes.** translations and commentaries of Averroes. A Latin version of the translations of Averroes, made from a Hebrew one, was the principal source from which the earlier Schoolmen derived their knowledge of all the writings of Aristotle, except his logical works, which had been translated by Boethius. This barbarous version continued in use even after a more accurate translation from the original Greek had been made by William of Moerbecke, under the direction of Thomas Aquinas. The merits of Averroes as a commentator have been variously estimated. Ludovicus Vives speaks of him with great contempt. "Nomen est commentatoris nactus, homo qui in Aristotele enarrando nihil minus explicat quam eum ipsum quem suscipit declarandum." With this may be contrasted the eulogy of Keckermann. "Nemo tam veterum interpretum videri potest proximus Aristotelis menti atque hic Arabs." The modern critic will probably take a middle course between the two.

While his commentaries may be pronounced somewhat prolix, and inferior in elucidating the text of Aristotle to those of the Greeks, particularly of his rival commentator Alexander; his general view of the Organon and its parts has much of the clearness which distinguishes the abridgments of Avicenna and Algazel[p]."

To the Arabian philosophers may be traced the beginning of those attempts to fix the definition and province of Logic as a branch of mental science which afterwards appear in a more developed form in the writings of the Schoolmen[q]. To the Arabians also are probably owing some of the distinguishing features, though certainly not the origin, of the ¯Scholastic Realism.

The period at which the Scholastic Philosophy may be said to have commenced, is a point of considerable dispute. It cannot, like various Greek schools of philosophy, be traced to a single founder; but was the gradual result of a collection of various doctrines and methods of teaching. Some have traced it up to John of Damascus, and even to St. Augustine[r]. Some commence with John Scotus Erigena in the ninth century, some with the nominalism of Roscelin in the eleventh[s]; while by others it has been brought down, at least as far as Theology is concerned, as low as the thirteenth century, the era of Albertus Magnus and Thomas Aquinas[t]. The name of Schoolmen appears to have been taken from the teachers of the cathedral and conventual schools established by

The Schoolmen. Scholastic Philosophy.

---

[p] St. Hilaire, *Mémoire*, vol. ii. p. 191. Roger Bacon, (Opus Majus, p. 37. ed. Jebb,) speaks of Averroes as " Homo solidæ sapientiæ, corrigens dicta priorum et addens multa, quamvis corrigendus sit in aliquibus et in multis complendus.

[q] See below, p. lviii. and p. 21, note m.

[r] Brucker, vol. iii. p. 716.

[s] Hallam, *Literature of Europe*, vol. i. p. 18.

[t] Hampden, *Bampton Lectures*, p. 72.

Charlemagne and his successors, and was eventually applied to all who, whether professedly teachers or not, adopted in their writings the method and matter which finally formed the course of education in these and similar establishments. The distinguishing feature of Scholasticism, the union of a theological matter with a dialectical method, is found at least as early as the writings of Lanfranc in the eleventh century. Commencing from this point, Scholasticism may be divided into three periods. 1. Its infancy, extending from the eleventh to the middle of the thirteenth century. 2. Its prime, from the latter period to the middle of the fifteenth. 3. Its decline, extending to the end of the sixteenth century [a].

Scholastic Logic.

The Logic of the Schoolmen is a phrase frequently employed, and often very inaccurately. It is incorrect to apply this name to the various applications of the syllogistic method, in Theology, in Metaphysics, in Physics, or in Psychology. These are merely treatises on their proper subjects, with a somewhat more ostentatious display of logical art than has been usual at other periods. But the applications of Logic to reasonings on this or that branch of material science have nothing in them which is more peculiarly the property of the Schoolmen than of any other reasoners. The *Logica utens* is one and the same to all generations of men; all who reason soundly, reason consciously or unconsciously by logical laws; and the open display of the instrument in use does not make it a distinct instrument from that which others employ in a more concealed manner.

A historical account of the Scholastic Logic ought therefore to confine itself to commentaries and treatises

[a] Cousin, *Ouvrages d'Abélard*, Introduction, p. lxv.

expressly on the science; and the scholastic contributions to the matter of Logic should be confined to such additions to the Aristotelian text as have been incorporated into the *Logica docens.* In this respect the Schoolmen did much to fix the technical terms of the science, particularly in respect of the relation of thought to language. Most of the distinctions of the different uses and significations of words are due to them ;—distinctions, however, carried to an useless and wearisome minuteness in the grammatical subtleties of the *parva logicalia.* They also contributed considerably to that which is most wanting in Aristotle, an exact conception of the nature and office of Logic; though their definitions were not always consistent with the rest of their treatment; the text of Aristotle being seldom modified to suit the theory of the science. But the most remarkable contribution of this period is to be found in that singular system of logical mnemonics by which, from the time of Petrus Hispanus, nearly all the forms and processes of Logic might be learned by rote and performed almost mechanically, by the aid of a memorial word or line. The controversy between the Realists and the Nominalists, though introduced into the pages of professedly logical treatises, cannot be regarded as an accession to the science. Its real bearings on the text of Aristotle and Porphyry were not seen by the disputants on either side[x]; and the controversy, as conducted by them, must be regarded as a metaphysical excrescence, introduced out of its place in a logical system.

The earliest scholastic writings on Logic proper are those of Abelard, the greater part of which have recently been published for the first time in the volume edited by M. Cousin. This volume contains, besides a theological

[x] See p. 25, note r, and Appendix, note A.

treatise called *Sic et Non*, a fragment on Genera and Species, erroneously ascribed to Abelard[y], and some genuine logical writings, consisting of glosses on the original and translated works of Boethius, and a distinct treatise called Dialectica. The glosses are of little value, but the Dialectica is one of the most important monuments of the scholastic philosophy. At first sight it appears to be a commentary; but, though the titles of the work follow Aristotle, Porphyry, and Boethius, it is in many respects an original and independent treatise[z].

The writings of Abelard and his contemporaries in the early part of the twelfth century form the commencement of a new epoch in the mediæval Logic, which may be regarded as that of the scholastic teaching properly so called. In the previous centuries the Organon of Aristotle appears to have been directly known only in those portions which had been illustrated by the Commentaries of Boethius, viz. the Categories and the De Interpretatione, the translations of the other books being unknown. With the twelfth century commences a direct acquaintance with the entire Organon, partly through the translations of Boethius, and even with some trace of other sources[a]. The other writings of Aristotle appear to have remained unknown till a somewhat later period[b].

---

[y] On the authorship of this fragment, see Prantl, ii. pp. 101, 113, 143. He remarks that its true title should be *De Divisione*.

[z] Cousin, Introduction, p. xxiii.

[a] See Prantl, vol. ii. pp. 4, 98, 102. Cousin, on the other hand, (Introduction, p. li,) is of opinion that the latter portions of the Organon were not known at this time in any direct translation, but only through the writings of Boethius on the same subjects. A direct translation of these books certainly existed among the writings of Boethius, though it is uncertain when this translation first became known to the mediæval logicians.

[b] Abelard died in 1142. About the middle of this century the study of Aristotle's physical and metaphysical philosophy commenced, by means of translations of the Arabic expositions and commentaries of Alfarabi

Contemporary with Abelard was Gilbert de la Porrée, Gilbert de la Porrée. whose *Sex Principia*, an expansion of the six last categories cursorily treated by Aristotle, was adopted in most of the scholastic logical treatises down to the sixteenth century[c].

Towards the end of the twelfth century we come John of Salisbury. to a work of great importance in the history and philosophy of the scholastic Logic, the *Metalogicus* of John of Salisbury. The work purports to be a defence of Logic, under which is included Grammar and Rhetoric, against a sciolist of the day, to whom he gives the name of Cornificius[d]. It contains an interesting account of the author's own preparation for dialectic studies, notices of the origin of Logic, and a good analysis of the Organon with criticisms. Among other points, it is worthy of notice that he considers the Aristotelian doctrine of the predicables, given in the Topics, to be preferable to the common account, derived from Porphyry. He highly praises Abelard; and his testimony is the more valuable, as he himself appears to incline to the doctrines of the Realists[e].

Avicenna and Algazel. (See Jourdain, *Recherches Critiques*, p. 227.) Some of these expositions M. Jourdain supposes to have been the books condemned by the Council of Paris in 1210. Aristotle's own physical and metaphysical writings were probably not translated till about the middle of the 13th century, (Jourdain, p. 37.)

[c] Hauréau, *Philosophie Scholastique*, vol. i. p. 298.

[d] This name M. Hauréau explains as follows. " *Cornifex, Cornificius,* signifiera ' celui qui fait des cornes.' Mais de quelles cornes peut-il être ici question ? Sans doubt de ces *cornua disputationis* dont parle encore Cicéron ; ce qu'on appelle, en logique, les cornes d'un dilemme. A ce compte, nos Cornificiens auraient été d'aigres disputeurs, des logiciens acérés, d'intraitables sophistes." *Philosophie Scholastique*, p. 344. Prantl on the other hand, with more probability, supposes that a historical name has been figuratively applied, and traces the origin of the appellation to the poet Cornificius, mentioned in Donatus's Life of Virgil, c. xvii. " Cornificius ob perversam naturam illum non tulit."

[e] St. Hilaire, vol. ii. p. 215. His opinions in this respect however are doubtful. See Hauréau, vol. i. p. 354.

Petrus Hispanus. In the second period of Scholasticism, contemporary with Albertus Magnus and Thomas Aquinas, is Petrus Hispanus, raised to the papal chair as John XXI. He died in 1277. His *Summulæ Logicales* may be regarded as the earliest scholastic treatise on Logic which professes to be any thing more than an abridgment of or commentary on portions of the Organon. But this work is especially remarkable, as introducing for the first time the memorial verses which form so striking a feature of the Logic of the Schoolmen. Nearly the whole of the ordinary logical mnemonics occur in this treatise, which appears to have had no predecessor, except perhaps the imperfect syllogistic mnemonic attributed to Blemmidas, which, even if genuine, was probably unknown to the Author. The last treatise of the Summulæ[f], called *Parva Logicalia*, contains sundry additions to the text of Aristotle, in the form of dissertations on *suppositio, ampliatio, restrictio, exponible propositions*, and other subtleties, more ingenious than useful, and belonging rather to Grammar than to Logic. To these are added notices of some popular sophisms, worthy of Eubulides or Chrysippus; which are curious, as shewing that the Scholastic Logic, like the Aristotelian, had its eristic predecessors, whose names the reviving literature of the period has not rescued from oblivion.

Albertus Magnus. We now come to the two chief names in the Scholastic philosophy, Albert of Cologne, surnamed the Great, and his pupil, Thomas Aquinas, known as the Angelic Doctor. These have been called the Plato and Aristotle of Scholasticism; and, as regards the Theology of the Schools, there is some truth in the comparison. The master was the first to combine into a system the

---

[f] The original edition of the Summulæ is divided into two parts; the abridgment of the Organon and the *Parva Logicalia*. Subsequent Editors subdivide it into seven treatises. See Hauréau, vol. ii. p. 241.

unconnected reasonings which formed the beginnings of the School Philosophy. The disciple carried out that system in detail, and elaborated its minutest parts[s].

As a commentator, Albert was the main instrument in introducing the writings of Aristotle into the Schools; his laborious expositions, however, have been frequently corrupted by Platonic and Arabian glosses[h]. His logical works are comprised in commentaries on the Organon, and treatises on Universals and on Definition. Aquinas has left also commentaries on the Hermeneia and Posterior Analytics; and some independent logical treatises; the principal one being "Summa totius Logicæ," which contains an abstract of the Isagoge of Porphyry and of the first four treatises of the Organon. The Topics and Sophistic Refutations are omitted in this work; but the latter form the basis of a separate treatise on the Fallacies. He has likewise written Opuscula on Demonstration, on Modals, on the four Opposed Terms, on Genus and Accident, and on the Nature of the Syllogism. The directly logical writings of Aquinas do not materially differ from Aristotle. Logic, however, is defined as *scientia rationalis*, and the three operations of the reason are brought within its province. Some of the mnemonic formulæ occur here, as in Hispanus.

John Duns Scotus, the Subtle Doctor, flourished at the end of the thirteenth and the beginning of the fourteenth century. He has commented on the Isagoge of Porphyry, under the title of *De Universalibus*, and on the several parts of the Organon. In common with Aquinas, he held Logic to be a Science; but maintains

(margin: Aquinas.)

(margin: Duns Scotus.)

[s] Encyclopædia Metropolitana, art. *Aquinas*, (by Bishop Hampden,) p. 796.
[h] See Hauréau, vol. ii. p. 10.

that its object is not the three operations of the reason, but the Syllogism[i]. His commentaries bear out his cognomen; consisting for the most part of minute distinctions, suggested by the text of his author, with arguments on both sides precisely stated, and distinctions drawn to the extreme of subtlety. Scotus, like Aquinas, was a Realist, and the more consistent of the two. He held that the universal existed in the individual, not *really*, as his predecessor had taught, but *formally*[k]. Hence the rival sects of Thomists and Scotists, the latter of whom ultimately adopted the name of Formalists. Both agreed, however, in opposition to Nominalism.

Occam.

From the school of Scotus, however, arose the great reviver of Nominalism, William Occam, the Invincible Doctor, the ablest writer in Logic whom the Schools have produced. His doctrine, like that of Abelard, was really Conceptualism[l]. The *Summa totius Logicæ* of Occam is the most valuable contribution of the middle ages to the *Logica docens*. If we do not subscribe to the hyperbole of his editor, Mark of Beneventum, who, borrowing from the well-known eulogy of Plato, declares that if the Gods used Logic, it would be the Logic of Occam, we may fairly allow, with M. St. Hilaire, that it is the clearest and most original of the works of that period. Occam, like Petrus Hispanus, departs from the ordinary arrangement of treating consecutively the Isagoge of Porphyry and the several books of the Organon. He commences with the different divisions of terms, of which his account is much more complete than that of the *Summulæ Logicales*. He then proceeds to the predicables, introduced by a defence of the nominalist view of universals, then to definition, division, and the cate-

---

[i] Scotus *de Univ.* Qu. 3. *Smiglecii Logica*, Disp. ii. Qu. 1.
[k] On this distinction, see Hauréau, vol. ii. p. 385.
[l] See Cousin, Abélard, Introduction, p. clv.

gories, and concludes the first part with an account of the supposition of terms. The second part treats of propositions, and the third of syllogisms and fallacies.

Between Scotus and Occam comes in order of time the most eccentric genius of the scholastic period, Raymond Lully. He is principally known as the author of the *Ars Magna*, by which he professed to teach a man ignorant even of letters the whole encyclopædia in the course of three months. This work is nominally logical, but has little in common with the Aristotelian Logic, being principally a mechanical contrivance for connecting different philosophical terms with each other[m]. But in his *Dialectica*, Lully condescends to follow the beaten track, and has composed a clear and concise synopsis of Logic, framed principally on that of Petrus Hispanus[n].

The writings of Occam, as well as those of Scotus, contributed especially to raise Logic to the rank of a distinct science, independent of its applied uses[o]. But they approached it from opposite sides. The principles of Occam, developed by modern philosophy, would lead us to the Logic of Kant: those of Scotus, almost to the Logic of Hegel. The science of the former would acquire a clear and distinct object in the province of Thought: that of the latter would gradually absorb all else, as coextensive with Being. Occam is the last great

Raymond Lully.

Later Schoolmen.

[m] St. Hilaire, *Mémoire*, vol. ii. p. 225.
[n] An account of Lully's system will be found in Keckermann, *Præcognita*, ii. 2. 39. and in Gassendi, *de Origine Logicæ*, c. 8. See also Hallam, *Literature of Europe*, vol. i. p. 310.
[o] Cf. Hauréau, vol. ii. p. 310. 425. 447 sqq. St. Hilaire, vol. ii. p. 226. M. Hauréau appears to regard Scotus as the author of the distinction between the *logica docens* and *utens;* which is not the case. Cf. Aquinas, *in* iv. *Metaph.* Lect. 4. Indeed, it is substantially contained in the διαλεκτικὴ χωρὶς πραγμάτων and ἐν χρήσει πραγμάτων of the Greek Interpreters.

name among the Schoolmen: the triumph of Nominalism involved the downfall of the principal applications of the scholastic method. Buridan, his disciple, the reputed author of the sophism called *Asinus Buridani*[p], developed the doctrines of Nominalism to a still further extent, but has the character of having pushed to an extreme point the subtleties distinctive of the scholastic system. Another philosopher of the same period, Walter Burley, is the author of some commentaries on the Logic and Physics of Aristotle, and deserves mention as the author of an attempt to extend the narrow historical knowledge of the period by a work entitled *de vita et moribus philosophorum et poetarum*. This work, of which the philosophical portion extends from Thales to Seneca, is in part compiled from Laertius, whose work the author seems to have possessed in a more complete form than that which is now extant[q]. In itself however it is of small value and contains many errors[r].

The reaction against the Scholastic Logic began in the fifteenth century. Laurentius Valla, Rodolphus Agricola, and Ludovicus Vives, successively attacked the system in 1440, 1516[s], and 1531. Their attacks were directed, partly against the Latinity, partly against the matter of the School Logic. The additions proposed by these reformers are chiefly rhetorical innovations from Cicero and Quintilian.

Buridan.

Burley.

Early Reformers.

---

[p] See Hamilton on Reid, p. 238.

[q] See Donaldson, *Literature of Ancient Greece*, iii. p. 280.

[r] Brucker, vol. iii. p. 856. Tennemann, viii. p. 906. Burley appears to have held a middle course between Nominalism and Realism. See Hauréau, vol. ii. p. 476. Brucker classes him with the nominalists, Tennemann with the realists.

[s] Agricola died in 1485. His three books *De Inventione Dialectica* were a posthumous work, first published in an imperfect form at Louvain in 1516.

A more formidable assault was made in 1543 by Ramus, Ramus. who not only devoted a special work to the criticism of Aristotle[t], but, adopting the dialectical and rhetorical innovations of the earlier reformers, composed a new system of Logic in opposition to the Aristotelian. He complains of the want of a definition of Logic in Aristotle, and treats it himself as the *Art of Dissertation;* its principal parts being *Invention* and *Judgment.* These he investigates at length in his *Dialecticæ Institutiones* and *Scholæ Dialecticæ,* and in his *Dialectique,* the earliest work on the subject in the French language. *Invention* he treats chiefly rhetorically, giving an account of arguments artificial and inartificial, and loci for establishing them. *Argument* in Ramus denotes any term of a question, not, as in Cicero, the middle. Of *Judgment* he admits three degrees, Axiom, (proposition,) Syllogism, and Method. In the earlier editions of his Dialectic he admits the three Aristotelian figures, but afterwards rejects the third. Each figure has six moods, two *general* (universal), two *special* (particular), and two *proper* (singular). Method he divides into *Methodus Doctrinæ,* and *Methodus Prudentiæ.* He rejects, as extralogical, the Categories, the Hermeneia, and the Examination of Fallacies. Ramus, as may be seen even from the above cursory notice, introduced many needless alterations in the language of Logic. In his logical innovations, he is partly indebted to Rodolphus Agricola and Johannes Sturmius; and, for some of his attacks on the Aristotelians, to Valla and Vives[u].

---

[t] *Aristotelicæ Animadversiones,* a title also given to the *Scholæ Dialecticæ.* The two works must not be confounded together.

[u] For a fuller account of Ramus and his system, see Waddington-Kastus, *De Petri Rami Vita, Scriptis, Philosophia,* Paris, 1848.

On the other hand, the Aristotelian Logic, purified of many of its scholastic accessions, was defended and taught by Melanchthon. The earlier editions of his *Erotemata Dialectica* preceded the attacks of Ramus[*]; but in 1547 he published a new edition, in the introduction to which he says, " Ego veram, incorruptam, nativam Dialecticen, qualem et ab Aristotele et aliquot ejus non insulsis interpretibus, ut ab Alexandro Aphrodisiensi et Boethio accepimus, prædico. . . . Etsi multi Aristotelicos libros vituperant, et tanquam tabulas dispersas fractæ navis esse dicunt, tamen, si quid ego judicare possum, affirmo eos Dialecticen recte tradere, et ab iis, qui liberali doctrina exculti sunt, intelligi posse." Melanchthon however agrees with Ramus in considering Logic as an Art. " Dialectica," he says, " est ars seu via recte, ordine, et perspicue docendi ; quod fit recte definiendo, dividendo, argumenta vera connectendo, et male cohærentia seu falsa retexendo et refutando." Under their united sanction, this became the prevailing doctrine of Logicians. The authority of Melanchthon established the Aristotelian Logic in the Protestant schools of Germany and Holland, and in Britain. At a later period, a conciliation was attempted between this system and that of Ramus. Burgersdyck, in 1626, classes the Logicians of his day in three schools, the Aristotelians, the Ramists, and the mixed school represented by Keckermann, Aristotelian in matter, Ramist in method[y]. These were called Philippo-Ramists, or Semi-Ramists ; and were rejected by the genuine disciples of Ramus, as Pseudo-Ramists. Among the English Ramists of the seventeenth century, the most learned

Later Logicians.

---

[*] Keckermann, *Præcognita*, Tr. ii. c. v.

[y] Of these, Sanderson says, " Invehuntur ipsi palam in Rameos, laudant Peripateticos : sed tamen in Systematibus suis Logicis Ramei magis sunt quam Peripatetici."

and important as a Logician is George Downame, Downame. Prælector of Logic at Cambridge, afterwards Bishop of Derry, the author of a Commentary on the Dialectic of Ramus; but the name most interesting to the general reader is that of John Milton, who published Milton. in 1672, two years before his death, a small volume entitled, " Artis Logicæ Plenior Institutio ad Petri Rami Methodum concinnata."

It would be impossible to give any thing like a complete history, or even a list, of the host of logical writers of the sixteenth and subsequent centuries. A brief account of most of them, down to his own time, will be found in the *Præcognita* of Keckermann, published in 1603. A cursory account of the modern schools is all that my present limits will allow.

Of the great schools of modern philosophy, down to Modern Logicians. the time of Kant, it is remarkable, that, though we have no treatise on Logic from the hand of any of the leaders and representatives of the several sects, we find in every case a work of the kind supplied and adapted to their fundamental principles by one or more of their most eminent followers. Bacon, Descartes, and Locke have left no logical writings, and Leibnitz only a few fragments. To call the *Novum Organum,* or the *Discours de la Méthode*[z], or the *Conduct of the Understanding,* a treatise on Logic, is simply to assume for the Aristotelian Logic a purpose never contemplated by Aristotle or his followers, and then to classify under the same head works pursuing this supposed end by totally different

---

[z] The *Regulæ ad directionem ingenii,* a posthumous work of Descartes, is sometimes called his Logic. See Hallam, *Literature of Europe,* vol. ii. p. 454 ; Franck, *Histoire de la Logique,* p. 250. But Descartes in this work expressly rejects the rules and forms of Logic, as useless for the discovery of truth, and mentions in one place (rule 13.) the only point in which his system has any thing in common with the dialecticians. In fact, this work, though fuller, is in principle the same as the *Discours de la Méthode.*

means.   To entitle any work to be classed as the Logic
of this or that school, it is at least necessary that it
should, in common with the Aristotelian Logic, adhere
to the syllogistic method, whatever modifications or
additions it may derive from the particular school of its
author.   In this point of view, the Baconian school may
be represented by the Logics of Hobbes and Gassendi ;
the Cartesian, by those of Clauberg and Arnauld; that
of Locke, by Le Clerc and 'S Gravesande[a]; that of
Leibnitz, by Wolf, Baumgarten, and his editor Meyer.

Hobbes. The Logic of Hobbes was the natural result of the
utilitarian spirit predominant in the method of Bacon.
The results, indeed, which Hobbes deduced, would probably in many points have been rejected by his master ;
but the indirect influence of Bacon is manifest throughout.   The end of knowledge, according to Hobbes,
is power, and the scope of all speculation is the performance of some action, or thing to be done.   In this we
recognise the echo of the words of Bacon, " Meta scien-
tiarum vera et legitima non alia est quam ut dotetur vita
humana novis inventis et copiis[b]."   Reasoning, according to Hobbes, is computation, the adding and sub-

---

[a] The sensationalist school of France, professing to be an offshoot of that
of Locke, has produced more than one treatise nominally on Logic ; the
principal ones being those of Condillac and Déstutt de Tracy.   But
these have nothing in common with the Aristotelian system.   Condillac
regards Logic as an art of thinking, but thought is identified with sensation,
and the process of reasoning is nothing but the analysis of our sensations
by means of language.   Hence his declaration, *tout l'art de raisonner se réduit
à l'art de bien parler.*   In the system of De Tracy, Logic is the science of
the characteristics and causes of truth and error in the combination of
our ideas.   His work is strictly psychological, examining, on the extreme
sensationalist hypothesis, into the formation of ideas and their different
modes of combination.

[b] *Nov. Org.* P. 1. Aph. 81.   In the same spirit Socrates, according to
Xenophon, μέχρι τοῦ ὠφελίμου πάντα καὶ αὐτὸς συνεπεσκόπει καὶ συνδιεξήει
τοῖς συνοῦσιν.   *Mem.* iv. 7.   On the influence of Bacon on Hobbes, see
Morell, *Hist. of Modern Philosophy,* vol. i. p. 86.

tracting of our thoughts and of their signs. A proposition is but the addition of two names, and a syllogism the adding together of three. In a proposition, two names are so coupled together, that he that speaks conceives both to be names of the same thing; from whence it follows that truth and falsehood consist only in speech, and that the first truths were arbitrarily made by those who first imposed names on things. A full criticism of this doctrine would exceed my present limits. I can only observe that the main error of Hobbes does not lie, as is sometimes said, in his theory of *notions*, but in that of *judgments*. He has overlooked the fact, that apprehension is primarily the analysis of judgment, not judgment the synthesis of apprehensions.

The Baconian influence is also manifest in Gassendi, Gassendi. the friend of Hobbes and the antagonist of Descartes. Like Hobbes, he describes reasoning as a computation, and he anticipates Condillac in tracing all knowledge to sensation. He adopts the fourfold division of Logic, into Apprehension, Judgment, Reasoning, and Method, which had virtually been invented by Ramus and accepted by the Semi-Ramists, and which was shortly afterwards adopted by the Port Royal Logic. He admits two figures only of Syllogism, an affirmative and a negative, (answering to the affirmative and negative moods of the first figure in Aristotle;) and it is worthy of remark, that in the order of the premises, he returns to the arrangement of the Greek Logicians, (the reverse of that of the Latins,) and places the minor before the major. His theory of reduction, by which he brings every syllogism ostensively to his two figures, contains some curious blunders.

Clauberg, called by Wolf *optimus omnium confessione* Clauberg. *Cartesii interpres*[c], published his *Logica Vetus et Nova*

[c] *Ontologia*, §. 7.

in 1654. It contains more of Cartesianism even than the Port Royal Logic, and is divided into four parts, *Logica Genetica, Logica Analytica, Hermeneutica Genetica,* and *Hermeneutica Analytica.* The two last parts are a series of rules for interpreting and criticising the writings of others. The second treats of methods of teaching, and the qualifications for a good teacher and learner. The first, or Logic proper, is interspersed with numerous psychological precepts, chiefly taken from the *Discours de la Méthode* of Descartes. Many of his examples are also taken from the Cartesian philosophy. His rules for induction are fuller than in the old Logic, and those of syllogism shorter.

Port Royal Logic. The Port Royal Logic, or Art of Thinking, is considered as the Logic *par excellence* of the Cartesian school. This work has been attributed to several authors; but is now generally allowed to have been written by Arnauld, assisted by Nicole. The first edition appeared in 1662. In addition to the logical merits of this work [d], the elegance and simplicity of its style contributed immensely to spread and popularize doctrines which had hitherto been reserved for the study of the learned in the dry formulas of the schools [e]. The authors, however, must be admitted to have sacrificed in some degree scientific accuracy to popularity; and in their attempt to convey miscellaneous instruction in logical examples, they have unfortunately given their high authority to the support of that spurious utilitarianism which has so often defaced the simplicity of logical science.

Buffier. Father Buffier is also entitled to honourable mention among the French Logicians. In his *Principes du*

[d] For an account of the scientific merits of the Port Royal Logic, see the Introduction to Mr. Baynes's Translation, p. xxix.

[e] St. Hilaire, vol. ii. p. 271.

Raisonnement, the rules of the syllogism are reduced to a single principle, *that which is in the contained is in the containing*. This formula, an important step towards the true law of syllogism, the Principle of Identity, is perhaps originally due to Leibnitz[f]. Buffier has had the good fortune to receive high praise from two very opposite quarters, and on very different grounds. He has been celebrated, on the one hand, as one of the earliest who attempted to found philosophy on certain primary truths, given in certain primary sentiments or feelings; and, on the other hand, as having advanced some important steps in the direction of the sensationalism of Condillac[s].

Le Clerc, (Joannes Clericus,) the friend and disciple Le Clerc. of Locke, published his Logic in 1692, three years after the first edition of Locke's Essay, of which he had previously seen the Epitome. This work is principally based on the views of Locke, with some additions from the Port Royal Logic, and the Recherche de la Vérité of Malebranche. The fourth book, on Argumentation, does not materially differ from the Aristotelian view; though, like Locke, he has not a high opinion of the syllogism, and considers it to be mainly an instrument of disputation. He adds a chapter on the Socratic method of discussion, which he considers more valuable than the Aristotelian syllogism. The Logic and Metaphysics of 'S Gravesande, published in 1736, is highly 'S Gravesande. praised by M. St. Hilaire, as simplifying with great clearness the ancient Logic, in connection with the principles of Locke. The doctrines of Locke, modified by Cartesianism, had also considerable influence on the Logic of Watts, in which a somewhat incongruous union Watts.

[f] See St Hilaire, vol. ii. p. 274.
[s] See Hamilton on Reid, p. 786. and Destutt-Tracy, *Elémens d'Idéologie*, P. iii. p. 130.

of Logic, Metaphysics, Psychology, and Educational Precepts is put forth as the Art of using Reason well in our inquiries after truth, and the communication of it to others. Equally vague in its conception and unsystematic in its

Bentham. contents is the fragment on Logic by Jeremy Bentham. According to his definition, Logic is " the art which has for its object or end in view, the giving, to the best advantage, direction to the human mind, and thence to the human frame, in its pursuit of any object or purpose to the attainment of which it is capable of being applied." In the same spirit as Hobbes, he considers Logic from the utilitarian point of view, as a means to the augmentation of happiness. But the treatise, except as regards some severe and by no means just criticisms of Sanderson, has little in common with the Aristotelian system. A more just and philosophical view of Logic will be

Kirwan. found in the works of another English writer, Dr. Kirwan, whose " Logic, an Essay on the elements, principles, and different modes of Reasoning," was published in 1807. Dr. Kirwan deserves honourable mention as one who has profited by, without servilely following, the teaching of Locke. While adopting much that is valuable in the writings of Locke and his successors, particularly Berkeley and Condillac, he has ably defended the Aristotelian Logic against the depreciating criticisms of Locke and his followers. He has however taken too narrow a view of the field of Logic, in confining it to the single process of Argumentation, in which, as well as in his definition of it as both a Science and an Art, he has been followed by Archbishop Whately; while, on the other hand, his treatment of the argumentative process contains much which from the formal point of view must be condemned as extralogical.

Wolf. The most important work on Logic from the School of Leibnitz is the *Philosophia Rationalis* of Wolf, first published in 1728. Wolf is regarded by Kant as the representative of the dogmatic philosophy. Philosophy with Wolf is the science of things possible, so far as they are possible, and contains three principal branches, Theology, Psychology, and Physics. The criterion of the possible is the principle of contradiction. Whatever is not contradictory is possible[h]. Logic directs the mind in the knowledge of all being; its principles being drawn on the one side from Ontology, on the other from Psychology. The *Logica Docens* is defined by Wolf as a Practical Science; the *Logica Utens* as an Art; the former being acquired by teaching, the latter by practice. The details of Wolf's Logic are principally Aristotelian, with one or two ingenious but perverse refinements. Thus, he reduces subaltern opposition to a syllogism with an identical minor premise, and all immediate consequences to abridged hypothetical syllogisms. Induction he regards, like Archbishop Whately, as a syllogism with the major premise suppressed. Wolf is also the author of a smaller Logic in German, of which there is a good English translation, published in 1770.

To the same school as Wolf belong Baumgarten and Meyer. Baumgarten is highly praised by Kant for his concentration of the Wolfian system. An annotated copy of Meyer's Logic is the foundation of that of Kant himself[i]. Baumgarten, Meyer.

Lambert, whose *Neues Organon* appeared in 1764, may be regarded as uniting in a great measure the doctrines of the antagonist schools of Locke and Leibnitz, and as the precursor of the Critique of Kant. His system is divided into four principal parts, contributing conjointly to the investigation and communication of truth: *Dianoiology,* or the doctrine of the laws and Lambert.

---

[h] On this criterion, see Hamilton on Reid, p. 377.
[i] See the Preface to Rosenkranz's edition of Kant's Logic.

power of the understanding in thought; *Alethiology*, or the doctrine of truth as opposed to error; *Semiotic*, or the doctrine of signs and their influence to the knowledge of truth; and *Phenomenology*, or the doctrine of false appearances and the means of avoiding them. In his first part, he principally follows Wolf, but differs from him in his view of the Syllogistic figures; the three last figures being regarded as resting on independent axioms, coordinate with the *dictum de omni et nullo*. These axioms are distinguished as *dictum de diverso, dictum de exemplo*, and *dictum de reciproco*. In his second part, which treats of simple and complex notions, and of truth and error, Lambert acknowledges his obligations to Locke. In the third, the theory of language and its relation to thought is treated with considerable fulness. The fourth part, which treats of appearance as distinguished from reality, has more of a metaphysical and psychological than of a logical character, with some mixture of physiology.

Ploucquet. Another German Logician who deserves mention, not so much for the importance as for the eccentricity of his views, is Godfrey Ploucquet of Tubingen, a contemporary of Lambert's, the author in 1763 of a "Methodus calculandi in Logicis," afterwards included with other writings in his "Commentationes Philosophicæ selectiores," published in 1781. Ploucquet's work is remarkable as an attempt to exhibit the reasonings of Logic in the form of an algebraical calculus, an attempt recently carried out to a greater extent by the "Neue Darstellung der Logik" of Drobisch, and in the logical writings of Professors De Morgan and Boole. A severe criticism of the principle of Ploucquet's Calculus will be found in Hegel's Logic, vol. ii. p. 143. The geometrical illustrations of the syllogism by Euler and Lambert are not of sufficient importance to require a separate notice.

A short account of these, as well as of Ploucquet's system, is given in the Appendix to Professor De Morgan's "Formal Logic," p. 323.

Kant has done more for logical science than any philosopher since Aristotle; partly in his distinct treatise on the subject, and still more in the exact examination of the forms and functions and limits of thought which runs through the Critique of Pure Reason. To Kant is owing, what has been so long needed, a definition of Logic, which secures for it a distinct and positive field of inquiry, as the *Science of the Necessary Laws of Thought.* Kant also did great service in banishing to a separate region, under the name of Applied Logic, the psychological precepts which his predecessors, especially the Cartesians, had incorporated with the body of the science, and giving thereby to formal thought its proper position as the object of Pure Logic. His demonstration that an universal material criterion of truth is not only impossible, but self-contradictory [k], has furnished us with the principle of a more liberal and enlightened appreciation of the real character and value of formal thinking than can be supplied by the whole previous history of philosophy.

At the same time, it must be admitted that the logical system of Kant is chargeable with one serious deficiency, which has been prominently shewn in the subsequent history of the science. He divorces altogether his *à priori* science from all connection with the psychological phenomena of consciousness, from all examination of the actual characteristics of any determinate operation of thought [1]. These matters he rejects as empirical; but without such empiricism, Logic and all pure science is impossible. It is matter of each man's personal experi-

[k] *Logik*, Einleitung, vii.
[1] See *Kritik der r. V.* p. 58, 276. ed. Rosenkranz.

ence that he actually thinks; and, without examination of the phenomena of special acts of thought, it is impossible to ascertain the necessary laws of thought in general[m]. Logic and Psychology thus necessarily form portions of one and the same philosophical course, and, without a knowledge of the latter, it is impossible to have any sound criticism or accurate estimate of the former.

Later German Logicians. The writings of Kant have had immense influence on the subsequent Logic of Germany. It is true that the two greatest of his immediate successors, Fichte and Schelling, have produced no direct logical work; and have openly expressed their low estimate of the science[n]. But a host of able writers have notwithstanding arisen, as numerous as the Logicians of the sixteenth and seventeenth centuries, to promulgate, to correct, or to oppose the Kantian Logic. Some of these, as Hoffbauer and Kiesewetter, adhere for the most part to the Kantian limits. Others, as Krug and Fries, are mainly Kantian, though they have materially enriched the science from their own resources; and the latter has especially noticed the want of a psychological relation, as the main defect of Kant's system. The most eminent name among the strictly formal Logicians since Kant is Herbart; but both he and his disciple Drobisch have pushed to an extreme Kant's error in an exclusively *à priori* view of the science.

Hegel. On the other hand, the Logic of Hegel reconstructs from the opposite side the metaphysical fabric which Kant had overthrown. After the Kantian Critique, it

[m] Cf. Cousin, *Leçons sur Kant*, p. 180.

[n] Fichte, in his "Vorlesungen ueber das Verhältniss der Logik zur Philosophie," altogether repudiates the ordinary Logic to make way for a transcendental system, and complains that this was not sufficiently done by Kant. Schelling in his "Bruno" holds the same view. "Welche Hoffnung zur Philosophie für den, welcher sie in der Logik sucht? Keine."

was impossible to bring a philosophy of the Absolute within the received compass of human thought: there remained only the attempt to expand thought to the immensity of the object, by a gigantic scheme of Intellectual Pantheism, in which the personal consciousness and its limits should be absorbed in the processes of the one Infinite Mind. Such is the fundamental principle of the Logic of Hegel, a Logic constructed, not in obedience to, but in defiance of, the laws of thought, which are held to be valid only for the finite understanding dealing with finite objects; the philosophy of the infinite being based on their abrogation.

It is not easy to give in a short compass an account of Hegel's Logic, which shall be intelligible to an English reader. If we were to describe it as an attempt to develope a Philosophy of Being in general, by reproducing the Divine Thought in the act of Creation, we might support the view by sufficient quotations from the work; but it would convey an erroneous impression to one who did not bear in mind the total suppression of *personality*, divine as well as human, in the Hegelian philosophy. It may perhaps be better characterized as an illegitimate expansion of the fundamental principle of the Cartesian philosophy, modified in some degree by the Kantian. "Cogito, ergo sum" is true within the limits of the personal consciousness. I exist only in so far as I am conscious of my existence; and I am conscious only as being affected in this or that determinate manner. Within these limits Thought and Being are identical, and every modification of the one is a modification of the other. But if the same principle is to be accepted in its Hegelian extent, I must commence by ascending from my personal consciousness to a supposed Universal Thought, identical with Being in general. Here personality disappears altogether; and the problem is, to deduce from the identity of Thought and Being in general, the several identical determinations of the one and the other. Such a process is not thought, but its negation. If the Universe had one consciousness, the system might be possible; for Thought and Being are identical only in and through consciousness. But such universal consciousness could not be *my* consciousness; and thus the Hegelian assumption cannot be grasped by any act of human thought. On the other hand, thought without consciousness is inconceivable; since it implies a negation of the one essential characteristic under which all thought is presented to the human mind. The logical notion which is not a function of my own personal thought, is a mere empty abstraction, inconceivable by reason; and the system deduced from it is incompatible with those regulative truths that are above reason. Vulgar Rationalism subjects belief to thought; it has been reserved for Transcendental Philosophy to subject it to the annihilation of thought.

Speculative philosophy has had three great periods, each of which has been consummated by a critical system of which Formal Logic has been a constituent portion. The Eleatic and Platonic metaphysics found their consummation in Aristotle; the Scholastic Philosophy in Occam; that of the seventeenth and eighteenth centuries in Kant. But from the Kantian philosophy has arisen another phase of speculation, not less dogmatic in its positions, not less extravagant in its aims, not less unstable in its foundations. A criticism which shall sift thoroughly the pretensions of this philosophy, it remains for the present generation to accomplish.

PART II. CRITICAL.

" THAT Logic," says Kant, " has even from the earliest
times advanced in the sure course of a science, is manifest
from the fact that since Aristotle it has taken no back-
ward step." " It is worthy of remark however," he continues, " that it has also up to this time been able to
take no step forward, and thus to all appearance seems
to be concluded and perfected." This remark is true
as regards what Aristotle did; but on the other hand, as
regards what Aristotle left undone, it is no less true that
the whole subsequent history of the science exhibits
scarcely any thing but the ebb and flow of unsettled
opinion. The master left behind him a collection of
writings; and to the substance of that collection his
disciples have, for the most part, faithfully adhered;
but he left no definition of the science on which he
wrote, and no principle for determining its boundaries;
and these accordingly have been matter of controversy
ever since.

Clitomachus compared the Logic of his day to the
moon, which never ceases waxing and waning°. The
cause of complaint has assuredly not been diminished
by the labours of subsequent expositors down to the
present time. Few logicians have in their practical
treatment materially added to or taken from the original
body of the system : few on the other hand are theore-
tically agreed as to what it is that they are expounding.
Ask of almost any writer, " What is Logic ?" the reply
is almost unanimous, that it is the subject treated of in
Aristotle's Organon. Ask what is this subject; and
nearly every commentator has a different definition.

° Κλειτόμαχος εἴκαζε τὴν διαλεκτικὴν τῇ σελήνῃ, καὶ γὰρ ταύτην οὐ
παύεσθαι φθίνουσαν καὶ αὐξομένην. *Stobæi Ecl.* Serm. lxxx.

Let us bring together a few of these conflicting witnesses. Logic is a part of philosophy[p]. It is not a part, but an instrument[q]. It is both a part and an instrument[r]. It is both a science and an art[s]. It is neither science nor art, but an instrumental habit[t]. It is a science and not an art[u]. It is an art and not a science[x]. It is the science of argumentation[y]—of the operations of the mind so far as they are dirigible by laws[z]—of the syllogism[a]—of the understanding in relation to evidence[b]—of the laws of thought[c]. It is the art of thinking[d]—of reasoning[e]—of the right use of reason[f]—of dissertation[g]—of teaching[h]—of directing the mind to any object[i]—of forming instruments for the direction of the mind[k].

Let us endeavour to disentangle some of the confusion in which the reader may be involved by this multitude of definitions. Logic was divided by the Schoolmen into

[p] The Stoics. See Ammonius, Prooem. in Categ. Philoponus, Prooem. in Anal. Prior.

[q] The Peripatetics. See Ammonius, Prooem. in Categ. Philop., Prooem. in Anal. Prior.

[r] The Academics. See Ammonius, l. c. Philoponus, l. c. and Brandis, Scholia, p. 140, b. 31.

[s] Petrus Hispanus, Suarez, Ruvius, Æmilius Acerbus, Bentham, Kirwan, Whately, J. S. Mill.

[t] The Greek Commentators, Zabarella, Smiglecius.

[u] Albertus Magnus, Aquinas, Scotus, Wolf, Kant.

[x] Ramus, Keckermann, Burgersdyck, Sanderson, Aldrich.

[y] Albertus Magnus, Alfarabi, Avicenna, Algazel.

[z] Aquinas.

[a] Scotus.

[b] J. S. Mill.

[c] Kant, Hoffbauer, Krug, Sir W. Hamilton.

[d] Gassendi, Arnauld.

[e] Le Clerc, Crakanthorpe, Wallis, Kirwan, Whately.

[f] Clauberg, Watts.

[g] Ramus.

[h] Melanchthon.

[i] Bentham.

[k] Burgersdyck, Sanderson, Aldrich.

the *Logica docens* and the *Logica utens*, and the same
division had been made before by the Greek Commentators, under the title of Logic without and with
application to things[1]. The former denotes Logic in its
theoretical character, as concerned merely with the laws
and forms of thought; the latter is the practical application of thought to this or that object matter. The
discrepancies in the definition of Logic, as Science or
Art, may partly be traced to a confusion between these
two.

The *Logica docens* is properly a Science and not an
Art. It is not correct to say, as has frequently been
said or implied by modern Logicians, that every Science
is an Art, because all knowledge admits of a practical
application. " The truth is," says Bentham, " that how-
soever clearly distinguishable in idea, the two objects,
Art and Science, in themselves are not, in any instance,
found separate. In no place is any thing to *be done*,
but in the same place there is something to *be known*;
in no place is any thing to be known, but in the same
place there is something to be done." The terms thus
extended are too vague to be of any value, and tend to
confuse rather than to distinguish. Science is not Art,
though scientific knowledge may be the basis of artistic.
A Science admits of a practical employment under

---

[1] " Intelligendum est tamen quod Logica dupliciter consideratur. Uno
modo in quantum est docens, et sic ex necessariis et propriis principiis
procedit ad necessarias conclusiones, et sic est scientia. Alio modo in
quantum utimur ea applicando eam ad illa in quibus est usus, et sic non
est ex propriis, sed ex communibus; nec sic est scientia." *Scotus, super
Univ. Porph.* Qu. 1. " Est Logica docens, quæ tradit præcepta, quibus
docetur quid, quomodo faciendum : utens vero est, quæ ex præceptis efficit
opera ipsis conformia, sicut cum artifex ex præceptis artis efficit opera
artis." *Smiglecii Logica*, Disp. ii. Qu. vi. For the parallel distinction
between Logic without and with application to things, (χωρὶς πραγμάτων,
συμβιβαζομένη τοῖς πράγμασιν, ἐν χρήσει καὶ γυμνασίᾳ πραγμάτων,) see
Ammonius, Prœm. in Categ. Philoponus, Prœm. in Anal. Prior.

certain conditions; but it does not become an Art until those conditions are complied with, and it may exist as a Science without them. The ordinary distinction between the man of theory and the man of practice is a proof of this. A man may have a scientific knowledge of music, and yet have no power of playing on any instrument. He may be acquainted with the principles of perspective, without any skill in the use of the pencil. He may know the mathematical principles of Optics, and yet be sadly at a loss if required to make a pair of spectacles. He may have studied the anatomy of the human frame, and yet be unable to perform a surgical operation. He may talk like a Curius, and live like a Bacchanal. And in like manner, he may be familiar with *Barbara, Celarent,* and *Baralipton,* but in practice be a weak and inconclusive reasoner. On the other hand, he may possess Art without Science, that is to say, he may have considerable dexterity in the practice of any operation, without being able to give a clear account of the principles on which it is conducted. Science is no more Art because the man of science may become an artist, than a boy is a man because he may grow up into one. Nay, far less so; for the boy becomes a man in the course of nature, without any effort of his own; while the man of theory may remain a man of theory all his life, without ever learning to apply his knowledge to practice.

When we are asked, What is Logic? it is clearly meant, What is the object of which books on Logic treat. No treatise on Logic can give all its practical applications. It can at best select only a few specimens, and these by way of example, not as an essential part of the theory. But it professes to give, and is bound to give, the entire principles of reasoning, or rather of thinking in general, even though it illustrates its teaching by no other examples than algebraical symbols. A treatise on Logic is not designed primarily to give men facility in the practice of reasoning, any more than a treatise on Optics is intended to improve their sight; and it would be as correct for a writer on the mathematical principles of Optics to entitle his work, " Optics, or the art of improving defective vision," as it is for a writer on the principles of Logic to adopt for his title, " Logic, or the art of reasoning." Yet we do not therefore deny that a knowledge of Optics is useful in making spectacles, nor that a knowledge of Logic is valuable in the practice of reasoning.

Art, in the strict sense of the term, is acquired by practice, Science by study[m]. A man who has learnt to reason accurately by practice in special cases, without a knowledge of the laws of the syllogism, has the art of reasoning, but not the science. He who knows the theory, but does not practise it, has the science of reasoning, but not the art. The Logic to be found in treatises on the subject, i. e. the *Logica docens,* is thus clearly a science and not an art; for it is gained by study and not by exercise. But there is a further distinction between *speculative* and *practical* science, according as the knowledge which it conveys is considered as an end in itself, or only as a means to be applied to some further purpose[n]. And here again,

---

[m] See Wolf, *Philosophia Rationalis, Proleg.* §. 10. " Omnis Logica utens est habitus, qui proprio exercitio comparatur, minime autem discendo acquiritur, adeoque et ipsa doceri nequit. Quamobrem, cum Logica omnis sit vel docens vel utens, neque enim præter regularum notitiam atque habitum eas ad praxin transferendi tertium concipi potest; sola Logica artificialis docens ea est quæ doceri adeoque in numerum disciplinarum philosophicarum referri potest. Atque ideo quoque Logicam definivimus per scientiam, minime autem per artem vel habitum in genere, quod genus convenit Logicæ utenti."

[n] Arist. *Metaph.* A minor, c. 1. Ὀρθῶς δ' ἔχει καὶ τὸ καλεῖσθαι τὴν φιλο-

Logicians of eminence, who are agreed as to the genus of Logic, are at issue as to its species. Granted that Logic is a science, is it speculative or practical? Wolf, the ablest of the German writers on Logic before Kant, while distinguishing accurately between Science and Art, regards Logic as belonging to the practical, not to the speculative sciences, the knowledge which it furnishes being subservient to the discipline of the mind and the acquisition of further truths. Accordingly he defines Logic as "Scientia dirigendi facultatem cognoscitivam in cognoscenda veritate [o]." On the other hand, Kant, who defines Logic as "the Science of the necessary laws of the Understanding and the Reason," considers and treats it as speculative [p], and the same view is well maintained by the excellent French translator of the Organon, M. St. Hilaire, whose language may be quoted as an accurate and admirably expressed statement of the true purpose of Logic and the spirit in which it should be studied. "Sans la logique, l'esprit de l'homme peut admirablement agir, admirablement raisonner; mais sans elle, il ne se connaît pas tout entier: il ignore l'une de ses parties les plus belles et les plus fécondes. La logique la lui fait connaître. Voilà son utilité: elle ne peut pas en avoir d'autre [q]."

That this latter is the true view is manifest, as soon as we distinguish accurately between the essential contents of Logic and its accidental applications. The benefits performed by Logic as a medicine of the mind, however highly we may be disposed to rate them, are

σοφίαν ἐπιστήμην τῆς ἀληθείας. Θεωρητικῆς μὲν γὰρ τέλος ἀλήθεια, πρακτικῆς δ' ἔργον.

[o] *Philosophia Rationalis*, §. 61. This was also the opinion of Occam and others. See Æmilius Acerbus, Quæst. Log. Qu. v.

[p] *Logik, Einleitung* I. This was also the opinion of Scotus and others. See Æmilius Acerbus, l. c.

[q] *Préface*, p. xlii.

accidental only, and arise from causes external to the science itself: its speculative character, as an inquiry into the laws of thought, is internal and essential. To the twofold character of Logic, two conditions are necessary. Firstly, that there should exist certain mental laws to which every sound thinker is bound to conform. Secondly, that it should be possible to transgress those laws, or to think unsoundly. On the former of these conditions depends the possibility of Logic as a speculative science: on the latter, its possibility as a practical science. Now if we look at these two conditions with reference to the actual contents of pure Logic, it is manifest that the abrogation of the first would utterly annihilate the whole science; whereas the abrogation of the second would at most only necessitate the removal of a few excrescences, leaving the main body of logical doctrine substantially as it is at present. Suppose, for example, that the difference between sound and unsound reasoning could be discerned in individual cases as a matter of fact, but that we had no power of classifying the several instances of each and referring them to common principles. It is clear that under such a supposition, the present contents of Logic, speculative and practical, could have no existence. The number of sound and unsound thinkers in the world might remain much as it is now; but the impossibility of investigating the principles of the one and applying them to the correction of the other, would make a system of Logic unattainable. But let us imagine, on the other hand, a race of intelligent beings, subject to the same laws of thought as mankind, but incapable of transgressing them in practice. The elements of existing Logic, the Concept, the Judgment, the Syllogism, would remain unaltered. Logic, as a speculative science, would investigate the laws of unerring reason, as Astronomy investigates the unvarying laws of the heavenly phenomena; but a practical science of Logic, to preserve the mind from error, would be as absurd as an Astronomy proposing to control and regulate the planets in their courses. From these considerations it follows that, even granting Logic to be, under existing circumstances, both a speculative and a practical science, yet the former is an essential, the latter an accidental feature; the one is necessarily interwoven with the elements of the system, the other is a contingent result of the infirmities of those who possess it.

On the other hand, the *Logica utens* may be either Science or Art, according to the purpose to which it is applied[r]. Whenever reasonings are employed on any special object of knowledge, there we have an instance of the *Logica utens*. The opposite view, which is sometimes taken on account of Aristotle's distinction between the *logical* and the *analytical* or *physical* syllogism, arises from a confusion between the Aristotelian and the later senses of the term *logical*.

It would be both tedious and unnecessary to discuss in detail the various accounts that have been given of the object of Logic, by those who are agreed as to its genus. Many of these may be passed over, as being merely verbal varieties of the same fundamental view[s]. One or two statements, however, require a brief notice,

---

[r] " Distinctio peccat, quia auctores distinctionis vocant Logicam utentem solum usum partis Topicæ, cum Logica utens vel conjuncta rebus potissimum dicatur, et de aliis partibus Logicæ rebus conjunctæ numquid non poterunt applicari rebus ea quæ de definitione et divisione demonstrationeque præcepta traduntur? Ex quo sequitur ut Logica utens sit quandoque vere Scientia, ut puta Physica vel Metaphysica, vel siqua alia est, physicus enim demonstrans mixtum ex elementis esse corruptibile est Logicus utens, et talis Physica est Logica utens et vere Scientia." *Acerbi Quæst. Log.* Qu. IV.

[s] Thus the opinion of Aquinas is virtually identical with Kant's, and that of Scotus with Archbishop Whately's.

as having been maintained by eminent authors in recent times, and involving views which it is important to a clear understanding of the nature and legitimate contents of Logic to distinguish from each other.

According to Archbishop Whately, Logic may be defined as the Science and Art of *Reasoning*[t]. In this point of view, the processes of apprehension and judgment are considered not in themselves as independent acts of thought, but as subordinate to argumentation. "This view," says Sir William Hamilton[u], "which may be allowed in so far as it applies to the Logic contained in the Aristotelic treatises now extant, was held by several of the Arabian and Latin Schoolmen; borrowed from them by the Oxford Crakanthorpe, it was adopted by Wallis; and from Wallis it passed to Dr. Whately. But, as applied to Logic, in its own nature, this opinion has been long rejected, on grounds superfluously conclusive, by the immense majority even of the Peripatetic dialecticians; and not a single reason has been alleged by Dr. Whately to induce us to waver in our belief, that

---

[t] In another passage, Archbishop Whately maintains that Logic is *entirely conversant about language;* adding, "If any process of reasoning can take place in the mind, without any employment of language, orally or mentally, (a metaphysical question which I shall not here discuss,) such a process does not come within the province of the science here treated of." That language in its most extended sense, i. e. some system of signs, verbal or other, is essential not merely to the communication, but to the formation of thought, appears to be proved by universal experience and by the character of conceptions as distinguished from intuitions. But notwithstanding this, language must be regarded only as the secondary and accidental object of Logic, which is primarily conversant about the laws of thought, not about the instrument by which it is formed or communicated. And if any process of human thought were possible without language, (which Archbishop Whately appears to consider as at least conceivably true,) the laws of such a process would, equally with any other, be matters of logical investigation. On the question of the relation of language to thought, see *Prolegomena Logica*, p. 15.

[u] *Edinburgh Review*, No. 115, p. 206. reprinted in his *Discussions*, p. 135.

the *laws of thought*, and not the *laws of reasoning*, constitute the adequate object of the science."

" The error," continues Sir W. Hamilton, " would be of comparatively little consequence, did it not induce a perfunctory consideration of the laws of those faculties of thought; these being viewed as only subsidiary to the process of reasoning." Of the truth of this charge there can be no question. A student might read through nearly every one of the popular treatises on Logic, without finding the slightest hint of the fact, that in the processes of conception and judgment, as well as in that of reasoning, there is a distinction to be made between the form of the thought and the matter, the former being equally in all three processes accurately and completely determinable by logical rules; the latter being equally in all three beyond the domain of the science. A thought may violate its own laws, and thus virtually destroy itself; or it may be perfectly consistent with itself, but at variance with the facts of experience. The result in the one case is a product logically illegitimate, or the *unthinkable*, in the other the empirically illegitimate, or *unreal*.

In both cases alike the mind is supposed to be already in possession of the necessary data for thinking at all. Where there is a material deficiency in the conditions preliminary to an act of thought, we cannot be said to think logically or illogically; for we cannot attempt to think at all. Thus, if we are told to conceive objects which have never been presented in their proper experience, a colour for instance which we have never seen, or a scent which we have never smelt; or if we are required to form a judgment, other than identical, with less than two concepts, or a syllogism with less than two premises, we are in the position of a builder without materials, who can neither obey nor disobey the rules of architecture. In every art or science, in every inquiry speculative or practical, the existence of the objects of inquiry is presupposed. The astronomer is not required to create the heavens, nor the grammarian to supply rules of speech to the mute fishes, nor the logician to analyse the laws of thought where no act of thought can be attempted.

Thought is *representative;* its primary materials are *presentations,* either of the external or the internal sense. In the product of any act of thought, it is necessary to distinguish between the *matter* and the *form.* The former is all that is given out of and prior to the thinking act; the latter is all that is conveyed in and by the act itself[x]. To conception are *given* attributes; to judgment are *given* concepts; to reasoning are *given* judgments. By the act of conceiving, the attributes are *thought* as representing one or more objects; by the act of judging, the concepts are *thought* as related to one or more common objects; by the act of reasoning, the judgments are *thought* as necessitating another judgment as their consequence.

The thinking process itself may also be distinguished as material or formal. It is *formal* when the matter given is sufficient for the completion of the product, without any other addition than what is communicated in the act of thought itself. It is *material* when the data are insufficient and the mind has consequently to go out of the thinking act to obtain additional materials. If, for example, having given to me the attributes A, B, C, I can think those attributes as coexisting in an object, without appealing to experience to discover what objects actually possess them, this is *formal conceiving.* If,

---

[x] Cf. Hoffbauer, Logik, §. 11. "*Materie des Denkens* sind Vorstellungen, aus welchen Gedanken erzeugt werden können, und die *Form des Denkens* ist die Art und Weise, wie dieses geschicht."

having given to me the concepts P and Q, I can pro-
nounce " P is Q," or " P is not Q," without a similar
appeal, this is *formal judging*. If, having given to me
the judgments " W is X," " Y is Z," I can elicit a conclusion from them alone, this is *formal reasoning*. The
term *experience* is here used in a wide sense, for all
accidental knowledge, all that is not part and parcel of
the thinking act itself.

One condition of formal conceiving is, that the attributes given must not contradict one another. There
is no contradiction between the notions of a horse's
body and a man's head. A centaur therefore is as
conceivable as a man or a horse, whether such a
creature exists in nature or not. But if we try to
conceive a surface both black and white in the same
portion, the attempt to individualize the attributes by
applying them to an object shews at once their incompatibility. Such a combination of attributes is incapable
of representing any possible object. Hence we have a
law of thought, or condition of logical possibility; namely,
that whatever is contradictory is inconceivable. This
is the well-known Principle of Contradiction, the most
general expression of which is, " nothing can be A and
not A," or " no object can be conceived under contradictory attributes."

Another law of thought may be derived from the fact
that all thought is representative of possible objects of
intuition[y]. Hence, whatever limits our constitution im-
poses *à priori* on the presentations of intuition, the same
limits hold good of the representations of thought. Now
intuition is possible only under the condition of limitation by differences. An object of intuition, as such,
possesses definite characteristics, by which it is marked

[y] On the meaning of the term *intuition*, as distinguished from *thought*,
see below, p. 2, notes c and d.

off and distinguished from all others : otherwise it would not 'be an object, but the universe of all objects. In the act of conception, therefore, when we regard certain given attributes as constituting an object, we conceive it as thereby limited and separated from all other objects, as being *itself* and nothing else. The indefinite ideas, therefore, corresponding to the general terms, Thing, Object, Being in general, are not concepts, as containing no distinctive attributes; and the general object denoted by such terms is inconceivable. This law of thought is expressed by the Principle of Identity, " Every A is A," or " Every object of thought is conceived as itself."

Attributes which comply with these laws are *logically* conceivable; but for an act of material conception, or rather of conception combined with perception or memory, more than this is required. A centaur, as has before been observed, is logically as conceivable as a horse ; and, as mere thoughts, one is as legitimate as the other. But the senses or other evidence must further assure me of the reality of the objects, before I can think of either horse or centaur as having any existence out of my imagination. This assurance is not the result of a law of thought, but of a fact of perception. Hence as a general rule : all imaginary objects are conceived as such formally ; all real objects are conceived as such materially, that is to say, not by an act of pure conception, but by uniting that act with the presence or remembrance of other sources of information.

Formal judging is possible, *affirmatively*, whenever one of the given concepts is contained in the other ; *negatively*, whenever one of them contradicts the other. If the concepts P and Q have no attributes in common or contradicting each other, I cannot determine whether they coexist in any object without an appeal to experience; but if Q contains the attributes O, P, I can by a law of thought alone determine that all Q is P, or if Q contain an attribute contradictory of P, I can in like manner determine that no Q is P. The Laws of Identity and Contradiction are here again called into operation. Hence as a general rule : all analytical judging is formal : all synthetical judging is material.

Formal reasoning is possible when the given judgments are connected by a middle term under such conditions of quantity and quality that the mere act of thought necessarily elicits the conclusion. If any addition to the data is required, the consequence is material. Purely formal mediate reasoning or syllogism is dependent on the same laws as formal judging, the Law of Identity governing the affirmative categorical syllogism and the Law of Contradiction the negative*; while the subordinate Law of Excluded Middle is called into operation in the immediate inferences of Opposition and Conversion*. A single example must suffice. In a syllogism in Barbara we reason in this form. " All A is [some] B, all C is [some] A, therefore all C is [some] B." The law which determines the conclusion is, that whatever is identical with a portion of A is identical with a portion of that which is identical with all A. Here is again the Principle of Identity. " Every portion of a concept is identical with itself." The other forms of syllogism may easily be analysed in the same manner.

The critical province of Logic is coextensive with the constructive. As the logician can form concepts, judgments, reasonings, in a certain manner from certain

---

* Hypothetical and Disjunctive judgments and reasonings are omitted, as being either extralogical or reducible to Categorical form. See this question discussed in the Appendix, Note I.
* See *Prolegomena Logica*, p. 200. (2nd ed. p. 216.)

data, so he is competent to examine all that is or professes to be formed in like manner from like data. To
distinguish the apparent from the real is the purpose
of logical criticism[b]: that which presents no false appearance is beyond its field. If a thought professes to
be based solely on formal grounds, to be guaranteed
as legitimate by the laws of thought alone, Logic is
competent to examine and decide upon its pretensions.
If it professes to rest in any degree on extralogical
foundations, on a sensible experience for example, or on
suppressed premises, Logic neither accepts nor rejects
its claims to a material validity, but dismisses it to be
tried before another tribunal. Accordingly when Logic
is defined to be the science of the laws of formal thinking,
or the science of the laws of thought as thought, (not as
modified by experience,) it follows that it can adequately
determine the *conceivability* of an object, the truth or
falsehood of an *analytical* judgment, or the validity of
a *professedly formal* reasoning, in which the given premises
are stated as the complete conditions of the conclusion.
On the other hand, it cannot determine the *real existence*
of an object, the truth or falsehood of a *synthetical* judgment, or the validity of a reasoning *professedly material*,
in which the premises are given as a part only of the
conditions of the conclusion. Formal thinking can be
called into operation by itself. Material thinking can
only operate in conjunction with an act of perception or
memory; and the laws of thought alone are no guarantee
for the trust-worthiness of the concomitant process. It
is of course open to any innovator to attempt to extend
the boundaries of the science by material additions; but

---

[b] Arist. *Soph. Elench.* c. 11. Ἡ γὰρ πειραστικὴ ἐστι διαλεκτική τις καὶ
θεωρεῖ οὐ τὸν εἰδότα ἀλλὰ τὸν ἀγνοοῦντα καὶ προσποιούμενον. Ὁ μὲν οὖν
κατὰ τὸ πρᾶγμα θεωρῶν τὰ κοινὰ διαλεκτικός, ὁ δὲ τοῦτο φαινομένως ποιῶν
σοφιστικός.

he does so in the teeth of Kant's demonstration, that a criterion of material truth is not only impossible, but self-contradictory. In attempting to enlarge the field of Logic, he only makes it impossible to assign to it any definite field whatever. If a single intruder is admitted from the province of material knowledge, no barrier can be devised which shall not with equal facility give access to all.

On this ground objections may be taken against the view of another eminent English writer on Logic, whose work has attained to a high and in many respects a well-deserved reputation. According to Mr. Mill, Logic may be defined as " the science of the operations of the understanding which are subservient to the estimation of evidence : both the process itself of proceeding from known truths to unknown, and all intellectual operations auxiliary to this^c." In accordance with this definition, his treatise on Logic is based on a combination of the Old and the New Organon ; and the Baconian rules for the interrogation and interpretation of nature are combined with the Aristotelian principles of the syllogism, as part and parcel of the same science.

This definition appears as much too wide as that of Archbishop Whately is too narrow. The latter is open to objection, because it excludes from the province of Logic processes of thought dependent upon precisely the same laws, and subject to the same method of discovery and criticism, as that of reasoning. The present definition is open to objection, because it includes within the province of Logic processes governed by different laws, involving fundamentally different methods, and implying essentially distinct conceptions, united and confused by the ambiguities of a common language.

^c Mill's Logic, vol. i. p. 13.

In the first place: the purpose of the Aristotelian Logic is to investigate the laws under which the subject thinks; the purpose of the Baconian Logic is to investigate the laws under which the phenomena of the object take place[d]. They are thus respectively occupied with the two opposite poles of human knowledge, the *ego* and the *non ego*. The questions of the former are to be answered by an examination of the internal consciousness; the questions of the latter by an examination of external nature. The two systems are thus diametrically opposed to each other in their *objects*. In the second place: the Aristotelian laws are laws of thought *as it ought to be*. The Baconian laws are laws of nature *as it is*. The former are principles resting upon their own evidence; certain *à priori* as laws, whether actually complied with or not; approving themselves to consciousness the instant they are enunciated; and irreversible in thought, because thought itself is under their control. The latter are laws resting upon the evidence of the facts to which they relate; valid only in so far as they are actually complied with; and ceasing to be laws at all, the instant that an exception to them is discovered. And, however universally true in nature, they are always reversible in thought; for prior to their discovery we had no reason to think of them at all, and afterwards we have only to discard an adventitious knowledge. The two systems are thus distinct in their *evidence*; the opposite of the one being the mentally inconceivable, that of the other the physically impossible. In the third place: in the applications of the Aristotelian Logic we proceed from the law to the facts, constructing types of reasoning according to given principles, and accepting or rejecting all actual cases, according as they do or do not exemplify the law. In the applications of the Baconian Logic we proceed from

[d] See Sir W. Hamilton, *Reid's Works*, p. 712.

the facts to the law, accepting as genuine all that actually occurs, and rejecting every law that does not account for the facts. The two systems are thus opposed in their *methods*.

On account of these differences, the fundamental conceptions of the two systems cannot be expressed in the same terms without ambiguity. *Law* in the Aristotelian system implies a consciousness of obligation, which exists whether realised or not in practice. *Law* in the Baconian system means an uniform sequence, which exists only as it is realised in practice. In the field of nature, the conceptions of *cause* and *effect* imply no more than the antecedent and consequent phenomenon. In the field of thought, the *cause* is the consciously productive self, the *effects*, the thoughts which by its own power and under its own laws it produces. *Necessity* in the one case denotes what *invariably is;* in the other, what *cannot but be thought.* In short, there is hardly a term in the one which can be transferred to the other, except by analogy. In all that is phenomenal, the facts of the philosophy of matter can only be applied by imperfect analogy to the philosophy of mind. In all that is real, the facts of the philosophy of mind can only by imperfect analogy be made use of in the philosophy of matter. The Aristotelian Logic, like Mathematics and Moral Philosophy, is constructed *à priori* from conceptions; and its principles and conclusions are primarily true of the conceptions, secondarily only of actual objects, on the supposition that they conform to the conceived model. The type of perfect reasoning is the same, though there may not be such a thing as a perfect reasoner in the world; just as the standard of morality is the same, though no man is morally perfect, and as the demonstrations of Geometry hold good of conceived figures, though such figures in their mathematical exactness are never met with in practice. On the other hand, the Baconian Logic, like the subordinate branches of physical science, is constructed *à posteriori* from the observed uniformities of nature; and its principles and conclusions are true primarily of the facts as they exist in nature, secondarily only of our conceptions, so far as they are accurate representations of the facts. Hence the truth of the system entirely depends on the real existence of the objects of which it treats; and the whole fabric would fall to the ground if the objects were annihilated or their constitution reversed. Hence too a conception not in accordance with facts is worse than useless : if it is not the representation of nature as it is, it cannot claim to be accepted as the representation of nature as it should be.

An error of this sort becomes serious in its consequences. It is a great mistake to treat various definitions of Logic as mere matters of opinion, in which each person is at liberty to expand or contract the boundaries of the science according to his own leading conception. The whole province of the practice of reasoning may be affected by an error in its theory. For example. A writer who treats the Organon of Aristotle and the Organon of Bacon as parts of the same system is in consistency obliged to regard the so-called laws of thought as being in reality laws of external nature[e]; and the same obligation extends to all cognate branches

---

[e] Thus Mr. Mill (*Logic*, vol. i. p. 235.) observes: "So long as what were termed Universals were regarded as a peculiar kind of substances, having an objective existence distinct from the individual objects classed under them, the *dictum de omni* conveyed an important meaning; because it expressed the intercommunity of nature, which it was necessary upon that theory that we should suppose to exist between those general substances and the particular substances which were subordinated to them. That every thing predicable of the universal was predicable of the various individuals contained under it, was then no identical proposition, but a statement of what was conceived as a fundamental law of the universe."

of knowledge. Hence the laws of physical causation are introduced without modification into the moral and intellectual world; and, instead of an ideal science of man as he ought to think or act, we are presented with an empirical science of the observed relations between thoughts or actions as they actually take place. Thus in the place of a system of Ethics based upon the theory of a free will as it ought to be determined by moral obligations, is substituted Ethology, or the science of the actual phenomena of habits formed by a necessary agent under the laws of an invariable causation[f]. And in consistency, as a part of the same system, we ought also to be presented with an *à posteriori* science of Geometry, based upon the measurement of figured bodies as actually found in nature. This alone is needed to furnish the consummation, and at the same time the *reductio ad absurdum*, of the whole system[g].

On the above grounds, we are justified in rejecting Mr. Mill's definition of Logic as too wide for scientific accuracy, as that of Archbishop Whately is too narrow

---

[f] The reader need scarcely be reminded, that this is Mr. Mill's actual conception of Ethology as the Exact Science of Human Nature. See his *Logic*, B. VI. Chap. V.

[g] This indeed is almost implied in the conception of M. Comte, who regards it as the principal office of Mathematics to furnish a substitute for the measuring rod. To quote his own words. "Nous devons regarder comme suffisamment constatée l'impossibilité de déterminer, en les mesurant directement, la plupart des grandeurs que nous désirous connaître. C'est ce fait général qui nécessite la formation de la science mathématique. Car, renonçant, dans presque tous les cas, à la mesure immédiate des grandeurs, l'esprit humain a dû chercher à les déterminer indirectement, et c'est ainsi qu'il a été conduit à la création des mathématiques." *Cours de Philosophie Positive*, t. i. p. 123. With this may be contrasted the language of Plato, *Rep*. vii. p. 527. Λέγουσι μέν που μάλα γελοίως τε καὶ ἀναγκαίως· ὡς γὰρ πράττοντές τε καὶ πράξεως ἕνεκα πάντας τοὺς λόγους ποιούμενοι λέγουσι, τετραγωνίζειν τε καὶ παρατείνειν καὶ προστιθέναι, καὶ πάντα οὕτω φθεγγόμενοι· τὸ δ' ἔστι που πᾶν τὸ μάθημα γνώσεως ἕνεκα ἐπιτηδευόμενον.

for scientific completeness. Between these two, the views of Kant, which have been substantially adopted in the preceding pages, hold an intermediate position, and one which promises more effectually than either to secure for the science what it has long needed, an exact definition and a systematic treatment. In accordance with these views, the conception of Logic which has been taken as the basis of the present work is that of the Science of the Laws of Pure or Formal Thinking, or, in the language of Sir William Hamilton[h], " the Science of the Laws of Thought as Thought."

[h] *Reid's Works*, p. 698.

ARTIS LOGICÆ

RUDIMENTA.

ARTIS LOGICÆ

RUDIMENTA.

————

CAP. I.

De Terminis Simplicibus.

§. 1. MENTIS operationes in universum tres sunt[a]. 1. *Simplex Apprehensio*. 2. *Judicium*. 3. *Discursus*[b].

[a] *Mentis operationes tres sunt.* More correctly : the *products* of pure thought are three, the Concept, the Judgment, and the Syllogism. Whether these are to be referred to three distinct operations of mind, is a psychological, not a logical question. At any rate, the three operations must be regarded as a merely logical division, invented as a convenient mode of classifying the products of thought, which are the proper objects of Logic. Cf. Herbart, *Psychologie als Wissenschaft*, Th. ii. §. 119.

[b] " Sicut dicit Philosophus in tertio de Anima, duplex est operatio intellectus. Una quidem, quæ dicitur indivisibilium intelligentia, per quam scilicet apprehendit essentiam uniuscujusque rei in se ipsa. Alia est operatio intellectus, scilicet componentis et dividentis. Additur autem et tertia operatio, scilicet ratiocinandi, secundum quod ratio procedit a notis ad inquisitionem ignotorum. Harum autem operationum prima ordinatur ad secundam : quia non potest esse compositio et

B

1. *Simplex Apprehensio,* est nudus rei conceptus intellectivus[c], similis quodammodo perceptioni sensitivæ[d]; sicut enim *Imago* rei est in

divisio, nisi simplicium apprehensorum. Secunda vero ordinatur ad tertiam : quia videlicet oportet quod ex aliquo vero cognito, cui intellectus assentiat, procedatur ad certitudinem accipiendam de aliquibus ignotis. Cum autem Logica dicatur rationalis scientia, necesse est quod ejus consideratio versetur circa ea, quæ pertinent ad tres prædictas operationes rationis." Aquinas in Periherm. Lect. 1. Cf. Opusc. xlviii. Tract. de Syll. cap. 1. The passage alluded to by Aquinas is De An. iii. 6. 1. ἡ μὲν οὖν τῶν ἀδιαιρέτων νόησις ἐν τούτοις περὶ ἃ οὐκ ἔστι τὸ ψεῦδος· ἐν οἷς δὲ τὸ ψεῦδος καὶ τὸ ἀληθές, σύνθεσίς τις ἤδη νοημάτων ὥσπερ ἐν ὄντων. 'Αδιαίρετα are either ἀριθμῷ or εἴδει. Metaph. ix. 1. 4. The latter only are νοητά, the former αἰσθητά. Cf. Anal. Post. i. 24. 11.

[c] Simple Apprehension, in the only sense in which it can have any connection with Logic, is an operation of *Thought,* and is more properly called *Conception.* It is necessary to distinguish Thought, which is *representative,* and whose immediate object is an *universal notion,* gained by comparison and indifferently applicable to many individuals, from the various intuitive faculties, which are *presentative,* and whose immediate object is an *individual* thing, act, or state of mind, existing without or within ourselves. This distinction is properly psychological, but must be carefully borne in mind in reference to the logical character of Thought. A fuller explanation is given in *Prolegomena Logica,* Chap. I.

[d] Among various intuitive faculties, it is necessary to distinguish between *Sensation, Perception,* and *Imagination.* The two former are distinguished by Stewart, *Outlines of Moral Philosophy,* §. 15. " *Sensation* expresses merely that change in the state of the mind which is produced by an impression upon an organ of sense ; of which change we can conceive the mind to be conscious without any knowledge of external objects. The word *Perception* expresses the knowledge we obtain, by means of our sensations, of the qualities of matter."

oculo, ita *Idea* in animo[e] : estque *Incomplexa* vel *Complexa*.

Apprehensio simplex Incomplexa, est unius objecti, ut *calami,* vel etiam plurium, confuse ; ut *calami, manus,* &c. *Complexa,* plurium, sed cum ordine quodam et respectu ; ut *calami in manu*[f].

And so M. Royer Collard, Jouffroy's Reid, vol. iii. p. 329. " Il y a dans l'opération du toucher sensation et perception tout ensemble : changement d'état ou modification intérieure, c'est la sensation : connaissance d'un objet extérieur, c'est la perception." This distinction originated with Reid : by earlier writers Perception was used widely, as coextensive with Consciousness in general. See Hamilton's Reid, p. 876. *Imagination* is properly the consciousness of an image in the mind resembling an absent object of intuition. The image, like the object which it represents, is individual. By the earlier writers, logical and psychological, this and other processes of intuition are confounded with those of thought. Thus Gassendi, from whom Aldrich has borrowed, treats *Imagination, Simple Apprehension, Conception, Notion,* and *Intellection,* as identical, and employed in the formation of *images, ideas, concepts,* or *phantasms* of things.

[e] *Idea.* In the later and post-Cartesian sense of the word ; in which sense, it is defined by Locke, " whatsoever is the object of the understanding, when a man thinks." For the history of this word, see Sir W. Hamilton, *Discussions,* p. 70.

[f] *Confuse.* This *confused* apprehension of many objects is in truth only a succession of single apprehensions : thus in the example, we have two apprehensions, first of *calami,* and then of *manus.* Aldrich's distinction between *incomplex* and *complex* apprehension is inaccurate, and depends merely on an accident of language. In respect of thought, it is indifferent whether we express the same notion in many words, as *an animal with the head of a man and the body of a horse,* or in one word, as *Centaur.* Complex Apprehension should properly be applied only to the apprehension of the proposition, (the

2. *Judicium,* est quo mens non solum percipit duo objecta, sed, quasi pro tribunali sedens, expresse apud se pronuntiat, illa inter se convenire aut dissidere[g].

Arist. de Int. i. 3. Est enim Judicium aliud *Affirmativum,* quod vocatur etiam *Compositio*[h]*;* aliud *Negativum,* quod et *Divisio.*

Porro, tam particula *Est,* quæ affirmando convenientiam exprimit, quam *Non-Est,* quæ negando Dissidium, appellatur *Copula;* (sicut et Grammatica *Conjunctiones Disjunctivas* habet;) atque hanc sub determinatione cognoscendo differt Judicium ab Apprehensione complexa.

E. g. Si quis dixerit *Triangulum æquilaterum esse æquiangulum,* possum Apprehensione Simplici

---

oratio perfecta,—Aquinas, Opusc. xlviii. de Int. c. 3.) as distinguished from that of a term or an imperfect sentence.

[g] *Percipit duo objecta,* This expression is only accurate in the earlier and wider sense of *perceives = is conscious of.* The elements united in the logical judgment proper are general notions, the objects of Conception. With this explanation, Aldrich's definition is tolerably accurate as regards the logical judgment, formed by the union of two concepts represented each by its separate sign in language. But this must not be confounded with the psychological judgment, which takes place in every act of consciousness. The latter is a conviction of the presence of the object of consciousness, either internally in the mind or externally in space. This judgment does not require the aid of language, and to it Aldrich's definition is not applicable. Cf. Cousin, Cours de Philosophie, leçon 23. Hamilton on Reid, p. 243, 375. Prolegomena Logica, p. 53, (2nd ed. p. 62.)

[h] Compositio—σύνθεσις. Divisio—διαίρεσις. See de Int. i. 3.

incomplexa intelligere quid sibi velint singula Orationis hujus vocabula, complexa vero quid tota sibi velit Oratio[i] : Quin et ipsius Naturæ lumine[j] intelligo, Duo quælibet objecta vel inter se convenire, vel non convenire, et proinde altera Copularum esse jungenda : Nondum tamen feci judicium donec Copulam determinaverim, i. e. apud meipsum statuerim hæc Duo Objecta, *Triangulum æquilaterum*, et *Triangulum æquiangulum*, hac Copula *Est*, non autem altera *Non-Est*, oportere conjungi.

3. *Discursus*[k], est motus sive progressus mentis

---

[i] Conception, the Apprehension of Logic, implies considerably more than the mere understanding of the meaning of words or sentences. A word or sentence may be intelligible when the notion signified is inconceivable ; indeed, the meaning of a word must be understood, before we can say whether the corresponding object is conceivable or not. Conception consists in an *unity of representation*, i. e. in the power of forming a mental image of the several attributes given in any word or combination of words. It is thus imagination relatively to a concept. Cf. Hamilton on Reid, p. 377. Prolegomena Logica, p. 24.

[j] *Ipsius Naturæ lumine.* This so-called *light of nature* is in truth one of the laws of thought, commonly known as the Principle of Excluded Middle. (*Principium exclusi medii inter duo contradictoria.*)

[k] " Additur tertia operatio quæ est discursus, ab uno composito vel diviso ad aliud : hoc tamen fit per argumentationem. Est autem argumentatio oratio significativa discursus rationis ab uno cognito ad aliud incognitum, vel a magis cognito ad minus cognitum. Sunt autem argumentationis quatuor species, scilicet syllogismus, enthymema, inductio, et exemplum." Aquinas, Opusc. xlviii. Tract. de Syll. cap. 1.

ab uno Judicio ad aliud; quod et Ratiocinium dicitur; et significatur Copula Illativa, qualis est *Ergo,* aut alia similis. v. g. *Qui est extra fortunæ potestatem est beatus. Sapiens est extra fortunæ potestatem.* Ergo, *Sapiens est beatus.*

Singulis operationibus sui accidunt defectus[1].

The definition is too wide, being applicable to the immediate inferences of Opposition and Conversion, as well as to the mediate by Argumentation. In all there is a progress from one judgment to another. *Discursus* is more properly the progress from two connected judgments to a third resulting from their connection. Cf. Port Royal Logic, Introd. " On appelle *raisonner* l'action de notre esprit, par laquelle il forme un jugement de plusieurs autres."

Of this division of the operations of the mind, Sir W. Hamilton has observed, that " it never was proposed as a *psychological* distribution of the cognitive faculties *in general :* but only as a *logical* distribution of that section of them which we denominate *discursive,* as those alone which are proximately concerned in the process of reasoning." *Reid's Works,* p. 242, 692. Hence Aristotle's division, which is *psychological,* will not exactly correspond. The nearest approach to Simple Apprehension is ἡ τῶν ἀδιαιρέτων νόησις ; but νόησις is variously used, and in its widest sense will embrace all the logical operations, and even φαντασία, which belongs rather to the perceptive soul. See *de Anima,* iii. 3. 8. Judgment will correspond nearly to the ὑπόληψις of *de An.* iii. 3. 7. (Cf. Trendelenburg, *Arist. de Anima,* p. 469.) The latter term however is inapplicable to the cognition of axiomatic truths. Discursus answers to διάνοια and λογισμός, the former term being applied both to the faculty and its operation. But there is much uncertainty in the use of all the above terms. Cf. Biese, vol. i. p. 89, 327. Hamilton's Reid, p. 768.

[1] The service supposed to be performed by Logic in relation to these three defects is more fully and clearly stated

Apprehensioni, *Indistinctio ;* Judicio, *Falsitas ;* Discursui, *Mendosa Collectio.* Quæ cum Sapientes animadverterent, et opportuna illis remedia

by Burgersdyck *Inst. Log.* l. ii. c. 1. " Mens nostra quadruplici defectu laborat, cum occupata est in investiganda rerum cognitione : vel enim non assequitur propositæ rei essentiam, sed circa illius accidentia solum hæret ac sensibiles notas ; vel essentiam rei confuse tantum concipit, et ratione minime distincta ; vel in dubiis non reperit quid statuat, aut etiam statuit quod falsum est ; vel denique non servat ordinem in commentando, qui cum natura rerum consentit. Hisce quatuor malis opponit Logica totidem remedia. Definitio exhibet menti essentiam rerum : divisio efficit cognitionem distinctam : syllogismus tollit animi incertitudinem et errorem circa themata complexa : methodus ἀραξίαν sive confusionem." Hence it appears that falsity of judgment simply was not regarded as remediable by Logic, but only falsity in relation to the syllogism, i. e. so far as it depends on the assumed truth or falsity of other judgments. But the above statement requires considerable limitation. Every process of thought is liable to a *formal* defect, as violating its own laws, and to a *material* defect, as inconsistent with experience. Thus a concept may be obscure or indistinct formally, as implying attributes which cannot be thought in conjunction, as when its different parts contradict one another : a judgment may be formally false, for the same reason : and a reasoning may be formally inconsequent, as transgressing the laws of the syllogism. In all these cases the fault may be detected by Logic. On the other hand, a concept may be materially obscure or indistinct, as containing attributes which we have never met with in our own experience : a judgment may be materially false, as being at variance with facts : a reasoning may be materially inconsequent, as not warranted by the laws or analogies of nature. In all these cases, the fault can only be detected and remedied by experience. Cf. *Prolegomena Logica*, p. 238, (2nd ed. p. 257.)

excogitâssent, præcepta sua in unum compegêre ;
eorumque Scientiam dixere *Logicam,* sive *Artem
Rationis* [m].

Est igitur *Logica,* Ars instrumentalis dirigens
mentem in cognitione rerum [n] : ejusque partes tres

---

[m] *Logicam.* " Logica dicta est ἀπὸ τοῦ λόγου. Λόγος duplex
est Aristoteli, ὁ ἔσω καὶ ὁ ἔξω λόγος, id est, *sermo internus et
externus.* Sermonem internum vocat τὸν ἐν τῇ ψυχῇ λόγον, id
est, *sermonem qui in anima est:* Plutarchus, Damascenus,
aliique appellant λόγον ἐνδιάθετον id est *sermonem intus conceptum;* et externum, λόγον προφορικὸν, id est, *sermonem foras
prolatum,* sive pronunciatum. Λόγος ἐνδιάθετος sive internus,
nihil est aliud quam ratio sive cogitatio, hoc est, actio mentis
res objectas earumque nomina concipientis. Mens enim non
solum res ipsas concipit atque intelligit, sed et idonea vocabula
excogitat ad conceptus suos aliis indicandos atque explicandos :
atque ita quodammodo in seipsa loquitur. Λόγος προφορικὸς
atque externus, est sermonis interni cogitationumque interpres,
atque (ut Damascenus loquitur, *lib. 2. de Orth. Fid. cap. 21.*)
ἄγγελος τοῦ νοήματος, id est, *nuncius cogitationis.* Ab utroque
sermone appellata est Logica, (utrumque enim regit ac
format) sed ad interno, quem nihil aliud esse diximus quam
mentis rationem sive cogitationem, præcipue nuncupatur ;
ab externo sermone, sive ab oratione, tantum secundario.
Logica enim regit cogitationes animi nostri per se ; orationem
non per se, (hoc enim Grammaticæ convenit) sed eatenus
tantum, quatenus rationis nostræ sive cogitationum interpres
est." *Burgersdicii Inst. Log.* l. i. c. 1. Cf. Arist. *Anal. Post.*
I. 10. 6 Οὐ πρὸς τὸν ἔξω λόγον ἡ ἀπόδειξις, ἀλλὰ πρὸς τὸν ἐν τῇ ψυχῇ,
ἐπεὶ οὐδὲ συλλογισμός. Ἀεὶ γὰρ ἔστιν ἐνστῆναι πρὸς τὸν ἔξω λόγον,
ἀλλὰ πρὸς τὸν ἔσω λόγον οὐκ ἀεί. The terms ἐνδιάθετος and προφορικὸς appear to have originated with the Stoics. See Wyttenbach on Plutarch, II. 44. A. (Plutarchi Moralia, vol. vi. p. 378.)
Compare Prantl, I. p. 420, 507.

[n] *Est igitur Logica.* This definition is more fully given by
Burgersdÿck, *Inst. Log.* l. i. c. 1. " *Logica est ars conficiens*

sunt, pro operationibus mentis quas dirigit. 1. *De Simplici Apprehensione.* 2. *De Judicio.* 3. *De Discursu.*

§. 2. QUONIAM vero, inter docendum et disputandum, neque res aliqua, neque conceptus, cui

instrumenta, iisque intellectum dirigens in cognitione rerum. *Logica docens* dicitur quæ præcepta tradit; *utens,* quæ præceptis utitur. Officium Logicæ docentis, est tradere præcepta et modum efficiendi instrumenta, quibus mens dirigitur in cognitione rerum, instrumentorumque naturam describere. Instrumenta Logica sunt quatuor, *definitio, divisio, syllogismus* et *methodus.* Officium Logicæ utentis, est instrumenta, cum opus est, efficere, iisque mentem dirigere, ne in quærenda rerum cognitione hallucinetur." From this it appears that the *knowledge of things* was regarded by this school as only the remote object of the *Logica utens,* as applied to this or that matter, and hence not to be gained from any logical treatise. Thus the distinction insisted upon by some critics between *in cognitione* and *in cognitionem,* is of no value; both being merely verbal variations in expressing the same view. This definition of Logic as an Art arose from the dialectical and rhetorical innovations introduced by the reformers of Logic in the latter part of the fifteenth century, and was adopted universally by Ramus and his followers, as well as by the Peripatetico-Ramists of the school of Keckermann, and afterwards by the Cartesians. Among the earlier philosophers, the Peripatetics considered Logic to be neither Art nor Science, but an Instrument. The Stoics regarded it as a Science, in which they were followed by the Schoolmen. Subsequently, in the schools of Wolf and Kant, Logic again obtained the name of Science, though the former regarded it as a practical, the latter, more correctly, as a speculative science. Cf. Zabarella *de Natura Logicæ,* lib. i. Smiglecii *Logica,* Disp. II. Qu. V. Sir W. Hamilton, *Discussions,* p. 132, *Lectures on Logic,* i. p. 9, ii. p. 233.

subjacet, commode in medium afferri potest ; necesse est vicaria utriusque signa substituere, quorum usum idoneum docendo, Logica mentem una ad bene operandum instruit.

Hujusmodi signa apud homines recepta, sunt *Voces :* Nam *Vox* est signum rei vel conceptûs[o] ex instituto vicarium[p] : et in significando, primo quidem *declarat* conceptum, deinde *supponit* pro re[q]. Dico autem *ex instituto,* quia soni inarticu-

De Int. 1. 2.

---

[o] Primarily of the conception, secondarily of the thing.   Cf. de Int. i. 2.   Καὶ ὥσπερ οὐδὲ γράμματα πᾶσι τὰ αὐτά, οὐδὲ φωναὶ αἱ αὐταί· ὧν μέντοι ταῦτα σημεῖα πρώτως ταῦτὰ πᾶσι παθήματα τῆς ψυχῆς, καὶ ὧν ταῦτα ὁμοιώματα, πράγματα ἤδη ταὐτά.   On the distinction between σημεῖον and ὁμοίωμα, see Waitz, vol. i. p. 324.

[p] What Aldrich calls simply *Vox,* is called by Aristotle φωνὴ σημαντική, and by Boethius and Petrus Hispanus, *Vox significativa ad placitum.*   In the latter case, *Vox* is extended to the grammatical word; in the former, it is limited to what may be called the *Vox Logica.*   Logic differs from Grammar, in considering language simply as the *interpretation of thought,* (the ἑρμηνεία of Aristotle,) not as in any way expressive of the passions or the will.   Logic therefore solely regards words as the signs of an operation of the reason; and hence its simplest words are the noun and the verb, which alone are *per se* signs of conceptions. Syncategorems, being not significative but consignificative, are excluded from Logic, but recognised by Grammar.   So Aristotle, in the De Interpretatione, treats only of the noun and the verb.   In the Poetics, ch. 20. he adds the φωναὶ ἄσημοι, the conjunction and the article.   Cf. Harris, *Hermes,* ch. iii. On the distinction between the logical and the grammatical proposition, some good remarks will be found in Du Marsais, *Principes de Grammaire,* p. 321.

[q] *Supponit pro re.*   The *supposition* (as it was called) of a term being posterior to its *signification.*   The doctrine of the supposition of terms, which is not found in Aristotle, is one

lati, vocesque quas Natura sponte suggerit, extra artem censentur.

Jam, quæ simplicem Apprehensionem exprimit, *Vox Simplex* est ; quæ Judicium, *Complexa*[r] ; quæ Discursum, *Decomplexa.* Nam argumentum omne

of the subtleties of the *parva logicalia*, a scholastic addition to the Organon, rather grammatical than logical. *Suppositio* was defined to be " Acceptio termini substantivi pro aliquo ;" thus the term *homo*, naturally applicable to men of all generations, is, in the proposition *homo currit*, accidentally limited to existing individuals. In this case it was said, in not very classical Latin, " homo *supponit* pro præsentibus." For further information on the various kinds of supposition, the curious reader may examine Sanderson's Logic, b. ii. ch. 2.

[r] *Vox complexa* (φωνὴ συμπεπλεγμένη) in Aristotle signifies a compound word ; his example is ἐπακτροκέλης, of which each part has a meaning in composition. *Vox simplex* (ἁπλῆ) where the parts have no meaning. The later meaning of *vox complexa* properly corresponds to Aristotle's λόγος (oratio), and is not limited, as by Aldrich, to the *Proposition* (oratio enunciativa). Thus Petrus Hispanus : " Vocum significativarum ad placitum alia complexa, ut *oratio*, alia incomplexa, ut nomen et verbum. Orationum perfectarum alia indicativa, ut *homo currit* ; alia imperativa, ut *Petre fac ignem ;* alia optativa, ut *utinam esset bonus clericus ;* alia subjunctiva, ut *si veneris ad me dabo tibi equum ;* alia deprecativa, ut *miserere mei Deus.* Harum autem orationum, sola indicativa oratio dicitur esse propositio." Sum. Log. Tract. 1. Cf. Boeth. de Syll. Cat. p. 582. With regard to the *vox decomplexa ;* as λόγος is defined by Aristotle as a species of φωνή, and syllogism as a species of λόγος, the latter may without error be called *vox.* But the distinction is unnecessary ; the syllogism, *as far as apprehension is concerned*, being only three several propositions. The connexion between them is not a matter of apprehension, but of reasoning.

resolvitur in tres *Propositiones,* sive sententias, et propositio omnis complectitur voces, non semper numero, sed sensu semper tres; 1. *Subjectum,* sive de quo aliud dicitur. 2. *Prædicatum,* sive id quod dicitur. 3. *Copulam,* quæ utrisque media intercedit*. Nam Subjectum et Prædicatum quoad sensum semper extrema sunt, et vocantur ideo *Termini Propositionis.*

Atque hinc adeo vulgo dicitur Pars prima Logicæ versari circa *Terminos simplices,* i. e. voces simplices, Apprehensionem simplicem exprimentes ᵗ: secunda circa *Propositionem,* sive Vocem com-

---

ˢ The Latin Logicians distinguish between propositions *secundi adjacentis,* in which the copula and predicate form one word, e. g. " Homo currit," and propositions *tertii adjacentis,* in which they are separated, e. g. " Homo est animal." The distinction originates with Aristotle, see *De Int.* 10. 3. But Aristotle does not maintain that propositions of the former kind are to be resolved into the latter. On the contrary, the early part of the *De Interpretatione* is adapted exclusively to propositions *secundi adjacentis;* and in order to make it applicable to such propositions as " Homo est animal," we must consider the copula and predicate as equivalent to a single verb ᵃ.

ᵗ In Aldrich's limitation of the terms, *Vox simplex, Vox categorematica,* and *Terminus simplex,* are synonymous: syncategorems not being voces (logicæ) at all. But in this usage he is not always consistent.

ᵃ In De Int. 1. 4. it seems at first sight as if λευκὸν alone was a ῥῆμα. That this is not the case is clear from Poetics, 20. 9. τὸ μὲν γὰρ ἄνθρωπος ἢ λευκὸν οὐ σημαίνει τὸ πότε, τὸ δὲ βαδίζει ἢ βεβάδικε προσσημαίνει τὸ μὲν τὸν παρόντα χρόνον τὸ δὲ τὸν παρεληλυθότα. In fact, λευκόν, by a common Greek idiom, is equivalent to λευκόν ἐστι.

plexam, quæ Judicium exprimit : tertia vero circa
Syllogismum, sive Vocem decomplexam, qua Argumentatio sive Discursus exprimitur.

§. 3. PRIMA igitur pars Logicæ versatur circa
Terminos Simplices[u] ; i. e. ejusmodi voces, quæ
solitariæ in propositione prædicari vel subjici possunt ; et vocantur ideo *Categorematicæ,* ut *homo,
lapis*[x]. Quædam etiam Vocabula sunt tantum
Syncategoremata, sive compartes Subjecti aut Præ-
dicati, ut *omnis, nullus ;* Quædam etiam mixta[y], ut
semper, i. e. omni tempore; *nemo,* i. e. nullus homo ;
Currit, i. e. est currens ; quo etiam modo verbum
omne Grammaticum resolvi potest.

De Int. c.
2. and 3.

[u] Aristotle's *Simple terms,* (ὅροι, εἰς οὓς διαλύεται ἡ πρότασις,)
or, as others call them, *categorematic words,* are the *noun* as
subject, and the *verb* as predicate, " *homo currit.*" The oblique
cases of the noun and past or future tenses of the verb are
not simple terms, being only πτώσεις ὀνόματος or ῥήματος· The
noun and verb are thus the only two parts of speech recognised by Logic. See Boethius, Introd. ad Syll. p. 561.
and Petr. Hisp. Tract. I. But it would be more accurate to
say that Logic analyses language on a different principle,
and hence does not recognise the grammatical parts of
speech at all. The logical proposition should be of the form
tertii adjacentis, and its predicate forms a part of the grammatical verb. Cf. *Prolegomena Logica,* p. 274, (2nd ed. p. 293.)

[x] The terms *categorematic* and *syncategorematic* are not Aristotelian, though the distinction is of course implied in his
theory of the Proposition. Κατηγόρημα in Aristotle means a
predicable, e. g. *de Int.* 11. 4. Cf. Trendelenburg, *Elementa,*
§. 3. Waitz, vol. i. p. 267.

[y] *Mixta.* This is clearly a cross division. Every mixed
word must, of course, be categorematic or syncategorematic.

Verbum igitur *Logicum* (nempe *purum*) præter Copulam nullum est: cætera ex participio et copula coalescunt[x].

De Int. 2.1.   *Nomen Logicum,* est Terminus simplex sine tempore significativus[a].   Nam ex antedictis, *Terminus simplex* idem valet atque Vox articulata et recta, et ex instituto significans: siquidem exclusæ sunt voces inarticulatæ, quasque natura sponte suggerit; voces autem obliquæ sunt Syncategoremata.

Multæ sunt Nominis Divisiones; quarum tres[b]

---

[x] The copula has an apparent resemblance to the grammatical verb, as being the only part of a logical proposition capable of personal inflection.   But inflection is one of the accidents, not one of the essentials of a verb, and belongs to particular, not to universal grammar.   The essence of a grammatical verb lies in its signification, being a combination of an attribute and an assertion.   Cf. Stoddart, *Universal Grammar,* p. 121.   Latham, *English Language,* p. 461.   The copula must of course not be confounded with the verb *est,* which predicates existence, as " Homo est."   The whole question is ably treated by Pacius on *de Int.* ch. 3.   Cf. Biese, *Philosophie des Aristoteles,* vol. i. p. 95.

[a] *Nomen.*—Arist. de Int. 2. 1. ὄνομα μὲν οὖν ἐστὶ φωνὴ σημαντικὴ κατὰ συνθήκην ἄνευ χρόνου.   *Sine tempore,* as opposed to the verb, the other simple term, τὸ προσσημαῖνον χρόνον.   " *Currit,*" e. g. in addition to its principal notion of running, signifies as an adjunct the present time, (see Ammonius, Scholia, p. 105. b. 29.)   This distinction is lost when we resolve the verb into copula and predicate.

[b] *Tres,* i. e. the three employed in his definition of *prædicabile,* viz. those into singular and common, univocal and equivocal, first and second intention.

sufficiunt hujus loci instituto; sed ob multiplicem earum usum, quinque alias adjungam.

1. Nomen *singulare,* est quod rem unam et solam significat, ut *Socrates: Commune,* quod plura, et eorum singula significare potest, ut *homo.* [De Int. 7. 1.]

[2. *Transcendens,* quod solis omnibusque veris Entibus convenit, ut *ens, res, aliquid, unum, verum, bonum*[c]. *Supertranscendens,* quod omnibus etiam fictis, ut *imaginabile, cogitabile: Non-transcendens,* omne aliud nomen.]

3. *Finitum,* est cui abest particula *non: Infi-*[De Int. 2. 3.] *nitum*[d], cui præfigitur, ut *non homo,* i. e. omnia præter hominem: unde particula *non,* dicitur *infinitans.*

4. *Positivum*[e], est quod significat rem quasi præsentem: *Privativum,* quod dicit absentiam rei a subjecto capaci: *Negativum,* quod ab incapaci. Sic *homo* est vox *positiva; videns* dicitur de homine

---

[c] These are usually called the six transcendents, and are regarded as predicable of the several categories *analogously,* not *univocally.*

[d] *Infinitum.* So translated by Boethius. It should be *indefinitum;* see Hamilton on Reid, p. 685. The translation is censured by Vives, de Caus. Corr. Art. lib. 3.

[e] In these divisions there is much clumsiness and self-repetition. The distinction between positive and privative nouns is repeated below, under the four *opposita. Negative* nouns have no business here at all, being opposed, not to *positive,* but to *affirmative,* and belonging to another kind of opposition, the *contradictory. Relatives* also form another member of the same fourfold division; and *Repugnants* include all the four *opposita,* and other nouns to boot.

positive;   *cæcus* de homine *privative;*   *cæcus,* seu potius *non videns,* de lapide *negative.*

5. *Univocum*[f], est cujus una significatio æque convenit multis, ut *homo: Æquivocum,* cujus diversæ, ut *Gallus: Analogum,* cujus una inæqualiter ut *pes.* [Vox ipsa dicitur *Univocum Univocans:* res significata *Univocum Univocatum,* et sic de cæteris.]

6. *Absolutum*[g], est cujus tota significatio spectat

---

[f] *Univocum (univocatum)—συνώνυμον: æquivocum, (æquivocatum)—ὁμώνυμον.* Ὁμώνυμα λέγεται ὧν ὄνομα μόνον κοινόν, ὁ δὲ κατὰ τοὔνομα λόγος τῆς οὐσίας ἕτερος, οἷον ζῷον ὅ τε ἄνθρωπος καὶ τὸ γεγραμμένον. Συνώνυμα δὲ λέγεται ὧν τό τε ὄνομα κοινὸν καὶ ὁ κατὰ τοὔνομα λόγος τῆς οὐσίας ὁ αὐτός, οἷον ζῷον ὅ τε ἄνθρωπος καὶ ὁ βοῦς. (Cat. ch. 1.) Analogous nouns are but one out of many species of equivocal, belonging to the *æquivoca consilio,* (ἀπὸ διανοίας,) of the Greek interpreters; to which are opposed the *æquivoca casu,* (ἀπὸ τύχης.) See Scholia, p. 42, a. 37, 47. Boethius in Prædicamenta, lib. 1. p. 117. (Cf. Arist. Eth. Nic. i. 4. 12.) The συνώνυμα of Aristotle must be distinguished from the modern synonyms, which answer to the πολυώνυμα of Speusippus, (Schol. p. 43. a. 31.) and the *multivoca* of Boethius, and are defined by the latter, " quorum plura nomina, una definitio est." Συνώνυμα was used in this sense by the Stoics, and the same sense may also be found in Aristotle, Rhet. iii. 2. 7. and perhaps Top. viii. 13. 2.

[g] It is not easy to distinguish accurately the two divisions of terms into absolute and connotative, abstract and concrete, respectively. The following attempt is made with some doubt as to its success. In the second chapter of the Categories, Aristotle divides all ὄντα into four classes, Universal Substances, Singular Substances, Universal Attributes, and Singular Attributes. Substances of both kinds exist *per se;* attributes can only exist in substances. Hence the scholastic distinction between Subjects of Predication and

rem per se sumptam, [ut *Justitia: Connotativum,* quod eandem quasi alteri nexam, ut *Justus.*]

Subjects of Inhesion. The universal substances are predicable of the singular, as genera and species of individuals. " Socrates is a man." In this case the individual is a subject of *predication.* Attributes are not in their original state predicable of substances. Whiteness exists in snow ; but we cannot say, " Snow is whiteness." Here, then, the subject is not one of predication, but of *inhesion.* But, by an act of the mind, an attribute may be so connected with a subject as to become predicable of it as a differentia, property, or accident; e. g. " snow is white." Predicates thus formed from attributes are called *connotative,* being said to signify *primarily* the attribute, and to *connote* or *signify secondarily* (προσσημαίνειν) the subject of inhesion. Hence a connotative term may be defined, " One which primarily signifies an attribute, secondarily a subject." Whereas the original universals, whether substances or attributes, as " man," or " whiteness," were called *absolute.* Again, by an act of the mind, the terms signifying substances, may be conceived in the form of attributes, so as to be no longer predicable of the individuals; thus " homo" becomes " humanitas." All such terms, not predicable of singular substances, whether primarily attributes, as " whiteness," or secondarily conceived as attributes, as " humanity," are called *abstract* terms; all that are predicable of the individuals, whether primarily, as " homo," or secondarily, as " white," are *concrete.* Hence the two divisions are distinct in principle, though some of the members of each cross. For example : *Homo* is concrete and absolute, *albus* concrete and connotative, *albedo* abstract and absolute; but no abstract term is connotative.

The above account differs considerably from that given by Mr. Mill, Logic, b. i. chap. 2. He inverts the phraseology, describing the attribute instead of the subject as connoted, and extends connotative terms, so as to include all concrete general names. This is in some respects an improvement on the scholastic distinction, but it must not be confounded with

Concretum, quod rem quasi sua natura liberam, sed jam implicitam subjecto, ut *Justus :* Abstractum, quod rem quasi sua natura nexam, sed jam subjecto

Cat. 1. 5. exemptam, ut *Justitia.* [Denique, si Concretum sola terminatione diversum sit ab Abstracto, ut *justus a justitia,* hoc *Denominans* dicitur, illud *Denominativum,* Subjectum vero *Denominatum*[h].

Cat. 8. 27. Denominativis accensentur aliquando *Derivativa* illa, quæ vel solam nominis Analogiam, vel solam rei vim, non utramque retinent, ut *Studiosus studii et virtutis.* Sed ista verius *Conjugata* sunt[i].

Connotativum quoque dicitur de nominibus

it. The materials of the present note are chiefly from Occam, Logic, p. i. chap. 5, 10. It must be admitted, however, that there is some licence in the use of the word *connotative.*

[b] Παρώνυμα δὲ λέγεται ὅσα ἀπό τινος διαφέροντα τῇ πτώσει τὴν κατὰ τοὔνομα προσηγορίαν ἔχει, οἶον ἀπὸ τῆς γραμματικῆς ὁ γραμματικὸς καὶ ἀπὸ τῆς ἀνδρείας ὁ ἀνδρεῖος. Cat. i. 5. The word παρώνυμα is translated by Boethius *denominativa.* It should have been *denominata.* From the same authority denominatives have been limited by the Schoolmen to concrete adjectives, predicable of a subject possessing the abstract attribute. Cf. Aquinas, Opusc. xlviii. Tract. 2. cap. 1. The limitation is not warranted by Aristotle, and is expressly rejected by his Greek Commentators. See Simplicius, Scholia, p. 43. b. 5. τῶν δὲ παρωνύμων ἂν εἴη, φησὶν ὁ Πορφύριος, καὶ τὰ πατρωνυμικὰ καὶ τὰ συγκριτικὰ καὶ τὰ ὑπερθετικὰ καὶ τὰ ὑποκοριστικά.

[i] *Studiosus* is used in Scholastic Latin as a translation of the Greek σπουδαῖος into the two senses of " diligent" and " virtuous." In the former, it is a denominative from *studium.* In the latter, not, as is observed by Aristotle, Cat. 8. 27. The name *conjugata* is more properly applied to derivatives from the same primitive, as *sapiens, sapienter, sapientia ;* the σύστοιχα of Aristotle. Cf. Arist. Top. ii. 9, 1. Cic. Top. c. 3.

quorum conceptus se mutuo ingrediuntur, ut *Pater et Filius:* nam et illa opponuntur absolutis; sed vocantur proprio nomine *Relativa.*]

7. *Convenientia,* sunt quæ possunt de eodem simul dici, ut *doctus et pius: Repugnantia,* sive *Opposita,* quæ non possunt, ut *album et nigrum* [j].

[Oppositio [k] *incomplexa,* sive terminorum simpli- Cat. 10. 1. cium, est omnino quadruplex : 1. *Relativa,* inter terminos relativos, ut *Patrem et Filium.* 2. *Contraria,* inter *contrarios,* i. e. absolutos se mutuo pellentes ex subjecto alterutrius capaci, ut *album et nigrum.* 3. Privativa, inter privativum et positivum, ut *videntem et cœcum.* 4. *Contradictoria,* inter positivum et negativum, intellige finitum et infinitum, ut *hominem et non-hominem.* Hæc est oppositionum maxima, quia nullum admittit medium; neque *Participationis,* quale est fuscum respectu Cat. 10. 8. *albi* et *nigri;* neque *Abnegationis,* quale est lapis

[j] *Repugnantia* should not be considered as synonymous with *opposita.* There are many repugnants which are not included under any of Aristotle's four modes of opposition; e. g. *red* and *blue* are repugnant, but not opposed.

[k] Λέγεται δὲ ἕτερον ἑτέρῳ ἀντικεῖσθαι τετραχῶς, ἢ ὡς τὰ πρός τι, ἢ ὡς τὰ ἐναντία, ἢ ὡς στέρησις καὶ ἕξις, ἢ ὡς κατάφασις καὶ ἀπόφασις. Ἀντίκειται δὲ ἕκαστον τῶν τοιούτων ὡς τύπῳ εἰπεῖν ὡς μὲν τὰ πρός τι οἷον τὸ διπλάσιον τῷ ἡμίσει, ὡς δὲ τὰ ἐναντία, οἷον τὸ κακὸν τῷ ἀγαθῷ, ὡς δὲ τὰ κατὰ στέρησιν καὶ ἕξιν, οἷον τυφλότης καὶ ὄψις, ὡς δὲ κατάφασις καὶ ἀπόφασις, οἷον κάθηται οὐ κάθηται. Cat. 10. 1. Cf. Metaph. iv. 10. Contraries are the two most opposite qualities of the same class of subjects, e. g. *black* and *white,* as colours of bodies; *virtue* and *vice,* as habits of the soul. Cf. Cat. 11. 5.

inter *videntem* et *cæcum*[1].   Relativa contra, omnium minima ; nam Relata non sunt opposita, nisi ad idem sumantur.]

8. Nomen[m] *Primæ intentionis*, est Vox in com-

---

[1] *Medium Participationis.* i. e. no object can be conceived as both A and not-A. This law of thought is called the Principle of Contradiction. *Medium Abnegationis*, i. e. no object can be conceived as neither A nor not-A. This law of thought is called the Principle of Excluded Middle. See above, p. 5. note j.

[m] On the meaning of the word *intentio*, see Zabarella, *De Rebus Naturalibus*, (Francof. 1607. p. 871.) '' Ego dico intentionem nil aliud esse quam attentionem, ac diligentiam animæ in alicujus rei consideratione, quo fit ut intentum etiam sumamus pro attento : hæc est vere Latina hujus vocis significatio ; sed traducta postea a Philosophis nostris hæc vox est ad omnem animi conceptum significandum, etiamsi absque diligentia fiat, et omnem speciem, sive sensilem sive intellectilem : hæc enim, quatenus est species spiritalis reale objectum repræsentans, dicitur esse ejus intentio, id est, imago in anima : hinc orta est distinctio illa, qua omnes utuntur, primarum et secundarum intentionum.'' '' Of the *first intention*,'' says Hobbes, '' are the names of things, a *man, stone*, &c. of the *second* are the names of names and speeches, as *universal, particular, genus, species, syllogism*, and the like.'' Except that the language is too much adapted to the ultra nominalism of the author, this passage exactly expresses the true distinction. A *first intention* or *notion* is a conception under which the mind regards *things*, whether facts of external or of internal perception. Thus the individual Socrates is regarded by the mind as *man, animal, body, substance*. All these are first intentions. And a mental state may be successively regarded as *a smell, a sensation, a fact of consciousness*. These again are first intentions. A *second intention* or *notion* is a conception under which the mind regards its first intentions as related to each other. Thus the relation of *animal* to *man*,

muni usu posita. *Secundæ,* Vox artis, quam ex communi sermone sumptam Philosophia recudit denuo et moderatur.

and of *man* to *animal,* is expressed in the second intention *genus* or *species.* First intentions, as conceptions of things, are predicable of the individuals conceived under them. Thus we may say, " Socrates is man, animal, &c." Second intentions are not so predicable : we cannot say, " Socrates is species, genus, &c." Hence when we are told that a predicable is *commune, univocum, secundæ intentionis,* it is not meant that all universals are *in themselves* second intentions ; but that every predicate *viewed in relation to its subject* may be comprehended under one of Porphyry's five classes of pre-dicables ; all which are second intentions. So when Genus is said to be predicable of Species, it is not meant that we can predicate the one second intention of the other, so as to say, " Species is Genus;" but that the first intention " animal " is predicable of the first intention " man ;" the relation of the one to the other being expressed by the second intentions " genus " and " species." For this reason Logic was said to treat of *second intentions applied to first.* See Aquinas, Opusc. lvi. Scotus, Sup. Univ. Qu. 3. Zabarella, De Natura Logicæ, lib. i. cap. 19.

The distinction between first and second intentions is generally considered as of Arabian origin. And this is perhaps true, as far as regards the assigning of second intentions as the proper object matter of Logic. In this point of view, Avicenna, in the beginning of his Logic, dis-tinguishes between those essences of things which are in the things themselves, and those which are in the intellect; and, in the second chapter of his Metaphysics, says, " Subjectum Logicæ sunt intentiones intellectæ secundo, quæ apponuntur intentionibus primo intellectis, secundum hoc quod per eas per-venitur de cognito ad incognitum." But the distinction itself, and even the name, may be found much earlier. Boethius, in the beginning of his commentary on the Categories, distinguishes,

§. 4. *Vox Singularis,* dicitur alio nomine *Individuum,* ejusque significatum *Unum numero :* neque enim singulare est quicquid Unum dici potest; sed multa, quæ sunt invicem similia, eatenus Unum censentur. Vocantur enim uno eodemque nomine; quod ipsa Vocis definitio[n] non patitur, nisi in illis reipsa sit, vel saltem concipi possit, una aliqua eademque Natura, quæ huic nomini respondeat.

Talem reperit intellectus, dum plura contemplando *abstrahit*[o] ab eorum differentiis; i. e. spectat

in language very similar to that of Hobbes, between the *prima* and *secunda positio nominis;* the first, " ut nomina rebus imponerentur," the second, " ut aliis nominibus ipsa nomina designarentur;" and it is perhaps on account of this passage that Scotus (Sup. Univ. Qu. 3.) attributes the origin of the distinction to Boethius. A similar distinction however between the πρώτη and δευτέρα θέσις τῶν ὀνομάτων is given by Porphyry, in his Exposition of the Categories, (Paris, 1543, f. 3.) Cf. Ammonius in Porph. f. 42. ed. Ald. and Boethius in Porph. p. 61. For scholastic expositions, see Aquinas, Opusc. xlii. c. 12. xlviii. Tract. I. cap. 1. in 1 Sent. Dist. 2. Qu. 1. Art. 3. Scotus, in 1 Sent. Dist. 23. In Univ. Qu. 11. Occam, Logic, P. i. cap. 11. A good account of the formation of second intentions is given by Burgersdyck, *Inst. Log.* lib. i. cap. 2. Aldrich's definition, which is extremely vague though not positively erroneous, was probably suggested by Crakanthorpe, who in his Proœmium calls second intentions *Voces Artis Logicæ.* It is scarcely necessary to add, that the explanation of Abp. Whately is altogether erroneous.

[n] *Vocis definitio.* Since Vox is " signum *rei vel conceptus,*" not *rerum vel conceptuum.*

[o] *Abstrahit,* i. e. abstracts its attention from the distinctive features of the objects presented. The terms *abstract* and

in rebus ea tantum quæ conveniunt, neglectis
omnibus quibus dissident ; adeoque fundamentum

abstraction have been used in various applications ; retaining
however in all the primary signification of *withdrawing* the
attention from one portion of certain phenomena given in
combination to fix it on the rest. In this sense Geometrical
Magnitudes are called by Aristotle τὰ ἐξ ἀφαιρέσεως, (*An. Post.*
I. 18. 1.) ; because the Geometer considers only the properties
of the *figure*, separating them from those of the material in
which it is found. (See *An. Post.* I. 5. 6. *Metaph.* x. 3. 7.)
On similar grounds is formed the scholastic distinction of
abstract and *concrete* terms ; since in the former the attribute
is considered apart from the subject in which it is perceived
by the senses : e. g. sight presents to us only *alba ;* the mind
forms the conception *albedo.* And so Universals are gained
by *abstraction*, i. e. by separating the phenomena in which a
given group of individuals resemble each other from those in
which they differ. For this reason Locke calls all universals
abstract ideas ; a phrase etymologically allowable, but liable to
be confounded with the scholastic use of the word *abstract* in
a different sense. For this reason it is better to adhere to the
term *universals :* which has at the same time the advantage of
leaving the Logician, as such, uncommitted to any metaphysical
hypothesis as to their nature ; since the Realist may interpret
Universal *Substances*, the Nominalist, Universal *Names*, the
Conceptualist, Universal *Notions*.

Generalization, which some modern writers distinguish from
Abstraction, is properly a species of abstraction ; viz. the divest-
ing the presentations of consciousness of the conditions of
existence in *space* and *time*, which are characteristic of individuals. This is done by the aid of signs, verbal or other,
which are at first signs of individual objects, and subsequently
of general notions. Other abstractions may exist without generalization ; but these are not processes of thought, but of perception, internal or external. Thus, to fix the eye or ear on
a particular sight or sound exclusively, is in the widest sense
an *abstraction*, but not a *generalization*. The psychological

omne discriminis, præter numerum, eximit. **Quare naturam sic abstractam, cum sit omni singulorum differentiæ superstes, concipi par est, non ut in singulis diversam, sed ut in omnibus eandem ;** adeoque *Universale* quiddam sive *Ens unum in multis :* ejusque signum idoneum erit, Nomen *commune, Univocum, Secundæ intentionis,* uno verbo, *Prædicabile*[p], sive Vox apta prædicari, i. e. Univoce dici de multis.

§. 5. *PRÆDICABILIUM*[q] *capita,* constitui et

controversies concerning abstraction cannot be discussed here. See *Prolegomena Logica,* p. 25, (2nd ed. p. 29.)

[p] " Prædicabile (Græce κατηγορούμενον) et universale, etsi reipsa non differant, (omne enim universale prædicari potest, et omne prædicabile debet esse universale,) ratione tamen diversa sunt. Nam universale, quatenus universale est, prædicatur de inferioribus, in quæstione qua quæritur quid sint : at prædicabile, quatenus est prædicabile, prædicatur etiam de coordinatis, idque in quæstione quâ quæritur qualia sint. Itaque, cum quinque sint prædicabilia, tantum duo tamen universalia sunt, genus et species. Nam differentia, proprium, et accidens, quatenus talia sunt, non sunt universalia, sed tantum quatenus sunt genera aut species eorum quæ sub illis continentur. Ex. gr. Sensus est proprium animalis ; sed non est universale, quatenus ut proprium de animali prædicatur, sed quatenus prædicatur de visu, auditu et cæteris sensibus, ut genus." *Burgersdicii Inst. Log.* l. i. c. x. The addition of *univocum, secundæ intentionis* is superfluous. The latter has been explained in a former note. The former, though a necessary result of the abstraction here described, is not a necessary part of the notion of a predicable. Indeed, other Logicians distinguish between *æquivocal, univocal,* and *denominative* predication. See Sanderson, l. i. c. 6.

[q] The five Heads of Predicables are an addition to the

definiri possunt ad hunc modum. Quicquid in multis reperiri potest, vel est tota eorum essentia, vel ejus pars, vel cum essentia conjunctum[r]. Quare Universalia vel (quod eodem redit) Prædicabilia sunt quinque, et non plura ; videlicet, *Genus, Species, Differentia, Proprium, Accidens.*

Aristotelian Logic, taken from the Isagoge or Introduction to the Categories by Porphyry, written in the third century. Aristotle's doctrine, as far as it can be gathered from the Topics, differs from that of Porphyry in several points; as does the latter from the view adopted by Aldrich.

[r] *Quicquid in multis,* &c. These definitions are taken from Albertus Magnus, (de Prædicab. Tract. II. cap. 1.) and were generally adopted by the Realists, in the form of introduction to, or commentary on, the Definitions given by Porphyry. The Nominalists, on the other hand, expressly denied that any predicable was of the essence of the individual. See Occam, Logica, p. i. cap. 20, 21. To discuss the full bearings of this controversy would exceed the limits of a note. It will be sufficient to observe, that a considerable portion of the language adopted by Aldrich is not even intelligible, except on realistic principles; and that whenever the same language is adopted by a Nominalist, he is inevitably involved in inconsistencies and self-contradictions. The same is in some degree true of the original exposition of Porphyry, though the latter professes to leave the question of Nominalism and Realism open. But the question of the existence of universals *a parte rei* is metaphysical, not logical, and no theory on this point ought to influence the language of Logic. The rules of Logic are primarily regulative of *thoughts;* and equally so, whatever opinion we may hold concerning the essence of *things.* For this reason, it is necessary to alter nearly the whole of Aldrich's language, in speaking of the logical predicables. On the realist point of view, see further, Appendix, note A.

Porph.
Isag. 3. 17.   Nam 1. *Genus,* est quod prædicatur de pluribus ut eorum essentiæ *pars materialis* sive communis ; ut *animal*".   2. *Differentia,* quæ ut essentiæ *pars* Isag. 3. 1.
17, 20. *formalis* sive discretiva; ut *rationale.*   3. *Species,* quæ ut tota essentia ; ut *homo.*   4. *Proprium,* quod ut essentiæ junctum necessario ; ut *risibile.* 5. *Accidens,* quod ut essentiæ junctum contingenter ; ut *album, nigrum, sedere*[t].

    [*] " Genus speciebus *materia* est. Nam sicut æs, accepta forma, transit in statuam, ita genus, accepta differentia, transit in speciem." Boethius *de divisione.* But as logicians, we are not warranted in introducing any portion of the essence of *things,* but only of *concepts* or *general notions.* The whole essence of a concept is the sum of the attributes which it comprehends, and this can only be fully declared by its *definition,* not, as Aldrich says, by *species.* The *Genus* or *material part* of *two given concepts,* (to speak of the material or formal part of a *single concept* is nonsense,) is the sum of those attributes which are common to both ; as the *difference* or *formal part* is composed of those attributes which are peculiar to each. Thus, if there be given three concepts, containing respectively the attributes, *ab, ac, bc. a* is the genus of the first compared with the second, *b* and *c* the respective differences. But if the first is compared with the third, *b* becomes the common genus, *a* and *c* the respective differences. In this, the only tenable logical point of view, there can be no such thing as an absolute genus or difference.

    [t] *Necessario—Contingenter.* This distinction is based on the supposition that certain attributes are necessarily connected with others, from which they flow, as effect from cause. Thus *risibility* was described in the scholastic philosophy as necessarily flowing from *rationality,* in the same manner as having the angles at the base equal to each other necessarily results from the equality of two sides in an

Patet hinc 1°. De iis *dici Prœdicabile* quibus *inest Universale.* *Genusque* adeo, quod est plurium essentiarum vel specierum pars communis, de *specie differentibus,* h. e. de diversis speciebus quas ingreditur, dici; ut *animal* de *homine* et *bruto.* *Speciem* vero, de *numero differentibus,* h. e. de diversis individuis, quorum singula habent essentiam speciei vocabulo significatam; sic *homo* de *Socrate* et *Platone* dicitur, et de omnibus, quibus natura inest humana. Reliqua vero Prædicabilia, (prout inferius patebit) eadem de causa, tam de specie quam numero differentibus dicuntur.

Et N. B. ex recepto more loquendi, Genus et Speciem *prædicari in* (i. e. respondere quæstioni factæ per) *Quid*[a]*;* Differentiam in *Qualequid*;

Isag. 2. 11. 6. 3.

Top. iv. 2. 11.
Isag. 2. 13. 10. 5. 11. 5. 15. 2.

isosceles triangle. But this theory, originally borrowed from the mathematics, is not true of any succession of physical phenomena. As a matter of fact, we experience that certain events are invariably conjoined, but there is not, as in mathematical demonstrations, any necessity that they must be so. Invariable succession, in fact, is the highest positive notion of causality to which we can attain in the case of sensible phenomena, though this limitation does not include the moral causality of which we are conscious in volition. Necessity, however, in any sense is untenable as a logical criterion of property, since it presupposes an acquaintance with the laws of any given physical phenomena, of which the Logician as such knows nothing. A better logical distinction between property and accident is that given by Aristotle, of the *convertible* and *non convertible* attribute. See Appendix, note A.

[a] *Prædicatur in Quid;* i. e. is expressed by a noun substantive: *in Quale;* by an adjective. See Aquinas, *Opusc.* xlviii. cap. 2. (Cf. (Pseudo) Abelard, *De Gen. et Sp.* p. 528. ed. Cousin.)

Proprium et Accidens in *Quale*. Unde facile est conficere vulgatas Prædicabilium definitiones. Nam *Genus* definitur, *Prædicabile quod prædicatur* de pluribus specie differentibus in Quid. Differentia, quod de pluribus specie vel numero differentibus in Qualequid &c.[1]

Isag. 2. 8.
2. 21.

Isag. 3. 17.

Patet 2°. *Genus* esse *Totum* quiddam, nempe *Logicum,* sive in modo loquendi ; quatenus continet (i. e. prædicationis ambitu complectitur) species tanquam *partes* sui *subjectivas. Speciem*

Arist.
Metaph.
IV.25.2,3.
Isag. 8. 8.

That the distinctions of substance, quality, and the other categories, are founded on grammatical grounds, is shewn by Trendelenburg, *Elem. Log. Arist.* §. 3.

The reader of Locke must not confound this distinction with that between *substances* and *modes; Essay,* b. ii. ch. 12. (Cf. Descartes, *Princ.* i. 48. Port-Royal Logic, p. i. ch. 2.) A quality is predicated *in quid* of another quality, as well as a substance of a substance ; e. g. " Prudence is a virtue." Cf. Pacius on Top. i. §. 3. Port-Royal Logic, part i. ch. 7.

The distinction between *Qualequid* and *Quale* is not warranted by Porphyry. According to him, Differentia, Proprium, and Accidens are all predicated, ἐν τῷ ὁποῖόν τί ἐστιν. Boethius distinguishes them as *Quale in substantia* and *Quale non in substantia.* The *vulgatæ definitiones* which follow are the original definitions of Porphyry, adopted by most subsequent Logicians.

[1] *Specie vel numero,* i. e. generic difference *de specie differentibus;* specific, *de numero differentibus.* But this would not be allowed by Porphyry, according to whom differentia is always predicated *de specie differentibus.* The remaining definitions might be supplied as follows ; *Species, quod de pluribus numero differentibus in Quid. Proprium, quod de pluribus numero differentibus in Quale. Accidens, quod de pluribus genere vel specie vel numero differentibus in Quale.* The two last, however, are not given as definitions by Porphyry.

quoque *Totum* esse, nempe *Metaphysicum,* sive in modo concipiendi ; quatenus continet (i. e. ad perfectionem sui postulat) Genus tanquam *partem* sui *essentialem*[y]. Unde Differentia Generi accedens, dicitur *Genus* ipsum *dividere,* quatenus ejus significata distinguit, et *speciem constituere,* quatenus ejus essentiam complet.

Isag. 3. 7, 13.

§. 6. *GENUS* aliud *Summum,* aliud *Subalternum* est : *Species* quoque, in *Subalternum* et *Infimam* distinguitur[z]. Genus summum, est quod

Isag. 2. 23, 28.

Isag. 2. 23, 29.

[y] *Totum Logicum—Totum Metaphysicum.* The propriety of this nomenclature may be questioned. " Universale," says Burgersdyck, " totum quoddam est; quippe multa complectitur ut partes. Dicitur *totum Logicum,* quia Logicæ munus est de universis disputare. Genus et differentia distinguuntur sola ratione ; ideoque compositio ex genere et differentia non est vera compositio, sed compositio rationis. Hoc totum solet appellari *totum Metaphysicum,* quia Metaphysica versatur circa ea fere, quæ non tam reipsa quam ratione diversa sunt," *Inst. Log.* 1. i. c. 14. But in truth, as regards mere notions, the potential extension and comprehension are both within the province of Logic ; and as regards things, the real essence of a species and the actual subdivisions of a genus are both equally without. The distinction itself is of great importance, and has been expressed in various ways, by the terms *potential* and *actual* whole, whole in *predication* and in *definition, universal* and *essential* whole, &c. The best is that adopted by the Port-Royal Logicians, who distinguish the *extension* or subjects of which a notion is predicable from the *comprehension* or attributes which it involves in itself. Thus genus is a whole in extension, species a whole in comprehension. On this important distinction, see Sir W. Hamilton's Lectures on Logic, I. p. 141. Mr. Baynes's Translation of the Port-Royal Logic, p. xxxii. or Bp. Thomson's Outline of the Laws of Thought, p. 79, 5th ed.

[z] The *Summum Genus* and the *Infima Species,* as here

nulli*, Species infima, quæ omni *cognato* *Generi*

described, are both merely imaginary limits, never arrived at in any process of actual thought. The notion of *Being* or even of *Substance* in general, apart from this or that special combination of attributes, and that of a combination so complex as to admit of no additional attributes in thought, are both psychologically inconceivable. A Highest Genus and a Lowest Species may be admitted in any material science, as the limits at which the investigations of that science begin and end; but such a limitation is made entirely on material grounds, relatively to the purpose of that particular science, and cannot be recognised by Logic. See Appendix, note A.

ᵃ The Aristotelian Logicians consider the *summa genera* as ten in number, viz. the ten Categories or Predicaments of Aristotle. These are οὐσία, ποσόν, ποιόν, πρός τι, ποῦ, ποτέ, κεῖσθαι, ἔχειν, ποιεῖν, πάσχειν; usually translated, Substance, Quantity, Quality, Relation, Place, Time, Situation, Possession, Action, Passion. The Categories have by different commentators been regarded as a classification of names, of things, and of both; and have been alternately banished to Metaphysics and recalled to Logic. Whatever position they may hold in the Metaphysical writings of Aristotle, in his Logical ones they are expressly declared to be a division of the notions signified by simple terms. *Ens* (τὸ ὄν) was not regarded as a *summum genus* to the several Categories, being considered by Aristotle and his followers as predicable of them, not *univocally*, but *equivocally*, or rather *analogously*. But a classification of Categories is out of place in Formal Logic. From the analysis of any notion, whether given in itself or as forming part of a judgment, I can by mere thinking arrive at the simplest elements it contains; but I cannot by mere thinking determine that all notions so analysed will lead me to exactly ten such elements, neither more nor less. This requires a knowledge, not merely of all the forms of thought, but also of all the characteristics of the objects about which we can think. On the principle of the Aristotelian Cate-

subjicitur: Genus vel Species subalterna[b], quæ et cognato Generi subjicitur, et de cognata Specie præedicatur. Voco autem *Cognata,* quæ ex iisdem Individuis perpetua abstractione colliguntur; ut *Homo, Animal, Vivens, Corpus, Substantia:* quæ ex *Socrate, Platone* &c. expurgatis continue differentiis oriuntur.

Isag. 2. 24, 30.

[Hanc seriem ita placuit describi ut quodammodo referret arborem: saltem a Porphyrio sic descripta *Porphyrianœ Arboris*[c] nomen habet. Hujus *truncum* referebat *linea directa,* in qua Genera et Species scribebantur: in *suprema* Tabula Genus summum, in *ima* Species infima; unde Nomina. Inter hæc Media Subalterna, suo ordine.

Differentiæ ad latus sunt dispositæ; ad quas ductæ a Generibus suis lineæ *Ramorum* instar pertinebant. Individua sub specie infima oblique descripta sunt, quasi propagines Radicis.]

gories and the objections raised against them, see Appendix, note B.

[b] *Species subalterna.* Here the word *species* has changed its meaning. In the original definition it meant a certain relation in which a predicate may stand to its subject. Man is a Species to Socrates. It now means a certain relation in which a subject may stand to its predicate. Man is a Species to Animal. These are generally distinguished by Logicians as the *species prædicabilis* and the *species subjicibilis.*

[c] By the Greek Logicians it was sometimes called the *ladder* (*κλίμαξ*) of Porphyry.

ARBOR PORPHYRIANA [d].

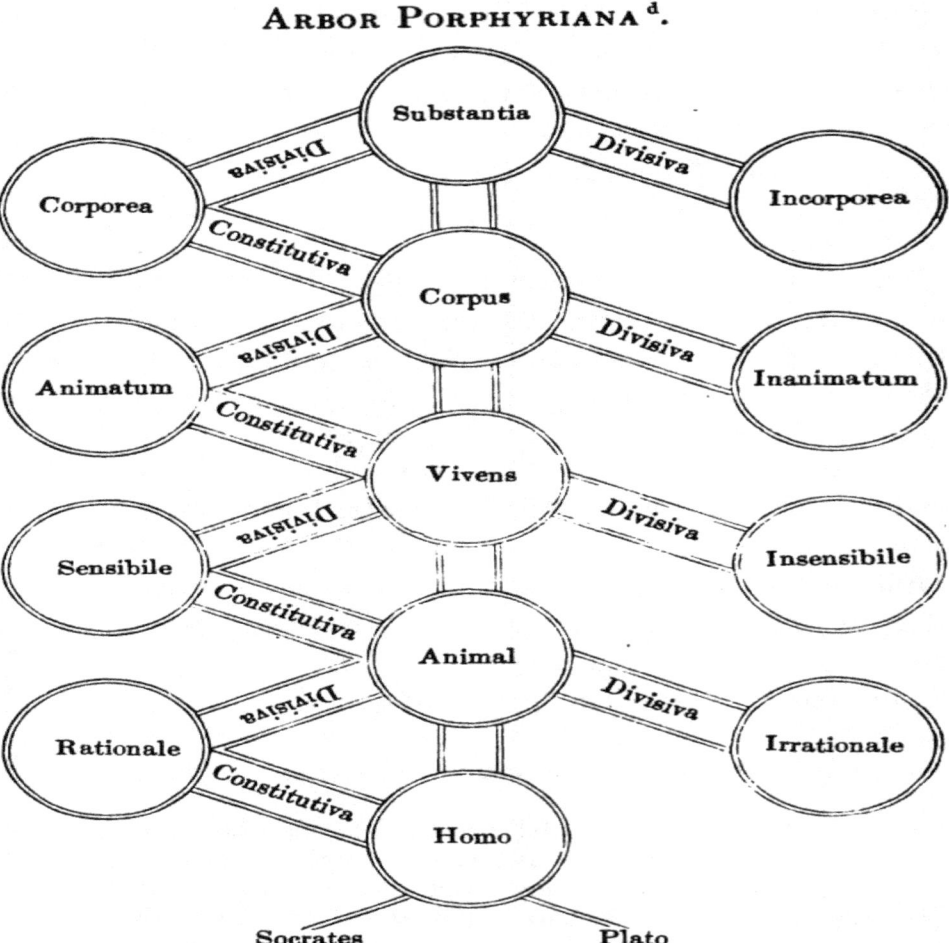

[d] This delineation of the Arbor Porphyriana is first given by Aquinas, Opusc. xlviii. Tract. ii. cap. 3. In all the earlier specimens, *Animal Rationale* is placed between Animal and Homo as the *proximum genus*, and divided into *mortale* and *immortale*, in accordance with Porphyry's definition of Man.

Quare 1. *Differentia* est vel *Generica,* quæ [Isag. 3. 6, 14.] constituit Speciem Subalternam ; vel *Specifica*[e], quæ infimam : hæc est, quæ de numero differentibus, illa, quæ de specie differentibus prædicatur. Exempla, *Sensibile* et *Rationale.*

2. *Proprium*[f] quoque, vel *Genericum* est, quod necessario comitatur essentiam Generis summi vel subalterni[g] ; atque ex illa adeo fluere atque oriri

[e] The term *specific difference* (διαφορὰ εἰδοποιός) has a different meaning in Porphyry. It is opposed to *accidental difference,* (διαφορὰ κατὰ συμβεβηκός,) and marks the differentia proper, which distinguishes species from species, (whether subaltern or infima,) as opposed to accidents, which only distinguish between individuals.

[f] *Proprium.* In formal logic, which cannot take into account the realist theory of essence, it becomes necessary to change slightly the language which expresses the distinction between *proprium* and *differentia.* The essence of a concept is the sum of the attributes which it comprehends. Whatever does not form a part of the *comprehension* of the concept or of the *signification* of its name, is not *part of* but *joined to* the essence : i. e. it is found in all or some of the individuals of the class, but is not implied in the name or notion of the class itself. Thus it is no part of the notion of a triangle that its angles are equal to two right angles ; and it is no part of the notion of a body to have weight. These then are *properties,* not *differences,* and, when predicated of their respective subjects, form what Kant calls *synthetical,* as distinguished from *analytical* judgments. Thus the *non-essential* are distinguished from the *essential* predicables. The further distinction of property from accident, as *necessarily* or *contingently* joined, has been already noticed as extralogical.

[g] A *summum genus* can manifestly have no constitutive differentia ; but it may have properties. There may be attributes forming no portion of the universal nature (or conception) of substance, which are notwithstanding found in all

D

dicitur : vel *Specificum,* quod fluit ab essentia
speciei infimæ : Illud itaque de pluribus speciebus,
hoc, de una specie et pluribus Individuis prædicatur. Exempla, *Mobile* et *Risibile.*

Isag. 4. 1.　　Proprium tamen aliunde quadrifariam dicitur[h].
1. Quod convenit soli, sed non omni ; scil. soli
Speciei, sed non omni ejus Individuo ; ut *homini*

substances and at all times. Such properties of the summum
genus are enumerated by Aristotle, Categ. ch. 5. These
were in the scholastic theory regarded as flowing from the
simple essence ; those of all subordinate classes from the
differentia.

[h] Porphyry, following Aristotle, does not distinguish Property from Accident as flowing necessarily from the essence,
but as coextensive and simply convertible with its subject.
In this he is followed by Boethius : the other distinction, however, appears as early as in the commentary of Albertus Magnus,
and seems to have been derived from the Arabians. (Cf. Albert
de Predicab. Tract. vi. cap. 1.) The ἴδιον of Porphyry answers
to the fourth kind of property mentioned in the text. The
other three are *accidents ;* the first and third separable ; the
second inseparable, but still only an accident, as being predicable of more subjects than *homo.* On the scholastic theory,
it is also an accident, as not flowing necessarily from *rationale,*
the differentia. Aristotle, who defines man ζῷον πέζον δίπουν,
would regard *bipes* as a differentia. It may be observed that,
upon the principles of Aristotle and Porphyry, a generic
property can only be regarded as a property with respect to
the highest species of which it is predicable. As regards all
subordinate species, it must be considered as an *accident.*
Mobile, for example, a property of *corpus,* is an accident to
animal, and to *homo,* as not convertible with them. This may
be fairly inferred from Top. ii. 3, 5. and is also maintained by
Avicenna and Albertus Magnus : see Albert. de Predicab.
Tract. ix. cap. 1. On the theory of *necessary connection,* it may
remain a property ; but on this authorities are divided.

esse Grammaticum. 2. Quod omni, sed non soli; ut *homini esse bipedem.* 3. Quod omni et soli, sed non semper; ut *homini canescere.* 4. Quod omni, soli, et semper; ut *homini risibilitas.* Hujusmodi Isag. 14. 7. Proprium est, quod constituit Quartum Prædicabile.

Accidens, cum essentiæ junctum sit contin- Isag. 5. 1. genter, adesse igitur vel abesse potest, salva interim essentia subjecti; cui tamen aliquando tam tenaciter inhæret, ut cogitatione sola divelli atque separari possit; ut *Mantuanum esse, a Virgilio.* Quare vocatur *Inseparabile*[1]. Quod autem actu sive reipsa separari potest, ut albedo a pariete, dicitur *Separabile.*

§. 7. QUEMADMODUM Vox Singularis dicitur *Indi-* An. Pr. I.
31. 1.
An. Post.

[1] We must distinguish between the accidents of a class and II. 5. 1. those of an individual. Of the former, those are *inseparable*, II. 13. 7. which, though not connected with the essence by any law of causation, are as a matter of fact found in all the members of the class, and can be the predicates of an *universal* proposition; e. g. " all crows are black." The *separable* accidents are found in some members of the class and not in others, and therefore can only be predicates of *particular* propositions; e. g. " some horses are black." This distinction between the separable and inseparable accidents of a class has been transferred by Archbishop Whately to distinguish between accident and property. Of the accidents of the individual, the inseparable can be predicated of their subject at all times; e. g. " Virgil is a Mantuan;" the separable only at certain times; e. g. " Virgil is sitting down." Aldrich's distinction, between *separable in thought* and *separable in fact*, is extralogical. Logic is concerned only with thought, not with physical changes.

D 2

viduum, ita et Communis *Dividua* dici potest. Eam enim per Metaphoram dividere dicitur, qui plura ejus significata recenset; nam in uno multa distinguit. Ita qui *animal* dicit *esse* (i. e. vocabulum animal *significare*) *hominem* et *brutum,* dicitur *animal in hominem brutumque dividere.*

Quare *Divisio*[k], est distincta enumeratio plurium,

---

[k] Division was employed by Plato and others as a method of demonstrating definitions. Aristotle shews that the reasoning is unsound, and always involves a *petitio principii.* For this reason he calls it a kind of weak syllogism, though he allows it to be useful for testing definitions when gained : see Appendix, note C. Among the later Peripatetics, Division seems to have been held in higher estimation; a separate treatise on the subject having been composed by Andronicus Rhodius. From them it descended to Boethius, whose book *de Divisione* is the principal authority from which subsequent Logicians have drawn.

According to Boethius, the word Division is used in three principal senses. 1. Division of a genus into species. 2. Division of a whole into parts. 3. Division of an equivocal term into its several significations. Of these, according to Cicero, Top. ch. 6. the first is properly called *Divisio,* the second, *Partitio.* "In partitione quasi membra sunt; ut corporis, caput, humeri, manus, latera, crura, pedes, et cetera: in divisione, formæ sunt, quas Græci ideas vocant; nostri, si qui hæc forte tractant, species appellant." Cf. Quintil. v. 10. vii. 1. In Division, the whole or its definition can be predicated of each part, as " Homo est animal," " Homo est vivens sensibile." In Partition this cannot be done. Boethius, however, includes under his second head, not only the enumeration of the component parts of an individual, but also that of the individuals contained under an *infima species.* " Ut cum dico domus aliud esse tectum, aliud paries, aliud fundamentum ; cumque hominis dicimus partes esse Catonem, Virgilium, Ciceronem." The last in one respect

quæ communi nomine significantur. Estque ana-
loga distributioni totius in partes. Unde et nomen
ipsum Commune dicitur *Totum Divisum,* et distincta ejus significata, *Partes* sive *membra divi-*
dentia, et bene dividendi leges statuuntur tres.

1. [1]Dividentia sigillatim minus contineant (i. e.

more resembles division proper; as the name and definition of
the whole are predicable of each part. But on account of the
infinite number of individuals, and consequent impossibility
of exhausting the species, this is not generally reckoned as a
division proper.

The division of an equivocal term, as *canis* into *animal,*
sidus, piscis, is sometimes called *Distinction.* The test of this
is, that the name is predicable of each member, but not the
same definition. This is useful for separating the senses of
an ambiguous term before defining it. See Top. vi. 2. 1.

[1] For the due observance of these rules, it is desirable that
the division consist of as few members as possible. Some
recommend *dichotomy,* or a division of every genus into two
species by means of opposed differentiæ. Of the four kinds
of Opposition, Boethius admits for this purpose contraries,
positive and privative terms, and also contradictories as sometimes unavoidable; but rejects relatives. Aristotle censures
the use of privative and indefinite terms, and approves of
division by *contraries.* See Top. vi. 6. 3. de Part. Anim. i. 3.
Here dichotomy is only practicable when the contraries admit
no medium between them. Cf. Cat. 10, 18. Top. vi. 6. 1.
Examples of dichotomy by contraries may be found in the
Arbor Porphyriana. For a threefold division of the same kind,
see Eth. Nic. vii. 6, 5. τῶν γὰρ ἡδέων ἔνια φύσει αἱρετά, τὰ δ' ἐναντία
τούτων, τὰ δὲ μεταξύ. Dichotomy by *contradiction,* which Aristotle
censures, had been a favourite method with Plato, as it afterwards was with Ramus and his followers. See Hamilton's
Reid, p. 689. Cf. Trend. Elem. §. 68, Erläuterungen, p. 106.

But none of the above methods of division can be regarded
as a strictly formal process of thought. Any concept A is

Top. VI. 6. arctius significent) quam Divisum. Nam Totum
1.
est majus partibus singulis. 2. Dividentia con-
junctim plus minusve ne contineant quam Divisum.
Nam Totum est æquale partibus universis. 3. Membra Divisionis sint opposita, (i. e. in se invicem ne
contineantur :) nam sine distinctione frustra est
partitio.

§. 8. DIVISIONEM excipit[m] (quæ per Metapho-

potentially divisible into A which is B, and A which is not B;
and experience alone can determine whether either of these
members includes under it really existing individuals or not.
Logically, the division of animal into mortal and immortal is
as good as that into rational and irrational. But this division
is not strictly formal; for B, the dividing attribute, not being
part of the comprehension of A, has to be sought for out of
the mere act of thought, after A has been given. This has
been observed by Hoffbauer and Fries, who hence rightly
maintain, against Kant, that even dichotomy by contradiction
is not an act of formal thinking. Cf. Hoffbauer, *Logik*, §. 138.
Fries *System der Logik*, §. 92.

The only strictly formal process of this kind is that
distinguished as *Determination*, which consists in the reunion of
a genus and difference previously elicited by analysis from
a given concept. Formal Division thus presupposes Definition. See Drobisch, *Neue Darstellung der Logik*, §. 17, 29, 30.

[m] *Excipit.* The reason of this order is given by Abelard:
" Quoniam vero divisiones definitionibus naturaliter priores
sunt, quippe ex ipsis constitutionis suæ originem ducunt, in
ipso quoque tractatu divisiones merito priorem locum obtine-
bunt, definitiones vero posteriorem." Dialectica, ed. Cousin.
p. 450. This is true in a material point of view; the matter
of a definition being sometimes gained by division. But
formally, the reverse order is preferable; a formal division
or determination being only possible after definition. See
the last note.

ram quoque dicitur) *Definitio ;* cujus est, assignare conceptus et voces, quibus ea, quæ ab invicem distincta volumus, velut agrorum fines, ex limitibus suis dignoscantur. Quæ cum definitis notiora esse debeant magisque obvia, Definitio vulgo dicitur *Oratio explicativa definiti.* *Oratio* (inquam) ut a Top.I.5.1. nomine distinguatur ; *Explicativa* quoque, nam et nomen *exprimit.*

Definitio alia, *Nominalis* est, quæ vocis signifi- An. Post. cationem aperit ; alia, *Realis,* quæ rei[n] naturam. II. 7. 5.

[n] *Rei.* i. e. of an universal notion existing in the mind ; without entering on the question whether there exists any external universal nature corresponding to it. Since all such notions are represented by words, a *real,* or more correctly speaking a *notional,* definition, will at the same time unfold the meaning of the word by which the given notion is represented. Still the two kinds of definition must not be confounded. A real definition has primarily for its object to analyse a complex notion into its component parts. Words are employed *secondarily,* though unavoidably, as signs, both of the whole notion, and of the simpler notions of which it is composed. But the object of nominal definition is to determine of what notion, simple or complex, a given word is the sign. The notion may be already known, more or less clearly, by means of other signs, though we were not aware of its connexion with the word in question. A different distinction between nominal and real definition is given by Leibnitz, *Nouveaux Essais,* l. iii. c. 3.

If this account of real definition is correct, it will follow that the same notion admits of only one definition ; since the same notion cannot be a combination of more than one group of attributes. And nothing can be more clear than Aristotle's testimony on these points, nothing more positive than his repudiation of the so-called *accidental* and *physical* definitions. (Cf. Top. vi. 4, 2. vi. 14, 5. i. 8. 2, 3. Metaph. vi.

Realis iterum vel *Accidentalis,* sive *Descriptio,* quæ definito accidentia (puta causas, effectus, proprietates aliaque id genus) assignat; vel *Essentialis,* quæ partes essentiæ constitutivas.   *Essentialis* denique, vel *Metaphysica* sive *Logica°,* quæ Genus

11, 15.)   Nevertheless, on the strength of a misunderstood passage in the De Anima, (i. 1. 16.) the threefold division of real definition has been fathered on the Stagirite.   For a fuller account of Aristotle's doctrine, see Appendix, note C. Before quitting this subject, it may be observed, that Logicians have perpetually confounded the *thing* or *notion* within the mind with the *things* or *individuals* without.   Thus Abp. Whately observes, that Logic is concerned with nominal definitions only; because all that is requisite for the purposes of reasoning is, that a word shall not be used in different senses; a real definition of any thing belongs to the science or system which is employed about that thing.   On the contrary, Logic is concerned with *real* or *notional* definitions only: its object being to produce *distinctness* in *concepts*, which are the *things* of Logic.   Nominal definitions belong to the grammars or dictionaries of particular languages.   Even Kant (*Logik,* §. 106.) has not quite avoided this confusion.

° *Metaphysica sive Logica.*   On this point the two great sects of the Schoolmen were at issue.   The Realists, following the Arabians, divided Logic into two parts; one, which treated of the essence of incomplex notions and things by *definition;* the other, of the truth of propositions as determined by *argumentation.*   To this latter the greater part of the Aristotelian Logic was regarded as belonging.   The former was supposed to have formed a lost portion of the ancient science. The Nominalists, on the other hand, and more correctly, maintained that to investigate the essences of things belonged to the province of Metaphysics; the Logician, as such, assigning no actual definitions, but borrowing them as mere examples from the science to which they properly belong.   As authorities for the two views, compare Albert, de Prædicab. Tract. i. chap. 5, 6. with Occam, Logic, part i. chap. 26.

et Differentiam ; vel *Physica*[p], quæ partes Essentiæ physicas, i. e. realiter distinctas : nam Genus et Differentia sola mente distinguuntur.

E. g. Definitur homo *Nominaliter*[q], qui ex humo.

[p] Physical definition is rejected by Aristotle, (Metaph. vi. 11.) on the ground that the physical parts are not parts of the species, but of the individuals. Aldrich's expression, "partes *essentiæ* physicas." cannot be tolerated, unless we regard universal notions as not merely real substances, but corporeal. In the example given by Aldrich, the so-called Physical definition may be regarded as merely an indirect mode of expressing the same notion that the Metaphysical definition expresses directly. It is thus merely an accidental variation of language, easily reduced to the direct form, and is so regarded by Albert, de Præd. Tract. i. chap. 6. and by Occam, pt. i. ch. 26. In all other cases it is no definition at all.

[q] Most Logicians reckon two principal methods of nominal definition: 1. by a synonymous term, e. g. "ensis est gladius:" 2. by Etymology, as in Aldrich's example. The former is in fact *translation*, it being indifferent whether the synonyms belong to the same language or not; the latter will in many cases be no definition at all; a large number of words having quite lost their etymological meaning. Neither of these methods is countenanced by Aristotle; see Appendix, note C. The former may be traced to the Greek Commentators; see Alexander, in Metaph. p. 442. ed. Bonitz. The latter is an innovation borrowed from the Rhetoricians, by whom it was called *Notatio*. See Cicero, Top. ch. 8.

" In Mathematics, and in all strict Sciences," says Abp. Whately, "the Nominal and the Real Definition exactly coincide; the *meaning of the word*, and the *nature of the thing*, being exactly *the same*." This remark is based on Locke ; (*Essay*, b. iii. c. 3. §. 18.) but it confounds the *Real Essence* of Locke, i. e. the unknown constitution of each *individual* with the *Logical Essence* or contents of a *general notion*. Cf. Zabarella *De Methodis*, l. i. p. 159.

Accidentaliter[r], Animal bipes implume. *Metaphy-sice*[s], Animal rationale. *Physice,* Ens naturale constans corpore organico et anima rationali.

Bonæ Definitionis leges potissimum tres sunt.

Top. VI.
1. 1.
1. Definitio sit adæquata definito : alias non explicat definitum. Quæ enim angustior est, explicat tantum *partem,* cum definitum sit *totum ;* quæ laxior, explicat *totum,* cum definitum sit
Top. VI. 4.
2, 7.
tantum *pars.* 2. Ut *per se* clarior[t] sit et notior

---

[r] Accidental definition is composed of genus and one or more *properties.* Accidents properly so called are expressly rejected as useless in definition by Porphyry, Isag. 3. 15. and by Boethius, Opera, p. 3, though admitted by some subsequent authorities. Hence *animal risibile* would be a better example than Aldrich's *animal bipes implume.* But the majority of Logicians have very properly regarded accidental definition, in any form, as no definition, but merely *description.* It does not analyse the contents of a *notion,* but enumerates marks by which one *individual* may be distinguished from each other. The same notion can have but one *definition;* the same individual may have many *descriptions.* Cf. Albert. l. c. Occam, pt. i. ch. 27. Wyttenbach. *Præcept. Log.* p. iii. c. v. §. 14. Drobisch, §. 104.

[s] Metaphysical definition, the only proper definition in the strict sense of the term, being by genus and differentia, (or more correctly by genus and *differentiæ;* see Top. i. 8, 3. and above, p. 26, note s.) it will follow, that all definable notions must be *species.* Hence *summa genera,* which have no differentiæ, and *individuals,* which are distinguished only by accidents, are not definable. See Arist. Metaph. iv. 3, 6. (where for εἰς read οὐ, supported by two Mss. and by Alexander, Schol. p. 693, a. 8.) vi. 15. 2. The supposed difference on this point between Aristotle and Locke, or rather Descartes, may be reduced to a verbal question. See Appendix, note C.

[t] *Per se clarior;* i. e. composed of parts greater in extension

definito : alias non explicat omnino. *Dico* tamen
per se, quia *per accidens* potest minus intelligi
quod notius est sua natura.   3. Ut justo vocum
propriarum numero absolvatur : nam ex Meta-
phoris oritur ambiguitas, ex nimia brevitate obscu-
ritas, ex prolixitate confusio.

Top. VI. 2.
4.
Top. VI. 2.
3. IV. 3. 4.

than the *definitum*, though less in comprehension ; as are the
genus and differentia, as compared with the species.   For the
more universal notions are γνωριμώτερα φύσει, though individuals
and lower species are γνωριμώτερα ἡμῖν.   See An. Post. i. 2. 5.
Top. vi. 4. 7, 9.

   ⁿ *Vocum propriarum ;* i. e. words in common use, called in
the Rhetoric, (iii. 2, 2.) κύρια ὀνόματα, i. e. *sanctioned* by popular
use ; " quem penes arbitrium est et jus et norma loquendi."
Cf. Poet. 21. 5. λέγω δὲ κύριον μὲν ᾧ χρῶνται ἕκαστοι.   In the
Topics, (vi. 2. 4.) they are called *established* names, (κείμενα
ὀνόματα.)

CAP. II.

De Propositione Categorica pura.

§. 1. SECUNDA Pars Logicæ agit de *Propositione*[a] sive *Enuntiatione;* quod est signum secundæ operationis Intellectus, sive Judicium verbis expressum.

Quare, ad Propositionem legitimam requiritur.

DeInt.5.1.   1. Quoad vocem, ut sit *Oratio affirmans*[b] *vel negans,* quæ est ejus *essentia.*

DeInt.4.3.   2. Quoad sensum, ut *verum vel falsum significet,* (id. scil. quod res est, vel secus, dicat,) quod essen-

---

[a] "Sed cum disseramus de Oratione, cujus variæ species sunt,......est una inter has ad propositum potissima, quæ pronunciabilis appellatur, absolutam sententiam comprehendens, sola ex omnibus veritati aut falsitati obnoxia : quam vocat Sergius *effatum,* Varro *proloquium,* Cicero *enunciatum,* Græci *protasin* tum *axioma ;*......familiarius tamen dicetur *propositio.*" Apuleius de Dogm. Platonis, lib. iii. He has not distinguished between ἀπόφανσις and πρότασις,—the former of which is rendered by Boethius *enunciatio,* the latter *propositio.* See Trendelenburg, Elem. §. 2. "᾽Απόφανσις quum ad syllogismum instituendum tanquam propositio quæ vocatur præmissa adhibetur, πρότασις dicitur." And so Aquinas, Opusc. xlviii. Tract. de Enunc. cap. 1. "Propositio nam solum dicitur de præmissis ipsius syllogismi, sed enunciatio tam de præmissis quam de conclusione." The distinction, however, is not implied in the definitions of the two by Aristotle, de Int. 5. 5. and Anal. Pr. i. 1. 2.

[b] *Oratio affirmans,* κατάφασις—*negans,* ἀπόφασις. These are literally rendered by Apuleius, *Propositio dedicativa* and *abdicativa.* The ordinary renderings, *affirmatio* and *negatio,* are first used by Boethius. See Prantl, i. p. 521.

tiæ necessario nexum, et proinde *proprietas* est. Unde et

3. Non est ambigua; sic enim orationes esset. Nec 4. Solœca vel mutila; sic enim nihil significaret.

Quare, ea demum Propositio legitima censebitur, quæ, juxta definitionem vulgatam, est *Oratio Indicativa*°, *congrua et perfecta, verum vel falsum significans, sine ambiguitate.* ~~De Int.5.5.~~ Anal. Pr. I. 1. 2.

§. 2. EJUS Divisiones variæ sunt;

1. *Categorica*ᵈ est, quæ enuntiat absolute; ut, *Homo est risibilis. Hypothetica,* quæ sub conditione; ut, *si homo est rationalis est risibilis. Vel dies est vel nox.*

Quod Categorica dicit, nihilo nexum est; quasi per se subsistens: quod Hypothetica, conditioni substat. Unde et hæc Divisio peti dicitur a *Substantia* Propositionis; et per ejus membra respondetur interroganti, *Quæ est Propositio?*

Categorica rursus dividitur in *Puram* et *Modalem*ᵉ. Hypothetica in *Conditionalem, Disjunctivam,*

ᶜ The proposition is defined by Aristotle, λόγος ἀποφαντικός, which is translated by Petrus Hispanus, *Oratio indicativa,* and better by Boethius, *Oratio enunciativa.* The rest of Aldrich's definition is superfluous.

ᵈ *Categorica.* In Aristotle κατηγορικὸς always signifies *affirmative,* and is opposed, not to ὑποθετικός, but to στερητικός. The latter sense probably originated with Theophrastus, who first expounded the hypothetical syllogism. See Sir W. Hamilton, *Discussions,* p. 152.

ᵉ Aristotle, in de Int. ch. 12. 1. enumerates four modes;

Anal. Pr. &c. Categorica pura, sive *Propositio de inesse*[f],
I. 2. 1.
De Int. 12. est quæ pure affirmat vel negat; i. e. simpliciter

the *necessary*, the *impossible*, the *contingent*, and the *possible*.
(ἀναγκαῖον—ἀδύνατον—ἐνδεχόμενον—δυνατόν.) These he afterwards,
Anal. Pr. i. 2. 1. reduces to two, the necessary and the contingent. See St. Hilaire's Translation, Preface, p. 66. That
he adds the *true* and the *false* is questionable; the words
ἀληθές, οὐκ ἀληθές, in de Int. 12. 10. are perhaps only intended
to mark the previous four pairs as contradictories, of which
the one must be true, the other false. Subsequent Logicians,
following the Greek Commentators, have multiplied the
number of modes *ad infinitum*. Any adverb annexed to the
predicate, "*homo currit velociter,*" or even an adjective qualifying
the subject, "*homo albus currit,*" was regarded as forming a
modal. The *name* τρόπος, as applied both to the modes of
propositions and to those of syllogisms, is not Aristotelian,
but comes from the Greek Commentators. (Ammonius, Schol.
p. 130. a. 16.)

The post-Aristotelian modes affect the subject or the
predicate alone, not the relation between them. They are
thus only pure propositions with complex terms, as is remarked by Melanchthon, *Erotemata Dialectica*, p. 132, ed. 1568.
Aristotle's modes affect the copula and the manner of
thinking, and are psychologically distinct *forms* of the proposition, as they are rightly treated by Kant, *Kritik der r. V.*
p. 71. But in a logical point of view, the distinction of
modals is unimportant, as not influencing any further process
of pure thinking. For this reason they are out of place in the
logical writings of Kant and his followers. See further,
Prolegomena Logica, note G. (2nd ed. note H.)

[f] *De inesse,*—τοῦ ὑπάρχειν. We find two expressions in
Aristotle, both of which are sometimes rendered by "*being in.*"
1. ὑπάρχειν, by which the *predicate* is said to be in the *subject*.
This is equivalent to κατηγορεῖσθαι. Τὸ Α ὑπάρχει παντὶ τῷ Β = τὸ
Α κατηγορεῖται κατὰ παντὸς τοῦ Β = *A inest omni B*. 2. εἶναι ἐν,
by which the *subject* is said to be in the *predicate*. Α ἐστιν ἐν
ὅλῳ τῷ Β = *Omne A est B*. This is exactly the reverse of

dicit Prædicatum inesse, vel non inesse, subjecto ;
ut, *Homo est animal.* *Homo non est lapis.* Mo-
dalis, quæ cum *Modo,* h. e. vocabulo experimente
quomodo Prædicatum insit subjecto ; ut *Necesse
est hominem esse animal.* *Impossibile est hominem
esse lapidem.* De Categorica pura, et quidem sola,
impræsentiarum loquor ; de cæteris alibi dicturus.

2. *Affirmativa*[g], est cujus Copula affirmativa est ; De Int.6.1.
ut, *Homo est animal.* *Non progredi est regredi.*
Negativa, cujus negat ; ut, *Homo non est lapis.*
Nullus avarus est dives. *Vera,* quæ quod res est
dicit; ut, *Homo est animal.* *Falsa*[h], quæ secus ; ut,

κατηγορεῖται. The English language is defective in not having,
like the Greek and Latin, a proper copula to express the
relation of comprehension as well as that of extension. Thus
the relation expressed by ὑπάρχει and *inest* can only be strictly
rendered into English by a circumlocution, " A is a quality
belonging to B." With the ordinary copula both relations
must be translated into the language of extension : τὸ A ὑπάρχει παντὶ τῷ B == *All B is A.* τὸ A ἐστιν ἐν ὅλῳ τῷ B == *All A is B.*
The memorable question at issue between Reid and Gillies,
(see Hamilton on Reid, p. 684.) turns on the above distinction. The former uses " being in " as a translation of
ὑπάρχειν, the latter, of ἐν ὅλῳ εἶναι.

[g] Κατάφασίς ἐστιν ἀπόφανσίς τινος κατά τινος· Ἀπόφασίς ἐστιν
ἀπόφανσίς τινος ἀπό τινος. Aristotle de Int. 6. 1. "Affirmatio est
enunciatio alicujus de aliquo. Negatio est enunciatio alicujus
ab aliquo." Boethius, de Int. p. 332. Aldrich's definition is
directly applicable only to propositions *tertii adjacentis.*

[h] *Vera—Falsa.* This is material, not logical truth and falsehood, and admits of no criterion from Logic nor from any
single science, but only from the proper experience of each
separate case. But even in this relation Aldrich's definition
is not quite accurate. Material truth does not consist in the
conformity of thought with the nature of things *per se :* for

Homo est lapis. Et cum per hasce species bene respondeatur interroganti, *Qualis est Propositio ?* (respondent enim per Differentiam et Proprium quæ in quale prædicantur) dicuntur hæ duæ divisiones peti a *Qualitate* Propositionis. Prior a *Qualitate Vocis,* sive *Essentiali ;* Posterior a *Qualitate Rei,* sive *Accidentaria.*

De Int.7.1.
An. Pr. I.
1. 2.

3. *Universalis*[i], est quæ subjicit terminum communem (cum signo universali, *omnis, nullus,* &c. adeoque) pro universis suis significatis distributive sumptum. *Particularis,* quæ terminum communem (cum signo particulari *aliquis, quidam,* &c. adeoque) ex parte tantum significantem. *Singularis,* quæ vocem (vel sponte, vel ex signo saltem) Individuam[k]; ut, *Socrates legit.* *Hic*

things are known to *us* only in their relation to some one or other of our faculties. Material Truth consists rather in the conformity of the object as represented in thought with the object as presented to the senses or to some other intuitive faculty. Formal or Logical Truth consists in the conformity of thought to its own laws; and of this, Logic furnishes an adequate criterion.

[i] *Universal,* καθόλου. *Particular,* ἐν μέρει, or κατὰ μέρος. *Indefinite,* ἀδιόριστος, An. Pr. I. 1. 2. *Singular,* καθ' ἕκαστον, (De Int. 7. 1.) *Omnis* is the sign of an universal proposition only when taken *distributively,* as, *Omnis homo est animal:* when taken *collectively,* as, *Omnes Apostoli sunt duodecim,* the proposition is singular.

[k] Individual names are distinguished as *individua signata,* expressed by a proper name, as *Socrates; individua demonstrativa,* by a demonstrative pronoun, *hic homo ; individua vaga,* by an indefinite pronoun, *aliquis homo, quidam homo:* a distinction found in the Greek commentators, Schol. p. 148, b. 23. Cf. Albert, de Prædicab. Tract. 4. cap. 7. Aquinas, Opusc.

homo est doctus. *Indefinita*[1]*,* quæ (terminum com-munem sine signo, et proinde) ancipitem : nam manente formula, vim recipit diversam ; ut, *Homo est animal,* nempe *omnis : Homo est doctus, aliquis* scilicet.

Petitur hæc Divisio a *Quantitate* Propositionis : nempe numero eorum pro quibus subjectum sup-ponit : unde et per has species bene respondetur interroganti, *Quanta sit Propositio?* Hanc doc-

---

xlviii. de Int. cap. 7. Of these, the two first will clearly form singular propositions. With regard to the last, it has been doubted whether they properly form singulars or particulars. Vives maintains them to be singulars ; observing, that *quidam* is not more indefinite than *Socrates* to one who is not ac-quainted with the man. But there is this difference. If we say, " quidam concionatur," " quidam legit," there is no evidence that the same person is spoken of in the two pro-positions ; while *Socrates,* except by a mere quibble, will always designate the same person. There may indeed be two persons of the same name ; but in this case the name fails to accom-plish the intended distinction, and we must specify Socrates the son of Sophroniscus. Hence *aliquis* and *quidam* are pro-perly called particulars. Cf. Wallis, Logic, lib. 2. cap. 4.

[1] " The term *indefinite* ought to be discarded in this relation, and replaced by *indesignate.*" Hamilton on Reid, p. 692. This proposition has no claim to a place in Logic, being only the negation of any logical quantity at all. The true in-definite proposition is in fact the particular ; the statement " some A is B " being applicable to an uncertain number of instances, from the whole class down to any portion of it. For this reason particular propositions were called indefinites by Theophrastus. See Ammonius *in de Int.* f. 63 a. ed. 1546. Alexander *in Anal. Pr.* f. 26 b. Cf. Prantl, *Gesch. der Logik,* I. p. 356.

E

trinam Scholastici hujusmodi carmine sunt com-
plexi ;

Quæ ?   *Ca.* vel *Hyp.* *Qualis ?*   *Ne.* vel *Aff.*
Quanta ?   *Uni. Par. In. Sing.*^m

§. 3. Propositio Singularis in Syllogismo æque
potest Universali".   Nam Subjectum ejus supponit
pro omni suo significato.   *Socrates est homo,* Universalis est, quia omnis ille Socrates tantum unus
est.   Indefinitæ quantitas judicatur ex materia
Propositionis, sive habitudine connexionis extre-

^m This, and the greater part of the scholastic memorial
verses, are found for the first time in the *Summulæ Logicales*
of Petrus Hispanus, afterwards Pope John XXI. who died in
1277.   He does not, however, profess to be the author of
them ; indeed some, including the present, are also noticed
by his contemporary Aquinas, as established mnemonics.   In
slight measure he has been anticipated by the Greeks.   A
mnemonic for the opposition of modals is found in the synopsis
attributed to Psellus, and one for the syllogistic moods in
Nicephorus Blemmidas.   But the genuineness of that portion
of the works of Aquinas has been questioned, and the treatise
which goes under the name of Psellus is probably a translation of the Summulæ of Hispanus.   The latter work is thus
our earliest undoubted authority for these curious specimens
of scholastic ingenuity.   See below, p. 84. note z.

" This is argued at some length in a thesis appended to
Wallis's Logic ; and is, to say the least, by far the most convenient way of bringing singular propositions under the
existing rules of the syllogism.   At the same time it may be
remarked that the employment of singular terms as predicates
is unnatural, and the reasoning, at least in affirmative syllogisms, worthless.   See An. Pr. i. 27. 3.   Indeed it may be
questioned whether the ἔκθεσις of Aristotle (see below, p. 61.)
was regarded by him as a syllogism at all.   Cf. Aquinas,

morum, quæ triplex est; 1. *Necessaria*°, quando extrema essentialiter conveniunt; 2. *Contingens,* quando accidentaliter tantum; 3. *Impossibilis,* quando essentialiter differunt. Unde Propositio Indefinita pro Universali habetur in materia impossibili et necessaria; pro Particulari vero, in contingenti.

Quare, Quantitas Propositionis, quatenus ad Syllogismum facit, est duplex : *Universalis* et *Particularis.* Et nota, quod Universalis affirmans

Opusc. xlvii. Zabarella, de Quart. Fig. cap. 7. Some additional remarks will be found in the Appendix, note E.

° Aristotle does not recognise this account of matter as *understood* in every *pure* proposition, but only as *expressed* in a *modal.* (See above, p. 46.) In the latter case it is no test of quantity, as there are universal and particular propositions of each mode. The distinction in the text, however, seems to have been early introduced. It is implied in the commentary of Ammonius on de Int. 7. (Scholia, p. 115. a. 14.) And Petrus Hispanus defines the three kinds of matter thus : *Necessary*, when the predicate is of the essence, or a property : *contingent*, when it is an accident to the subject : *impossible*, when a repugnant quality. In this point of view, the supposed criterion of quantity is inapplicable to propositions in which the predicate is an inseparable accident. But the whole question of matter is clearly extra-logical. See Sir W. Hamilton, *Discussions,* p. 148. The *Logician* cannot determine a proposition to be necessary or contingent, unless stated as such. The point must be ascertained from the Science to which the proposition materially belongs. The Logician, however, may use indefinites as particulars, not assigning a quantity from the matter, but admitting an indefinite premise (and therefore conclusion) where the rules of the figure do not require an universal. Hence the minor premise in fig. 1. may be indefinite, but not the major. See An. Pr. i. 4. 9.

symbolum habet A ; negans E : Particularis affirmans symbolum I ; negans O.

Asserit A ; negat E : Universaliter ambœ.

Asserit I ; negat O : sed Particulariter ambo[p].

In Universali, signum affirmans distribuit tantum Subjectum[q] : Negans, etiam Prædicatum. Nam ut verum sit *Omne a est b,* sufficit aliquod *b* convenire omni *a :* sed falsum est *nullum a esse b,* si vel aliquod *b* conveniat alicui *a.* Eodem argumento, ut sit verum *Aliquod a est b,* sufficit si vel aliquod *b* conveniat alicui *a :* sed falsum est quod *aliquod a non est b,* nisi illud *a* differat a quovis *b.*[r] Et proinde

[p] On these lines Wallis remarks, " Nam tam erant soliciti de syllabarum quantitate, aut syntaxeos ratione, quam ut Rhythmus constet aut ὁμοιοτέλευτον. Alii tamen, quo constet versus, pro *sed universaliter,* substituunt *verum generaliter ;* et, quo Syntaxi prospiciatur, pro *ambo,* neglecto Rhythmo, substituunt *ambæ ;* respicientes vocem subintellectam, *propositiones.*"

[q] In opposition to this, the almost unanimous doctrine of former Logicians, the New Analytic of Sir William Hamilton is founded on the principle that both terms in every proposition have a determinate quantity always understood in thought, and which ought to be expressed in words. That a quantified predicate must be admitted, in certain cases at least, as an addition to the ordinary logical forms, is unquestionable ; but its systematic introduction into the present work would not be possible without a complete rewriting of Aldrich's text.

[r] Aldrich assumes the distribution of the predicate in a negative, to prove the simple conversion of E. Those who adopt Aristotle's proof of the latter, (see below, p. 61.) might deduce the former from it. Both however may fairly be allowed to stand on their own evidence.

In particulari, nullus terminus distribuitur, præter negantis prædicatum, quod semper distribuitur.

Quanquam igitur fieri potest, ut prædicatum distribuatur in affirmante, tamen non est necessarium ; sed *per accidens* fit, et *virtute significati,* non *virtute signi.* In statuendis autem Propositionum legibus, spectandum est id tantum, quod structura postulat, non quidquid sensus admittit : cum illud essentiale, et perpetuum sit ; hoc mutabile, et incertum.

Hæc igitur regula generalis esto, quod in Propositione A, subjectum tantum distribuitur ; in O, tantum Prædicatum ; in I, neutrum ; in E, utrumque.

§. 4. PROPOSITIONIBUS [a] accidunt *Oppositio* et *Conversio. Opponi* dicuntur duæ, quæ, cum subjecta habeant et prædicata omnino eadem, Quantitate tamen, vel Qualitate vocis, vel utraque pugnant.

Oppositionis [t] doctrina tota colligitur et demon- De Int. 7. Anal. Pr. II. 15.

[a] *Opposed Propositions,—*ἀντικείμεναι προτάσεις, Arist. a term sometimes limited to Contradictories.

[t] As Logic can take no cognisance of *understood* matter, the " necessary, impossible, and contingent" should be omitted from the table of Opposition. It is no part of the province of the Logician to determine *when* a given Proposition is materially true or false ; but only what formal inferences may be made upon the assumption of its truth or falsehood. Hence the Canons of Opposition should be expressed only in the hypothetical form. They may be briefly given thus :

1. If A is true ; O is false, E false, and I true.
2. If A is false ; O is true ; E and I unknown.

stratur ex apposito Schemate, in quo, A. E. I. O.
sunt quatuor Propositiones quantitate sua et qualitate signatæ; quæ
sunt *v. f.* (hoc est,
veræ vel *falsæ*) pro
materia *n. i. c.*
(hoc est, *necessaria,
impossibili, contin-
gente ;*) quod ex
ipsa materiæ defi-
nitione satis patet.
De *necessaria;* quia
Propositionis ex-
trema in ea essenti-
aliter conveniunt :
de *impossibili;* quia

n. v.
i. f.   A.   Contrariæ   E.
c. f.

f. n.
v. i.
f. c.

Subalternæ

Contradictorie
Contradictione

Subalternæ

n. v.
i. f.   I. Subcontrariæ   O.
c. v.

f. n.
v. i.
v. c.

in ea essentialiter differunt : de *contingenti;* quia
secus non esset materia contingens. Inspecto
igitur hoc Schemate facile est

  1. Oppositionis[t] *species* numerare ; quæ sunt

  3. If E is true; I is false, A false, and O true.
  4. If E is false; I is true; A and O unknown.
  5. If I is true; E is false; A and O unknown.
  6. If I is false; E is true, O true, and A false.
  7. If O is true; A is false; E and I unknown.
  8. If O is false; A is true, I true, and E false.

So that from the *truth* of an universal, or the *falsehood* of a particular, we may infer the accidental quality of all the opposed
Propositions ; but from the *falsehood* of an universal, or *truth*
of a particular, we only know the quality of the Contradictory.

  [t] *Contradictory,* ἀντιφατικῶς (ἀντικείμεναι). *Contrary,* ἐναντίως.
Arist. The term *Subcontrary* (ὑπεναντίως) is not used by Aristotle

vulgo quatuor : *Contradictoria, Contraria, Subcontraria, Subalterna.*

2. Singularum definitiones conficere. V. g. *Oppositio Contradictoria, est inter* (A. O. vel E. I. hoc est) *duas Categoricas quantitate pariter et qualitate pugnantes.* *Contraria, inter* (A. E. h. e.) *duas universales qualitate pugnantes* &c.

3. Oppositarum Canones quatuor eruere et demonstrare hunc in modum.

1. Contradictoriæ A. O. vel E. I. sunt in nulla materia simul veræ ; in nulla simul falsæ ; sed in quacunque una vera, falsa altera.

Sed notandum est, ad Contradictionem requiri quatuor : nempe loqui de eodem 1. *eodem modo.* 2. *secundum idem.* 3. *ad idem.* 4. *in eodem tempore*[a] ;

Soph. Elenc 5. 5.

---

to denote the opposition of particulars ; though he admits the opposition itself, *de Int.* ch. 7. In *Anal. Prior.* ii. 15. he calls it an opposition κατὰ τὴν λέξιν, but not κατ' ἀλήθειαν. The term is used by the Greek commentators, (Ammonius, *Schol.* p. 115. a. 15.) followed by Boethius, *Int. ad Syll.* p. 564. Subaltern propositions (ὑπάλληλοι) are not noticed at all by Aristotle. The laws of subaltern opposition are first given by Apuleius, *De Dogmate Platonis,* lib. 3. though he does not give it a name. He is followed by Marcianus Capella. The name is given by Boethius, *Intr. ad Syll.* p. 566. and in the Commentary on the *De Interpretatione.* The treatise of Apuleius, if genuine, is a production of the second century, contemporary with, or a little prior to, the works of Alexander of Aphrodisias. The three first kinds of opposition are called by him *Alterutræ, Incongruæ,* and *Suppares.*

[a] *Secundum idem, ad idem.* Cf. Plato, Rep. iv. p. 436. Δῆλον ὅτι ταὐτὸν τἀναντία ποιεῖν ἢ πάσχειν κατὰ ταὐτὸν γε καὶ πρὸς ταὐτὸν οὐκ ἐθελήσει ἅμα.

quarum conditionum si defuerit aliqua, possunt *Est* et *Non est* inter se bene convenire. E. g. 1. Cadaver hominis *est* et *non est* homo : *Est* enim homo mortuus ; *Non est* homo vivus. 2. Zoilus[v] *est* et *non est* niger : *Est* enim crine ruber, niger ore. 3. Socrates[w] *est* et *non est* comatus : nempe *est*, ad Scipionem, *non est*, ad Xenophontem comparatus. 4. Nestor *est* et *non est* senex : *Est* enim, si de tertia ejus ætate, *non est*, si de prima loqueris.

2. Contrariæ A. E. in nulla simul veræ ; in Contingenti, simul falsæ ; in ceteris, una vera, falsa altera ; nempe in Necessaria, vera A. falsa E ; in Impossibili, vera E. falsa A.

3. Subcontrariæ I. O. in Contingenti, simul veræ ; in nulla simul falsæ ; in Necessaria, vera I. falsa O ; in Impossibili, vera O. falsa I.

4. Subalternæ A. I. vel E. O. et simul veræ, et

---

[v] *Zoilus*, see Martial, lib. xii. ep. 54.

   Crine ruber, niger ore, brevis pede, lumine læsus,
   Rem magnam præstas, Zoile, si bonus es.

[w] Aldrich has not before mentioned the opposition of *singulars*. " Socrates is wise," " Socrates is not wise." These are contradictories ; though the definition does not strictly include them, having inadvertently been worded solely with reference to universals. But they have the essential feature of contradictories, that one is always true, and the other false; (de Int. 7, 8.) and the definition given, Anal. Post. i. 2. 6. will include them :—'Αντίφασις δὲ ἀντίθεσις ἧς οὐκ ἔστι μεταξὺ καθ' αὐτήν. Some Logicians call the opposition of singulars, *secondary contradiction*. Boethius, p. 618, regards them as contradictories. See also Wallis, lib. ii. cap. 5.

simul falsæ, et una vera, falsa altera esse possunt. Nam in Necessaria, simul veræ sunt A. I ; in Impossibili, simul veræ E. O ; in eadem, simul falsæ, A. I. et in Necessaria, simul falsæ E. O ; in Contingenti, (propter A. E. falsas, I. O. veras) A. I. vel E. O. sunt una vera, falsa altera.

Possunt etiam aliter hi Canones Oppositarum, cum pluribus aliis, tum hoc quoque modo demonstrari.

1. Contradictoriæ A. O. vel E. I. nec *simul veræ* nec *simul falsæ* esse possunt. Quod enim una negat, idem altera de eodem, secundum idem, affirmat : Id vero fieri nec natura patitur, nec sensus ipse communis. Quare,

α. Si Universalis vera sit, Particularis, quæ sub ea continetur, vera est. Et

β. Si Particularis falsa sit, Universalis, quæ eam continet, falsa est : Quoniam enim Subjectum in Universali distribuitur, fit, ut in ea, et in Particulari, idem, de eodem, secundum idem, dicatur : vere igitur et falso simul dici, (hoc est, affirmari simul et negari) nequit.

2. Contrariæ A. E. non possunt esse *simul veræ :* sed in materia contingenti sunt *simul falsæ.* Nam 1°. Exponatur Universalis vera ; Ergo particularis vera per 1. *a* ; Ergo quæ particulari contradicit falsa per 1. Sed hæc est Expositæ contraria[x].

---

[x] *Exponatur—exposita.* Aldrich's use of these terms in relation to opposition and conversion has been censured by Sir W. Hamilton, *Lectures on Logic*, vol. I. p. 263. Perhaps

2°. Exponatur Universalis de materia contingenti ; Ergo et hæc falsa est, et Particularis vera, vi materiæ : Ergo quæ particulari contradicit falsa per 1. Sed hæc est Expositæ Universali contraria.

3. Subcontrariæ I. O. *simul falsæ* esse non possunt : sed *simul veræ,* vel *una vera, falsa altera,* esse possunt. Sunt enim duæ duarum Contrariarum Contradictoriæ, ut in Schemate patet, cum contrariis decussatim comparandæ. Quare, (per 1. et 2.) Subcontrariæ sunt in nulla materia simul *falsæ;* quia contrariæ in nulla *simul veræ :* Subcontrariæ in contingenti simul veræ ; quia Contrariæ in eadem simul falsæ. In Impossibili vero, et Necessaria, eadem utrisque lex est, ut sit una vera, falsa altera.

however it may be defended by analogy, if not by actual precedent. *Exponere* is properly to appeal to the senses, by selecting an individual instance. (See below, p. 61. note d.) It may thus without any great impropriety of language be employed, as here, to denote the selection of a single instance to exhibit the working of a rule. In this sense *proponere* is used by Boethius, *Introductio ad Syllogismos Categoricos.* The use of the corresponding word *conversa,* as employed by Aldrich, is sanctioned by Boethius, *ibid;* and may thus be regarded as more accurate historically, as well as more appropriate in itself. Many logicians however employ it in an opposite sense. Thus the Oxford predecessors of Aldrich, Crakanthorpe, Sanderson, and Wallis, all use *conversa* for the proposition given to be converted, *convertens* for that inferred from it. See further, Hamilton, *Lectures on Logic,* I. p. 262. II. p. 256.

4. Subalternæ A. I. vel E. O. et *simul veræ*, et *simul falsæ*, et *una vera, falsa altera* esse possunt. Nam 1°. Si subalternans (nempe Universalis) vera sit, Subalternata (sive Particularis) vera est (per 1. α.) 2°. Si Subalternata falsa, Ergo Subalternans falsa (per 1. β.) 3°. Si Subalternans falsa, Ergo quæ illi contradicit vera (per 1.) Ergo hujus Subcontraria, quæ est Expositæ Subalternata, vera vel falsa esse potest (per 3.) 4°. Si Subalternata vera, Ergo quæ illi contradicit falsa (per 1.) Ergo hujus Contraria, quæ est expositæ Subalternans, vera vel falsa esse potest (per 2.)[y]

§. 5. *CONVERTI* dicitur Propositio, cujus extrema An. Pr. I. 2.

[y] On the doctrine of Opposition in general, it may be remarked, 1. That Subalterns are improperly classed as *opposed* propositions, and should be referred to a separate table as *immediate inferences*. 2. That the Greek expressions πᾶς—οὐ πᾶς, οὐδεὶς—ἔστι τις, are better adapted to signify the relations both of opposition and of immediate inference than their English substitutes *all, none*, and *some*. *Some men* is naturally understood as meaning more than one, whereas *not all men* includes one or any number short of the whole. Hence the Aristotelian examples, πᾶς ἄνθρωπος λευκός, οὐ πᾶς ἄνθρωπος λευκός, express a complete contradiction more accurately than *all men are white, some men are not white;* as the latter admits of a third possibility, *one man is not white.* 3. That there may be *material* as well as *formal* consequences in opposition and immediate inference, as well as in mediate inference. Thus, *all men are white, all men are black*, are materially, but not formally, contrary to each other. *A is greater than B, therefore B is less than A*, is a material immediate inference. The formal consequences alone come under the cognisance of Logic.

transponuntur *.   Variis id modis fieri potest, sed præsertim duobus ª : 1. *Simpliciter,* quando tam

* The logical, as distinguished from the grammatical proposition, is properly of the form distinguished as *tertii adjacentis,* and the copula is always in the present tense. For Logic considers words only as the signs of thought: and the copula indicates the present union of two notions in the mind of the thinker, not the past or future connection of facts narrated or predicted. Every proposition should therefore, before conversion, be stated in the form *A is B*, which by conversion becomes *B is A*, with a change, if necessary, in the quantity. To give more minute directions would be to encroach upon the province of the Grammarian : we must be guided by the idiom of the language we are using. In Latin, e. g. the substantive acquires an adjective power, and the adjective a substantive, without change of form ; e. g. " nullus sapiens est iracundus," " nullus iracundus est sapiens." In English we must say, "No angry *man* is wise." Rules on this point are extra-logical.

The directions of some Logicians as to the conversion of past and future time, e. g. " nullus senex erit puer," are also, logically speaking. out of place here, though practically helps to a beginner. For these tenses not being logical copulæ, the sentence is not, as it stands, a logical proposition ; and should be reduced to such, before it comes into the hands of the converter.

ª Aristotle's account of conversion differs somewhat from this. He divides conversion into universal and particular, according to the quantity of the proposition after *conversion.* Consequently E is converted *universally,* A and I *particularly.* He does not recognise any conversion of O. Simple conversion, (ἀπλῆ ἀντιστροφή,) is mentioned by Philoponus, Scholia, p. 148. b. 21. Boethius uses the terms *generalis* and *per accidens.* In the system of Sir W. Hamilton, by assigning a quantity to the predicate of every proposition, the various kinds of conversion are reduced to that of simple conversion alone.

quantitas, quam utraque qualitas servatur. 2. *Per accidens*[b], quando servata qualitate, quantitas mutatur.

f Ec I Simpliciter convertitur Ev A per Acci[c] et conversio utrobique illativa est.

Nam 1. sit vera E[d], puta *Nullum A est B :* Ergo

---

[b] *Per accidens;* so called because it is not a conversion of the universal *per se*, but by reason of its containing the particular. For the proposition " Some B is A," is *primarily* the converse of " Some A is B," *secondarily* of " All A is B." See Boethius, de Syll. Cat. p. 589.

[c] *A st O, per contra ; sic fit conversio tota.*
Conversion by contraposition, which is not employed by Aristotle, is given by Boethius in his first book, *De Syllogismo Categorico.* He is followed by Petrus Hispanus, who first gives the mnemonic, as above. It should be observed, that the old Logicians, following Boethius, maintain, that in conversion by contraposition, as well as in the others, the *quality* should remain unchanged. Consequently the converse of " All A is B " is " All not B is not A," and of " Some A is not B," " Some not B is not A." It is simpler, however, to convert A into E and O into I, (" No not B is A ;" " Some not B is A,") as is done by Wallis and Abp. Whately ; and before Boethius by Apuleius and Capella, who notice the conversion, but do not give it a name. The principle of this conversion may be found in Aristotle, Top. ii. 8. 1. though he does not employ it for logical purposes.

[d] *Sit vera E.* This is the proof given by Theophrastus and Eudemus. (Alexander, Scholia, p. 148. b. 29.) Aristotle proves it by the method called ἔκθεσις, i. e. by the *exhibition* of an individual instance, (ἐκτιθέναι *exponere sensui;* whence a syllogism with singular premises is called *syllogismus expositorius.*) Thus, No A is B, therefore No B is A, for if not, Some *individual* B, say C, is A. Then C is both A and B,

(cum uterque terminus distribuatur) quodvis A differt a quovis B. Ergo vicissim : Ergo *Nullum B est A*. 2. Sit vera I : Ergo falsa est ejus Contradictoria E : Ergo et contradictoriæ simpliciter conversa : Ergo quæ conversæ contradicit, (i. e. expositæ simpliciter conversa,) est vera. 3. Sit vera E. Ergo et ejus simpliciter conversa : Ergo et conversæ subalternata : quæ est expositæ conversa per accidens. 4. Sit vera A ; Ergo et ejus subalternata : Ergo et subalternatæ simpliciter conversa : quæ est expositæ per Accidens e.

and therefore it will not be true that No A is B ; which was the original proposition. Aristotle does not assume the conversion of I to prove that of E, which would be arguing in a circle. For a fuller account, see Hamilton on Reid, p. 696.

Alexander himself offers a third proof by syllogism in the first figure. No A is B, therefore No B is A ; for suppose " Some B is A," and " No A is B," ∴ Some B is not B.

Having proved the conversion of E, those of A and I will follow from it. " All A is B, therefore Some B is A ;" or else No B is A, and therefore (by conversion) No A is B ; whereas we assumed All A is B. And again, Some A is B, therefore Some B is A ; or else No B is A, and therefore No A is B.

For these proofs, the only assumption necessary is the principle of contradiction. But proof of any kind is superfluous. Conversion and other immediate inferences are necessary results of the laws of thought, equally evident and more direct than the mediate inferences by syllogism. Neither process is dependent on the other.

e In Conversion, as in Opposition, Singular Propositions have been neglected by Aldrich. Concerning these, the following extract from Wallis may assist the learner. " Propositio *Singularis*, (sive Affirmativa sive Negativa,) cum semper *Universalis* sit, observat leges aliarum Universalium. Puta,

Ceteræ Conversiones^f, cum sint partim ambiguæ, partim falsæ, partim ad præcepta Syllogismorum inutiles, in Logica negliguntur^g.

Virgilius est Poeta; ergo *Aliquis Poeta est Virgilius.* Item, *Virgilius non est Græcus;* ergo *Nullus Græcorum est Virgilius.* Atque in aliis similiter.

" Si autem *Convertendæ* propositionis *Prædicatum* sit *Individuum,* (quodcunque habuerit Subjectum,) *Convertentis Subjectum* (quippe quod fuerat *Convertendæ Prædicatum*) *Individuum* erit; propterea et Propositio *Convertens* (siqua sit) necessario erit *Singularis,* adeoque *Universalis.*" See also Reid's Works, ed. Hamilton, p. 697.

^f *Cæteræ conversiones.* For the benefit of the curious, we quote the following : " Tres igitur sunt famosæ apud Logicos conversionis species. Dico famosæ, quoniam nonnulli moderni invenerunt duas alias conversionis species, quarum una est conversio propositionum nullius quantitatis, ut exclusivæ et reduplicativæ. Nam sic convertitur exclusiva ; tantum homo est rationalis, omne rationale est homo : reduplicativa autem sic convertitur : homo in quantum homo est rationalis, rationale est homo in quantum homo. Item propositionum modalium, ut hominem esse album est possibile, ergo possibile est hominem esse album. Item alii imaginati sunt duas alias species, Prima est quando mutatur qualitas et non quantitas, ut hic ; omnis homo est animal, omne animal non est homo. Secunda est quando mutatur quantitas et qualitas, ut hic ; omnis homo est animal, aliquod animal non est homo. Verum quia hujusmodi conversiones non sunt in usu, nec nobis deserviunt pro reductione syllogismorum, ideo immorabimur circa primam et secundam speciem, tangentes breviter de tertia, omnibus aliis relictis." Javellus, de Propositione, cap. ii.

^g Is the converse an inference from the original proposition, or, as Whately says, the same judgment in another form ? This was an early point of dispute among the Schoolmen. See Albert. in Anal. Pr. Tract. i. cap. 8. Aristotle clearly

considers it an *inference;* otherwise it would be absurd to prove it. Reid, in his Account of Aristotle's Logic, defines it as an inference, and the definition is accepted by his learned Editor. Kant, too, regards both conversion and opposition as *syllogisms of the understanding,* the new judgment being always different in form, though not in matter, from the old. As regards conversion *per accidens,* the original proposition is clearly not identical with the converse; as it cannot be substituted for it, but may be false, while the converse is true. But on the new system of Sir W. Hamilton, the predicate being quantified, and the proposition reduced to an equation between the terms, it is better to consider the converted proposition as identical with the original.

CAP. III.

De Syllogismo Categorico puro.

§. 1. Tertia pars Logicæ agit de *Argumento* [a] sive *Syllogismo,* quod est signum tertiæ operationis intellectûs; nempe *Discursus,* vel *Ratiocinium* Propositionibus expressum.

Quare, cum Discursus [b] sit progressus mentis ab uno judicio ad aliud, perspicuum est in eo requiri 1. Aliquid unde discursus ordiatur. 2. Aliud quo perveniat. 3. Ea sic ab invicem pendere, ut unum ex alio, et aliûs vi innotescat; secus enim, unum post aliud cognoscere, est tantum sæpe judicare.

Jam, ex quo aliud cognoscendum est, ipsum certe præcognosci debet; et proinde quasi sine discursu notum, *antecedere, poni, præmitti;* et ex eo reliquum *concludi, colligi, inferri* et *sequi* dicitur. Est autem duplex *consequentia:* Anal. Post.
I. 1. 1.

1. *Materialis;* quando ex Antecedente Consequens infertur, sola vi Terminorum [c], quæ est

---

[a] *Argument* is not properly synonymous with syllogism, but with the middle term only. See Hamilton's *Discussions,* p. 149.

[b] See before, p. 5. note k.

[c] The *force of the terms* leads to a conclusion by suggesting to the mind certain additional truths concerning the things spoken of, which are not *given* in the premises. But this additional knowledge is clearly extralogical. See Appendix, note D. The *matter* of the syllogism is all that is given *to and out of* the act of reasoning: the *form* is what is conveyed

Argumenti materia: ut, *Homo est animal.* Ergo *est vivens.*

2. *Formalis;* quando infertur propter ipsum colligendi modum, quæ est *argumenti forma;* ut, *B est A. C est B.* Ergo *C est A.* Mutatis terminis et servata eorum dispositione, Materialis plerumque fallit, Formalis semper obtinet: et proinde hæc solum in Logica spectatur, illa, tanquam mutabilis et lubrica, negligitur.

Anal. Pr.
I. 1. 6.
Top. I. 1. 2. Hisce intellectis, opinor satis constare quo sensu definiatur *Syllogismus;* [d]*Oratio in qua positis qui-*

in and by the act itself. The former is expressed in the *terms* of which the reasoning is composed, and which vary in every different act of thought; the latter appears in the *relation* in which those terms are thought to one another, as constituting *premises* which necessitate a *conclusion.* This remains within certain fixed limits in every different act of thought. The same principle of distinction may be applied to discern between the matter and form of concepts and judgments. The logical forms of the syllogism are exhibited in *mood* and *figure,* as those of the proposition in *quality* and *quantity.* Cf. Burgersdyck. *Inst. Log.* l. ii. c. 6. "Forma syllogismi est apta trium propositionum dispositio ad conclusionem ex præmissis necessario colligendum. Hæc aptitudo posita est in figura et modo." A distinction slightly varying from the above will be found in Crakanthorpe, *Logica,* l. iii. c. 13. and another in Kant, *Logik,* §. 59. The latter has been censured by Krug, *Logik,* §. 72.

[d] Arist. Anal. Pr. i. 1. 6. Συλλογισμὸς δέ ἐστι λόγος ἐν ᾧ τεθέντων τινῶν ἕτερόν τι τῶν κειμένων ἐξ ἀνάγκης συμβαίνει τῷ ταῦτα εἶναι. See also Top. i. 1. 2. The latter definition is translated by Aulus Gellius, xv. 26. "Oratio in quâ, consensis quibusdam et concessis, aliud quid, quam quæ concessa sunt, per ea, quæ concessa sunt, necessario conficitur." The word *concessis*

busdam atque concessis, necesse est aliud evenire præter et propter ea quæ posita sunt atque concessa.

§. 2. Multæ sunt ejus species ; sed una tantum præsentis instituti ; nempe *Categoricus simplex,* i. e. qui constat tribus Propositionibus de inesse[e]. E quibus duæ priores sunt Antecedens, tertia Consequens ; quæ extra Syllogismum spectata (scil. quamdiu hæret in incerto) *Problema*[f], et Quæstio[g] dicitur ; in Syllogismo autem (nempe post fidem factam) *Conclusio.* Quæstionis duo sunt extrema, Subjectum et Prædicatum ; quorum de Convenientia vel Dissidio inquiritur, ope termini

Anal. Pr.
I. 4. 15.
I. 26. 1.
Anal. Post
II. 1. 1.

is too limited ; being strictly true only of the topical syllogism. Cf. Trendelenburg, *Elementa,* §. 21. On the charge of *petitio principii,* sometimes brought against the syllogism, see Appendix, note E.

[e] i. e. pure Categoricals.

[f] Τὸ γὰρ αὐτὸ γένει πρόβλημα καὶ λῆμμα καὶ ὁμολόγημα καὶ συμπέρασμα καὶ ἀξίωμα· πάντα γὰρ προτάσεις τῇ σχέσει τὴν διαφορὰν ἔχοντα· προτιθέμενον γὰρ εἰς δεῖξιν ὡς μὴ γνώριμον πρόβλημα καλεῖται, λαμβανόμενον δὲ εἰς ἄλλου δεῖξιν λῆμμα καὶ ὁμολόγημα· ἀξίωμα δὲ ὅταν ἀληθὲς ᾖ καὶ ἐξ ἑαυτοῦ γνώριμον, δεδειγμένον δὲ συμπέρασμα, Alexander, Schol. p. 150, b. 40. This accords with the sense of πρόβλημα in Anal. Pr. i. 4. 15. i. 26. 1. The dialectical use of the term in disputation is not very different. Cf. Topics, i. 4. 1, 3. i. 11. 1. Schol. p. 256, a. 14.

[g] *Quæstio;* τὸ ζητούμενον, Anal. Post. ii. 1. 1. which term, however, has a more extensive application than is here assigned ; for two of the *Quæstiones Scibiles, an sit* and *quid sit,* cannot in all cases be determined syllogistically. See An. Post. ii. 3. and Appendix, note C.

alicujus tertii ; idque propter Canones sequentes[h], in quibus vis omnis Syllogistica fundatur.

1. Quæ conveniunt in uno aliquo eodemque tertio, ea conveniunt inter se.

[h] These Canons are an attempt to reduce all the three figures of syllogism directly to a single principle ; the *dictum de omni et nullo* of Aristotle, which was universally adopted by the scholastic Logicians, being directly applicable to the first figure only. This reduction, so long as the predicate of propositions has no expressed quantity, is illegitimate ; the terms not being equal, but contained one within another, as is denoted by the names *major* and *minor*. Hence, as applied to the first figure, the word *conveniunt* has to express, at one and the same time, the relation of a greater to a less, and of a less to a greater,—of a predicate to a subject, and of a subject to a predicate. In the system of Sir W. Hamilton, by assigning a quantity to the predicate, the terms of every proposition are equal in extent ; and the Canons become legitimate representatives of the syllogism ; but in this case they are only narrower statements of the true syllogistic laws ; which are given in the Principles of Identity and Contradiction. (Every A is A ; No A is not A.) These, with the Principle of Excluded Middle, (Every thing is either A or not A,) are the highest and most exact statements of the Necessary Laws of Thought. Cf. *Prolegomena Logica*, p. 223. (2nd ed. p. 240.)

Wallis mentions the Canons as recent innovations in Logic. " Nonnulli autem Logici, (nostri seculi aut superioris,) posthabita veterum probatione per *Dictum de Omni et de Nullo*, aliud substituunt illius loco Postulatum ; nimirum, *Quæ conveniunt in eodem tertio conveniunt inter se*. *Inst. Log.* l. iii. c. 5. Cf. Bacon. *Nov. Org.* l. ii. aph. 27. Melanchthon (*Erotemata*, p. 172, ed. 1568.) mentions them as adopted by a sect of Logicians in his day. The earliest writer in whom I have found them is Rodolphus Agricola, *De Inv. Dial.* i. 2. He describes at considerable length the office of the middle term as a measure of equality or inequality.

2. Quorum unum convenit, alterum differt uni et eidem tertio, ea differunt inter se.

3. Quæ non conveniunt in uno aliquo eodemque tertio, ea non conveniunt inter se.

Sunto enim A et C, nec assignari possit ejusmodi tertium, Ergo nihil habent commune ; Ergo non conveniunt inter se.

4. Quorum neutri inest quod non sit in alio, ea non differunt inter se[i].

5. Quæ non probantur convenire in uno aliquo eodemque tertio, ea non probantur convenire inter se. Dubitari enim potest utrum detur ejusmodi tertium, et dubitatio ista non tollitur.

6. De quibus non probatur, convenire unum eidem alicui tertio cui alterum differt, ea non probantur differre inter se. Dubitari enim potest, utrum detur ejusmodi tertium, h. e. utrum alterutri insit quod non est in reliquo : et dubitatio ista non tollitur[k].

---

[i] The third and fourth Canons relate to conditions under which no syllogism *can* exist. " Two things, which have not a point in common, are totally distinct." "Two things, which have not a point of difference, are undistinguishable." But if there is no such point, there is no middle term, and therefore no syllogism.

[k] The fifth and sixth Canons relate to conditions under which no syllogism *does* exist. " If no point has been assigned, whether of agreement or difference." But if so, there is no syllogism.

Hence these four cannot be called Canons of syllogism. They may be useful, however, for examining the illogical positions of an opponent.

§. 3. Ex sex hisce Principiis Syllogismi structura sic deducitur.

Anal. Pr.
I. 25. 1.
1. In omni Syllogismo sunt tres, et tres tantum, termini. Nam Syllogismus[1] omnis probat aliquam conclusionem : Et in illâ sunt duo tantum extrema : Et illa neque convenire, neque differre probatur, sine uno, unoque tantum, tertio.

Anal. Pr. I.
4. 8. I. 5. 1.
I.6.1.I.5.7.
Jam, Prædicatum Quæstionis dici solet *majus extremum*[m], *major terminus ;* Subjectum Quæstionis,

Anal. Pr. I.
32.8.I.4.3.
I.5.1.I.6.1.
minor ; Terminus vero tertius, cui quæstionis extrema comparantur, Aristoteli *Argumentum,* vulgo *Medium*[n] : Nam Prædicatum Quæstionis plerumque amplius est Medio ; hoc minori.

[1] Aristotle adopts an inverse method ; first examining the structure and stating the laws of each separate figure of syllogism, in An. Pr. i. ch. 4, 5, 6. and afterwards enumerating, as the result of the examination, the general laws applicable to all, in An. Pr. i. 23 sqq. On the respective merits of the two methods, see Pacius on An. Pr. i. 4. Reid, ed. Hamilton, p. 700.

[m] *Majus extremum ;* τὸ μεῖζον ἄκρον, (also τὸ πρῶτον, An. Pr. i. 31. 2.) *minus ;* τὸ ἔλαττον, (also τὸ ἔσχατον, An. Pr. ii. 8. 8.) *Terminus,* ὅρος, for the various meanings of which, see Waitz, vol. i. p. 370. *Major term :* μείζων ὅρος : *minor ;* ἐλάττων ὅρος, An. Pr. i. 5. 7. The definitions of the major and minor terms given in the text are condemned by Pacius, (on An. Pr. i. 7.) as inapplicable to the indirect moods. Aristotle gives a separate definition of the three terms in each figure. But the indirect moods may, without loss, be dispensed with. An account of various theories of the distinction between the major and minor term will be found in Sir W. Hamilton's *Discussions,* 2d Ed. p. 670. Aldrich's *prædicatum quæstionis* corresponds to the distinction maintained by Alexander and Averroes.

[n] More correctly, "Aristoteli *medium*, Ciceroni aliisque *argumentum*." See Hamilton's *Discussions,* p. 150. The nearest

2. In omni Syllogismo sunt tres, et tres tantum, propositiones. Duæ præmissæ[o], in quibus Medium cum extremis seorsim conferatur, (nempe *Major*, in quæ cum majori; *Minor*, in qua cum minori;) una *Conclusio*, in qua extrema invicem committantur. Anal. Pr. I. 23. 5. I. 25. 8. I. 32. 8. Anal. Pr. II. 10. 6.

N.B. 1. Quod Major dici solet simpliciter *Propositio*; Minor, *Assumptio*[p]. 2. Quod Medium non ingreditur conclusionem, alias idem per idem probaretur: adeoque non essent tres termini.

3. Ancipiti medio nihil conficitur. Neque enim affertur in hoc casu unum aliquod idemque tertium vel in quo extrema conveniant, vel cui unum conveniat, alterum differat. Anal. Pr. I. 32. 10. Soph. Elench. 4. 1.

4. Medium non distributum[q] est anceps. Esto Anal. Pr. I. 24. 1.

Greek equivalent to *argumentum* is πίστις, which, however, as employed by Aristotle, is a rhetorical, not a logical term. The origin of Aldrich's blunder it is difficult to conjecture.

[o] *Major premise*; ἡ πρὸς τῷ μείζονι ἄκρῳ πρότασις. *Minor premise*; ἡ πρὸς τῷ ἐλάττονι ἄκρῳ πρότασις. *Conclusion*; συμπέρασμα, which also signifies *minor term*, Anal. Pr. ii. 14. The *premise* is not, properly speaking, called ὅρος by Aristotle. In such expressions as καθόλου ὄντων τῶν ὅρων, (Anal. Pr. i. 5. 2.) there is an ellipsis of πρὸς τὸν ἕτερον, and the phrase means strictly, that one *term* is predicated *universally* of the other, i. e. of the whole of the other.

[p] As by Cicero, de Invent. i. 37. Fortunatianus, Rhet. lib. ii. Cassiodorus, de Art. ac Disc. ch. 2. Boethius, de Syll. Hyp. p. 614. The terms are of Rhetorical origin. Quintilian calls the major premise, *Intentio*; Inst. Orat. v. 14. The conclusion is called *complexio*; a term also applied by Cicero to the Dilemma; de Inv. i. 29.

[q] *Distribution* is not an Aristotelian term. It forms part of

enim B terminus communis in b et *β* divisibilis ; Ergo b et *β* sunt opposita : et tamen vere dicitur Aliquod B est b, et Aliquod B est *β*. Quare aliquod B est Medium anceps.

5. Quare Medium in præmissis semel ad minimum distribui debet ; sufficit tamen, si vel semel distribuatur. Nam 1. ad probandum A est C, conveniat C alicui B, et A omni ; Ergo eidem alicui B : Ergo affertur unum aliquod idemque tertium &c. 2. ad probandum A non est C, conveniat C alicui B, et A differat omni ; Ergo eidem alicui B : Ergo affertur &c.

6. Processus ab extremo non distributo in præmissis, ad idem distributum in conclusione, vitiosus est. Nam ex *aliquo* non sequitur *omne*. Esto enim verum quod aliquod ; Ergo potest esse verum quod aliquod non ; (nam Subcontrariæ possunt esse simul veræ ;) Ergo de aliquo potest affirmari quod non de omni. Esto rursus verum

what the Schoolmen call *parva logicalia ;* a kind of appendix to analyses of the Organon ; containing matters, some evolved from, though not distinctly treated of by Aristotle, others complete innovations, more properly belonging to Grammar than to Logic. The greater part of these first appear in Petrus Hispanus. See *Summulæ Logicales*, Tr. 7.

The syllogistic rules concerning distribution are of course implied in Aristotle's account of each figure, though not enunciated separately as common to all. Thus, to say that the major premise in fig. 1. must be universal, or one premise in fig. 2. negative, is equivalent to a rule for distributing the middle term. The particular conclusion in fig. 3. in like manner forbids an illicit process of the minor term.

quod aliquod non : Ergo potest esse verum quod
aliquod : Ergo de aliquo potest negari quod non
de omni.

7. Præmissis negantibus nihil probatur : Affer- _{Anal. Pr.}
tur enim tertium cui utrumque extremum differt ; ^{I. 24. 1.}
non autem cui vel utrumque conveniat, vel unum
conveniat, alterum differat.

8. Si præmissarum altera sit negativa, erit etiam
Conclusio. Nam præmissarum reliqua est affirmativa : Ergo extremorum unum differt medio, alterum convenit : Ergo extrema differunt inter se :
Ergo conclusio est negativa.

9. Contra, si Conclusio sit negativa, erit etiam _{Anal. Pr.}
altera præmissarum. Nam extrema differunt inter ^{I. 24. 4.}
se : Ergo eorum unum convenit medio, alterum
differt : Ergo præmissarum altera affirmat, reliqua
negat.

10. Præmissis particularibus nihil probatur. Nam _{Anal. Pr.}
præmissarum altera affirmat : Ergo in illa medium ^{I. 24. 1.}
non distribuitur : Ergo distribui debet in reliqua :
Ergo illa est negativa in qua medium prædicatur :
Ergo conclusio negativa : Ergo prædicatum ejus
distribuitur, quod in præmissis non est distributum ; Fuit enim vel affirmativæ terminus alter,
vel subjectum·negativæ ; horum vero nullus distribuitur.

11. Si præmissarum altera particularis sit, con- _{Anal. Pr.}
clusio quoque particularis est. Sit enim 1. Præ- ^{I. 24. 3.}
missarum altera particularis affirmativa ; Ergo in
illa nec extremum suum nec medium distribuitur :

Ergo medium distribuitur in reliqua, quæ etiam Universalis est, sitque 1. Affirmativa : Ergo in illa medium subjicitur, et extremum medio attributum non distribuitur : Ergo neutrum extremorum distribuitur in præmissis : Ergo neutrum in conclusione : Ergo conclusio particularis affirmativa est. Sit 2. Negativa : Ergo conclusio negativa : sed debet habere extremum non distribụtum : Ergo particularis negativa est.

Sit 2. Præmissarum altera particularis negativa : Ergo Reliqua Universalis affirmativa : Ergo in præmissis duo tantum termini distribuuntur : Ergo Conclusio habet extremum non distributum : Ergo cum negativa sit, erit etiam particularis.

An. Pr. I.
24. 3. 12. Quod si Conclusio[r] particularis sit, non necesse est præmissarum alteram particularem esse. Fieri enim potest, ut instituto meo sufficiat subalternata, quando subalternans potuit inferri. Et cum illæ sint simul veræ, liberum est utramvis inferre. Quanquam stricte loquendo, Argumentatio non est accurata ; nam Subalternatæ veritas non immediate deducitur ex præmissis, sed ex subalternante.

---

[r] This rule is given by Aristotle, not with reference to the subaltern moods, but to the third figure, in which two universal premises only warrant a particular conclusion. An inverse rule of inference holds with regard to truth and falsehood : two true premises necessitate a true conclusion ; but the truth of the conclusion does not guarantee that of the premises. Cf. An. Pr. ii. 2. 1.

Syllogismi generales regulas complectitur hoc Tetrastichon*.

Distribuas medium ; nec quartus terminus adsit.
Utraque nec præmissa negans, nec particularis.
Sectetur partem Conclusio deteriorem.
Et non distribuat, nisi cum præmissa, negetve.

§. 4. SUPEREST per hasce regulas inquirere, quot modis componi possunt tres Propositiones de inesse, ut Syllogismum conficiant. Qua in inquisitione duo spectanda sunt.

1. *Modus*[t], sive legitima determinatio Pro-

---

* An earlier form of this mnemonic is given in some editions of Petrus Hispanus :

>Partibus ex puris sequitur nil, sive negatis.
>Si qua præit partis, sequitur conclusio partis.
>Si qua negata præit, conclusio sitque negata.
>Lex generalis erit, medium concludere nescit.

[t] Mood (τρόπος) is not in this sense an Aristotelian expression, (unless possibly in An. Pr. i. 28. 14 ?); but it is found in his Greek commentators. See Alexander, Schol. p. 150, b. 3. Aristotle in the same sense employs πτῶσις, An. Pr. i. 26. 1. He does not adopt an arithmetical calculation of possible moods distinct from considerations of figure, but shews, in each figure separately, what combinations of propositions are admissible, and what not. It may be observed, that the earliest scholastic Logicians do not consider Mood as composed of three propositions, but of the two premises only. Thus Petrus Hispanus defines " ordinatio *duarum* propositionum in debita qualitate et quantitate;" so Aquinas, in Opusc. xlviii. de Syll, ch. 4. In this case the number of possible moods is only sixteen.

This computation is preferable to Aldrich's, because simpler; but neither has any *logical* value. The *legitimate*

positionum secundum Quantitatem et Qualitatem.

2. *Figura,* sive legitima dispositio Medii cum partibus Quæstionis.

Modi sunt in universum 64. Nam, ut supra ostensum est, ad Syllogismum faciunt Propositiones tantum quatuor A. E. I. O. Quare concipi potest Quadruplex tantum Major in Syllogismo ; cuilibet vero Majori quadruplex tantum Minor adjungi ; unde 16. paria præmissarum : et singulis præmissis quadruplex tantum Conclusio ; unde 64. Modi Syllogismorum.

AAA. AAE. AAI. AAO. *AEA. AEE. AEI. AEO. *AIA. AIE. AII. AIO. *AOA. AOE. AOI. AOO.

EAA. EAE. EAI. EAO. *EEA. EEE. EEI. EEO. *EIA. EIE. EII. EIO. *EOA. EOE. EOI. EOO.

IAA. IAE. IAI. IAO. *IEA. IEE. IEI. IEO. *IIA. IIE. III. IIO. *IOA. IOE. IOI. IOO.

OAA. OAE. OAI. OAO. *OEA. OEE. OEI. OEO. *OIA. OIE. OII. OIO. *OOA. OOE. OOI. OOO.

Ex his excluduntur sedecim per Regulam 7.

determination ought to be such as the laws of Logic require ; not one which arises from a mere arithmetical calculation. On logical grounds, there are eight valid combinations of premises ; viz. AA. AE. AI. AO. EA. EI. IA. OA. The conclusion, being determined by the premises, cannot properly be reckoned as an independent element in the combinations. Cf. *Fries, System der Logik,* §. 57.

propter præmissas negantes, viz. EEA. EEE. EEI. EEO. *EOA. EOE. EOI. EOO. *OEA. OEE. OEI. OEO. *OOA. OOE. OOI. OOO. Duodecim per Reg. 10. propter præmissis particulares, viz. IIA. IIE. III. IIO. *IOA. IOE. IOI. IOO. *OIA. OIE. OII. OIO. Duodecim per Reg. 8. quia præmissarum altera negat, sed non conclusio, viz. AEA. AEI. AOA. AOI. *EAA. EAI. EIA. EII. *IEA. IEI. *OAA. OAI. Octo per Reg. 11. quia præmissarum altera particularis est, sed non conclusio, viz. AIA. AIE. AOE. *EIE. *IAA. IAE. *IEE. *OAE. Denique quatuor per Reg. 9. quia conclusio negativa est sed neutra præmissarum, viz. AAE. AAO. AIO. *IAO.

Excluduntur igitur in universum Modi $52 = 16 + 12 + 12 + 8 + 4$. e quibus multi contra plures regulas peccant, quamvis una tantum notetur.

Supersunt $(64 - 52 =)$ 12 Modi ad Syllogismum utiles, viz. AAA. AAI. AEE. AEO. AII. AOO. *EAE. EAO. EIO. *IAI. IEO[n]. *OAO.

§. 5. FIGURÆ[x] Syllogismorum sunt 4. Nam

---

[n] IEO has been condemned ever since the days of Apuleius, as far as the second and third figures are concerned. It was sometimes allowed in the first, as the indirect mood Frisesmo, but should not have been retained by Aldrich, who does not recognise the indirect moods. With a direct conclusion, it manifestly produces an illicit process of the major term.

[x] Figuræ, σχήματα, An. Pr. i. 4. 15. "Figuras Syllogismorum, quæ dicuntur (Apuleius ' formulas' vocat), ab Aristotele appellatas esse Jul. Pacius putat, quia figuris geometricis ad-

Medium, quod cum utroque extremo comparatur, vel 1. subjicitur majori et tribuitur minori, et fit

scriptis syllogismi ab eo illustrati sint. Equidem hanc vocem non tam a geometricis petitam quam de ipso ordine terminorum accipiendam putaverim, quem σχῆμα appellari licebit, etiam si de geometricis figuris non cogitetur : sic enim supra commemoravimus τὰ σχήματα τῆς κατηγορίας (Metaph. v. 2. 1.), τὸ σχῆμα τῆς ἰδέας (Metaph. vi. 3. 2.). τὰ σχήματα τῆς λέξεως (Poet. 19. 7.), σχῆμά τι δημοκρατίας (Polit. vi. 4. 5.)." Waitz, vol. i. p. 384. On the other hand, Sir W. Hamilton, in a very interesting paper in the second edition of his *Discussions*, p. 666. maintains the opinion of Pacius, and proposes a restoration of the Aristotelian diagrams. This dissertation contains a fund of valuable matter on the history and philosophy of Logic, which will well repay a careful perusal.

Aristotle acknowledges only three figures ; looking rather to the extension of the middle term, as compared with the other two, than to its position in the two premises. In this point of view there are only three figures possible ; for the relative extensions of the major and minor terms being given, the middle can only have three positions ; between the other two, as in the first figure ; greater than both, as in the second ; or less than both, as in the third. See Trendelenburg, Elem. §. 28. Waitz on Anal. Pr. i. 23. 7. The invention of the fourth figure is attributed by Averroes (on Anal. Pr. i. 8.) to Galen. The latter may possibly have first called the five moods by that name, but they were known at a much earlier period as indirect moods of the first figure. An indirect mood is one in which we do not infer the immediate conclusion, but its converse. Consequently, the predicate of the conclusion, which in a direct mood is the *major* term, is in an indirect one the *minor*. The five indirect moods of the first figure were called Baralip, Celantes, Dabitis, Fapesmo, Frisesmo. The three first are clearly Barbara, Celarent, Darii, with the conclusions converted. With regard to the two last, the process is a little more intricate. They have negative minor premises, and thus offend against a

figura prima; vel 2. tribuitur utrique, et fit *secunda;* vel 3. subjicitur utrique, et fit *tertia;* vel 4. tribuitur majori et subjicitur minori, et fit *quarta.* Quæ omnia sequenti Schemate declarantur.

Dispositio trium terminorum, scilicet majoris A. medii B. minoris C. in Figura.

1.	2.	3.	4.
B. A.	A. B.	B. A.	A. B.
C. B.	C. B.	B. C.	B. C.
C. A.	C. A.	C. A.	C. A.

Quare quælibet Figura excludit adhuc sex modos[y]. Nempe

special rule of the first figure; but this is checked by a counterbalancing transgression. For by simply converting O, we alter the distribution of the terms, so as to avoid an illicit process. Thus,

All B is A (fap)	Some B is A (fris)
No C is B (esm)	No C is B (esm)
Therefore Some A is not C (o)	Therefore Some A is not C (o)
Where to infer " Some C is not A," would involve an illicit process of the major term.	Where to infer " Some C is not A," would involve an illicit process of the major term.

The invention of these indirect moods is attributed to Theophrastus; not, however, on the authority of Apuleius, as asserted by M. St. Hilaire, but on that of Alexander, Schol. p. 153, a. 47. But they were clearly recognised by Aristotle; the last two in Anal. Pr. i. 7. 1. the first three in Anal. Pr. ii. 1. 2. The passage in Apuleius does not refer to the *indirect*, but to the *indefinite*, syllogism.

[y] Certain moods, not excluded by the general rules of syllogism, are rejected in some one figure, by what are called

1. **Propter Medium non distributum.** Prima duos IAI. OAO. Secunda quatuor AAA. AAI. AII. IAI. Quarta duos AII. AOO.

2. **Propter processum majoris illicitum.** Prima quatuor AEE. AEO. AOO. IEO. Secunda duos IEO. OAO. Tertia quatuor AEE. AEO. AOO. IEO. Quarta duos IEO. OAO.

3. **Propter processum minoris illicitum.** Tertia duos AAA. EAE. Quarta duos AAA. EAE.

Supersunt Modi certo et necessario concludentes 24. sex in qualibet Figura.

I.

*b*A*r*	Omne	B	est	A	
*b*A	Omne	C	est	B : *Ergo*
*r*A	Omne	C	est	A.	

the *special rules* of that figure. These special rules are given as follows by Petrus Hispanus.

Fig. 1. { 1. Minore existente negativa nihil sequitur.
{ 2. Majore existente particulari nihil sequitur.

Fig. 2. { 1. Majore existente particulari nihil sequitur.
{ 2. Ex puris affirmativis nihil sequitur.
{ 3. In secunda figura semper concluditur negative.

Fig. 3. { 1. Minore existente negativa nihil sequitur.
{ 2. In tertia figura conclusio debet esse particularis.

These rules are all to be found in An. Pr. i. ch. 4, 5, 6. Of the fourth figure three special rules have been framed; viz. 1. " Quando major est affirmativa, minor semper est universalis." 2. " Quando minor est affirmativa, conclusio est semper particularis." 3. " In modis negativis, majorem universalem esse oportet."

*c*E	Nullum	B	est	A
*l*A	Omne	C	est	B : *Ergo*
*r*E*nt*	Nullum	C	est	A.

*d*A	Omne	B	est	A
*r*I	Aliquod	C	est	B : *Ergo*
I	Aliquod	C	est	A.

*f*E	Nullum	B	est	A
*r*I	Aliquod	C	est	B : *Ergo*
O	Aliquod	C	non est	A.

A	Omne	B	est	A
A	Omne	C	est	B : *Ergo*
I	Aliquod	C	est	A.

E	Nullum	B	est	A
A	Omne	C	est	B : *Ergo*
O	Aliquod	C	non est	A.

II.

*c*E*s*	Nullum	A	est	B
A	Omne	C	est	B : *Ergo*
*r*E	Nullum	C	est	A.

*c*A*m*	Omne	A	est	B
E*s*	Nullum	C	est	B : *Ergo*
*tr*E*s*	Nullum	C	est	A.

G

*f*E*s*	Nullum	A	est	B		
*t*I	Aliquod	C	est	B :	*Ergo*	
*n*O	Aliquod	C	non est	A.		

*b*A*r*	Omne	A	est	B		
O*k*	Aliquod	C	non est	B :	*Ergo*	
O	Aliquod	C	non est	A.		

E	Nullum	A	est	B		
A	Omne	C	est	B :	*Ergo*	
O	Aliquod	C	non est	A.		

A	Omne	A	est	B		
E	Nullum	C	est	B :	*Ergo*	
O	Aliquod	C	non est	A.		

III.

*d*A*r*	Omne	B	est	A		
A*p*	Omne	B	est	C :	*Ergo*	
*t*I	Aliquod	C	est	A.		

*f*E*l*	Nullum	B	est	A		
A*p*	Omne	B	est	C :	*Ergo*	
*t*O*n*	Aliquod	C	non est	A.		

*d*I*s*	Aliquod	B	est	A		
A*m*	Omne	B	est	C :	*Ergo*	
I*s*	Aliquod	C	est	A.		

*b*O*k*	Aliquod	B	non est	A	
A*r*	Omne	B	est	C :	*Ergo*
*d*O	Aliquod	C	non est	A.	

*d*A*t*	Omne	B	est	A	
I*s*	Aliquod	B	est	C :	*Ergo*
I	Aliquod	C	est	A.	

*f*E*r*	Nullum	B	est	A	
I*s*	Aliquod	B	est	C :	*Ergo*
O*n*	Aliquod	C	non est	A.	

IV.

*br*A*m*	Omne	A	est	B	
A*n*	Omne	B	est	C :	*Ergo*
*t*I*p*	Aliquod	C	est	A.	

*c*A*m*	Omne	A	est	B	
E*n*	Nullum	B	est	C :	*Ergo*
E*s*	Nullum	C	est	A.	

*d*I*m*	Aliquod	A	est	B	
A*r*	Omne	B	est	C :	*Ergo*
I*s*	Aliquod	C	est	A.	

*f*E*s*	Nullum	A	est	B	
A*p*	Omne	B	est	C :	*Ergo*
O	Aliquod	C	non est	A.	

_fr_**Es**	Nullum	A	est	B	
I**s**	Aliquod	B	est	C.:	_Ergo_
O**n**	Aliquod	C	non est	A.	

A	Omne	A	est	B	
E	Nullum	B	est	C :	_Ergo_
O	Aliquod	C	non est	A.	

Barbara[a], _Celarent, Darii, Ferioque_, prioris :
Cesare, Camestres, Festino, Baroko, secundæ :
Tertia, _Darapti, Disamis, Datisi, Felapton_,

[a] _Barbara, Celarent_, &c. This mnemonic first appears in
the _Summulæ Logicales_ of Petrus Hispanus, (see on p. 50.)
But in his version the fourth figure is omitted, and its moods
given as indirect moods of fig. 1. This earliest edition of
these celebrated lines runs thus :

> Barbara, Celarent, Darii, Ferio, Baralipton,
> Celantes, Dabitis, Fapesmo, Frisesomorum,
> Cesare, Camestres, Festino, Baroco, Darapti,
> Felapton, Disamis, Datisi, Bocardo, Ferison.

Several other versions are found in later writers. A Greek
mnemonic of the same kind is inserted in editions of the
Organon preceding that of Pacius. (See Buhle's Aristotle,
vol. ii. p. 628.) It runs thus :

> Fig. 1. γράμματα—ἔγραψε—γραφίδι—τεχνικός.
> Fig. 2. ἔγραψε—κάτεχε—μέτριον—ἄχολον.
> Fig. 3. ἅπασι—σθεναρός—ἰσάκις—φέριστος—ἀσπιδι— ὅμαλος.

This mnemonic is attributed by M. St. Hilaire to Nicephorus
Blemmidas. It is found, in a more complete form, in the
margin of the Augsburg MS. of the Synopsis attributed to
Psellus, though omitted in Ehinger's Edition. (See Prantl,
vol. ii. p. 275.) Sir W. Hamilton, in a note appended to the
second edition of his _Discussions_, p. 669, maintains that the
Greek mnemonic is in all probability only an imperfect attempt
at conversion into Greek of the Latin memorial of Hispanus.

Bokardo, Ferison, habet : Quarta insuper addit
Bramantip, Camenes, Dimaris, Fesapo, Fresison.
Quinque *Subalterni,* totidem *Generalibus* orti,
Nomen habent nullum, nec, si bene colligis, usum.

§. 6. ATQUE omnes quidem 24. eatenus concludere, quod in iis convenientia vel dissidium
extremorum certo atque necessario colligatur, ex
Principio primo et secundo abunde constat.

Quod aliter demonstrat Aristoteles ad hunc
modum.

Statuit primo Theorema, quod Scholastici vocant Anal. Pr. I.
*Dictum de Omni et Nullo*ᵃ, scil. "Quod prædicatur 1. 8.

ᵃ Λέγομεν δὲ τὸ κατὰ παντὸς κατηγορεῖσθαι, ὅταν μηδὲν ᾖ λαβεῖν τῶν
τοῦ ὑποκειμένου, καθ᾽ οὗ θάτερον οὐ λεχθήσεται· καὶ τὸ κατὰ μηδενὸς
ὡσαύτως, An. Pr. i. 1. 8. The same principle is implied in
the first antipredicamental rule, Categ. 3. 1. ὅσα κατὰ τοῦ κατη-
γορουμένου λέγεται πάντα καὶ κατὰ τοῦ ὑποκειμένου ῥηθήσεται. Indeed,
Aldrich's version is more nearly a translation of the latter
than of the *Dictum* properly so called. Cf. Petr. Hisp. Tract. iv.
" Dici de omni est, quando nihil est sumere sub subjecto, de
quo non dicatur prædicatum. Dici de nullo est, quando nihil
est sumere sub subjecto a quo non removeatur prædicatum."
The *Dictum de Omni et Nullo* is most improperly called a
Theorem. This term in Aristotle is synonymous with ζήτημα,
and means a proposition, the truth of which is to be inquired
into, not one laid down as an axiom. See Topics, i. 11. 1.
Alexander, Scholia, p. 259, a. 38.
The *dictum* is directly applicable only to the first figure,
which is considered by Aristotle as the type of all syllogisms,
and to which the others have to be reduced, as a necessary
test of their validity. In this he is followed by Kant, *Logik*,
§. 69. Other Logicians enunciate distinct axioms for the
second and third figures. This has been done by Lambert,

" Universaliter de alio, (i. e. de termino distributo,)
" sive affirmative, sive negative, prædicatur similiter
" de omnibus sub eo contentis."

Neues Organon, part i. ch. 4. §. 232. but he is far from happy
in his enunciation of the dicta. We may state them as follows,
in a somewhat improved form.

Principle of second figure. *Dictum de Diverso.*

If a certain attribute can be predicated (affirmatively or
negatively) of every member of a class, any subject, of which
it cannot be so predicated, does not belong to the class.

Principles of third figure. I. *Dictum de Exemplo.*

If a certain attribute can be affirmed of any portion of the
members of a class, it is not incompatible with the distinctive
attributes of that class.

II. *Dictum de Excepto.* If a certain attribute can be denied
of any portion of the members of a class, it is not inseparable
from the distinctive attributes of that class.

The natural use of the second figure, according to Lambert,
is for the discovery and proof of the differences of things: that
of the third, for the discovery and proof of examples and
exceptions.

Concerning Lambert's imaginary principle of the fourth
figure, see p. 93, note n. Lambert's principles are criticised
by Krug, *Logik*, §. 109. According to Sir W. Hamilton,
(*Discussions*, 2d Ed. p. 666.) " it was Melanchthon who first
excogitated, as he thought, the various principles on which
proceed the various syllogistic figures." The following may
be gathered from his *Erotemata Dialectices.*

Principle of first figure. Posito genere, necesse est speciem
poni.

Principle of second figure. Remoto genere, removetur species.

Principle of third figure. Posita specie, necesse est genus
poni, sed particulariter.

There is a third manner of treating the syllogistic figures;
viz. by regarding them as all equally direct applications of
one and the same principle. This has been attempted by
Aldrich and others in the Canons; (see p. 68.) but inaccurately.

Admisso hoc Theoremate (quod axioma sponte perspicuum est) constat una, modos quatuor priores in prima certo atque necessario concludere. Nam eorum major ostendit majus extremum prædicari de medio distributo; et minor, minus extremum sub medio contineri.

Quare, Modi quatuor prædicti nihilo penitus indigent quo necessitas conclusionis appareat, præter ea quæ in præmissis posita sunt; et proinde quatuor illi sunt præ cæteris evidentes. Nam cæteri omnes aliquo vel aliquibus egent, quæ, utcunque per præmissas necessaria, in Syllogismo tamen non exprimuntur. Quare illos Aristoteles perfectos[b], hos *imperfectos* dicit; Scholastici *directos,*

Anal. Pr. I. 1. 7.

The three ultimate Laws of Thought are the Principles of Identity, of Contradiction, and of Excluded Middle. These are directly applicable to all the syllogistic figures alike. Other general principles, but less accurate, have been given by the Port-Royal Logic, part iii. ch. 10. by Buffier, *Principes du Raisonnement,* Let. vi. vii. and by Euler, *Lettres à une Princesse d'Allemagne,* p. ii. l. 36. ed. Cournot. For a criticism of the Port-Royal principle, cf. Duval-Jouve, *Logique,* p. 306.

[b] Τέλειον μὲν οὖν καλῶ συλλογισμὸν τὸν μηδενὸς ἄλλου προσδεόμενον παρὰ τὰ εἰλημμένα πρὸς τὸ φανῆναι τὸ ἀναγκαῖον, ἀτελῆ δὲ τὸν προσδεόμενον ἢ ἑνὸς ἢ πλειόνων, ἃ ἔστι μὲν ἀναγκαῖα διὰ τῶν ὑποκειμένων ὅρων, οὐ μὴν εἴληπται διὰ προτάσεων, Anal. Pr. i. 1. 7. With Aristotle, the "dictum de omni et nullo" is the principle of all syllogism; and the conversions, &c. required by the imperfect syllogisms, must be performed before their conclusions are admitted as valid.

The *direct* and *indirect* syllogisms of the Schoolmen must not be confounded with the *perfect* and *imperfect* of Aristotle. An indirect syllogism is one in which the minor term is the *predicate*, the major the *subject* of the conclusion. See Aquinas, Opusc. xlviii. de Syll. cap. 8. Scotus, super lib. I. Anal. Prior.

et *indirectos* vocant: quia per illos ad conclusionem, velut ad scopum, recta itur; per reliquos eodem perveniri potest, prius tamen alio deflectendum est.

An. Pr. I.
7. 3. 4.
I. 23. 1.

Perfici[c] igitur et *revocari* atque *reduci* dicimus indirectos, cum per modum aliquem directum illationis suæ vim demonstrant. Et definitur *Reductio*[d], imperfecti Modi in perfectum mutatio, quo necessitas illationis fiat ex inevidenti evidens. Fiet autem, quando evidenter (h. e. in prima) ostenditur conclusionem vi præmissarum vel 1.

An. Pr. I.
7. 3.

talem esse; vel 2. aliam esse non posse. Unde Reductio est vel *ostensiva* vel *ad impossibile*[e].

Quæst. xxii. sqq. Occam, Logica, p. iii. cap. 6. Of these in- direct moods, five were admitted in the first figure, two in the second, (by converting the conclusions of Cesare and Camestres,) three in the third, (by converting the conclusions of Darapti, Disamis, and Datisi.) Cf. Anal. Pr. i. 7. ii. 1. Of these, the five in the first figure are the most important, being sometimes regarded as a fourth figure. See p. 77, note x. The perfect and imperfect moods of Aristotle are sometimes called *immediate* and *mediate*. Cf. Aquinas, Op. xlviii. cap. 1. Occam, Log. p. iii. cap. 2. Boethius calls them *indemonstrable* and *demonstrable*.

[c] *Ferfici*,—τελειοῦσθαι, ἐπιτελεῖσθαι; (τελείωσις occurs An. Pr. i. 25. 8.) *Reduci*, ἀνάγεσθαι, (never ἀπάγεσθαι:) ostensively, δεικτικῶς.

[d] *Reductio.* The value of Reduction in Logic will depend on the principle adopted as the basis of the syllogism. In the systems of Aristotle and Kant, whose principles are im- mediately applicable only to the first figure, reduction is necessary. In the system of Lambert, in which each figure rests on a separate axiom, reduction is impossible; the process being then the destruction of one distinct reasoning, and the substitution of another. By reducing the laws of thought to their simplest form, in which they are applicable to all syllogisms directly, reduction is superfluous.

[e] *Reductio ad impossibile.* This phrase, though sanctioned

Utriusque praxin pro Modis nominatis docent ipsa Modorum nomina a Scholasticis in hunc finem conficta. Nam in iis tres vocales sunt totidem propositiones Syllogismi sua quantitate et qualitate signatæ. Consonæ initiales B. C. D. F. notant modum primæ, ad quem sit Reductio. S. P. propositionem, quam vocalis proxime antecedens designat, esse in Reductione convertendam : S simpliciter; P per accidens. M transponendas esse præmissas. K reductionem fieri per impossibile, i. e. pro præmissa, cujus symbolo adhæret, sumendam esse Conclusionis contradictoriam [f]. Quibus ex præscripto factis, colligitur in prima

by respectable authorities, is incorrect; as may be shewn by substituting the definition. What is the meaning of " the change of an imperfect to a perfect mood to the impossible ?" The error has been caused by the Aristotelian expression, ἀπαγωγὴ εἰς τὸ ἀδύνατον; in which, however, ἀπαγωγὴ does not mean reduction. The *deductio ad impossibile*, as it is usually rendered, (*abductio* would perhaps be better,) is one species of the συλλογισμὸς ἐξ ὑποθέσεως, (see Appendix, note I,) the object of which is, to prove the truth of a given problem, by inferring a falsehood from the assumption of its contradictory. This may be employed in the reduction of syllogisms, but it is also used for other purposes, as by Geometers, (Euclid. i. 7.) The correct expression is therefore *Reductio per deductionem ad imposssibile*, or elliptically, *Reductio per impossibile*. The ἀπαγωγὴ of An. Pr. ii. 25. will be explained hereafter.

Any mood may be reduced by the *deductio ad impossibile*, though in practice it is usually confined to Baroko and Bokardo.

[f] Whence the lines,

S vult simpliciter verti; P vero per acci :
M vult transponi; C [K] per impossibile duci.

conclusio vel expositæ eadem, vel eam inferens,
vel præmissæ contradictoria, ut in exemplo.

*c*E*s*	Nullum	A	est	B
A*r*	Omne	C	est	B : *Ergo*
E	Nullum	C	est	A.

ad

*c*E	Nullum	B	est	A
*l*A	Omne	C	est	B : *Ergo*
*r*E*nt*	Nullum	C	est	A.

*d*I*s*	Aliquod	B	est	A
A*m*	Omne	B	est	C : *Ergo*
I*s*	Aliquod	C	est	A.

ad

*d*A	Omne	B	est	C
*r*I	Aliquod	A	est	B : *Ergo*
I	Aliquod	A	est	C.

*b*A*r*	Omne	A	est	B
O*k*	Aliquod	C	non est	B : *Ergo*
O	Aliquod	C	non est	A.

ad

*b*A*r*	Omne	A	est	B
*b*A	Omne	C	est	A : *Ergo*
*r*A	Omne	C	est	B.[g]

---

[g] Archbishop Whately gives an ostensive reduction of
Baroko and Bokardo to Ferio and Darii, by converting the
major premise by contraposition. Logic, b. ii. c. 3. §. 5.

§. 7. REDUCTIONIS ostensivæ validitas sic ostenditur. Ex præmissis reducendi, per conversionem imperatam, necessario colliguntur præmissæ reducti : atque ex iis, per figuram primam, conclusio reducti : quæ vel ipsa conclusio reducendi erit, vel per illativam conversionem fiet.

Reductionis per Impossibile validitas sic ostenditur. Quoniam præmissæ ex hypothesi sunt semper veræ, ergo contradictoria præmissæ nunquam vera : ergo contradictoria conclusionis nunquam vera[h] : (nam has simul veras esse demonstratur in Barbara) ergo contradictoria conclusionis semper falsa : ergo conclusio ipsa semper vera.

[Reducitur etiam quilibet modus innominis, facto quod præcipitur, ad præmissas sui subalternantis. Tum vero conclusio, quæ colligetur in prima, erit vel expositæ subalternans, vel in expositam per accidens convertetur.

Reductiones[i] (cum primæ ad reliquas, tum An. Pr. I. 45. 1.

This had been done before; partly by Jung, in the *Logica Hamburgensis*, B. III. ch. 12. §. 15. and partly by Wolf, *Philosophia Rationalis*, §. 384.

[h] Since a false conclusion cannot be drawn without at least one false premise, see An. Pr. ii. 2. 1. But in the present syllogism, one premise is given true, being one of those of the original syllogism; the other, therefore, is false, which is the contradictory of the original conclusion. The syllogism *ad impossibile* will not always be in Barbara; though it is so in the reduction of Baroko and Bokardo.

[i] Of these reductions, it need only be observed, that they are only possible where the same problem can be proved in both figures; hence only negative syllogisms can be reduced

earum ad se invicem) bene multas, quod et obviæ sint, et instituto meo minus necessariæ, præter-

An. Pr. 1.
7. 5.

mitto.   Illud tamen notatu dignum est, quod cum *Darii* ad *Camestres,* et *Ferio* ad *Cesare* reducatur per impossibile, uterque igitur ad *Celarent;* omnisque adeo modus reducitur ad duos universales primæ.]

§. 8. PERSPICUUM est ex antedictis

1. Syllogismos simplices, certo atque necessario concludentes, fieri 24 modis : 6 in qualibet figura.

An. Pr. I.
26. 1.

II. Et in aliquo istorum modorum probari posse conclusionem quamlibet de inesse ; nempe A uno modo, E quatuor, I septem, O duodecim[k].   Et

An. Pr. I.
4. 15.
An. Pr. I.
5. 16.
An. Pr. I.
6. 17.

rursus ; in prima, conclusionem quamcunque : In secunda, omnes et solas negativas : In tertia, omnes et solas particulares : In quarta, quamlibet præter A.   De præmissis denique, quod in prima et secunda, major semper universalis est ; in prima et

---

to the second figure, and only particular syllogisms to the third. *Barbara, Baroko,* and *Bokardo,* cannot be ostensively reduced to any other figure, except by the use of conversion by contraposition.

[k] Rejecting the fourth figure and the subaltern moods, it will be better to say with Aristotle ; A is proved only in one figure and one mood, E in two figures and three moods, I in two figures and four moods, O in three figures and six moods. For this reason, A is declared by Aristotle to be the most difficult proposition to establish, and the easiest to overthrow ; O, the reverse.   And generally, universals are more easily overthrown, particulars more easily established.

tertia, minor affirmativa : In secunda, præmissarum altera negativa : aliaque ejusmodi ; quæ ipsa modorum nomina satis indicant[1].

Atque hinc facile colligitur, inspecto schemate modorum, quali medio probanda sit quæstio omnis de inesse. e. g. Quæstio A probatur in *Barbara ;* medio, de quo prædicatum quæstionis universaliter affirmatur, quodque de subjecto quæstionis affirmatur itidem universaliter ; et sic de cæteris.

Anal. Pr. I. 28. I. I. 32. 10.

Adverte tamen quod imperite disputantis est afferre modum innominem ; ponet enim in præmissis plusquam opus est ad conclusionem. Quare et innomines hactenus sunt incensi ; quamvis negari nequeant, sicubi per inscitiam adhibentur[m].

Adverte etiam, quod figura quarta tribus cæteris deterior est ; cum aliis de causis, tum ex hoc præsertim, quod medium dicat de majori, hunc de minori, minorem de medio, h. e. medium nugatorie de seipso[n].

---

[1] See p. 79, note y.

[m] The invention of the five anonymous moods is attributed by Apuleius to Aristo of Alexandria.

[n] This objection is brought against Galen by Averroes, on *Anal. Post.* I. 8. It might be better stated, *majorem nugatorie de seipso.* Reckoning backwards from the conclusion, we find that the major contains the minor, the minor the middle, the middle the major ; so that, in fact, the major contains itself.

The fourth figure has been defended by Lambert, who declares it to be useful for the discovery or exclusion of the species of a genus. He frames a principle for it, called *dictum de reciproco.* I. If no M is B, no B is this or that M (Camenes). II. If C is or is not this or that B, there are B's

III. Syllogismis etiam adnumerantur aliæ argumentorum species ; quæ nec stricte loquendo Syllogismi sunt, nec ita tamen peccant, ut propterea mereantur excludi : in quibus scilicet reticetur argumenti pars aliqua, sed quam proclive est cogitatione substituere.

Anal. Pr.
II. 27. 2
Rhet. I. 2.
8.

1. *Enthymema ;* cujus antecedens constat propositione et judicio ; nam judicium est propositio in mente° ; e. g. *Homo est animal ;* ergo *est vivens.*

which are or are not C. (Bramantip, Dimaris, Fesapo, Fresison.) The principle is sufficiently clumsy ; the utility questionable, since nothing can be established by this process which may not be proved more simply in other ways. It may be observed also, that the objection which Lambert urges, and with reason, against the conversion of the second and third figures, viz. that by conversion we often substitute an unnatural and indirect for a natural and direct predication, does not hold as regards the fourth. For, in the first three moods no conversion of premises is needed. By regarding the first stated as the minor, the second as the major, we obtain a much more natural conclusion in the first figure. Fesapo and Fresison establish *exceptions,* and therefore, on Lambert's theory, should more naturally fall into the *third* figure. The whole distinction, however, between *natural* and *unnatural* predication relates to the matter, not to the form of the thought.

° *Propositio in mente.* Aldrich had in his mind the absurd etymology from ἐν θυμῷ, or as Versorius gives it, " ab *en* quod est in, *thymos,* quod est mens, et *monos,* quod est unum, quasi in mente retinens unam propositionem." The erroneousness of this etymology (besides its intrinsic absurdity) appears from the word ἐνθύμημα being found in the Greek language before it assumed a technical meaning ; e. g. Soph. Œ. C. 292, 1199. Some Logicians attempt to distinguish between the

Dicitur etiam Aristoteli *Syllogismus Oratorius;* et, si integra ejus vis contineatur in unica propositione, *sententia Enthymematica;* utrumque Quintiliano *sententia cum ratione;* ut, *Mortalis cum sis, immortale ne geras odium.* Deest illi ad Syllogismum altera præmissarum; utrum vero major an minor, ex quæstione dignoscitur. Rhet. II. 21. 6.

2. *Inductio;* in qua ponitur quantum opus est de singulis, et deinde assumitur de universis; ut, *Hic et ille et iste magnes trahit ferrum;* ergo *omnis.* Est igitur Enthymema quoddam; nempe Syllogismus in Barbara^p, cujus minor reticetur. Anal. Pr. II. 23. 2.

3. *Exemplum;* (Aristoteli *Inductio Oratoria* ^q) Anal. Pr. II. 24. 1. Rhet. I. 2. 19.

Logical and the Rhetorical Enthymeme, (see Sanderson, b. iii. ch. 8.) The distinction is not authorized by Aristotle, and is liable to the objection which must always lie against a wanton alteration of the meaning of technical terms. For the Enthymeme of Aristotle, see Appendix, note F.

p The supposed minor is, of course, " All magnets are this, that, and the other." In this perversion, Aldrich has been preceded by Zabarella, De Meth. lib. iii. cap. 3. Archbishop Whately departs still further from Aristotle, and makes Induction a Syllogism in Barbara with the *major* premise suppressed. Thus:

" That which belongs to this, that, and the other magnets,
      belongs to all;
Attracting iron belongs to this, that, and the other;
Therefore it belongs to all."

So also Wolf, *Phil. Rat.* §. 479. For the real nature of Logical Induction, see Appendix, note G.

q Aldrich considers the Example as an Induction; i. e. according to his view, as a Syllogism in Barbara with the minor premise suppressed. The supposed minor, according

ubi quod ponitur de singulari noto, assumitur de simili ignoto : ut, *Sylla et Marius laceravere rempublicam ;* ergo *Cæsar et Pompeius lacerabunt.* Hujus etiam minor reticetur ; quapropter (ut in cæteris) quæstionem *assumi* dico ; neque enim *colligitur* nisi ex posito et subintellecto.

4. *Sorites*; in cujus Antecedente, ex ordinata

to this view, will be, " Cæsar and Pompey are Sylla and Marius." But the example proper is not a logical reasoning at all ; being a compound of an imperfect, and therefore illogical, Induction and a Syllogism. See further, Appendix, note H.

ʳ The Sorites is a series of propositions, in which the predicate of each is the subject of the next ; the conclusion being formed of the first subject and the last predicate. It may be expanded into a series of syllogisms in the first figure, the conclusion of each being the minor premise of the next. There will be as many syllogisms as there are intermediate propositions between the first premise and the conclusion ; the first being the only *minor* premise stated. Hence there can only be one particular premise in a Sorites, the first ; the others being major premises in the first figure. And the last is the only premise which may be negative : for any previous negative premise would produce a negative conclusion, which could not be used as a minor premise in the next syllogism.

The Sorites is not recognised as a distinct kind of reasoning by Aristotle. Nor is there any reason why it should have been ; as it is merely a combination of ordinary syllogisms, succinctly expressed. Its distinct exposition is attributed to the Stoics. But the principle, as Melanchthon observes, is implied in Categ. 3. 1. and the Sorites itself is alluded to in Anal. Pr. i. 25. 2, 11. There is another form of the Sorites, called the *regressive* or *Goclenian*, first given by Goclenius in his *Isagoge in Organum Aristotelis*, 1598, p. 255. In this, the subject of each proposition is the predicate of the next; the conclusion being

serie terminorum, præcedens quisque subjicitur sequenti, donec a subjecto quæstionis pervenitur ad prædicatum, v. g. *Homo est animal: animal est vivens: vivens est substantia;* ergo *Homo est substantia.* In Sorite igitur subaudiuntur Syllogismi quot sunt intermediæ propositiones; (vel si mavis, quot in antecedente termini intermedii;) unde et a cumulo nomen habet.

5. Soriti affinis est Syllogismus, cujus præmissarum altera est sententia Enthymematica*; ut, *Nullus injustus est amandus: Omnis Tyrannus (crudelis cum sit) est injustus;* ergo *Nullus Tyrannus est amandus.* Qui quidem Syllogismus peculiare nomen non habet ᵗ; Præmissæ autem

formed of the last subject and the first predicate. E. g. All D is E, all C is D, all B is C, all A is B; therefore all A is E. In this, when expanded, the conclusion of each syllogism is the major premise of the next. In this Sorites, only the first premise can be negative and the last particular. This, as Krug has remarked, should really be called the *progressive;* the ordinary Sorites the *regressive.* A much more complicated theory of Sorites is given by Herbart, *Lehrbuch zur Philosophie,* §. 70. and by Drobisch, *Logik,* §. 81.; but it is of little logical value.

The Sorites must not be confounded with the well-known fallacy of the same name, attributed to Eubulides of Miletus, and mentioned by Cicero, *De Divinatione,* ii. 11. For the history of the Sorites, name and thing, see Sir W. Hamilton's *Lectures on Logic,* vol. i. p. 375.

* On the Enthymematic sentence, see Arist. Rhet. ii. 21. 6.

ᵗ It is sometimes called an *epicheirema.* The word originally was synonymous with Dialectic Syllogism. See Top. viii. 11, 12. Of this *epicheirema* or *argumentatio,* the Rhetoricians enumerated various kinds, *tripartita, quadripartita, quinque-*

Anal. Pr.
I. 25. 11.
I. 28. 5.
Enthymematicæ Antecedens, Aristoteli *Prosyllo-gismus* est[u].

6. Huc denique revocandum est compendium illud disputandi opponentibus usitatissimum, reticendi scilicet conclusionem ; cum sit ipsa Quæstio, quam respondens non supponitur ignorare.

[Admittuntur denique in Scholis etiam Syllogismorum formulæ, quia contra regulas voce tantum, non sensu, peccant, et mutata phrasi ad canonicas facile revocantur. Suntque nihil aliud quam Licentiæ quædam Syllogisticæ, et in accurata disputatione non videntur admittendæ.

Anal. Pr.
I. 39.
1. Quando pro termino repetendo substituitur vox illi æquipollens. Ut in hoc, *Ens naturale constans corpore organico et anima rationali est homo : Socrates est ejusmodi :* ergo *est homo*, et similibus. Potest enim Sophista abuti ista libertate vel ad nugandum vel ad fallendum.

2. Quando fiunt Syllogismi ex obliquis, qualis est, *Omnis hominis equus currit : Socrates est homo ; ergo Socratis equus currit.* Pro minori rectius dixeris *Socratis equus est hominis equus,* alias con-

partita, *&c.* See ad Heren. ii. 2. ii. 19. Cic. de Inv. i. 37 sqq. Quint. Inst. v. 13. Finally, the name Epicheirema was limited to the quadripartite. Cf. Trendelenburg, Elem. §. 33. Schweighæuser on Epictetus I. 8. For some other variations in the use of the name, see Krug, *Logik,* §. 113.

[u] Not exactly. The prosyllogism, or antecedent syllogism, of Aristotle, is a syllogism employed to prove one of the premises of another syllogism. It need not be expressed in a curtailed form. See Pacius on Anal. Prior. i. 35. 3. Biese, vol. i. p. 157.

sequentia, licet bona, non erit immediata. Atque illo insuper laborat disputatio omnis ex obliquis, quod præter necessitatem aperit locum fallaciæ.

3. Quando propositio aliqua intelligitur contra quam sonat, e. g. *Quod non habet partes non interit per dissolutionem partium : Anima humana non habet partes :* ergo *anima humana non interit per dissolutionem partium.* Nam major sonat negative, intelligitur vero affirmate : puta, *Quod interit &c. habet partes.* Vel etiam singulæ propositiones intelliguntur affirmate, ac si esset Syllogismus, *Omne expers est incorruptibile : Anima humana est expers ;* ergo *anima humana est incorruptibilis.*

Eodem accenseri possunt Syllogismi quales Author *Artis Cogitandi*[a] vocat *Complexos,* in quibus etiam *dijudicandis* jactat se satis imperite. v. g. p. 164. laudat hunc Syllogismum, *Lex divina jubet Reges honorari ; Ludovicus XIV est Rex ;* ergo *Lex divina jubet Ludovicum XIV honorari.* Ubi valet certe Argumentum ; Syllogismus tamen est

---

[a] *Author Artis Cogitandi.* The work alluded to is " l'Art de penser," commonly called the Port-Royal Logic. This work has been ascribed to various authors, but was most probably written by Arnauld, assisted by Nicole : the first edition was published at Paris in 1662. Aldrich has on more than one occasion spoken too slightingly of this very valuable work, the Logic *par excellence* of the Cartesian Philosophy. For a better estimate of its merits, the reader is referred to Stewart's Preliminary Dissertation to the Encyclopædia Britannica, p. 80. and to the Introduction to the recent able Translation of the Port-Royal Logic, by Mr. Baynes.

H 2

falsissimus, cum habeat quinque terminos. Nam ex conclusione patet quod major terminus est *jubet Ludovicum XIV honorari*, et minor *Lex divina:* ergo minor Propositio *Lex divina jubet Reges honorari:* ergo Medius terminus *jubet Reges honorari:* ergo Major Propositio debuit esse, *Quod jubet Reges honorari, jubet Ludovicum XIV honorari;* et tum valeret Syllogismus; nec redundarent duo termini, qui in secunda propositione jam redundant.

P. 166. Syllogismum hunc improbat[*], *Debemus credere Scripturæ: Traditio non est Scriptura:* ergo *non debemus credere Traditioni;* quia eum scil. imperite reducit ad primam, cum tamen Syllogismus apertissime hoc dicat in secunda, *Objectum fidei divinæ est Scriptura: Traditio non est Scriptura;* ergo *Traditio non est Objectum fidei divinæ.*

Ibidem imperite autumat Syllogismum sequentem, in quo omnes propositiones videntur affirmativæ, esse in secunda; *salvari* vero, quia minor sensu exclusiva, negativam in se contineat. Quod si ipsos Syllogismi terminos rite dignoscere potuisset, vidisset sane Syllogismum esse in Barbara transpositis præmissis, v. g. *Bonus Pastor est paratus animam ponere pro ovibus; Pauci hoc sœculo sunt*

---

[*] *Syllogismum hunc improbat.* In this instance, it is scarcely necessary to observe that the Port-Royal Logicians are right, and Aldrich is wrong. The premise does not *state* that *nothing but Scripture* is to be believed; and therefore the conclusion drawn is illogical.

parati &c. ergo *Pauci hoc sæculo sunt Boni Pastores.* Hujus conclusio perspicue dicit (non de paucis, quod sunt Boni Pastores, sed) de Bonis Pastoribus, quod sunt hoc sæculo pauci. Quare Major terminus est *hoc sæculo pauci,* et Minor *Boni Pastores.* Ergo Minor Propositio, *Boni Pastores sunt parati* &c. et Medius terminus, *parati animam ponere pro ovibus.* Syllogismus vero hic est, *Qui parati sunt animam ponere pro ovibus sunt hoc sæculo pauci : Qui sunt Boni Pastores sunt parati animam ponere pro ovibus :* ergo *qui sunt Boni Pastores sunt hoc sæculo pauci*[y].

Hæc dixisse erat operæ pretium, nequis temere repudiaret eos qui, si non videntur, sunt tamen revera Syllogismi.]

[y] *Hoc sæculo pauci.* Aldrich's solution is untenable. "Few" is not predicated *distributively,* but *collectively.* From "wise men are few," we cannot infer, "Socrates is few." The syllogism, therefore, *as stated by Aldrich,* becomes a fallacy of division; though, when tested by common sense, it is unquestionably valid. The Port-Royal Logicians substitute for the minor premise, *Multi Pastores hoc sæculo non sunt parati,* &c. which is perhaps the most satisfactory way of treating the proposition, regarded as a single statement. But in fact it contains two distinct assertions; 1st, that some men are prepared; 2dly, that most men are not. The reasoning should thus be resolved into two distinct syllogisms. See Kant, *Logik,* §. 31.

CAP. IV.

De Syllogismis Hypotheticis*.

§. 1. *Syllogismus Hypotheticus,* est in quo una, duæ, vel tres propositiones hypotheticæ. v. g. *Si sapit, est beatus: Sapit; ergo est beatus.* Vel, *Qui sapit est beatus: Si est Philosophus, sapit; ergo Si est Philosophus, est beatus.* Vel, *Si sapit, est beatus: Si est Philosophus, sapit; ergo Si est Philosophus, est beatus.* Nos de eo tantum loqui instituimus qui est cæteris usitatior, in quo nempe Major Hypothetica[b].

* Hypothetical syllogisms, in the present sense of the term, are not treated of by Aristotle. An exposition of them was first sketched out by Theophrastus, which was afterwards further developed by Eudemus and the Stoics. None of these works, however, have come down to us. A few notices may be gathered from the Greek commentators; but our principal extant authority on the subject is Boethius. Of the συλλο-γισμοὶ ἐξ ὑποθέσεως of Aristotle, which Pacius has confounded, and M. St. Hilaire attempts to identify, with the hypotheticals of Theophrastus, some account will be given in the Appendix, note I. In the *Prolegomena Logica,* I have given a theory of hypotheticals different from that commonly adopted by Logicians. But that theory, though I believe it to be more accurate than that of Aldrich, differs too widely from his text to be admissible here. I have therefore transferred it to the Appendix, note I.

b This is the only kind of hypothetical syllogism in which the conclusion is categorical. If the minor premise, or both premises, are hypothetical, the conclusion is so too. A syllogism with all three propositions hypothetical was called by Theophrastus, δι' ὅλου ὑποθετικός, (Scholia, p. 179. a. 16.)

Propositio Hypothetica late sumta definitur, Plures Categoricæ per conjunctionem aliquam unitæ, et conjunctio vocatur *Copula;* estque *Conditionalis, Disjunctiva, Causalis*[c] &c. ut apud Grammaticos; unde totidem Hypotheticarum species, suis copulis cognomines. Sed ad Syllogismum non faciunt, Præter *Conditionalem,* et *Disjunctivam*[d]; quarum exempla, *Si sapit est beatus. Vel dies est vel nox.*

Conditionalis habit vim illativam. Unde *Conditio* ipsa, sive pars prior, quæ est instar inferentis, *Antecedens* dici solet; *Assertio,* sive pars posterior, quæ rationem habet illatæ, *Consequens;* partiumque inter se connexio, *Consequentia*[e].

[c] *Causalis,* e. g. " Because A is B, C is D." This is, of course, only a hypothetical in the loose sense of the above definition. In the same sense were admitted *temporal* hypotheticals, " When A is B, C is D;" *locals,* " Where A is B, C is D," &c. &c. The causal hypothetical proposition is really a curtailed hypothetical syllogism. " Because A is B, C is D," is equivalent to " If A is B, C is D, and A is B." Cf. Hoffbauer, *Logik,* §. 236.

[d] Nothing can be more clumsy than the employment of the word *conditional* in a specific sense, while its Greek equivalent, *hypothetical,* is used generically. In Boethius, both terms are properly used as synonymous and generic; the two species being called *conjunctivi, conjuncti,* or *connexi,* and *disjunctivi,* or *disjuncti.* See *Boethii Opera,* p. 610, Hamilton's *Discussions,* p. 150. The nomenclature of Boethius is followed by Ramus. With reference to modern usage, however, it will be better to contract the Greek word than to extend the Latin one. *Hypothetical,* in the following notes, will be used as synonymous with *conditional.*

[e] It has been questioned whether Hypothetical Syllogisms can be reduced to Categorical. This question must not be

Conditionalis cujusque sententia est, quod, data Conditione, datur Assertio; quod bifariam explicari

confounded with the inquiry, whether the hypothetical *proposition* is formally the same with the categorical. The latter is answered by Kant in the negative, but that decision does not affect the present question. The reduction of hypothetical syllogisms must be governed by the same rules as that of categoricals; and in the latter case, it is allowable to substitute for a given proposition another which, though not identical, is implied by it. For instance, a particular proposition may be employed in the place of an universal. So in hypotheticals, if the new propositions contain the same terms, and are immediately deducible from the original ones, the reduction is legitimate. This will generally be the case when the hypothetical proposition has but three terms; both clauses having the same subject or the same predicate. The following instances may thus be reduced:—

I. If All A is B, All A is C,   All B is C,
   But All A is B;   to   All A is B;
   ∴ All A is C.   ∴ All A is C.

II. If All A is B, All C is B,   All A is B,
    But All A is B;   to   All C is A;
    ∴ All C is B.   ∴ All C is B.

These syllogisms, indeed, were admitted by the Ramists, the great advocates of hypotheticals, to be categorical. But where the hypothetical has four terms, as, "If A is B, C is D," this mode of reduction is not practicable; yet even in this case a categorical syllogism may be constructed, whose propositions, though expressed in different terms, are implied in those of the original syllogism. Thus:

Constructive.

Destructive.

Every case of A being B, is a case of C being D.

Every case of A being B, is a case of C being D.

This is a case of A being B.

This is not a case of C being D.

∴ This is a case of C being D.

∴ This is not a case of A being B.

The above directions are all that can be given on the ordinary

potest.   1. *Si detur* Conditio, *danda est* Assertio ; unde *Regula prima :* Posita Antecedente, recte ponitur Consequens.   2. Si *daretur* Conditio, *danda esset* Assertio; unde *Regula secunda :* Sublata Consequente, recte tollitur Antecedens.

Porro hoc unum statuit, Antecedente vera, veram esse Consequentem; non autem ambas esse simul veras, aut simul falsas, aut una vera, falsam alteram : per illam igitur, sublata Antecedente, poni vel tolli potest Consequens ; aut posita Consequente, poni vel tolli Antecedens.   Unde *Regula tertia :* Sublata Antecedente, vel Posita Consequente, nihil certo colligitur[f].

Conditionalis igitur Syllogismi duæ sunt, nec plures, formulæ.

I. Quæ vocatur *Constructiva.*

Si   C. D.   tum   K. $\triangle$.
Sed   C. D.   ergo   K. $\triangle$.

theory of hypotheticals.   The first method of reduction is only approximately true ; and various ingenious examples have been framed by Logicians, to which it is inapplicable. See Krug, §. 82. Fries, §. 62.   The truth is, that the so-called hypothetical proposition is really the statement of a consequence, which is sometimes formal, sometimes material ; and in the latter case, the consequence is extralogical, and cannot be reduced to any logical form, without additional assumptions derived from the matter treated of.   See below, Appendix, note I.

[f] By adopting the above modes of reduction it may easily be seen, that the violation of this third rule is equivalent, in the case of denying the antecedent, to an illicit process of the major term ; in that of affirming the consequent, to an undistributed middle.

II. Quæ dicitur *Destructiva*[g].

    Si   C. D.   tum   K. △.
    Sed non K. △. ergo non C. D.

§. 2. QUÆ de *Conditionali* dicta sunt, *Disjunctivæ* satis cavent.   Ejus enim in Syllogismo positæ sententia conditionaliter efferri semper potest[h].

---

[g] The destructive syllogism is naturally reduced to the second figure in the categorical form, and cannot in most cases be brought to the first without considerable awkwardness.   This may be avoided by *converting* the hypothetical before reduction.   A hypothetical proposition is converted by *Contraposition;* thus, " If A is B, C is D," to, " If C is not D, A is not B."   The syllogism may then be treated as a constructive.   Cf. Hamilton on Reid, p. 697.   Whately's Logic, b. ii. ch. 4. §. 3.

Hypothetical as well as Categorical reasonings may be combined in a Sorites.   The Hypothetical Sorites consists of a series of propositions, in which the consequent of each is the antecedent of the next ; the conclusion being composed of the first antecedent and the last consequent.   Thus :

Constructive Sorites.	Destructive Sorites.
If A is B, C is D.	If A is B, C is D.
If C is D, E is F.	If C is D, E is F.
If E is F, G is H.	If E is F, G is H.
∴ If A is B, G is H.	∴ If G is not H, A is not B.

See Wolf, *Phil. Rat.* §. 470.

[h] With regard to the import of the disjunctive proposition, Logicians are at issue.   The majority (Kant among the number) regard it as stating all possible cases ; so that one only of its members can be true.   And Aquinas maintains that any disjunctive proposition in which this condition is not observed is *false.*   On this supposition all the four inferences given by Aldrich are valid.   But it may be questioned whether the incompatibility of the members appears in the *form* of

v. g. Si posita vel C vel D
Subsumatur
Sed C ergo non D
    D   non C
    non C ergo D
    non D   C
Pro exposita Disjunctiva
dic conditionaliter

every disjunctive proposition. *We may happen to know* that
two alternatives cannot be true together, so that the affirmation
of the second necessitates the denial of the first, and the
affirmation of the first the denial of the second; but this, as
Boethius observes, is a *material*, not a *formal* consequence,
whether it be stated in the hypothetical or disjunctive form.
It must be allowed that the examples sometimes adduced on
this side of the question have not been very happily chosen.
It sounds oddly enough to state a known truth as a possible
falsehood, as in the instance, " *Bellum Trojanum cecinit vel
Homerus vel Virgilius.*" But other and more natural specimens
have been given; e. g. " *Aut olim Troja fuit, aut historia de
bello Trojano est mera fabula.*" The case is still clearer when
both members of the disjunctive are negative, as in the
example given by Boethius, " Si enim quis dicat, aut non
est album aut non est nigrum, sive album non esse assumpserit, non necesse erit esse vel non esse nigrum : sive
nigrum non esse assumpserit, ut sit vel non sit album, nullam
faciet necessitatem." On this supposition only two of the
above syllogisms are valid, which may be reduced to hypotheticals as follows :

Constructive.	Destructive.
If A is not B, C is D.	If A is not B, C is D.
But A is not B.	But C is not D.
∴ C is D.	∴ A is B.

For a further account, see Wallis, Log. Thes. 2.

$$\begin{array}{ll} \text{Si C tum non D} & \\ \text{D} & \text{non C} \\ \text{non C tum} & \text{D} \\ \text{non D} & \text{C} \end{array}$$

§. 3. SUPEREST Syllogismus quidam Hypotheticus redundans, alio nomine *Dilemma*[1], quia ple-

[1] Of the word *Dilemma*, various etymologies have been proposed ; 1. a choice of alternatives offered to an adversary; 2. a double premise assumed (λῆμμα); 3. a not very probable one given by Keckermann, " a δὶς λαμβάνεσθαι, quia utrinque capit et constringit adversarium contra quem adducitur." The first seems to be adopted by Aldrich, and is perhaps supported by Cassiodorus, Expos. in Ps. 138, 9. " Dilemma, quod fit ex duabus propositionibus pluribusve, ex quibus quicquid electum fuerit, contrarium esse non dubium est." Cf. Victorinus in 1 Rhet. Cic. 86. But whatever be the origin of the word, it was certainly employed as synonymous with the *complexio* of Cicero, (de Inv. 1. 29.) This is expressly stated by Servius, (on Æn. ii. 675.) and the word had been previously used in a similar sense by the Greek rhetoricians. See Hermogenes, de Inv. p. 167, ed. Walz; Apsines, Ars Rhet. p. 524. In this sense it may be defined, (omitting the adversary, as belonging rather to Rhetoric or Dialectic than Logic,) " A syllogism, having a conditional major premise with more than one antecedent, and a disjunctive minor." Its different forms may be thus exhibited :

I. Simple Constructive.

If A is B, C is D ; and if E is F, C is D ;
But either A is B, or E is F ;
∴ C is D.

II. Complex Constructive.

If A is B, C is D ; and if E is F, G is H ;
But either A is B, or E is F ;
∴ Either C is D, or G is H.

rumque duo (etsi interdum plura) proponit adversario capienda; quorum utrumvis acceperit, causa cadet. Tale est illud Biantis, *Si uxorem ducas formosam, habebis* κοινὴν, *communem; si deformem,* ποινὴν, *pœnam:* ergo *Nulla est ducenda*[k].

[1] Hoc non valet, nisi ita comparetur, ut partem alteram accipi sit necesse; utraque autem feriat; nec possit retorqueri. Quæ si vidisset Bias, suo sibi Dilemmate minus placuisset; neque enim vel formosa uxor vel deformis necessario futura est; sed est media quædam pulchritudo, quam Ennius

III. Destructive, (always Complex.)

If A is B, C is D; and if E is F, G is H;
But either C is not D, or G is not H;
∴. Either A is not B, or E is not F.

There cannot be a *simple* destructive Dilemma of this kind, as is shewn by Abp. Whately, Logic, b. ii. ch. 4. §. 5.

There is another form of reasoning, sometimes called Dilemma, which is also a hypothetico-disjunctive reasoning, but which, instead of having the major premise hypothetical and the minor disjunctive, has both combined in the major; the *whole* of the disjunctive consequents being denied in the minor. E. g. "If A is B, either C is D, or E is F; but neither C is D, nor E is F; therefore A is not B." This form is given by Wallis, lib. iii. cap. 19.; as well as by Wolf and Kant. But it is a perversion of the Dilemma proper, and introduces no distinction whatever; being merely a common disjunctive syllogism, as is shewn by Wallis himself. It is, in fact, the *enumeratio*, not the *complexio*, of Cicero.

[k] See Gellius, Noct. Att. v. 11.

[1] These remarks entirely relate to the matter, and have nothing to do with the Logical character, of the Dilemma. See Whately, ii. 4. 5.

statam appellavit ; Favorinus eleganter *uxoriam.* Porro, nec formosa omnis est communis, nec deformis, pœna. Denique Dilemma facile retorqueri potest. Puta, *Si formosam duxero, non habebo pœnam ; si deformem, non habebo communem.*

Dilemma nihil aliud est, quam *Inductio Negativa*[m]; in qua Syllogismi Major Conditionalis est

Arist.Rhet. II. 23. 15.

---

[m] This remark is taken from Wallis, and is only applicable to the Dilemma in his sense of the term. The negative induction appears categorically in this form :

> There are no instances of C being D, nor of E being F.
> But these are all the possible instances of A being B.
> ∴ There is no instance of A being B.

The Dilemma of Aldrich cannot, as it stands, be reduced to this form. The categorical conclusion, e. g. *Nulla uxor est ducenda,* does not follow from the premises of the Dilemma of Bias ; but requires the additional assumption, that neither matrimonial nuisance is, under any circumstance, to be endured. This brings it to Wallis's form, thus :

> *Si ducenda est uxor, aut formosa ducenda est, aut deformis :*
> *Atqui non est ducenda formosa, neque deformis :*
> *Ergo, Uxor non est ducenda.* (Burgersdyck, *Inst. Log.* ii. 13.)

The Complex Dilemma, as given above, may be reduced, if required, to a series of hypothetical syllogisms, and so to categoricals : thus :

Constructive.	Destructive.
If E is F, G is H ;	If E is F, G is H ;
If A is not B, E is F ;	If C is D, G is not H ;
∴ If A is not B, G is H.	∴ If C is D, E is not F.
If C is not D, A is not B ;	If A is B, C is D ;
∴ If C is not D, G is H.	∴ If A is B, E is not F.

The reduction of the simple Dilemma is obvious enough.

cum consequente distributiva : puta, *Si omnino, tum sic, vel sic, vel sic ;* quam afferre Categorice adeo est proclive ut non indigeat præcepto.

But all such reductions, except as serving to vindicate the universality of the syllogistic model, are rather curious than useful.

CAP. V.

De Syllogismo quoad Materiam.

§. 1. Hæc de Syllogismo quoad *Formam* spectato. Jam de eodem quoad *Materiam,* h. e. *Certitudinem* et *Evidentiam* propositionum ex quibus componitur.

Certa autem propositio est, cui nihil occurrit in contrarium, vel quod occurrit instar nihili est; ut, *Omnis homo est risibilis**: *Evidens,* quæ simul

---

* This definition is vague enough : the example, however, shews more clearly what is intended. For *risibile* was regarded as a property, flowing from, and demonstrable by, the differentia *rationale.* We may therefore define a *certain* proposition as " a proposition capable of demonstration." It will thus be distinguished from an *evident* proposition, which is axiomatic and indemonstrable. Both are, of course, *necessary,* which is essential to demonstrative reasoning : but the former is the conclusion of a demonstration ; the latter, a premise. Waiving the physical question of the necessary connection of risibility and rationality, we may give as examples, of a certain proposition, " The angles of every triangle are equal to two right angles ;" of an evident, " Things which are equal to the same are equal to each other."

Such seems clearly to be Aldrich's meaning in the present passage ; in which *certa* and *evidens* correspond to what are commonly called *immediata immedietate subjecti,* and *immediata immedietate causæ.* (Cf. Sanderson, lib. 3. cap. 12. from whom this part is chiefly taken.) Aldrich's subsequent language, however, is by no means consistent.

ac percipitur assensum imperat; ut, *Totum est majus sua parte: Dubia,* in qua hæremus, cum illius pars utraque valde se probet intellectui; ut, *Astra regunt homines;* nam et regere et non regere videntur.

Dubitanti siquid aliud occurrat, quo pendens animus in alterutram partem propendeat, quod erat Dubium fit *Probabile* [b]. Et potest, quod pro- Top. I. 1. 3. batur, *Verum* esse, sed probanti tantum *Verisimile* est. Multis nihilominus assentimur isto modo, et assensui nomen est *Opinio* [c].

Est igitur *Opinio* propositionis *tantum probabilis;* An. Post. eique nulla competit certitudo; sed in ipsa sui I. 33. 2. ratione includit *formidinem oppositi.* Sunt Opinioni tamen *Gradus* quidam *ad certitudinem,* pro diverso pondere rationum quæ assensum movent, diversi. Est quod omnibus, quod plerisque, quod Top. I. 1. 3. sapientibus videtur; et quod horum singulis, quod plerisque, quod celeberrimis; quorum omnium dispar est probabilitas; quorumdam vero tanta, ut ad certitudinem quam proxime accedat.

§. 2. QUI *Opinionem* (h. e. assensum quemlibet scientia minorem) parit, Syllogismus appellatur

---

[b] Ἔνδοξα δὲ τὰ δοκοῦντα πᾶσιν ἢ τοῖς πλείστοις ἢ τοῖς σοφοῖς, καὶ τούτοις ἢ πᾶσιν ἢ τοῖς πλείστοις ἢ τοῖς μάλιστα γνωρίμοις καὶ ἐνδόξοις. Arist. Top. i. 1. 3. Such propositions form the premises of dialectical syllogisms.

[c] Λείπεται δόξαν εἶναι περὶ τὸ ἀληθὲς μὲν ἢ ψεῦδος, ἐνδεχόμενον δὲ καὶ ἄλλως ἔχειν. Τοῦτο δ᾽ ἐστὶν ὑπόληψις τῆς ἀμέσου προτάσεως καὶ μὴ ἀναγκαίας. Anal. Post. i. 33. 2.

I

Top. I. 1. 2. *Dialecticus,* Διαλεκτικὸς[d], i. e. probabiliter disserens : quæque proprie dicitur *Dialectica,* est pars Logicæ quæ de hoc agit Syllogismo. Multiplex autem est materia circa quam versatur Opinio, et per omnes sparsa disciplinas ; cujus infinitam pene varietatem ad pauca capita revocavit Aristoteles, et sub iis Effata Dialectica suis quasi in sedibus *locavit.* Hæc itaque capita, Τόπους, i. e. *Locos* appellat ; unde Syllogismus Dialecticus alio nomine *Topicus* dicitur[e].

De Locis Dialecticis et ad ea pertinentibus Effatis, sive (ut Scholastici vocant) Maximis[f] ;

---

[d] Διαλεκτικὸς δὲ συλλογισμὸς ὁ ἐξ ἐνδόξων συλλογιζόμενος. Top. i. 1. 2. On the origin and different uses of Dialectic, some remarks will be found in the Introduction. Its name had originally reference, not to the probable character of the matter, but to the colloquial form.

[e] The τόποι are general principles of probability, standing in the same relation to the dialectic syllogism as the axioms to the demonstrative. A definition is given, Rhet. ii. 26. 1. ἔστι γὰρ στοιχεῖον καὶ τόπος εἰς ὃ πολλὰ ἐνθυμήματα ἐμπίπτει. The origin of the name may be illustrated by calling it the *place* in which we look for middle terms ; with which may be compared Cicero's definition, Top. ch. 2. " Itaque licet definire, locum esse argumenti sedem : argumentum autem, rationem, quæ rei dubiæ faciat fidem." Cf. De Orat. ii. 174. Theophrastus' definition is given by Alexander, Schol. p. 252. a. 12. ἔστι γὰρ ὁ τόπος, ὡς λέγει Θεόφραστος, ἀρχή τις ἢ στοιχεῖον, ἀφ' οὗ λαμβάνομεν τὰς περὶ ἕκαστον ἀρχάς.

[f] The Schoolmen divided *Loci* into two kinds, which they called *Maximæ,* and *Differentiæ Maximarum.* The former were propositions expressing a general principle of probability, (or even of certainty, for the term was extended to include axioms ;) such as, " De quocunque prædicatur definitio, et definitum."

plura non loquor.   Pro exemplo tamen hoc accipe:
Inter Maximas Loci primi, qui est *Testimonium,* Top. III. 1. 2.
reperitur hæc; *Peritis credendum est in sua arte:*
ex qua elicitur hujusmodi Syllogismus Topicus.
Quod (Pythagoras) *Ipse dixit concedendum est:*
Migrare animas Ipse dixit; ergo *Migrare animas*
concedendum est.   Probatur Major; quia *Peritis*
credendum est in sua arte.

§. 3. *Certitudo* eadem videtur, quæ improprie
vulgo dicitur *Evidentia Moralis*[g]; quæque iis con-

The latter consisted of one or more words, expressing the
point in which one maxim differed from another; e. g. the
above maxim is said to be *ex definitione et definito:* so in
Aldrich's example the maxim is, *Peritis credendum est in sua*
arte; the differentia, *Testimonium.*   The latter were sometimes
called simply *Loci.*   Cf. Petr. Hisp. Tract. v.   The distinction
is not warranted by Aristotle, with whom the τόποι are always
Propositions.

The history of the word *Maxim* is given in a learned note
by Sir W. Hamilton, Reid's Works, p. 766.   He shews that
it originated with Boethius, by whom, however, it was merely
used as an adjective, in the phrase *maxima propositio.*   The
Schoolmen dropped the latter word, and employed *maxima* as
a substantive.

[g] This paragraph, Aldrich appears to have taken from the
Cartesians, and spoiled in the taking.   Thus Clauberg, *Logica,*
P. I. qu. 133.   " Quænam axiomata minimum habent veritatis
seu certitudinis? *Contingentia* seu contingenter vera, h. e. quæ
ita vera sunt ut falsa esse possint: ut si judicem matres amare
liberos suos.   Horum axiomatum certitudo vocatur vulgo
Moralis, non quod in rebus tantum ethicis seu moralibus
locum habeat, sed quod aliter de talibus statuendo contra
bonos mores plerumque peccetur."   And in the same manner,

venit effatis, de quibus nemo prudens dubitaverit : qualia præsertim sunt *Principia* ad vitam moresque pertinentia, cum conclusionibus quæ ab his legitime deducuntur. Nam hujusmodi propositiones videntur esse plusquam probabiles, nondum tamen evidentes : neque enim eas quisque amplectitur quamprimum apprehendit ; sed iis prudens sine ulla formidine assentitur.

Certitudo[h] duplex est ; alia *Objecti,* quæ est rei

moral certainty is distinguished from *metaphysical* by Descartes. *Méthode*, p. iv.   This is obviously a totally different sense of the word *certainty* from that given at the beginning of the chapter.   " Omnis homo est risibilis" can hardly by any stretch of language be called a *moral precept*.   Moral certainty is a very different thing from demonstrative certainty, being merely a high degree of probability.   But nothing can be more confused than the whole of this chapter.

[h] We have now got back again to demonstrative certainty. This part is taken from Sanderson, whose account is infinitely clearer than that of Aldrich.   " Demonstratio est *Syllogismus faciens scire.*   Scire autem unumquodque dicimur, cum causam cognoscimus propter quam res est, quod illius rei causa sit, nec possit res aliter se habere.   Unde duplex oritur scientiæ certitudo : altera objecti, vel *scibilis*, quando rei causa proxima apprehenditur : altera subjecti, vel *scientis*, quando sciens certus est rem non posse aliter se habere.   Per illam distinguitur *scientia* ab *errore:* per hanc ab *opinione*, quæ includit in ratione sui formidinem oppositi."   From the above account it is clear that there can be no degrees of either Certainty. For any obstacle as regards the object, renders the proposition no longer certain, but doubtful ; any consciousness of such in the subject, reduces the state of mind from knowledge to opinion.   The same may be said of Evidence, in the proper limitation of the term.   A proposition not *sponte perspicuum* may be certain, but is not evident.

percipiendæ ; alia *Subjecti,* quæ est Intellectûs percipientis[i]. Et utrique sui sunt *gradus.* Est enim **Certius** certitudine Objecti, id cui minus obest ; certitudine Subjecti, cui quod obsit minus percipitur. Evidentia similiter duplex est ; *Objecti* nempe, et *Subjecti ;* et utrique sui sunt *gradus.* Dispar enim evidentia est, prout id quod percipitur vel est sponte perspicuum ; vel a sponte perspicuo propius abest ; vel utrumvis horum videtur.

Atque hinc, rursus, *Evidentia*[k] multifariam divi-

---

[i] On the history of the terms *Object* and *Subject, Objective* and *Subjective*, see Sir W. Hamilton's note, *Reid's Works*, p. 806. and Trendelenburg, *Elementa*, §. 1. The variations between the scholastic and the modern sense of these terms are however in this particular relation unimportant. Where *knowledge* or *certainty* is spoken of, the subject of inherence (in the scholastic sense) is the mind as knowing; and the object proper is the thing as known ; and thus far, the modern use of the same terms is nearly coincident ; though when viewed out of relation to the act of knowledge, the two nomenclatures are exactly the reverse of each other. In our present point of view we may distinguish *certitudo objecti* as *a quality of the proposition as apprehended by the mind,* and *certitudo subjecti* as *a state of the mind as apprehending the proposition;* and in this sense the two are inseparable from each other, being only the same act of thought viewed from opposite sides. This is the only sense of *object* and *subject* with which Logic has any concern. The *subjective existence,* as the schoolmen would call it, or the *objective existence,* as the moderns would call it, of things out of the act of thought, belongs to a metaphysical inquiry, with which, as Logicians, we have no concern.

[k] Evidence is here extended so as to include not only axiomatic but demonstrated propositions. This licence

ditur. Sed nostro sufficit instituto, quod hæc, de qua loquimur, Propositionis *Evidentia*, vel est 1. *Axiomatis* sponte perspicui; cui proinde sine ulla probatione assentimur: vel 2. *Conclusionis* ab ejusmodi axiomatibus (*immediate* an *mediate* parum refert, modo) rite deductæ. Nam cum una sit Veritas, sibi constans, apteque cohærens; quodque verum, vel per se certum atque evidens sit, vel cum effatis quibusdam certis et evidentibus necessario connexum; fit, ut quamprimum apprehenditur hæc connexio, eadem omnia quasi luce perfusa, parem (specie) consequantur assensum.

An. Post.
I. 2. 2.
I. 4. 1.

§. 4. Qui postremæ huic evidentiæ competit assensus apud Logicos vocatur *Scientia.* Est igitur Scientia *conclusionis certæ et evidentis,* a præmissis certis et evidentibus legitime deductæ[1]. Certitudinem vero utramque intelligo; et utramque (tam Objecti scilicet quam Subjecti) evidentiam. Nam

An. Post.
I. 33.

per Objecti certitudinem Scientia distinguitur ab *Errore;* per Subjecti certitudinem ab *Opinione*[m].

Aldrich perhaps took from Crakanthorpe, who uses *certain* and *evident* as synonymous terms; but he departs from his principal authority, Sanderson, and is inconsistent with himself. *Evident* should be limited to the axioms, the original premises of demonstration; *certain,* to the conclusion.

[1] It would be better to say, " conclusionis certæ, a præmissis certis vel evidentibus." The premises in demonstration may be axiomatic principles, or the conclusions of previous demonstrations. In both cases the result is *scientia,* though in the latter the demonstration is not-*potissima.*

[m] Strictly speaking, objective and subjective certainty of

Si desit evidentia subjecti, nulla est *Scientia ;* ubi
sola adest, *persuasa* tantum, non *realis* evidentia
est.

Qui *Scientiam* parit Syllogismus appellatur An. Post.
Scientificus ; alio nomine, Ἀποδεικτικὸς *Demon-* I. 2. 2.
I. 4. 1.
strativus, et interdum *Demonstratio.* Conclusiones Top. I. 1.;
enim certas et evidentes apud Mathematicos repe-
riri multas in confesso est: cumque Illi, quæ

thought cannot be actually separated from each other, being
merely the same act of thought viewed from opposite sides.
Of objects out of the act of thought, the thinker knows
nothing. But in comparing two minds together, one of
whom is supposed to have a firm conviction of a true proposition on sufficient grounds, the other an equally firm conviction of a false proposition, the difference between them
will lie, not in the state of conviction which is common to
both, but in the object on which it is exercised ; and the
change from error to knowledge will be effected by the
substitution of one object for another. On the other hand,
if a truth known scientifically by one man is assented to with
hesitation by another, the difference lies in their respective
states of mind in relation to a common object, and the change
from opinion to knowledge will consist in a different mode of
contemplating the same truth. Hence, in strict accuracy, we
should say, that the characteristic of error is the attribution
of certainty to a wrong object ; that of opinion, the absence
of certainty in the subject. The criterion of knowledge from
error is strictly the character of the object as it appears to a
rightly informed mind ; and hence, among the later Logicians,
we find *respectu objecti* used as equivalent to *per se ;* and opposed
to *respectu subjecti,* as it appears to this particular thinker.
This forms the connecting link between the scholastic use
of *objective* to denote what exists only in thought, and the
modern use, to denote the absolute affections of things
without the mind.

docent, soleant adjuncto *Diagrammate* ostendere ; seque propterea non rem probare, sed (quod majorem innuit evidentiam) *demonstrare* dicant ; arcessito igitur ab illis vocabulo, *Syllogismus scire faciens* apud Logicos vocatur *Demonstratio.* Cumque in Scientia (siqua forte possibilitas, tamen) nullus sit erroris metus ; quod hujusmodi Syllogismis, sive uno, sive pluribus probatur, id libenter agnoscimus sicut perhibetur *ita esse ;* et *aliter* (saltem naturaliter) *se habere non posse.*

§. 5. Duæ sunt Demonstrationis species. Prima, quæ demonstrat ῞Οτι, sive *Quod res sit ;* probando, vel simpliciter et directe *rem ita esse,* et tum vocatur *Ostensiva,* seu potius *Directa ;* vel si *non sit,* absurdi aliquid necessario secuturum. Hæc est quæ Græce dicitur ᾿Απαγωγὴ [n], Latine, *ducens*

Anal. Pr.
II. 11. 1.
An. Post.
I. 26. 1.

[n] *ἀπαγωγή· ducens ad impossibile.* This is only a correct rendering of the Aristotelian ἀπαγωγὴ εἰς τὸ ἀδύνατον ; see p. 88, note e. The term ἀπαγωγή, when it occurs by itself, has a different meaning. It is a syllogism whose major premise is certain, and its minor either more probable or more easily demonstrable than the conclusion. It thus holds an intermediate place between the demonstrative and the dialectic syllogism. See Anal. Pr. ii. 25.

The connecting notion between these two senses of ἀπαγωγή seems to be that of a *change of question ;* a *turning off* from the immediate point to be proved to something else on which it may be made to depend. Thus, in the *deductio ad impossibile,* instead of proving the original question directly, we attempt to shew the falsehood of its contradictory ; and in the present case we abandon the immediate proof of the conclusion for that of the minor premise on which it depends.

ad absurdum, impossibile, incommodum, uno verbo recte dixeris *Obliquam.* Exemplum ejus dat reductio Syllogismi a *Baroko* vel *Bokardo* ad *Barbara.*

Ostensiva Directa fit duobus modis.

1. Quando aliquid demonstratur per *Effectum;* ut si diceres, *Luna Soli opposita nigra cernitur;* ergo *patitur Eclipsin.* 2. Quando per *Causam remotam;* ut si idem colligeres quia *Sol et Luna diametraliter opponuntur.* Quod si illud demonstrares per *Causam proximam,* quia nempe *Terra inter Solem et Lunam interponitur,* tum fieret

An. Post. I. 13. 1, 2.

An. Post. I. 13. 1, 5.

Secunda Demonstrationis species Διότι, i. e. quæ docet *Quare,* vel *Propter quid* res sit; causam ejus assignando, non quamcunque, sed *proximam* seu *immediatam°.* Sic enim statuunt Logici quod

An. Post. I. 13. 3. II. 16. 4, 6. II. 17. 3.

° *Immediatam.* The word ἄμεσος is used in two senses by Aristotle. 1. For a proposition not proved by any *higher* middle term; i. e. an axiomatic principle, forming the first premise of a demonstration. Such is the sense in Anal. Post. i. 2. 2. and ii. 19. 1. 2. For a premise immediate as regards its conclusion; i. e. not requiring the insertion of *lower* middle terms to connect its terms with those of the conclusion. Such is the sense in An. Post. i. 13. 1. This second sense is intended here.

Of an immediate proposition in the first sense, the favourite scholastic example was, *Omne animal rationale est risibile;* the predicate being regarded as flowing directly from the subject, not as connected with it by any intervening cause. Whereas in *homo est risibilis,* between predicate and subject intervenes the middle term *rationalis.* See Aquinas, Opusc. 48. de Syll. Demon. cap. 5. Zabarella, in I. Anal. Post. c. 2.

Scientia omnis est *Cognitio rei per causam,* sed *proprie dicta* per *propriam,* h. e. *proximam :* nam per remotam *Cur sit* aliquatenus ostenditur ; nihil amplius quam *Quod sit* demonstratur.

Utriusque Speciei membra gradu differunt. Nam obliqua ὅτι est deterior directa, quia non demonstrat *rem ita esse,* nisi quatenus docet *eam aliter se habere non posse;* quod tametsi eodem redeat, tamen animo minus satisfacit ; nam si par sit utrobique Certitudo, hujus tamen minor Evidentia est [p].

An. Post.
II. 18.

Habet et Διότι suos gradus ; quia potest esse causa proxima quæ non est *prima,* h. e. per se nota et indemonstrabilis : cujus ideo præfertur Evidentia, quia (contra quam cæteræ) sua luce est conspicua, et nihil indiget aliena. Quare, quæ

cont. 9. Hence the following specimen of a *demonstratio potissima :*

> *Omne animal rationale est risibile;*
> *Omnis homo est animal rationale;* ergo
> *Omnis homo est risibilis.*

Any subsequent demonstration from this conclusion ; e. g. *Omnis Philosophus est homo;* ergo *Omnis Philosophus est risibilis;* would be *per causam proximam, sed non primam.* Whether this distinction can fairly be traced to Aristotle is questionable. Some further remarks will be found, Appendix, note K.

[p] Here we have a third meaning of *evidentia.* It is now, not the evidentness of a *Proposition,* but that of a *Demonstration;* i. e. the clearness of connection between premises and conclusion.

hanc adhĭbet causam Demonstratio, et habetur, et nominatur *Potissima.*

Sunt igitur ex mente Logicorum Demonstrandi quatuor modi ; quorum alter alteri evidentia, adeoque dignitate, præstat[q]. *Valet* Demonstratio obliqua ; *Potens* est quælibet Directa ; *Potior* quæ per causam proximam, *Potissima* quæ per primam demonstrat. Hujus est vulgata illa Definitio, *Syllogismus constans veris, primis, immediatis, notioribus, prioribus, et causis Conclusionis*[r]. Exemplum, nisi forte apud Mathematicos, an uspiam occurrat nescio. An. Post. 1. 2. 2.

[q] The following table may assist the learner.

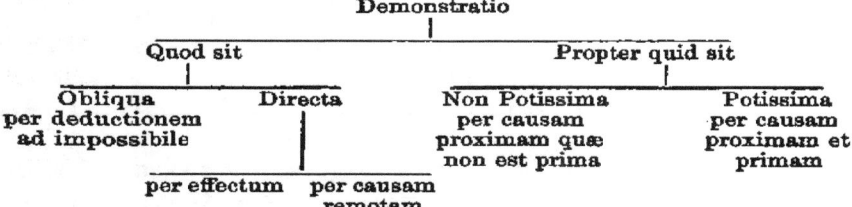

[r] This definition is translated from Aristotle. 'Απόδειξιν δὲ λέγω συλλογισμὸν ἐπιστημονικόν. 'Επιστημονικὸν δὲ λέγω καθ᾽ ὃν τῷ ἔχειν αὐτὸν ἐπιστάμεθα. Εἰ τοίνυν ἐστὶ τὸ ἐπίστασθαι οἷον ἔθεμεν, ἀνάγκη καὶ τὴν ἀποδεικτικὴν ἐπιστήμην ἐξ ἀληθῶν τ᾽ εἶναι καὶ πρώτων καὶ ἀμέσων καὶ γνωριμωτέρων καὶ προτέρων καὶ αἰτίων τοῦ συμπεράσματος. Anal. Post. i. 2. 2. See further, Appendix, note K.

CAP. VI.

*De Methodo*ᵃ.

§. 1. METHODUS est talis dispositio partium alicujus disciplinæ, ut integra facilius discaturᵇ.

ᵃ Μέθοδος in Aristotle is employed with various shades of meaning; 1. for any instrument of acquiring or communicating knowledge ; as in de An. i. 1. 4. πότερον ἀπόδειξίς τίς ἐστιν ἢ διαίρεσις ἢ καί τις ἄλλη μέθοδος. Cf. Philoponus, Scholia, p. 235, a. 10. 2. for knowledge reduced to system ; and thus as equivalent to ἐπιστήμη : Phys. Ausc. i. 1. 1. Eth. Nic. i. 1. 1. Top. i. 2. 2. 3. for a systematic treatise on any branch of knowledge, synonymous with πραγματεία : Polit. iv. 2. 1. vi. 2. 6. Eth. Nic. i. 2. 9. But Method, in the present sense of *arrangement*, is not treated of in the logical writings of Aristotle, with the exception of a few rules for the arrangement (τάξις) of a dialectical disputation in the eighth book of the Topics. A lost treatise, called *Methodica*, is mentioned in the Rhetoric, I. 2. Method, as a distinct part of Logic, was first introduced by Ramus, and from him passed to the logical writings of the Cartesians and of Gassendi, by whom it was treated as a fourth part of Logic. Like most of the additions to the Aristotelian system, it was originally the property of the Rhetoricians.

ᵇ Method has been treated of by Logicians in two principal senses. 1. As a process of inference from the known to the unknown ; which is the earlier sense of the term, and sanctioned by Aristotle and his Greek interpreters. 2. As an arrangement of truths already known, with a view of communicating them to others. The last corresponds to the Greek τάξις, and should rather be called *Ordo*. It is distinguished from the first by Zabarella and others. Aldrich's definition corresponds only to the second sense of *Methodus ;* but in his subsequent division he confounds it with the first.

Estque duplex. 1. *Inventionis,* quæ disciplinæ Eth. Nic. I. 2. 5.
præcepta invenit; 2. *Doctrinæ,* quæ tradit. Prior Phys.Ausc. I. 1. 1.
procedit a sensibilibus, et singularibus, quæ sunt
nobis notiora, ad intelligibilia, et universalia, quæ
sunt *notiora naturæ:* Posterior, contra*.

Method in either sense is not properly a part of Pure or
Formal Logic. It is an application of Logic to the discovery
or communication of truths in material science: its rules
cannot be determined *à priori* from the laws of thought; but
must be gathered empirically from the examination of particular sciences, and will require modification in many instances
from the particular matter with which they have to deal.

*The *Methodus Inventionis* can only be a process of inference:
for no *arrangement* of parts is possible before they have been
discovered. The *discovery* of general principles from individual
objects of sense, if limited to the inferential process itself,
will be *Induction.* The term, however, is sometimes extended
so as to include the preliminary accumulation of individuals.
In this wider sense it will embrace the four successive steps
given by Aristotle, Anal. Post. ii. 19. αἴσθησις, μνήμη, ἐμπειρία,
ἐπαγωγή.

But the *Methodus Inventionis* must not be absolutely limited
to Induction and its preliminaries, though these are the most
important instruments of discovery. In some sciences, as in
mathematics, truths are chiefly discovered by demonstration;
and, till so discovered, cannot, of course, be imparted to others
by the *methodus doctrinæ.*

Induction and Syllogism are the only two methods of
inference. The Greek commentators, Ammonius and Eu-
stratius, enumerate four, adding Division and Definition; but
in these last there is no reasoning process. See Zabarella,
de Methodis, lib. iii. cap. 5 sqq. If we extend the method of
discovery beyond the process of inference proper, so as to
include any accumulation of knowledge, we may distinguish
three principal instruments. 1. Pure experience, applicable to

Methodus Doctrinæ duplex est. [d]*Perfecta, ἀκροα-μaτικὴ*; et *Imperfecta, ἐξωτερική*. Perfecta rursus, vel *Universalis* est, qua integra disciplina, vel *Particularis,* qua aliqua disciplinæ pars docetur. Utraque duplex est.

An. Post.
I. 7. 1.
I. 10. 4.
Eth. Nic.
I. 2. 5.

1. *Compositoria* sive *Synthetica*[e], quæ inservit the acquisition of historical knowledge. 2. Demonstration, applicable to sciences of pure reasoning. 3. Induction, applicable to mixed sciences of reasoning and fact. Cf. Fries, *System der Logik,* §. 117.

[d] The *Methodus Doctrinæ* is not in the same sense a process of inference from known to unknown; for the parts are supposed to be known already to the teacher, and are methodically arranged for the benefit of the learner. This then corresponds rather to Order than to Method in the proper sense. It may be an arrangement either of the whole or of a portion of a subject; and is thus either universal or particular. Cf. Zabarella, de Methodis, lib. ii. cap. 20. The distinction between the Perfect and Imperfect Method is not usually recognised by writers on the subject. Aldrich is thinking of the *acroamatic* and *exoteric* teaching of Aristotle and others; the characteristic feature of the latter being the suppression of certain doctrines as not fitted for a promiscuous audience. Whereas the universal and particular Methods merely relate to the whole and the parts in the same exposition.

[e] On Synthesis and Analysis, and the various employment of both, some remarks will be found in the Appendix, note G. The notion of Synthesis in the present passage corresponds to that of Metaphysical parts and whole, which is there mentioned as applicable to a syllogistic process from a general principle to its particular application. Not so that of Analysis; which in the present passage is also a process from the universal to the particular, not from the particular to the universal. By *Subjectum* is meant the most general Subject whose properties the Science investigates; as Magnitude in Geometry.

disciplinis Theoreticis ; et a notione *Subjecti* incipiens, principia ejus et species investigat, donec a summo genere in ista disciplina perveniat ad infimam speciem[f]. 2. *Resolutoria* sive *Analytica*[g], quæ inservit disciplinis Practicis ; et

Eth. Nic.
VI. 13. 10.
VII. 9. 4.
Metaph.
VI. 7. 6.

The *Principia* are the ἀρχαὶ ἐξ ὧν, or axiomatic principles, from which the demonstration commences. *Species* are the subdivisions of the general Subject; as the square, the triangle, &c. Cf. Anal. Post. i. 10. 4. Πᾶσα γὰρ ἀποδεικτικὴ ἐπιστήμη περὶ τρία ἐστίν, ὅσα τε εἶναι τίθεται (ταῦτα δ' ἐστὶ τὸ γένος, οὗ τῶν καθ' αὑτὰ παθημάτων ἐστὶ θεωρητικὴ) καὶ τὰ κοινὰ λεγόμενα ἀξιώματα, ἐξ ὧν πρώτων ἀποδείκνυσι, καὶ τρίτον τὰ πάθη, ὧν τί σημαίνει ἕκαστον λαμβάνει. On the position of these in demonstration, some remarks will be found in Appendix, note C and K: see also Trendelenburg, Erläuterungen, p. 118.

[f] " Exemplum evidens in primis est in scientia physica, ubi primum tractatur de corpore naturali in genere, deque affectionibus ejus et principiis; post descenditur ad species corporis naturalis, videlicet corpus simplex, cœlum, elementum ; post mixtum, idque iterum vel imperfecte mixtum, vel meteora; post perfecte mixtum, idque iterum vel inanimatum, ut metalla, mineralia, vel animatum, idque vel vegetans, ut planta, vel sentiens : idque iterum vel irrationale, ubi tractantur omnia animalia bruta: vel rationale, ut homo ; atque ita a summo genere ad species infimas devenitur. Eadem methodus observatur in mathematica et physica." Keckermann, Syst. Log. lib. iii. Tract. ii. cap. 1. Cf. Zabarella, de Meth. lib. ii. cap. 7.

[g] The Analytic, as well as the Synthetic Method, observes a deductive order from premises to conclusion. Its name then refers, not to the metaphysical relations of Species and Genus as whole and part, but to that common illustration of Aristotle's, by which, in productive or practical operation, the product or end is represented as a whole, and the materials or means as parts. The order of teaching will be the same as that of deliberation ; the reverse of that of operation. The following

a notione *Finis* incipiens, subjectum, et tandem media investigat[h].

Regulæ Methodi generales hæ sunt. In tradenda disciplina 1. Nihil desit aut redundet. 2. Singulæ partes inter se consentiant. 3. Nihil tractetur quod non sit subjecto aut fini homogeneum. 4. Singulæ partes aptis transitionibus connectantur.

---

passages may illustrate the image. Eth. Nic. iii. 5. 11. ἀλλὰ θέμενοι τέλος τι, πῶς καὶ διὰ τίνων ἔσται σκοποῦσι, καὶ διὰ πλειόνων μὲν φαινομένου γίνεσθαι διὰ τίνος ῥᾷστα καὶ κάλλιστα ἐπισκοποῦσι, δι᾽ ἑνὸς δ᾽ ἐπιτελουμένου πῶς διὰ τούτου ἔσται κἀκεῖνο διὰ τίνος, ἕως ἂν ἔλθωσιν ἐπὶ τὸ πρῶτον αἴτιον, ὃ ἐν τῇ εὑρέσει ἔσχατόν ἐστιν· ὁ γὰρ βουλευόμενος ἔοικε ζητεῖν καὶ ἀναλύειν ὥσπερ διάγραμμα . . . καὶ τὸ ἔσχατον ἐν τῇ ἀναλύσει πρῶτον ἐν τῇ γενέσει. Eth. Nic. vi. 13. 10. οἱ γὰρ συλλογισμοὶ τῶν πρακτῶν ἀρχὴν ἔχοντές εἰσιν, ἐπειδὴ τοιόνδε τὸ τέλος καὶ τὸ ἄριστον. vii. 9. 4. ἐν δὲ ταῖς πράξεσι τὸ οὗ ἕνεκα ἀρχὴ ὥσπερ ἐν τοῖς μαθηματικοῖς αἱ ὑποθέσεις. An example of the deliberative and practical processes will be found, Metaph. vi. 7. 7.

By *subjectum* is meant the *subjectum operationis*, or *materia circa quam*, more properly called the *object;* by *media*, the means by which out of this matter the end is produced. In building, e. g. the house is the *end;* the materials the *subject;* the act of building, *the means.* In Ethics, as treated by Aristotle, happiness is the *end;* man the *subject;* virtue the *means.*

[h] Exemplum evidens methodi analyticæ ab Aristotele in Ethicis proponitur, ubi libro primo *finis* præcognoscitur, scilicet felicitas ; post *subjectum*, nimirum hominis appetitus, seu voluntas, et intellectus ; sequentibus libris *media* traduntur, per quæ finis introducitur, videlicet virtutes theoreticæ et practicæ." Keckermann, Syst. Log. lib. iii. tr. 2. cap. 1.

5. Præcedat in docendo, sine quo alterum intelligi non potest, ipsum vero sine altero potest.

§. 2. In tradendis disciplinis suis Mathematici hac utuntur methodo[i]. 1. *Vocum significationem* constituunt : h. e. *Vocabula artis* suo quodque loco sic definiunt, ut legem sibi statuant iis nusquam uti, præterquam in eo sensu quem explicat definitio. 2. Definitionibus subjungunt *Axiomata,* quas et κοινὰς ἐννοίας vocant[j] ; h. e. effata sponte perspicua, quibus in decursu operis utendum vident. 3. Posthæc adjiciunt *Postulata,* quæ ad praxin spectant ; suntque per se certa et evidentia ; quæ proinde sine probatione concedi suo jure *postulant.* 4. Hisce positis, propositiones demonstrant; ordine, et, quoad fieri potest, affirmate : una lege contenti, ut, quicquid demonstratum eunt, ex ante datis vel probatis manifestum faciant. Cætera, in quibus methodi præceptores multi sunt et odiosi, non morantur.

[i] *Hac utuntur methodo.* For a further account of the method of mathematical reasoning, see Appendix, note L, on the Logic of Geometry.

[j] The κοιναὶ ἔννοιαι of the Mathematicians correspond to the ἀξιώματα of Aristotle. The latter term is not used by Euclid; nor by any of the early Mathematicians in its Aristotelian sense. Among the Stoics, *axiom* was synonymous with *proposition,* and in this sense it is mentioned in a passage of Apuleius, quoted p. 44, note a. For a full history of the term and its several uses, see Sir W. Hamilton's note, Reid's Works, p. 764.

K

Mathematicorum methodum in cæteris artibus et scientiis, si tenere non liceat, æmulari certe licet. Quo ad hanc quæque proprius accedit, eo cæteris perfectior, et ad docendum aptior videtur. Sed ad ea quæ docentur retinenda, nihil est utilius absoluti operis Conspectu ; in quo, ea quæ sunt ante (extra ordinem fortasse) demonstrata, suis quæque in locis, h. e. servata Logicorum methodo, reponantur.

APPENDIX.

Solutio Sophismatum[a].

§. 1. Cujuscunque Syllogismi difficultas ad duas Species revocari poterit; alteram, quæ in *Argumenti Materia*, alteram, quæ in *Forma* consistit : nam qui has duas expedire noverit, is in tertia, quæ ex ambarum complexione oritur, non hærebit.

[a] The examination of Fallacies is extralogical, except when the consequence is formally invalid ; in which case it may be detected by the ordinary rules of syllogism. The following Sophisms are not all susceptible of this solution. They are mostly material fallacies, arising from ambiguity of language or falsity of assertion. But they are not treated of by Aristotle as belonging to the Science of Logic, but to the Art of Dialectic, of which, as has been before observed, a considerable portion is material. In fact, Aristotle's Treatise περὶ σοφιστικῶν ἐλέγχων is merely an account of the pseudo-refutations principally in use among the Sophists of his day, whether depending upon equivocal language, false assumption, or illogical reasoning. In relation to Logic, it has little more than a historical value. A strictly logical classification of fallacies should commence by distinguishing, in all the three operations of thought, between the *matter* which is given *to*, and the *form* which is given *by* the thinking act. Acts of conception, judgment, or reasoning which violate the laws of thought, and are therefore defective in form, should be classed as logical fallacies ; those which are faulty in the conditions preliminary to the act of thought should be classed as material. See further, *Prolegomena Logica*, p. 237. (2nd ed. p. 256.) and below, Appendix, note M.

K 2

Soph.
Eleuch.
9. 1.

Si inciderit *Materia* difficilis, unicum huic malo remedium est, disciplinam unde desumitur argumentum, fideliter didicisse ; quod ut facias, *Instrumenti* operam tibi Logica præstabit ; sed ulterius nihil confert. Proprium illi munus est Syllogismi Formam explorare ; h. e. Utrum Conclusio ex Præmissis consequatur propter ipsum Colligendi modum : Sed an ponendæ sint Præmissæ (nisi forte sint pure Logicæ) aliunde discendum est. Sicubi autem Syllogismus qui legitimus non est, videatur tamen ; aut contra ; (quorum utrumque sæpissime, et de causis pene infinitis accidit) Formalem ejus Consequentiam excutere est Artis Logicæ.

Qui hoc opus aggreditur, id sibi negotii datum sciat, ut Difficilem suum Syllogismum, primo in Categoricum purum, vel in plures, si opus sit, convertat ; tum ad Canonem accurate exigat ; cujus operis ratio præcedente Libro abunde declarata An. Pr. I.
32. 8. est. Summa rei huc redit. Consideranda est primo Conclusio ; ejusque Termini solerter distinguendi : Prædicatum enim est Major Terminus Syllogismi ; qui proinde Præmissam quoque Majorem indicabit ; Subjectum pariter Minorem ; et in utraque sese offeret Argumentum sive Terminus Medius : Unde et si desit Præmissarum alterutra, facile suppleri poterit. Hisce cognitis, nec Figura Syllogismi, nec Modus latebit ; qui si legitime, nec tamen vere concludere videatur, quærendum annon anceps sit aliquis trium Terminorum ? nam si in iis

nulla lateat ambiguitas, necessario falsa erit altera Præmissarum.

Hunc in modum licebit Syllogismum quemvis Categoricum purum explorare ; qualis si non sit qui proponitur, quam facillime fiet, per ea quæ priore Libro, extremo Capite tertio, et toto quarto sunt ostensa. Siquid amplius restet, id Exemplis melius quam Præceptis docebitur.

§. 2. ORDIĒMUR autem a facillimis ; nempe vete- Soph. rum Sophistarum *Fallaciis;* quarum 13 species Elench 4. 1. enumerat Aristoteles ; sex, quæ *multiplicitate dictionis;* septem, quæ aliquo *extra dictionem* vitio laborarent[b]. Et erat aliqua fortasse difficultas in

[b] Of the Aristotelian division of Fallacies into οἱ παρὰ τὴν λέξιν and οἱ ἔξω τῆς λέξεως, Archbishop Whately observes, that it has not hitherto been grounded on any distinct principle : he therefore adopts a conjectural explanation, according to which the former are interpreted as logical Fallacies, in which the conclusion does not follow from the premises ; the latter, as material Fallacies, where the conclusion does follow, the falsehood being in the assumption. This, however, is not the ancient principle of distinction, which is stated, with more or less clearness, by several Logicians. To go no higher than Sanderson ; we find, " Fallacia omnis in dictione oritur ex dictionis aliqua multiplicitate. Est autem Multiplex aliud actuale : quando dictio invariata multa significat ; ut in *æquivocatione*, et *amphibolia.* Aliud potentiale : quando dictio quoad prolationem aliquo modo variata, multa significat ; ut in *compositione, divisione,* et *accentu.* Aliud phantasticum : quando dictio unum reipsa significans, videtur tamen multa significare ; ut in *figura dictionis.* Fallaciæ extra dictionem sunt in quibus contingit deceptio, non tam ex multiplici aliquo latente in vocibus ipsis, quam ex ignoratione rerum."

earum aliquibus, juxta veterem disputandi (h. e. interrogandi) morem propositis; sed profecto nemo tam obtusus est, qui non easdem Syllogistice pro- positas agnoscat statim, et derideat. V. g. Erit for- tasse qui rogatus *Quod non amiserit utrum habeat necne?* non intelligat se captum iri, sive simpliciter habere se, sive non habere responderit: at proposito hujusmodi Syllogismo, *Quod non amisisti habes; Cornua non amisisti;* Ergo *habes:* Vel *Quod non amisisti non habes; Oculos non amisisti;* Ergo *non habes;* quid reponat nemo non videt.

This principle is found in Alexander of Aphrodisias, Scholia, p. 298, b. 28.; and still earlier, if the work be genuine, in the Treatise περὶ τῶν παρὰ τὴν λέξιν σοφισμάτων, ascribed to Galen. Indeed it may be gathered from Aristotle himself; Soph. Elench. 4, 1. 6, 2. 7, 3. Occam states the distinction still more clearly. " Fallaciæ in dictione sunt illæ penes quas secundum omnes modos peccant sophistica argumenta com- posita ex signis voluntarie institutis. Fallaciæ extra dictionem sunt illæ penes quas peccant argumenta tam composita ex signis voluntarie institutis quam composita ex signis naturali- ter significantibus." Logica, iii. 4. cap. 1. The former arise from defects in the arbitrary signs of thought, and hence are generally confined to a single language, and disappear on being translated into another. The latter are in the thought itself, whether materially, in the false application of notions to things, or formally, in the violation of the laws by which the operations of the reason should be governed; and thus adhere to the thought, in whatever language it may be ex- pressed. Under this head are thus included both false judgments and illogical reasonings. These Fallacies are connected with language only secondarily and accidentally; the former primarily and essentially. See further, Waitz, vol. ii. p. 532.

Fallaciæ *dictionis,* sive *in dictione,* sex sunt[c].

§. 3. 1. Fallacia *æquivocationis,* sive nata ex voce æquivoca; ut, *Canis est animal; Sirius est canis ;* Ergo, *Sirius est animal.* In hoc quatuor sunt termini; quorum duo, vox *Canis* æquivoce sumpta. _{Soph. Elench. 4. 1. 19. 1.}

2. Fallacia *amphiboliæ;* sive nata ex sententia *amphibola,* h. e. ancipitis structuræ; ut *Quod tangitur a Socrate illud sentit; Columna tangitur a Socrate;* Ergo *Columna sentit.* Vox *sentit,* non sponte, sed in hac structura est ambigua; cujus vi, in Majori significat *Sentit Socrates ;* in Conclusione, *Sentit Socratem ;.* Quare Syllogismus habet quatuor terminos. _{Soph. Elench. 4. 4. 19. 1.}

3. 4. Fallacia *Compositionis*[d], ubi datum in sensu _{Soph. Elench. 4. 6. 20. 1.}

---

[c] With the following account of the Fallacies may be compared the corresponding chapter in the Rhetoric, ii. 24. In doing so, however, it must be remembered, that the present sophisms occur in a disputation carried on in colloquial form between antagonists, and conforming to established rules; whereas those are introduced *ad libitum* by an Orator in the course of his speech. Hence, though the principle of deception may be similar, the manner of its application will not always correspond. The same caution is still more necessary in examining modern specimens of Sophistry.

[d] This Fallacy, as treated by Aristotle, includes a wrong composition of clauses in a sentence capable of two punctuations. In this extension, the examples *possibile est sedentem stare, &c.* are easily included under Composition; the sense varying according as *sedentem* is joined with *possibile est,* or with *stare.* The Fallacy of Division, in like manner, will include the separation of clauses which ought to be united.

diviso sumitur in sensu composito ; ut, *Duo et Tria sunt Par et Impar ; Quinque sunt Duo et Tria ;* Ergo *Quinque sunt Par et Impar*[e]. Fallacia *Divisionis,* quando datum in sensu composito sumitur in diviso ; ut, *Planetæ sunt septem : Sol et Luna sunt Planetæ ;* Ergo *Sol et Luna sunt septem.* Utroque modo quatuor sunt termini si aperte loquaris. V. g. Prioris Syllogismi mens est, Duo et Tria *seorsim accepta* sunt Par et Impar. Quinque sunt Duo et Tria *in unum composita,* &c. Posterioris vero, Planetæ *collective sumpti* sunt septem ; Sol et Luna sunt Planetæ *distributive sumpti* &c. Unde duplex utrobique Medius.

Soph. Elench. 4. 7. 20. 1.

Soph. Elench. 4. 6. 20. 4.

" Huc referri solent hujusmodi Orationes ; *Possibile est album esse nigrum ; Possibile est sedentem stare :* dubito an satis recte ; quia tanto " acumine non est opus. Potest quidem album " *fieri* nigrum ; et Possibile est *sedenti* stare ; at " si hæc velles, incongrue locutus es. Utraque " igitur Oratio est simpliciter neganda ; vel ut " aperte falsa si sit congrua, vel si non sit congrua, " quia non est Propositio."

Soph. Elench. 4. 8. 21. 1.

5. Fallacia *Accentus* seu *Prosodiæ*[f] potius, quando

[e] In these instances, the verbal defect lies in the copula. Two and three *are* (constitute) five. Two and three *are* (severally) even and odd.

[f] The *Fallacia Prosodiæ*, as Aristotle observes, is a Fallacy in writing only, not in speaking. *Lépores* and *lepóres* have no ambiguity when rightly pronounced. The first example (*servus ergo cervus*). supposing the pronunciation of both words to be the same, is not properly an instance of this Fallacy.

pro eodem sumuntur quæ vel Litera, vel Spiritu, vel Tempore, vel Accentu sunt diversa : ut, Est *servus* Ergo est *cervus ;* Est *ara* Ergo est *hara.* Est *malum* (an apple) Ergo malum (an evil). Venatur *lépores* Ergo et lepóres ; quibus qui falli potest, debet.

6. Fallacia *Figuræ dictionis,* quando propter dictiones similes, quod de uno datur de altero arripitur : idque vel *Grammatice*[s], ut *Musa* est

Soph. Elench. 4. 9. 22.

[s] *Grammatice,* i. e. inferring that *Poeta* is of the feminine gender, because the majority of words with the same termination are so. *Logice,* inferring that *videre* belongs to the category of ποιεῖν, because most infinitive moods of this form are included under it. Thus viewed, it may be classed as *in dictione,* because the rules of gender and conjugation are different in different languages.

But the more common form in which this Fallacy would be stated is that of an induction, or rather a number of examples, after the manner of Socrates. Indeed, this very sophism is put into the mouth of Socrates by Aristophanes, Nubes, 681 sqq. Stated in this form, the logical inconsequence is obvious ; as also if it is reduced to syllogism. " Such and such words are feminine ; Musa *resembles* such and such words." Here there is no middle term. This ambiguity is sometimes called *multiplex phantasticum.* Cf. Petr. Hisp. Summ. Log. Tract. vi. " Est autem multiplex phantasticum, quando aliqua dictio significat unum et videtur significare aliud, propter similitudinem quam habet in parte cum alia dictione : ut *videre* significat passionem, et videtur significare actionem, propter hoc quod est simile huic verbo, *agere.*" In this form, it would seem more naturally to belong to the class *extra dictionem.*

In Rhet. ii. 24. 2. Aristotle gives another form of this Fallacy ; viz. when a series of detached propositions are so enunciated as to appear logically connected, not being really so. See also Soph. Elench. 15. 5.

Fœminini generis, Ergo et *Poeta:* vel *Logice,* ut *Docere est agere,* Ergo et *Videre.* Hæc Materia potius quam Forma peccat: et operose solvi non postulat: ponit aliquid aperte falsum; quo negato evertitur.

Soph.
Elench.
4. 10.
Soph.
Elench.
6. 1. 24. 1. Fallaciæ *extra dictionem* sunt septem[h].

§. 4. 1. FALLACIA *Accidentis*[i]; quando *accidentarium* aliquod confunditur cum eo quod est *essentiale* seu principaliter intentum: ut, *Quod emisti comedisti, Crudum emisti;* Ergo *Crudum comedisti:* in quo, *Quod emisti,* et *Quale emisti,* confunduntur; unde quatuor termini.

Soph.
Elench.
5. 2. 25. 1. 2. Fallacia *a Dicto secundum Quid ad Dictum Simpliciter;* quando proceditur a voce determinate sumpta, ad eandem absolute positam: ut, *Æthiops est albus dentes;* Ergo *albus:* unde quatuor esse Terminos necesse est[k].

[h] Fallacies *extra dictionem* embrace all those in which the deception arises from any other cause than ambiguity of language; whether from a false assumption in the premise, or from the reasoning being unsound. Purely logical fallacies belong, not to the *in dictione,* but to the *extra dictionem.*

[i] The example of this Fallacy given by Aristotle is, Coriscus is different from Socrates; Socrates is a man; therefore Coriscus is different from a man. The Fallacy lies in assuming that whatever is different from a given subject is incompatible with all the predicates (τὰ συμβαίνοντα) of that subject. The reasoning is thus illogical: Socrates is a man; Coriscus is not Socrates; therefore Coriscus is not a man.

[k] The example as stated by Aristotle will run thus; *Æthiops*

3. Fallacia *Ignorationis Elenchi*. *Elenchus* [1] proprie Syllogismus est Adversarium redarguens: confirmando scil. quod illius sententiæ contradicat. Quare in hanc incidit Fallaciam qui se putat Adversarium redarguere, non servatis *Contradicendi Legibus,* (de quibus vide pag. 55.) Qui in his peccat, docendus est se nescire Quid sit Contradicere.

Soph.
Elench.
5. 5. 26. 1.
An. Pr. II.
20. 1.
Soph.
Elench.
6. 4.

4. Fallacia *a non-causa pro causa* [m]; sive sit a

Soph.
Elench.
5. 11. 29. 1.
An. Pr. II.
17. 3.

non est albus; Æthiops est albus dentes; Ergo, *qui est albus non est albus.* Here there are four terms, and the Conclusion, as Aristotle himself observes, is not drawn *syllogistically.*

[1] The Elenchus is defined by Aristotle, συλλογισμὸς ἀντιφάσεως, An. Pr. ii. 20. 1. Soph. Elench. 6. 4. The *Ignoratio Elenchi* consists in neglecting some of the conditions required by the rules of Dialectic for proving the contradictory of any given proposition. This is the case when the conclusion does not logically follow from the premises; or when the premises themselves are not admitted by the opponent; or when the conclusion, though legitimately deduced from allowed premises, is an apparent, not a real, contradiction of the opponent's position, failing in one of the four conditions of contradiction, viz. *eodem modo, secundum idem, ad idem, eodem tempore.* In this extended sense, every fallacy is an Ignoratio Elenchi, as is observed by Aristotle, Soph. Elench. 6. 1. though the name is especially applied to the last instance.

[m] This fallacy, according to Aristotle, most frequently occurs in the *deductio ad impossibile,* and consists in pretending that the proposition which we wish to refute is the cause of the false conclusion, which in reality follows from other premises; i. e. in maintaining that the conclusion is false because *that particular assumption* is false. This mode of deception has place in dialectical disputation, from the practice of asking the opponent to grant certain premises. An unnecessary proposition is asked and granted among the rest, and after-

non-vera pro *vera;* sive a *non-tali* pro *tali*[n]: ut
Cometa fulsit; Ergo *Bellum erit;* Nullo modo;
nam si fuerit, aliis de Causis futurum est. *Quod
inebriat prohibendum est; Vinum inebriat;* Nequa-
quam vero, sed Abusus vini. Hæc Fallacia bene
solvitur negando Causam falsam: melius, addu-
cendo germanam.

" Huc refertur ab aliquibus (qua de causa non
" video) hoc Sophisma; *Qui magis esurit, plus*
" *comedit; Qui minus comedit, magis esurit;* Ergo
" *Qui minus comedit, plus comedit.* Sed qui hoc,
" vel hujus simile attulerit (ut innumera afferri
" solent) docendus est congrue loqui: Hoc si
" fecerit, dicet in hoc casu, *Qui magis esurit* plus
" *comedet; Qui minus comêdit, magis esurit;* Ergo
" *Qui minus comêdit,* plus *comedet.*"

Soph.
Elench.
5. 8. 28. 1.

5. Fallacia *Consequentis*[o], quando infertur quod

wards selected as the false assumption. Aldrich's examples
refer rather to the rhetorical than to the dialectical form of
this fallacy. In this the speaker is guilty merely of a false
assertion, attributing a certain effect to a wrong cause. See
Rhet. ii. 24. 8.

[n] In the *non vera pro vera*, there is no connexion between
the effect and the supposed cause; in the *non tali pro tali*,
there is a connexion, but an insufficient one; wine, e. g. does
not intoxicate except in certain quantity. This instance,
however, more properly belongs to the fallacy *a dicto secundum
quid ad dictum simpliciter.* " Wine (in excess) intoxicates;
therefore, Wine (absolutely) is to be forbidden."

[o] The *fallacia consequentis* is an error in reasoning, as may
be clearly seen in the examples given Soph. Elench. 5. 8. and
Rhet. ii. 24. 7. e. g. Honey is yellow; Gall is yellow; there-

non sequitur: ut, *Animal est;* Ergo, *Est Homo.*
Hic memineris, quod si recte ratione uti volumus,
Consequentia aut directa, immediata, formalis, aut
plane nulla est; peccat enim contra aliquam Dialecticæ regulam; ad quam si provoces, refelletur.

6. Fallacia *Petitionis Principii*[p], cum ut datum
assumitur, quod probatum oportuit. V. g. Cum
probatur aliquid vel per seipsum, (quæ vocatur
Petitio statim,) ut, *Homo est,* Ergo, *est Homo:*
Vel per Synonymum; ut *Ensis est acutus;* Ergo,
Gladius: Vel per æque ignotum; ut *Hic est Pater
Melchisedek;* Ergo, *Hæc Mater:* Vel per ignotius;
ut, *Hoc Quadratum est hujus Trianguli duplum,*
Quia *huic Circulo æquale:* Vel per Circulum; re-
sumendo scilicet quod relictum est; ut si diceres,
Ignis est calidus, Ergo *urit:* et post pauca, *Ignis
urit,* Ergo *est calidus.*

Soph.
Elench.
5. 7. 27. 1.
Anal. Pr.
11. 16. 1.
Top. VIII.
13. 1.

7. Fallacia[q] *plurium interrogationum,* quando
plures quæstiones velut una proponuntur; v. g.
Suntne Mel et Fel dulcia? Estne homo animal et

Soph.
Elench.
5. 13. 30. 1.

fore gall is honey. Here the middle term is undistributed.
Another specimen cited by Aristotle is the reasoning of
Melissus; "Whatever is generated has a beginning; the
universe is not generated; therefore it has not a beginning."
Cf. Phys. Ausc. I. 3. 2. Here there is an illicit process of the
major term.

[p] On the *Petitio Principii,* see Appendix, note E. Aristotle
enumerates five varieties; which, however, are not the same
as those given by Aldrich. See Top. viii. 13.

[q] This is merely a dialectical fallacy; and consists in
entrapping an opponent into an answer partly false, by
artfully putting two questions as one.

lapsi?   Evertitur, ad singulas quæstiones distincte respondendo ; sicut fecit Menedemus Eretriensis, qui rogante eum Alexino, *Numquid Patrem verberare desiisset?   Nec verberavi*, inquit, *nec desii*[r].

Atque hæ sunt tredecim Sophismatum formulæ[s] Veteribus usitatiores, quæ Tironibus Logicis in exemplum proponi solent.   Poterant esse pauciores ;   nam videntur aliquæ coincidere ;   et præterea tres, *Non-causa pro Causa, Petitio. Principii,* et *Plures interrogationes,* non sunt Fallaciæ proprie dictæ, h. e. Syllogismi Forma peccantes[t] ; sed Vitia male Opponentis.   Poterant et plures[u] ; sed cum hic numerus Aristoteli satisfecisset, idem omnibus post illum Logicis satisfecit.

§. 5. Sophismatibus ex sententia veterum accen-

[r] Diog. Laert. ii. 135.

[s] These thirteen fallacies are comprised in the mnemonic lines,

Æquivocat, Amphi. Componit, Dividit, Acc. Fi.

Acci. Quid, Ignorans, Non causa, Con. Petit. Interr.

[t] Aristotle's definition of Fallacy will include logical deductions from false premises, as well as illogical deductions from any premises.   See Top. i. 1. 3. Ἐριστικὸς δ' ἐστὶ συλλογισμὸς ὁ ἐκ φαινομένων ἐνδόξων, μὴ ὄντων δέ, καὶ ὁ ἐξ ἐνδόξων ἢ φαινομένων ἐνδόξων φαινόμενος.   Aldrich's limitation to Syllogisms faulty in form is quite arbitrary.

[u] Aristotle does not profess to give a complete enumeration of the fallacies ; but only a list of such as may be solved by the Dialectician.   There may be innumerable false assumptions, on matters not belonging to Dialectic, which must be refuted from the principles of the Science or Art to which they belong.   See Soph. Elench. 9. 1.

sendæ sunt *Inexplicabiles* (ut vocantur) *Rationes,* quas Megarici, Stoici, aliique Eristicam professi, propriis nominibus insignivere, *Crocodilus, Mentiens, Obvelatus,* &c. quas plerasque collegit *Gassendus,* et retulit in *Libro de Origine et Varietate Logicæ:* Nos eodem fere ordine explorabimus quo ab illo sunt propositæ.

1. ACHILLES vocatur Argumentum quo usus est Zeno Eleates, non ut Motum tolleret, quod vulgo sed falso dicitur; sed ut ostenderet Continuum non esse infinite divisibile, quia hoc dato Motus tolleretur. Argumentum sic se habet. Sit Achilles quantum voles πόδας ὠκὺς, puta decuplo velocior Testudine. Quiescente illo, confecerit Testudo partem aliquam (puta decimam) spatii percurrendi. Tum procédat Achilles, idemque spatium percurrat: progredietur interim Testudo per partem ejus decimam, h. e. totius spatii centesimam; hanc conficiat Achilles, et percurret interim Testudo hujus centesimæ decimam; et sic deinceps in infinitum; quo fiet ut Achilles nunquam assequatur Testudinem[x].

Arist.Phys. Ausc. VI. 9. 3. Top. VIII. 8. 2. Soph. Elench. 24. 5.

---

[x] We must not confound the metaphysical difficulties connected with the infinite divisibility of space, with the logical difficulty of a false conclusion apparently deduced from true premises. Archbishop Whately evades the latter, by observing that the sophism cannot be exhibited in a Syllogism. But this confession is in fact a surrender of the syllogistic criterion, as a means of discriminating between sound and unsound reasoning. On the contrary, nothing is easier than to exhibit the reasoning in a Syllogism, and to shew thereby

Ineptum est hoc Sophisma. 1. Quia solvitur ambulando; quod fecit Diogenes[y]. 2. Quoniam ex ipsa Hypothesi, Dum Testudo quæ præcessit spatio A, conficit $\frac{1}{10}$ A, Achilles conficiet 2 A;

that the fallacy does not lie in the form, but in the matter. Thus, representing the whole space to be traversed by a,

"Any space equal to $\frac{a}{10} + \frac{a}{100} + \frac{a}{1000}$ &c. is infinite, (being the sum of an infinite series.) The space to be passed before Achilles overtakes the tortoise is equal to this sum. Therefore it is infinite."

The whole *logical* mystery of this famous fallacy lies in this, that *the major premise is false.* The sum of an infinite series may be, and in this case is, finite. This premise is equally false, whether space is or is not divisible *ad infinitum.* In this way the sophism is solved by Descartes, *Epist.* P. I. Ep. 118. On the metaphysical question connected with the matter of the sophism, see Hegel, *Werke,* vol. iii. p. 218. xiii. p. 294. Fries, *System der Logik,* §. 109. Herbart, *Einleitung in die Philosophie,* §. 139. Trendelenburg, *Logische Untersuchungen,* vol. i. p. 179. The solution attempted by Coleridge, (*Friend,* vol. iii. p. 93.) is refuted by Herbart.

It may be observed, that Aldrich is mistaken as regards Zeno's object in this sophism. It was proposed to support the leading tenet of Parmenides, of the unity of all things, by shewing that the identity of rest and motion is a necessary result from the contrary opinion. It does not appear, however, that Zeno advanced this argument seriously. His principal design was to retort the ridicule which had been thrown on the doctrine of Parmenides, by involving his ·opponents in the same absurdities which they professed to find in his theory. Cf. Plato, *Parm.* p. 128. Arist. *Soph. Elench.* 10. 2. 33. 4. Cousin. *Nouveaux Fragments, Zénon d'Elée.*

[y] The solution of Diogenes proves nothing. Zeno contends that reason contradicts the evidence of the senses. Diogenes replies that the evidence of the senses contradicts that of reason. Who denied that?

adeoque statim assequetur eam, et antecedet*. Sed hoc (inquies) in casu proposito nunquam fiet; Recte; Ne enim fiat, in ipso proponendi modo clam inseritur nova conditio. Nam 3. Argumentum aliis verbis hoc dicit: Si Achillem decuplo velociorem præcesserit Testudo; et *uterque meo pergat arbitratu;* Ego perficiam ne Achilles assequatur Testudinem: Quare prorsus nunquam assequetur. Quæ est *Fallacia a dicto secundum quid, ad dictum simpliciter.*

2. Diodorus Cronus, quod Sophismata Stilponis non solvisset, exinde ὄνος appellatus est*; id cognominis aliunde promeritus, quod ad hunc modum contra Motum disputaret. *Mobile movetur vel in quo est loco, vel in quo non est; At neutrum horum;* Ergo *Non omnino.* Unde facete illum lusit Herophilus, qui ut luxatum illi humerum restitueret rogatus, *Tuus* (inquit) *humerus vel in quo erat loco*

---

* The futility of this attempt at solution might have been learned from Aristotle, Soph. Elench. 24. 5. It only shews that the contradictory assertion rests also on seemingly valid reasoning; whereas the duty of the opponent is to shew where the fallacy of Zeno's reasoning lies.

* The facetious Iambics in which Diodorus was thus " writ down an ass" are as follows:

Κρόνε Διόδωρε, τίς σε δαιμόνων κακῇ
  Ἀθυμίᾳ ξυνείρυσεν
Ἵν' αὐτὸς αὑτὸν ἐμβάλῃς εἰς τάρταρον,
  Στίλπωνος οὐ λύσας ἔπη
Αἰνιγματώδη; τοιγὰρ εὑρέθης Κρόνος
  Ἔξω γε τοῦ ῥῶ κάππα τε.
See Diog. Laert. ii. 112.

L

existens excidit, vel in quo non erat. Sed neutrum horum ; Ergo *non omnino.* Diodori argumento breviter et perspicue respondet Gassendus, Quod movetur moveri *a loco* in quo erat, *per locum* in quo est (sive quem pertransit), *ad locum* in quo nondum est, sed futurum est[b].

3. RECIPROCUM vocat Argumentum *Gellius,* quod Græce dicitur Ἀντιστρέφον : cui illustrando conficta est Fabula quæ Græcorum vanitatem olet. Narrant enim inter Protagoram et Euathlum, vel (ut facetiæ locus sit) inter Coracem et Tisiam[c] convenisse, ut hunc ille Dialecticam doceret ; idque hac lege, ut dimidium mercedis statim ac-

---

[b] The true solution of the sophism of Diodorus is, that the disjunctive premise is false. "The place where a body is," is contradictory of "the place where a body is not;" as "Englishmen" is contradictory of "not-Englishmen;" but "moving in the place where it is," is no more contradictory of "moving in the place where it is not," than "an army composed of Englishmen" is contradictory of "an army composed of not-Englishmen." As it would be false to say, "Every army must be composed of Englishmen or not-Englishmen," to the exclusion of the third possibility of a mixed force ; so it is false to say, "Every body must move in the place where it is, or in the place where it is not," to the exclusion of the third possibility of moving partly in the one and partly in the other. This solution is substantially given by Hobbes, *Philosophia Prima*, P. II. c. 8. §. 11.

[c] The story is told of Protagoras and Euathlus by Aulus Gellius, v. 10. and by Apuleius, Florid. iv. 18. ; of Corax and Tisias, by the Scholiast to Homogenes, *Rhetores Græci*, ed. Walz, iv. p. 13. and by Suidas, *s. v.* Κακοῦ Κόρακος κ. τ. λ. See also Sext. Empir. adv. Math. II. 96. Cf. Menag. ad Diog. Laert. ix. 56.

ciperet ;   reliquum, cum discipulus causam vicisset.
Primam exinde litem cum Discipulo contestatus
est Magister, cum mercedis reliquum lege peteret ;
apud Judices vero sic agebat : *Ego si vicero, Tisia,
Tu solves ex sententia, sin minus, ex pacto ; utroque
igitur modo solvendum est.* Respondit Tisias, *Ego
nihil solvo ; Tu si viceris, ex pacto ; sin minus, ex
sententia.* Tanto utrinque acumine perculsi boni
judices, exclamarunt Κακοῦ Κόρακος κακὸν ὠόν,
causamque in longissimum diem distulerunt.

Ineptum erat Coracis Dilemma quia potuit tam
bene retorqueri. Nihilominus callide agebat, si id
Judices vidissent. Nam cum mercedem inique
peteret, causa cadere debebat ; Quamprimum autem
cecidisset, ei merces ex pacto debebatur.

§. 6. 4. MENTIENS qui est Græce Ψευδόμενος[d], Soph. Elench. 25. 3. Eth. Nic. VII. 3. 8. Chrysippi Syllogismus ne ab ipso quidem solutus, præter cæteros insolubilis habetur. Eum Cicero[e] sic enuntiat : *Si dicis Te mentiri, et verum dicis,
mentiris ; Sed dicis Te mentiri, et verum dicis ;
mentiris igitur.*

[d] This Fallacy is attributed to Eubulides of Miletus. See
Laert. ii. 188. It is mentioned by Aristotle, Eth. Nic. vii. 3. 8.
and consequently must be older than Chrysippus. For some
remarks upon it, see Hegel, *Gesch. der Philosophie, Werke,* xiv.
p. 116.

[e] Acad. Quæst. iv. 30. Its solution is obvious. No one can
lie without lying about something. The something is not
stated in the sophism. The question as it stands is un-
meaning. Is this thing very like ? Like what ?

Congrue loquere, Chrysippe, et intelliges Te vel nihil prorsus, vel nihil dicere difficile. Qui se dicit *mentitum*, et verum dicit, *mentitus est; Qui mentiturum, mentietur.* Horum utrumque verum est, et nemini obscurum. Sed qui ut verum simul dicat et mentiatur dicit unum aliquid, cujus partes sibi invicem contradicunt, is nec verum, nec falsum, sed omnino nihil dicit: quando enim sententiæ pars una evertit alteram, tota nihil prorsus significat, sed inaniter strepit.

Subtilius disputare videbantur qui sic agebant. *Cretenses esse mendaces dicit Epimenides Cretensis. Mentitur igitur;* Ergo *Illi sunt veraces;* Ergo *et Ille verum dicit;* Ergo *Illi rursus sunt mendaces* &c. Sed profecto nihil stultius est hoc Argumento, nisi vox *Cretenses* eos ad unum omnes significet, et Omnis mendax quicquid dicit mentiatur[f].

Videtur hic *Mentiens* peperisse subtilem illam Scholasticorum *de Insolubilibus* doctrinam. " Nam " talia argumenta (inquit *Occam*) non possunt fieri " nisi quando actus humanus respicit istum termi- " num *Falsum*, vel aliquem consimilem affirmative; " vel hunc terminum *Verum*, vel aliquem consimilem " negative[g]." Esse hæc *Sophismata* ante dixerat; nec vocari *Insolubilia*, " quia nullo modo solvi " possunt, sed quia cum difficultate solvuntur."

[f] This Fallacy is solved by Fries, §. 109. A man who is *always* a liar cannot possibly say or imply " I lie;" for this would be a truth, and thus he would not be always a liar.

[g] Occam, *Logica*, iii. 3. cap. 45.

Insolubilis exemplum sic proponitur. Incipiat Socrates sic loqui, *Socrates dicit falsum;* et nihil amplius loquatur : tum interroget aliquis, utrum vera an falsa sit hæc propositio. Respondeo, nec veram nec falsam esse, sed nihil significare, nisi aliquid aliud respiciat, quod a Socrate ante dictum supponitur. Qui enim profert hæc verba, *Socrates dicit falsum,* fert judicium de dicto Socratis ; quique fert judicium, necessario præsupponit aliquid de quo judicet : Unde cum sententia præsupponat objectum suum, clarum est eandem numero propositionem, et sententiam et ejus objectum esse non posse. Quare et Scholarum subtilitas hic nihil proficit ; nihilque opus est plura dicere de Insolubilibus.

5. FALLENS Διαλανθάνων[h], vel ut alii Διαλεληθὼς, de Juramento ludit sicut *Mentiens* de nuda affirmatione. E. g. *Qui jurat se falsum jurare et falsum jurat, vere jurat.* Quare eodem fere modo quo *Mentiens* explicatur.

§. 7. 6. 7. OBVELATUS, alio nomine ELECTRA, est Soph. *Fallacia a dicto secundum Quid ad dictum Simpli-* Elench. 24. 2. *citer.* Nam colligere pertendit, quod et Patrem

---

[h] The Διαλανθάνων is probably a similar Fallacy to the Electra and the Obvelatus. The honour of its invention is divided between Eubulides and Diodorus Cronus. The example given by Aldrich is a mere conjecture of Gassendi's. For a discussion of this and the following fallacies, see Hegel, *Gesch. der Philos. Werke,* xiv. p. 119.

Filius et Soror Fratrem, h. e. Electra Orestem *prorsus* nesciat, si eundem *velo obductum* se nescire fateatur[1].

8. 9. ACERVALIS et CALVUS[J], sunt ejusdem Sophismatis duo tantum Exempla. V. g. Si rogatus a Sophista, neges te *Calvum* fieri amisso crine uno, duobus, tribus, et sic deinceps ad 99, sed amissis centum concedas ; vel eodem modo neges 99 grana *Acervum* esse, centum autem esse fatearis ; concludet ille grano unico adjecto Acervum fieri ; crine unico amisso, Calvitiem. Facile autem respondetur, *Unum centesimum* non esse *Unicum;* nam est Unum cum nonaginta novem. Vel si

---

[1] The Fallacy of the Electra is founded on Sophocles, Elect. 1222. It is given as follows by Lucian, Vit. Auct. §. 22. παρεστῶτος γὰρ αὐτῇ τοῦ Ὀρέστου ἔτι ἀγνῶτος, οἶδε μὲν Ὀρέστην, ὅτι ἀδελφὸς αὐτῆς· ὅτι δὲ οὗτος Ὀρέστης, ἀγνοεῖ. The Obvelatus is of similar character. ΧΡΥΣ. Ἦν σοι παραστήσας τινὰ ἐγκεκαλυμμένον, ἔρωμαι, τοῦτον οἶσθα; τί φήσεις; ΑΓΟ. Δηλαδὴ ἀγνοεῖν. ΧΡΥΣ. Ἀλλὰ μὲν αὐτὸς οὗτος ἦν ὁ πατὴρ ὁ σός, ὥστε εἰ τοῦτον ἀγνοεῖς, δῆλος εἶ τὸν πατέρα τὸν σὸν ἀγνοῶν. Another variety of the same sophism will be found in Aristotle, Soph. Elench. 24. 2. where it is classed under the *Fallacia Accidentis.* Diogenes Laertius, ii. §. 108. attributes the *Electra* and *Obvelatus* to Eubulides, as well as the *Acervus, Cornutus,* and *Calvus.*

[J] These two Fallacies, which are in fact but one under different names, are alluded to by Horace, Ep. ii. 1. 45. and by Persius, Sat. vi. 80. The *Acervus* is frequently called *Sorites,* (cf. Cic. *Acad. Quæst.* iv. 16. *De Divin.* ii. 11. Diog. Laert. II. 108.) but must not be confounded with the series of syllogisms of the same name. For the history of the name *Sorites* in these two applications, see Hamilton, *Lectures on Logic,* I. p. 375.

mavis sic ; Fit Acervus, grano uno, sed adjecto ; adeoque non unico, sed cum pluribus aliis. Fit Calvities crine uno, sed post multos alios, amisso.

10. CORNUTUS et *Ceratinus, Ceratine, Ceratis,* et *Ceras*[k] dicitur Sophisma illud ante memoratum, *Quod non amisisti habes* &c. Quæ est *Petitio Principii ;* nam supponit Te cornua habuisse.

Ineptissima hæc Fallacia plus acuminis præfert juxta veterem Disputandi modum rogando proposita. Erit enim fortasse, qui rogatus, *Quod non amiserit, utrum habeat necne ?* · non intelligat se captum iri, si simpliciter respondeat ; sive habere se, sive non habere dicat. Nam eum adiget Sophista, ut vel se habere Cornua, vel non habere Oculos fateatur.

11. Acutus sibi videbatur Menedemus (Eretriensis scil. quem ἐριστικώτατον appellat Laërtius) quum ad hunc modum nugaretur. *Diversum, a Diverso Diversum est ; Prodesse est a Bono Diversum ; Prodesse igitur non est Bonum*[l]. Quæ est crassa et putida *Æquivocatio ;* et nihil amplius.

§. 8. 12. CROCODILUS[m] a Chrysippo inventus, qui ad Fallaciam Consequentis revocari poterit, sic proponitur. *Surripuerat infantem Crocodilus ;*

---

[k] See Laertius, vii. 187. Gellius, *N. A.* xvi. 2.
[l] Diog. Laert. ii. 134.
[m] This Fallacy is given at length by Lucian, Vit. Auct. §. 22.

redditurum se, hac lege pollicitus, ut divinet mater, utrum apud se reddere an non reddere constituerit. Si dicat mater *Non reddere ;* mentietur si infantem receperit : Si dicat *reddere ;* non reddet quia hoc est falsum. Quamobrem Chrysippus nihil esse putat difficilius quum responsum matri suggerere. Nec injuria, si lubricum putet divinare ; sed immerito, si in hoc (ut videtur) hæreat, Quod si puerum Crocodilus non reddere constituerit, quamvis id Mater divinaverit non reddet : quasi consilium quod primum intenderat Crocodilus, postquam indicatum est, repudiare non possit, et ex pacto non debeat : nam si Mater recte divinaverit, recepto puero, non mentitur illa, sed consilium mutat Crocodilus.

13. Metens Θερίζων qui vocatur, ita placuit Zenoni Stoico, ut Sophistæ a quo eum didicerat duplum pactæ mercedis numeraret. Proponente Ammonio[n] sic se habet. *Si messurus es, non fortasse metes, fortasse non metes, sed metes omnino ;* Pariter, *si non messurus es, non fortasse metes, fortasse non metes, sed prorsus non metes.* Atqui *vel metere te, vel non metere, necessarium est ; perit igitur* Fortasse, *quod in neutra hypothesi locum habet.* Fortunatum Sophistam! qui mercede dupla hunc fumum vendidit ; *Vel hoc, vel illud evenire est necesse ; Quare hoc et non illud necessario eventurum est.*

---

[n] *In de Interp.* sect. 2. cap. 10. f. 91. b. ed. 1546. Cf. Menage ad Laert. vii. 25.

Nihil amplius dicit qui sic dixerit, *Ut vel metas vel non metas est necesse:* Ergo *Vel necessario metes vel necessario non metes.* Breviter, hæc *Fallacia Divisionis* est; nam in Antecedente, Modus *Necessario,* non tribuitur nisi toti Disjunctivæ; sed in Consequente dicitur de ejusdem membris seorsim acceptis.

14. IGNAVA RATIO vel 'Αργὸς λόγος appellatur°, qui si valeat nihil est omnino quod agamus in vita. V. g. *Si Fatum est ægroto convalescere, sive medicum adhibuerit sive non adhibuerit, convalescet:* Pariter, *si illi Fatum est non convalescere, sive medicum adhibuerit, sive non adhibuerit, non convalescet: et alterutrum Fatum est; medicum ergo adhibere nihil attinet.* Lepide respondit Chrysippus posse esse *Confatalia* adhibere medicum et convalescere: Quemadmodum et Zeno, quando servum furem verberabat, *Furari sibi Fatum esse* dicenti, et *Vapulare* respondit. Sed commodius dici videtur, Si sit Fatum, hoc valere argumentum; idque vel solum sufficere ne Fatum esse concedamus. Argumentum hocce et quæ præcedunt pp. 145, 146. N°. 2. et 3. ex Dilemmatis legibus facile solvuntur.

§. 9. PLURA sunt apud Autores Inexplicabilium Rationum nomina; quorum exempla Gassendus quia nusquam invenisset, ipse reperit. Verum ea relinquimus studiosis; quibus etiam consulto est

---

° See Cicero, *de Fato*, c. 12.

relictum, ut quæ sunt hactenus explicata, illi explicent in Syllogismos conversa.   Exempla Gassendi ne desiderent qui libro carent, non pigebit exscribere.

Dominans, Κυριεύων.   Themistoclis filius nec Græcis imperat, nec de imperando cogitat : Verum imperat Matri, quæ imperat Themistocli, qui Græcis imperat ; *Dominatur* itaque Græcis, *et non-dominatur* [p].

Conficiens Περαίνων.   Multum itineris *conficit, et non conficit* Canis, qui in rota gradiens totum diem, ex eodem tamen loco non recedit.

Superpositus vel *Superlativus,* Ὑπερθετικὸς [q], Soriti forte affinis ; Ut si roges quota sit palea, quæ si mulo *super-imponatur* ille oneri succumbat ?

Soph.
Elench.
22. 12.   *Nullus,* Οὖτις.   Homo in Communi nec est hic, nec ille, nec alius homo singularis, Ergo *Nullus* [r].

[p] The anecdote is mentioned, but without any reference to this fallacy, by Plutarch, *De Lib. Educ.* c. 2. *Apophthegm*, p. 185.   Vit. Cat. Maj. c. 8.   The Fallacy Κυριεύων is mentioned by several writers, but not fully explained by any. Cf. Arrian, *Epicteti Dissert.* ii. 19.   Lucian, *Vit. Auct.* c. 22. Plutarch, *Sympos.* I. i. 5.   Gellius, *Noct. Att.* I. 2.   For a discussion concerning it, see W. A. Butler, *Lectures on Ancient Philosophy,* I. p. 414.   It probably derived its name rather from its supposed dignity as an argument than, as Gassendi conjectures, from the mention of a ruler.   The same may be said of the Περαίνων or *conclusive* sophism.

[q] This conjecture of Gassendi's is founded on the old reading of Epictetus, *Diss.* III. 2. 6 ; where however for ὑπερθετικοὺς we should probably read ὑποθετικούς.   See Schweighæuser's note, Epict. tom. ii. pars 2. p. 615.

[r] This sometimes appears in another form, as one of the

Vel ut tritum Sophisma : *Quod Ego sum, Tu non es ; Ego sum homo :* Ergo *Tu non es*[*]. Vel denique ut Chrysippus. *Qui est Megaris, non est Athenis ; Homo est Megaris ;* Ergo *Homo non est Athenis*[t].

Subjicit Gassendus ex Laërtio[u], has Chrysippi Rogatiunculas. 1. Qui non initiatis indicat mysteria, impie agit. Sed hoc facit Hierophantes ; *Ergo* Impie agit. 2. Est quoddam caput ; Id Tu non habes ; *Ergo* Caput non habes. 3. Id quod loqueris ex ore tuo egreditur : Currum loqueris ; *Ergo* Currus ex ore tuo egreditur.

§. 10. NON temperaturos sibi Juvenes satis scio quin dissiliant risu, ubi hæc tam futilia intellexerint a gravissimis Philosophis serio fuisse proposita ; et Veteribus adeo difficilia haberi, ut Philetas Cous

various expositions of the celebrated Fallacy of the *tertius homo*, alluded to by Aristotle, Soph. Elench. 22. 12. Metaph. i. 9. 8. It is given by Alexander, Schol. p. 314. b. 42. In the proposition, ἄνθρωπος περιπατεῖ, the subject is not the Platonic αὐτοάνθρωπος, who is immoveable, nor yet any individual man ; therefore there is a third man, distinct from the Idea and from the individuals. Several other forms of this Fallacy are given by Alex. in Metaph. p. 62. ed. Bonitz. Cf. Brandis, *de perditis Aristotelis libris*, p. 18. Cousin, *de la Metaphysique d'Aristote*, p. 164. Bonitz in Arist. Met. 990. b. 15.

[*] See Gellius, N. A. xviii. 13.

[t] Ammonius *ad Categ. Arist.* f. 58. οἱ Οὔτιδες παραλογισμοὶ κατὰ τὸν παρ' Ὁμήρῳ Ὀδυσσέα, ἐν καιρῷ Οὔτιν ἑαυτὸν καλέσαντα. Οὔτινος παραλογισμοῦ παράδειγμα. Εἴ τίς ἐστιν ἐν Ἀθήναις, οὗτος οὐκ ἔστιν ἐν Μεγάροις· ἄνθρωπος δέ ἐστιν ἐν Ἀθήναις· ἄνθρωπος ἄρα οὐκ ἔστιν ἐν Μεγάροις.

[u] vii. 186, 187.

præceptor Ptolemæi Philadelphi solius *Mentientis* explicandi studio confectus interierit[x]. Quamvis autem Aristotelis beneficio, videantur ista ut sunt levia, in iis tamen prompte atque artificiose solvendis non inutiliter sese Juvenes exercebunt: nam in gravissimis Disputationibus, hæc eadem recocta Novæ præsertim Philosophiæ cultores sæpissime reponunt.

V. g. *Gassendus* Vacuum quod appellat *disseminatum* eodem fere Sophismate demonstrare pertendit, quo olim Zeno *contra motum* utebatur: Suamque *Hobbius* de *Necessitate* sententiam iisdem propugnat Fallaciis quibus *Fatum* Stoici: aliaque plurima hujus generis, quæ sunt Nobis prætereunda, studiosis inter legendum occurrent.

Fefellit Virum satis alias perspicacem hæc sequela, quæ in Ambiguis distinguendis versatum minime (opinor) fefellisset; *Possum datæ peripheriæ trientem exhibere*[y]; *Possum igitur datam peripheriam trisecare:* cujus falsitatem ipsa Praxis redarguit; neque enim trientem exhibuit, sed alterius circuli peripheriam trienti parem: h. e. non *trientem* ipsum, sed *trientis valorem:* Paria fecisset qui oblatum sibi solidum trisecturus, ne attrectato quidem solido porrexisset drachmam[y].

---

[x] See Athenæus, *Deipn.* ix. 64.

[y] *Datæ peripheriæ trientem.* Aldrich appears to have mistaken the problem. There is no difficulty in trisecting the *entire circumference* of a circle, which may be done by inscribing an equilateral triangle, (Euclid iv. 2.) The true

§. 11. VOLENTEM hic desinere pungit scrupulus, qui nonnullos hodie Mathematicos male habet. Nam in Demonstrationibus quibusdam, Conclusionem ex sui Contradictoria, per legitimas necessariasque consequentias directe inferri volunt. Quod si ita sit, miror a Veteribus, præsertim Scepticis non fuisse animadversum; quippe hoc dato tota ruat Logica necesse est.

Dicunt tamen Theodosium demonstrasse quod *si Maris superficies non est Sphærica, est Sphærica.* Verum ille nihil tale demonstravit; sed tantum Maris superficiem *si nondum esset, fore Sphæricam:* siquid enim emineat (inquit) illud statim, ex natura humidi, subsidet : Unde si Maris superficies sit (ut non est) inæqualis, *fiet* perfecte Sphærica.

Videamus aliud Exemplum. Sunto numeri duo inæquales, et inter se primi; Dico quod eorum differentia ad minorem prima est. *Esto enim numerus aliquis qui metitur minorem;* idemque metiatur differentiam : Ergo metitur eorum summam ; Ergo metitur majorem, huic summæ parem; *Ergo non metitur minorem.*

Possum hoc loco dicere quod mendose colligitur; siquis enim numerus minorem metiatur ex sup-

problem is to trisect an *angle*, or the *arc* subtending a given angle. The solution to which Aldrich alludes appears to have been of this kind. If an arc be drawn subtending a given angle with a radius = a, and another with a radius = ½ a, the latter arc = ½ of the former. But the larger arc is not thereby trisected. For the materials of this note I am indebted to Professor De Morgan.

posito, et majorem ex demonstrato; colligendum erat *datos esse inter se compositos, quod est contra Hypothesin.* Verum ne pluribus exemplis sim molestus, malo generale responsum. Dico igitur, Quod nulla hujusmodi Demonstratio supponit solam suæ Conclusionis Contradictoriam; sed quælibet cum Contradictoria ponit aliquid quod eam evertit; et evertere, demonstrando ostendit. Quare Conclusionem non infert ex ejus Contradictoria; sed ex Contradictoria cum Contradictoriæ eversiva: quod si faciat nihil mirum. Nam *Si Socrates* v. g. *est homo, et irrationalis,* tum *Si est homo, non est homo:* Et *Si Socrates est mortuus, et scit se esse mortuum,* tum *Si est mortuus non est mortuus:* Et Universaliter, *Si et hæc est vera et quæ hanc evertit:* tum *Si hæc est vera, non est vera:* quibus omnibus inest una quæ est prorsus nulla difficultas. Ubi enim Hypothesis evertit suppositionem, quidni ex Hypothesi sequatur, quod Suppositioni contradicit?

APPENDIX.

———

A. On the Predicables.
B. On the Categories.
C. On Definition.
D. On Material and Formal Consequence.
E. Is the Syllogism a Petitio Principii?
F. On the Enthymeme.
G. On Induction.
H. On Example and Analogy.
I. On the Hypothetical Syllogism.
K. On the Demonstrative Syllogism.
L. On the Logic of Geometry.
M. On the Classification of Fallacies.

APPENDIX.

NOTE A.

ON THE PREDICABLES.

IT has been already observed that the ordinary logical account of the Predicables, even in its least objectionable form, as it occurs in the Isagoge of Porphyry, cannot be consistently maintained, except upon Realist principles. By this is meant, that there are portions of that account altogether untenable, except on the supposition that Genera and Species are not mere conceptions of the human mind, but have an independent existence in Nature. Whether they are to be regarded as existing separately, as in the Platonic theory of ideas, or in the individuals, according to the view sometimes attributed to Aristotle, (for both these opinions had their advocates among the Schoolmen*,) is in this respect immaterial; though it may be observed by the way, that of the various modifications to which Realism has at different times been subjected, the Platonic hypothesis. is by far the most consistent and intelligible. The

---

ᵇ Both were early, almost simultaneous, developments of the scholastic Realism, appearing as soon as the Nominalism of Roscelin compelled the antagonist doctrines to assume a definite form. The Platonic theory was advocated by Bernard of Chartres; the other, ultimately the prevailing doctrine, found its earliest scholastic supporter in William of Champeaux.

M

points which may be considered as especially demanding the Realist hypothesis are,

1. The admission, under any definition, of an *Infima Species*.

2. The definition frequently adopted of such Species, as being the whole essence of the individuals of which it is predicated.

3. The assumption that every such Species has one absolute differentia, convertible with the Species, and serving to distinguish it from every other.

It is not asserted that these views were held by none but professed Realists. The first, indeed, may be traced to Aristotle, who has by different writers been regarded as a Realist, a Conceptualist, and a Nominalist, in the strictest sense[b]; it is also to be found in Porphyry, who in the commencement of his treatise proclaims himself neutral: and it was subsequently adopted by the scholastic Nominalists[c]. The second is held by Boethius, who, as far as he had any definite views, rather inclines to Conceptualism[d]; and the third, though not formally established in the schools till the time of Aquinas, was afterwards adopted by Nominalists and Realists indifferently[e]. But this does not prove the compatibility of the doctrines, but only the inconsistency of their holders. The Realist, when pressed to declare why he has fixed the *Infima*

---

[b] See Hamilton on Reid, p. 405.

[c] Abelard, ed. Cousin, p. 537. Occam, Logic, pt. i. chap. 21.

[d] Boethii Opera, p. 72.

[e] The Porphyrian definition of man, "Animal rationale mortale," was adopted by the earlier Schoolmen, Abelard, Albertus Magnus, and Petrus Hispanus; though sometimes with the saving clause, that it must be understood with reference to the Stoical notions of the Gods. Aquinas was the first who expelled the Genus *animal rationale* from the Arbor Porphyriana, and, limiting rationality to men, distinguished Angels as *intellectuales*. Cf. Summa, P. i. Qu. lviii. 3. Opusc. xlviii. Tract. I. cap. 4. Tract. 2. cap. 3.

Species at *Homo,* has an obvious and sufficient answer. I did not make the world, he might say. Substances, universal as well as singular, exist independently of me : I state facts as I find them, and am not bound to determine why they are so. But let a Conceptualist or Nominalist' talk of a Lowest Species, and he is refuted at once by his own fundamental doctrine. The several Species are our own creation, as abstract ideas, or as significations of words. You have no right arbitrarily to declare that you will form complex conceptions thus low and no lower ; or, at least, if you fix such limits for your own convenience, you have no right to impose the same restriction on others.

The same remarks apply to the theory of an absolute differentia, such as *rationale*, predicable of all men and of none but men, and serving to distinguish that species, not from some other given species, but from all others whatever. Porphyry, as has been before observed, ad-

---

' Between Nominalism and Conceptualism there is no real difference, unless in conjunction with the latter we maintain the power of the mind to form Universal notions, unaided by verbal or other symbols. And even then, all Nominalism will be Conceptualism, though all Conceptualism will not be Nominalism. For Universals can only be identified with names by considering these as the signs of notions. Yet Nominalism has been accused as destructive of all Philosophy, and that by the advocates of Conceptualism. But the fundamental error of Hobbes and his followers is not their doctrine of Universal *Terms*, but their theory of the import of *Propositions*. The two, however, are not necessarily connected. We may adopt Locke's theory of abstract ideas, without maintaining with him that knowledge is the perception of the agreement or disagreement of two ideas ; and we may hold that general notions require the aid of language, without maintaining with Hobbes, that truth and falsehood depend on names, or with Condillac, that science is only a language well constructed. But, not to argue this point here, we may observe, that the Scholastic Nominalists. at least Abelard and Occam, were Conceptualists. With regard to Roscelin, it is hardly fair, upon the slight notices we possess of his views, to identify his Nominalism with that of Hobbes, whom Leibnitz rightly calls *plusquam Nominalis.* No one can suppose Abelard's *deductio ad absurdum* to be a fair statement of Roscelin's views.

mits only a *relative* differentia. His definition of man is ζῷον λογικὸν θνητόν; *rational* being the differentia of man when compared with brutes; *mortal*, when compared with the gods[s]. But if either of these attributes be selected as the differentia of man *absolutely*, we must again have recourse to Realism to justify the position. If species are made by Nature, they may have been so framed that each has a peculiar characteristic shared by no other. How this can be proved to be the case is another question; but there is no *à priori* impossibility in the supposition. But if the species is but a conception formed by the mind, what is to hinder us from forming four complex notions *abc, abd, acd, bcd,* of which no part is a differentia absolutely and *per se,* though *c* distinguishes the first from the second, *b* the first from the third, and *a* the first from the fourth?

With regard to the doctrine of the Infima Species being the *whole essence* of the individuals of which it is predicated, the case is still clearer; inasmuch as this language was expressly maintained by the Realists, and expressly repudiated by the Nominalists. It is true that it is previously to be found in Boethius; but here his authority is of little value; as he appears in the character of an interpreter rather than of a critic, and does not seem to have formed any decided opinion of his own. In one of his commentaries on Porphyry he uses the language of Realism; in the other, he is a professed Conceptualist[h]. But even had his views been more definite in favour of the latter hypothesis, it would only shew that he admitted details into his system incon-

---

[s] Isagoge, iii. 19.

[h] Cousin, Ouvrages d'Abélard, Introduction, p. 66. Cousin's remarks are partly supported by Baur, *Lehre von der Dreieinigkeit,* ii. p. 418. Rémusat (*Abélard,* i. p. 349.) takes a more favourable view, but allows that the opinion of Boethius himself is not decidedly expressed.

sistent, if pushed to their ultimate consequences, with its main positions.

In treating the doctrine of Predicables, two alternatives are open to the modern Logician. Either he may take the scholastic language as he finds it, and explain it with reference to the theories on which it was originally founded; warning, however, at the same time his readers or hearers, that the supposed Real Essences are deserving of the same amount of belief as the Deities of Heathen Mythology, or the Sylphs, Gnomes, and Salamanders of the Rosicrucians; or he may adopt a theory of Universals in conformity with views current in modern philosophy, and remodel the whole account of the predicables, so as to make it consistent therewith. But any attempt at a compromise between the two, any explanation of ancient language upon modern hypotheses, can produce nothing but inconsistency in the Teacher and confusion in the Pupil. In the first place, such explanation, even where most satisfactory, is founded merely on analogy, and hence will rather shew what the doctrines expounded ought to have been, according to modern criticism, than what they actually were. In the second place, the analogy in some important particulars will fail entirely, and the exceptional cases must either by some unnatural distortion be forced under the given classification, or be excluded altogether, to the serious detriment of the completeness of the theory.

To adopt then the first mode of explanation. We will suppose that Genera and Species are *substances*, having a real existence independently of us, and cognisable as to their nature, no matter how, by the human mind. Of these universal substances, some are more extensive, others less so, the limits at both extremities being fixed by nature, and the numbers in each degree settled and unalterable. The higher enter into the composition of the lower, the lowest not contributing to form any other Universal, but susceptible of Accidents, from which union are formed various Individuals. Man, for example, is a lowest species: to this are added certain accidental modifications which form Socrates, and at the same time others which form Plato. These modifications excepted, there is nothing in Socrates which is not at the same time in Plato, nor in Plato, which is not at the same time in Socrates[1]. Moreover, from these Universal Substances, or rather from the distinctive portion of each, certain qualities *flow*, or are produced as effect from cause. Others, not connected by causation, are found in the individuals of this or that Species, some universally in all, others partially, in some individuals only.

From a series of assumptions of this kind, the exposition of the Realist doctrine of Predicables is easy. And this, or some other of the various phases of Scholastic Realism, must of necessity be assumed, if our intention is to explain an old theory, not to construct a new one.

On the other hand, we have the modern Logician expounding somewhat in the following style. Genera and Species have no existence *a parte Rei*, but are notions formed by the mind from observing certain points of similarity in different individuals. But similarity must not be confounded with identity. The image

---

[1] " Homo quædam Species est, res una essentialiter, cui adveniunt formæ quædam et efficiunt Socratem: illam eamdem essentialiter eodem modo informant formæ facientes Platonem et cætera individua hominis; nec aliquid est in Socrate, præter illas formas informantes illam materiam ad faciendum Socratem, quin illud idem eodem tempore in Platone informatum sit formis Platonis. Et hoc intelligunt de singulis speciebus ad individua et de generibus ad species." Pseudo-Abelard, de Gen. et Spec. ed. Cousin. p. 513. This was the first doctrine of William of Champeaux. Other expositions of Realism might be given.

and superscription on two coins may present no discernible marks of distinction from each other; but if on that account we say that they are *the same*, we employ the word in an equivocal sense, which must be carefully distinguished from that in which we say that both are struck from *the same* die. In the latter sense, the attributes forming the humanity of Socrates are not the same with those forming the humanity of Plato; though the common notion *man* embraces both, and though, by availing ourselves of an ambiguity of language, we say that both are of *the same* species.

General notions thus framed by the mind, when expressed in language, form common terms. And the various attributes comprehended[k] in every such notion are its logical essence[l]. By this we do not mean any thing necessary to the physical existence of an object; but merely that, as general notions are formed from the observation of similar attributes in individuals, every individual must possess such attributes, if it is to be included under the extension of the notion and called by the corresponding common name. Proper names, on

---

[d] In a Pamphlet published under the name of " A Dissertation on the Heads of Predicables," I inadvertently adopted Mr. Mill's expressions of *connotation* and *denotation*, to distinguish between the attributes contained in a complex notion, and the subjects of which it is predicated. The distinction I still regard as most important, and one that is not perhaps sufficiently marked in modern language; but further study of the scholastic phraseology has led me to regard Mr. Mill's language as too wide a departure from the original use of the terms. For this reason I have preferred the expressions *Comprehension* and *Extension*, as better sanctioned by Logical authority. Cf. Port Royal Logic, P. I. chap. 6. " J'appelle *comprehension* de l'idée, les attributs qu'elle enferme en soi. J'appelle *étendue* de l'idée, les sujets à qui cette idée convient." For the Scholastic Connotation, see p. 16, note g.

[l] This is the *Nominal Essence* of Locke, which corresponds to the Logical Essence of other philosophers, though variously explained according to the different Metaphysical theories. The term *Real Essence* is used by the same philosopher to denote that generally unknown constitution of *individual things* on which their sensible properties depend.

the contrary, have no essence, as they have no general notion belonging to them, but are mere arbitrary marks imposed for the purpose of distinguishing individuals from each other.

But though our earliest complex notions may have been gained from real objects, there is no reason why such notions alone should be admitted in a theory of Predication. Such a theory only distinguishes the several relations which the subject and predicate of a proposition may bear to each other. With the objective existence of things corresponding to our general notions, we have for the present no concern. Whatever theory may be adopted as to the origin of our ideas, there can be no doubt that we have the power of forming combinations in the mind, which have not been observed to exist in nature[m]. And the relation of subject and predicate in propositions into which such notions enter, may be identified with some of the relations of other notions.

In constructing or explaining a theory of Predication in conformity with these views, there is one ambiguity which it is not possible to avoid, without a coinage of new terms. The distinctions of Genus and Differentia must be gained by comparing two terms not predicable of each other. Compare, for example, Man with Brute, the common Genus will be Animal, the respective Differentiæ, Rational and Irrational. But there is no absolute Genus or Differentia, and frequently, while the whole comprehension of the notion remains the same, the Genus and Differentia may change places, according as it is compared with this or that other notion. In the comparison, for example, of a plane triangle with a parallelogram, " rectilineal figure " is its common, " having three sides " its distinctive part. But compare a plane

---

[m] Cf. Locke, Essay, b. ii. ch. 2. §. 2.

with a spherical triangle, "having three sides" is common to both; the distinction being, that the sides in the one case are straight lines, in the other, arcs of great circles[n]. But when one only of the compared notions is employed as the subject of a proposition, and a portion of the attributes which it comprehends is predicated of it, that predicate cannot properly be called Genus or Differentia, the comparison from which these distinctions arise having ceased.

With this proviso, we may adopt, *mutatis mutandis*, the classification of the Predicables given by Aristotle himself, as furnishing a more satisfactory groundwork than either the Isagoge of Porphyry or its subsequent scholastic embellishments. Every Proposition, according to Aristotle, expresses one of four relations of the Predicate to its Subject; Genus, (under which may be included Differentia,) Definition, Property, or Accident[o]. For every Predicate must either be convertible with its Subject or not. If convertible, it either expresses the whole Essence (τὸ τί ἦν εἶναι) of the Subject or not. In the former case it is called Definition, in the latter, Property. If not convertible, it either expresses part of the Essence or not. In the former case it is Genus, in the latter, Accident.

This division, being founded on dichotomy by contradiction, must necessarily exhaust every possible mode of Predication. Interpreting the Essence, in accordance with our present view, as the sum of the attributes

[n] This has been remarked by Leibnitz, *Nouveaux Essais*, iii. 3. *Opera*, ed. Erdmann, p. 304. *Schreiben an Wagner, ibid.* p. 425.

[o] See Topics, i. 8. Sundry attempts have been made, not very successfully, to reconcile this account with that of Porphyry. But though some license of interpretation may be allowed, when the object is to reconcile an author with himself, it is scarcely necessary to strain his language into agreement with a writer who lived more than six centuries after him, and who does not even profess to be commenting on him.

comprehended in a notion, we shall find all four members admissible where the Subject of the proposition has both *comprehension* and *extension;* i. e. is a complex notion containing attributes, and is predicable of existing objects. For its Predicate may either express a whole or a part of the attributes comprehended in the Subject, or else some attribute not so comprehended, but possessed by the objects of which the Subject is predicable. In the latter case, where the Subject and Predicate are distinct in comprehension, they may be either equal or unequal in extension.

The two first cases will correspond to the class of Propositions called by Kant, Analytical Judgments, and by Mr. Mill, Verbal Propositions. In these the attributes composing the Predicate are a part or the whole of those composing the Subject. They therefore depend solely on the Principle of Identity. If Animal form part of the conception Man, the objects, whether actual or possible, thought under the latter must necessarily be identical with a portion of those thought under the former.

To avoid the introduction of new words, we may retain the Aristotelian nomenclature of *Genus* and *Definition* to express the relation of Predicate to Subject in these two classes of Propositions; though the former appellation, for the reason stated above, is not altogether free from objections. Under Definition may be also included a class of Propositions which are not, in the strict sense of the word, Analytical [p], and are not admitted by Aristotle to be Definitions proper; viz. those in which the Predicate is a single term synonymous with the Subject.

The last two cases will correspond to the Synthetical Judgments of Kant, and to the Real Propositions of

[p] Though Kant admits even tautological propositions (A is A) as explicitly analytical.

Mr. Mill. In these, the subject is neither a word nor a notion, but the several individual things of which a certain notion is predicable. For example, in the Proposition, "All men are mortal," we do not mean that the conception Man includes Mortality, but that the individuals possessing the attributes comprehended in the former notion possess also those comprehended in the latter.

In distinguishing a certain portion of these Propositions as predicating *Property*, we must divest ourselves altogether of the notion of necessary or contingent connexion, and regard the word purely as a translation of the Aristotelian ἴδιον. These Propositions assert, not merely that certain objects possess certain attributes, but that they alone possess them. This assertion, however, is very imperfectly expressed in the ordinary form of the affirmative proposition. The judgment, "all equilateral triangles are equiangular," does not by its mere form imply that all equiangular triangles are equilateral. This knowledge is conveyed by the geometrical matter, not by the logical form. To remedy this defect of language, it is necessary in a system of formal Logic to distinguish the propositions in which property is predicated from those in which accident is predicated, by attaching an universal sign to the predicate. "All equilateral triangles are all equiangular," will then denote that the predicate is a property of the subject; while "all men are some mortals," distinguishes by the particular sign that the predicate is an accident.

The distinction adopted by Aldrich between Property and Accident, as *necessarily* or *contingently* connected with the subject, is untenable in formal Logic. If not expressed in the copula, it implies the extralogical knowledge of a law of connexion existing or not between the objects signified by the terms; a law which cannot be indicated in the symbolical form of the proposition. If, on the other hand, a special form of the copula is adopted, and Property and Accident distinguished by the expressions A *must be* B, A *may be* B, the classification becomes no longer applicable to the pure form of the proposition, and requires the introduction of the extra-logical doctrine of Modality[q]. The adoption of a quantified predicate, on the other hand, is a necessary step when language is designed to express the pure form of thought, and every classification of logical forms should be adapted to this condition[r].

In the foregoing remarks, Genus and Definition express a relation of notions to notions, Property and Accident, one of attributes to things. Hence it will follow that notions thought as unreal, i. e. confessedly predicable of no objects existing elsewhere than in the mind, can only, as such, be the subjects of analytical judgments. Proper names, on the other hand, having no essence, can only be the subjects of synthetical judgments. The former have no Properties or Accidents ; the latter have no Genus or Definition.

Species is excluded from the Predicables, and confined to the *Species Subjicibilis*, the correlative of the Predicable Genus. By this we avoid an inconsistency of which the majority of Logicians are guilty, in employing the term Species sometimes to express a relation of a Predicate to a Subject, sometimes that of a Subject to a Predicate. The so-called *Species Prædicabilis*, is, in the manner of its predication, in no way distinguishable from Genus. *Man*, when predicated of *philosopher*, expresses a part only of the essence of its subject, i. e.

[q] On Modality as a Form, see *Prolegomena Logica*, note G. (2nd ed. note H.)

[r] This principle, the basis of Sir W. Hamilton's New Analytic, is well stated by Mr. Baynes, *Essay on the New Analytic*, p. 9.

a portion of the attributes which the subject notion comprehends ; precisely as does *animal*, when predicated of *man*.

A Lowest Species will be inadmissible, as it implies a notion so complex as to be incapable of further accessions. It is true that, in the continual formation of Species, we may arrive at combinations of attributes not realized in Nature ; but the classification of things is not the province of the Logician ; nor has he a right to conclude *à priori* that the field of physical research is exhausted, or that notions now regarded as imaginary may not hereafter be discovered to be real. But whether such discovery be made or not, it will not affect the *relation* of two notions to each other. Logic is concerned only with the necessary relations of concepts in thought. Every concept, being common to a plurality of objects, is potentially divisible into lower ones. A logical lowest species, if such were possible, would be a concept embracing all conceivable attributes not condemned by the laws of thought as contradictory of each other. This, as well as its opposite, the logical highest genus, or notion so simple as to have no distinctive attributes, are mere imaginary limits, never reached in any process of actual thought'. A material science may have its highest and lowest classes ; the former being the general class, embracing all the objects whose properties that science investigates ; the latter the classes at which that special investigation ends. In Geometry, for example, under the *summum genus* of magnitudes in space, we find three *infimæ species* of triangles, the equilateral, the isosceles, and the scalene. The geometrical properties of the figures are not affected by any further subdivision. But this limitation cannot be acknowledged by the Logician. He knows nothing of the geometrical or

* See *Prolegomena Logica*, p. 183. (2nd ed. p. 198.)

physical properties of this or that class of objects.   As
a mere concept, " an equilateral triangle whose sides are
two feet long," is a subordinate species to "equilateral
triangle;" and the subdivision may, as far as mere thought
is concerned, be continued *ad infinitum.*

Note B.

ON THE CATEGORIES.

Lists of the Categories, more or less complete, occur in different parts of Aristotle's works in slightly different relations. The following passages may be selected as the principal. *Categ.* ch. 4. Τῶν κατὰ μηδεμίαν συμπλοκὴν λεγομένων ἕκαστον ἤτοι οὐσίαν σημαίνει ἢ ποσὸν ἢ ποιὸν ἢ πρός τι ἢ ποῦ ἢ ποτὲ ἢ κεῖσθαι ἢ ἔχειν ἢ ποιεῖν ἢ πάσχειν. Ἔστι δὲ οὐσία μὲν ὡς τύπῳ εἰπεῖν οἷον ἄνθρωπος, ἵππος· ποσὸν δὲ οἷον δίπηχυ, τρίπηχυ· ποιὸν δὲ οἷον λευκόν, γραμματικόν· πρός τι δὲ οἷον διπλάσιον, ἥμισυ, μεῖζον· ποῦ δὲ οἷον ἐν Λυκείῳ, ἐν ἀγορᾷ· ποτὲ δὲ οἷον ἐχθές, πέρυσιν· κεῖσθαι δὲ οἷον ἀνάκειται, κάθηται· ἔχειν δὲ οἷον ὑποδέδεται, ὥπλισται· ποιεῖν δὲ οἷον τέμνει, καίει· πάσχειν δὲ οἷον τέμνεται, καίεται. *Topic.* i. 9. Μετὰ τοίνυν ταῦτα δεῖ διορίσασθαι τὰ γένη τῶν κατηγοριῶν, ἐν οἷς ὑπάρχουσιν αἱ ῥηθεῖσαι τέτταρες. Ἔστι δὲ ταῦτα τὸν ἀριθμὸν δέκα, τί ἐστι, ποσόν, ποιόν, πρός τι, ποῦ, ποτέ, κεῖσθαι, ἔχειν, ποιεῖν, πάσχειν. Ἀεὶ γὰρ τὸ συμβεβηκὸς καὶ τὸ γένος καὶ τὸ ἴδιον καὶ ὁ ὁρισμὸς ἐν μιᾷ τούτων τῶν κατηγοριῶν ἔσται· πᾶσαι γὰρ αἱ διὰ τούτων προτάσεις ἢ τί ἐστιν ἢ ποιὸν ἢ ποσὸν ἢ τῶν ἄλλων τινὰ κατηγοριῶν σημαίνουσιν. *Metaph.* iv. 7. Καθ' αὑτὰ δὲ εἶναι λέγεται ὅσαπερ σημαίνει τὰ σχήματα τῆς κατηγορίας· ὁσαχῶς γὰρ λέγεται, τοσαυταχῶς τὸ εἶναι σημαίνει. Ἐπεὶ οὖν τῶν κατηγορουμένων τὰ μὲν τί ἐστι σημαίνει, τὰ δὲ ποιόν, τὰ δὲ ποσόν, τὰ δὲ πρός τι, τὰ δὲ ποιεῖν ἢ πάσχειν, τὰ δὲ ποῦ, τὰ δὲ πότε, ἑκάστῳ τούτων τὸ εἶναι ταὐτὸ σημαίνει.

From these passages it appears that the Categories were regarded by Aristotle, 1. As an enumeration of the different significations of simple terms, apart from their connexion in the proposition. 2. As an enume-

ration of the several genera under which Aristotle's four
heads of predicables fall.   3. As an enumeration of the
different modes in which Being may be signified.   An
examination of the principle of classification is necessary, in order that we may determine how far the charges
of deficiency and redundancy, so frequently brought
against Aristotle's list, can be fairly maintained.

The most celebrated of these accusations is that of
Kant[a].   Assuming that Aristotle's design was identical
with his own, viz. to enumerate the pure or *à priori*
conceptions of the understanding, he asserts that the
classification was made upon no principle; that it was
found by the author to be defective, and the post-
predicaments added in consequence; that the list thus
enlarged is still defective; that it contains forms of the
sensibility as well as of the understanding; (*quando, ubi,
situs, prius, simul;*) that empirical notions are intruded
among the pure (*motus*), and deduced concepts classed as
original (*actio, passio*); and that some original elements
are altogether omitted[b].

A somewhat similar criticism is given in Mr. Mill's
Logic.   The Categories he supposes to be " an enumeration of all things, capable of being named; an enumeration by the *summa genera*, i. e. the most extensive
classes into which things could be distributed; which
therefore were so many highest Predicates, one or other
of which was supposed capable of being affirmed with
truth of every nameable thing whatsoever."   Thus viewed,
he pronounces the list to be both redundant and defective.   Action, passion, and local situation, ought to
be included under relation; together with position in
time (*quando*), and in space (*ubi*); while the distinction

---

[a] For an account of the earlier criticisms of the Categories by Plotinus,
Campanella, and others, see Trendelenburg, *Geschichte der Kateyorienlehre.*
[b] *Kritik der r. V.* p. 80. (ed. Rosenkranz.)   *Prolegomena,* §. 39.

between the latter and *situs* is merely verbal. On the other hand, all states of mind are omitted entirely; as they cannot be reckoned either among substances or attributes[c].

These objections will stand or fall, according as their authors have rightly or wrongly divined the purpose of Aristotle's classification. Kant is mistaken in supposing that Aristotle added the post-predicaments to complete his list of Categories. The post-predicaments were not so called by Aristotle, and have never been classed by commentators among the Categories. The term is of scholastic origin, and was employed to denote the five subjects treated of by Aristotle after the Categories proper. Kant is equally mistaken in supposing that Aristotle had any intention of classifying the pure forms of the understanding, independent of experience. On the contrary, the Categories belong to the matter of thought, are generalized from experience, and leave altogether untouched the psychological question of the existence of elements *à priori*[d]. Any objection, therefore, based on the inclusion of empirical or the exclusion of original elements, is untenable, and rests on a misapprehension of the philosopher's design. Nor yet can we adopt Mr. Mill's opinion, that Aristotle designed a classification of all things capable of being named; at least not in that point of view in which things are regarded according to their real characteristics as presented to consciousness. The Categories are rather an enumeration of the different modes of naming things, classified primarily according to the grammatical distinctions of speech, and gained, not from the observation

[c] Mill's Logic, vol. i. p. 60.
[d] See Sir W. Hamilton, *Discussions*, p. 26. Franck, *Histoire de la Logique*, p. 26. St. Hilaire, *Logique d'Aristote traduite en Français*, p. lxxx.

of objects, but from the analysis of assertions. This is manifest from the name and from the manner of treatment. Κατηγορία, κατηγορεῖν, κατηγόρημα, κατεγορούμενον, κατηγορικός, have all primarily reference to forms of speech; the term κατηγορία being used by Aristotle as well for any predicate term, as for the highest generalizations under which predicates can be classed[f]. In the beginning of the treatise on the Categories, terms as combined in a proposition are made to precede terms regarded separately[g]; and the proposition, as the only assertion capable of truth and falsehood, appears to be regarded as the unit of speech, of which the simple term is but a fractional element[h].

It is therefore probable, that the Aristotelian distinction of Categories arose from the resolution of the proposition and a classification of the grammatical distinctions indicated by its parts. The noun substantive leads us to the category of οὐσία, the adjectives of number and of quality to ποσόν and ποιόν, the adjective of comparison to πρός τι, the adverbs of place and time to ποῦ and ποτέ, the different forms of the verb, intransitive, præterite, active, and passive to κεῖσθαι, ἔχειν, ποιεῖν, and πάσχειν[i]. It is true that in his subsequent treatment the philosopher by no means adheres strictly to the grammatical point of view, and that his classification may, even on his own principles, be considerably simplified; but it must be remembered, that at that time the science of Grammar was in its infancy, that its forms of speech had not been analysed completely, nor its boundaries clearly separated from those of Logic and Metaphysics.

[f] See Trendelenburg, *Geschichte der Kategorienlehre*, p. 2. The Aristotelian expression σχήματα τῆς κατηγορίας will thus primarily mean *forms of predication*.

[g] See *Categ.* ch. 2.

[h] See *Categ.* ch. 3. Trendelenburg, *Kategorienlehre*, p. 12.

[i] Trendelenburg, *Elementa*, §. 3. *Kategorienlehre*, p. 23.

The omission, therefore, in the Aristotelian list, of separate heads of classification for mental states, cannot be charged as a defect in this point of view, so long as mind and its various states (whatever may be their difference in other respects) are represented by the same verbal forms as substances and attributes. And accordingly we find various mental states, faculties, passions, habits, and dispositions, classified together with corresponding affections of body, under the head of qualities[k]. A more valid objection in a grammatical point of view would be, that qualities in their abstract form are expressed by nouns substantive, and should therefore be classed under the category of substance. This objection would be tenable in relation to the distinctions of modern Grammar. But Aristotle appears to have limited the *substantive word* to terms expressive of the πρῶται οὐσίαι, or individual substances, and the δεύτεραι οὐσίαι, or their several genera and species. The latter denote properly the category of substance, or substance considered as one of the possible predicates of a proposition. Words denoting individual substances, being subjects only in the proposition, do not properly indicate a category[l].

In reference, therefore, to the treatise of the same name, we might fairly describe the Aristotelian Categories as an enumeration of the different grammatical forms of the possible predicates of a proposition, viewed in relation to the first substance as a subject. And this view is not materially departed from in the other writings of Aristotle. The passage quoted from the Topics, indeed, only continues the same view, stating that those predicates, which in their actual relation to their subjects in a proposition

---

[k] See Categ. ch. 8.

[l] *Categ.* 5. 27. 'Απὸ μὲν γὰρ τῆς πρώτης οὐσίας οὐδεμία ἐστὶ κατηγορία· κατ' οὐδενὸς γὰρ ὑποκειμένου λέγεται· τῶν δὲ δευτέρων οὐσιῶν τὸ μὲν εἶδος κατὰ τοῦ ἀτόμου κατηγορεῖται, τὸ δὲ γένος καὶ κατὰ τοῦ εἴδους καὶ κατὰ τοῦ ἀτόμου.

come under one of the four heads of Genus, Definition, Property, or Accident, come as simple terms under one of the ten Categories. The Metaphysical view of the Categories is not materially different. In that work, Aristotle enumerates the different senses in which the term *Being* (τὸ ὂν) is used, in order to determine in what sense it is applied to the object of metaphysical inquiries[m]. *Being* sometimes signifies the accidental connection of an attribute with a subject, or of two attributes with a common subject. It is also used co-extensively with the Categories in predication; thus we may say, ἄνθρωπος ὑγιαίνει, or ἄνθρωπος ὑγιαίνων ἐστίν, ἄνθρωπος τέμνει, or ἄνθρωπος τέμνων ἐστίν, the verb εἶναι being admissible as a copula in any proposition, whatever may be the category of its predicate[n]. But substance is the πρώτως ὄν, the proper object of metaphysics[o]. In this account, Aristotle does not appear to have distinguished between the verb substantive, as denoting real existence, and the copula as denoting the coexistence of notions in the mind; but, as in other places, the Categories are enumerated, not as an exhaustive catalogue of existing things, but as a list of different modes of predicating by the copula. They thus originally belong to Grammar, rather than to Logic or Metaphysics, though the treatment of latter philosophers, perhaps in some degree sanctioned by Aristotle himself, has brought them into closer connection with the latter sciences, and overlooked their proper relation to the former[p].

[m] See Trendelenburg, *Kategorienlehre*, p. 167.
[n] Metaph. iv. 7.
[o] Metaph. vi. 1.
[p] Trendelenburg, *Kategorienlehre*, p. 216.

Note C.

ON DEFINITION.

In the notes to Aldrich's account of Definition, I have endeavoured to explain his language in conformity with the views most commonly found in Logical Treatises. But as these views differ in many respects from those of Aristotle, on which they are supposed to be founded, and as a correct account of the doctrines of that Philosopher will materially assist in the solution of more than one of those *vexatæ quæstiones* which are most perplexing to beginners in Logic, I shall attempt a somewhat fuller exposition here.

In the second Book of the Posterior Analytics, Aristotle mentions three different forms of Definition, in the following words: Ἔστιν ἄρα ὁρισμὸς εἷς μὲν λόγος τοῦ τί ἐστιν ἀναπόδεικτος, εἷς δὲ συλλογισμὸς τοῦ τί ἐστι, πτώσει διαφέρων τῆς ἀποδείξεως, τρίτος δὲ τῆς τοῦ τί ἐστιν ἀποδείξεως συμπέρασμα[a]. This passage is a concise summary of the whole Aristotelian theory of Definition. Adopting it as our text, we proceed to comment as follows.

A necessary preliminary to the determining the Real Definition of any object, (τί ἐστι,) is to ascertain that such object exists (ὅτι ἐστι). Otherwise our Definition will be merely a nominal one[b]. But we have two classes of definable objects, of which the existence is determined in two different ways, producing a corresponding variety in the form of the Definition.

---

[a] Anal. Post. ii. 10. 4.

[b] Anal. Post. ii. 8. 3. Ἀδύνατον εἰδέναι τί ἐστιν, ἀγνοοῦντας εἰ ἔστιν. Ibid. ii. 7. 2. Ἀνάγκη γὰρ τὸν εἰδότα τὸ τί ἐστιν ἄνθρωπος ἢ ἄλλο ὁτιοῦν, εἰδέναι καὶ ὅτι ἔστιν· τὸ γὰρ μὴ ὂν οὐδεὶς οἶδεν ὅ τι ἐστίν, ἀλλὰ τί μὲν σημαίνει ὁ λόγος ἢ τὸ ὄνομα, ὅταν εἴπω τραγέλαφος, τί δ' ἐστι τραγέλαφος ἀδύνατον εἰδέναι.

I. Attributes, under which term are included all things belonging to any other Category than that of Substance. These exist only in Substances as their subjects, and their existence is properly determined by *Demonstration*[c]. When ascertained in any other way, we are said to know it only accidentally[d]. In the Demonstrative Syllogism, the minor term is the Subject, the major the Attribute; the Cause, by virtue of which the Subject is thus affected, being the middle term. When by such a Syllogism we have proved that all A is B, we know that the attribute B exists in the subject A.

II. Substances, which exist not in a Subject, but *per se*[e]. Of such the existence cannot be proved, but must be *assumed*, before any of their Attributes can be demonstrated. This assumption under the name of Hypothesis, forms one of the Aristotelian ἀρχαί, or Principles of Science, which must precede all Demonstration[f].

[c] Hence the Scholastic maxim, *Accidentis esse est inesse.* Cf. Aquinas, Opusc. xlviii. de Syll. Demonst. c. 11. I have preferred the term Attribute to Accident, inasmuch as the latter is frequently appropriated in a special sense to such Attributes as exist only contingently, and are therefore indemonstrable.

[d] Eth. Nic. vi. 3. 4. ὅταν γάρ πως πιστεύῃ καὶ γνώριμοι αὐτῷ ὦσιν αἱ ἀρχαί, ἐπίσταται· εἰ γὰρ μὴ μᾶλλον τοῦ συμπεράσματος, κατὰ συμβεβηκὸς ἕξει τὴν ἐπιστήμην.

[e] Categ. 5. 18. Κοινὸν δὲ κατὰ πάσης οὐσίας τὸ μὴ ἐν ὑποκειμένῳ εἶναι.

[f] The following table of the Principles of Science may be useful to the reader.

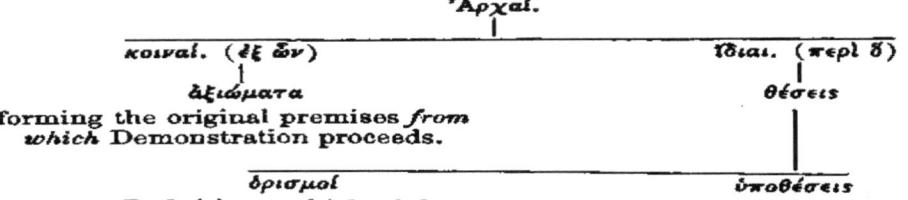

'Αρχαί.

κοιναί. (ἐξ ὧν)	ἴδιαι. (περὶ ὅ)
ἀξιώματα	θέσεις

forming the original premises *from which* Demonstration proceeds.

ὁρισμοί	ὑποθέσεις
Definitions, which of the Subjects are real, of the Attributes nominal.	Assumptions of the existence of the Subjects, as a necessary condition to their definition.
	[N.B. The Attributes are not *assumed* to exist, but *proved* to exist in their Subjects.]

In some passages, speaking in a stricter sense, Aristotle declares Substances alone to be capable of Definition[g]; but in the wider sense of the term which prevails throughout the Posterior Analytics, it is applicable both to Substances and to Attributes.   In both cases the inquiry into the Definition of a thing is identical with that into its cause; with this distinction, that in the case of Attributes, the Cause is to be sought, not in the Attribute, but in its Subject; whereas in the case of Substances which exist *per se*, the Cause is to be sought in themselves only[h].

Attributes are defined by the same cause which served as a middle term to prove their existence.   This is the mode of Definition described as $\sigma \upsilon \lambda \lambda o \gamma \iota \sigma \mu \grave{o} \varsigma$ $\tau o \tilde{\upsilon}$ $\tau \acute{\iota}$ $\grave{\epsilon} \sigma \tau \iota$, $\pi \tau \acute{\omega} \sigma \epsilon \iota$ $\delta \iota \alpha \phi \acute{\epsilon} \rho \omega \nu$ $\tau \tilde{\eta} \varsigma$ $\grave{\alpha} \pi o \delta \epsilon \acute{\iota} \xi \epsilon \omega \varsigma$.   As an example, he gives the definition of an eclipse.   The moon is proved to be eclipsed, because the sun's light is intercepted by the earth.   The same cause furnishes us at once with a middle term for demonstration, and with a definition of the attribute[i].   Why is the moon eclipsed?   Because

---

See Anal. Post. i. 2. 7. i. 10. 1. i. 32. 6. and Sanderson's Logic, b. iii. ch. 11. From this it will be seen that Mr. Mill has unjustly accused Aristotle of maintaining that the science of Geometry is deduced from Definitions. (Mill's Logic, vol. i. p. 197.) Hence may also be explained the contradiction which Stewart professes to find in Aristotle's doctrines.   (Elements, Pt. ii. ch. 3. sect. i.) The principles *from which* Aristotle demonstrates, are *Axioms*, of which he gives as a specimen, " If equals be taken from equals, the remainders are equal."   The necessity of *assuming* the existence of the subject is maintained by Aristotle as clearly as by Mr. Mill.   Cf. also Metaph. v. 1. 2. x. 7. 2.

g e. g. Metaph. vi. 5. 5. Cf. Metaph. vi. 4. 12.

h Anal. Post. ii. 2. 5. $\tilde{\omega} \sigma \pi \epsilon \rho$ $o \tilde{\upsilon} \nu$ $\lambda \acute{\epsilon} \gamma o \mu \epsilon \nu$, $\tau \grave{o}$ $\tau \acute{\iota}$ $\grave{\epsilon} \sigma \tau \iota \nu$ $\epsilon \grave{\iota} \delta \acute{\epsilon} \nu \alpha \iota$ $\tau \alpha \grave{\upsilon} \tau \acute{o}$ $\grave{\epsilon} \sigma \tau \iota$ $\kappa \alpha \grave{\iota}$ $\delta \iota \grave{\alpha}$ $\tau \acute{\iota}$ $\grave{\epsilon} \sigma \tau \iota \nu$. $T o \tilde{\upsilon} \tau o$ δ' $\mathring{\eta}$ $\grave{\alpha} \pi \lambda \tilde{\omega} \varsigma$ $\kappa \alpha \grave{\iota}$ $\mu \grave{\eta}$ $\tau \tilde{\omega} \nu$ $\grave{\upsilon} \pi \alpha \rho \chi \acute{o} \nu \tau \omega \nu$ $\tau \iota$, $\mathring{\eta}$ $\tau \tilde{\omega} \nu$ $\grave{\upsilon} \pi \alpha \rho \chi \acute{o} \nu \tau \omega \nu$. Anal. Post. i. 24. 6. $\tilde{\omega}$ $\gamma \grave{\alpha} \rho$ $\kappa \alpha \theta$' $\alpha \grave{\upsilon} \tau \grave{o}$ $\grave{\upsilon} \pi \acute{\alpha} \rho \chi \epsilon \iota$ $\tau \iota$, $\tau o \tilde{\upsilon} \tau o$ $\alpha \grave{\upsilon} \tau \grave{o}$ $\alpha \grave{\upsilon} \tau \tilde{\omega}$ $\alpha \breve{\iota} \tau \iota o \nu$.

i The reduction of this Demonstration to syllogistic form has been variously attempted.   The following is given by Aquinas, Opusc. 38. " Omne corpus naturale, illuminatum a sole, privatum luce a terræ objectu deficit; luna est hujusmodi, ergo luna deficit."   A more general, and so far preferable, major premise, is given by Crakanthorpe, Log. lib. iv. cap. 4.

the sun's light is intercepted by the earth. What is an eclipse? An intercepting of the sun's light from the moon by the earth. Thunder in the same way is defined, ἀπόσβεσις πυρὸς ἐν νέφει, the answer to the question διὰ τί βροντᾷ; being διὰ τὸ ἀποσβέννυσθαι τὸ πῦρ ἐν τῷ νέφει.

This kind of definition, as has been observed, differs from a demonstration in the position (θέσις) of its terms[j]; for it has the same terms (ἔκλειψις, ἀντίφραξις, σελήνη,—βροντή, ἀπόσβεσις πυρός, νέφος,) but not in the same order, and with some variety of grammatical form (πτῶσις[k]).

The Definition, then, of an Attribute is to be found in its Cause. But the Aristotelian Philosophy recognises four Causes, and sometimes more than one of these is concerned in the production of the same effect. Which of these is to be taken as the Definition? In Anal. Post. ii. 11. Aristotle shews that any one of the four may be used as a middle term in demonstration; but it by no means follows that each may be a Definition of the major term. On this point, Aristotle's opinion is not decidedly

"Omne corpus illuminatum ab alio, inter quod et corpus illuminans opacum corpus sic interponitur, ut umbra opaci corporis operiat et comprehendat corpus illuminatum, eclipsatur seu privatur suo lumine."

j The Definition is by some given as "an obscuration of light in the moon, caused by the interposition of the earth." But in this case, the major term of the Demonstrative Syllogism is not "eclipsed," but "obscured." If these two terms are synonymous, the Definition is merely nominal, and the latter part superfluous; if not, we do not define the attribute demonstrated (obscuration), but another (eclipse), contained under it as species under genus. I interpret Aristotle's words as referring to the complex form of the Definition, as given in question and answer, or in a proposition—τί ἐστιν ἔκλειψις; ἀντίφραξις ὑπὸ γῆς—ἡ ἔκλειψίς ἐστιν ἀντίφραξις ὑπὸ γῆς. So the third form of Definition mentioned An. Pr. ii. 10. resembles the conclusion of a Demonstration, as containing, in the same form, only the major and minor terms, (βροντή, νέφος) ἡ βροντή ἐστι ψόφος ἐν νέφει. Aristotle's text is not decisive, the one view being rather supported by ch. 8. the other by ch. 10. The question is by no means unimportant; the attempt to reduce these Definitions to a pseudo-Genus and Differentia has fostered a grave error, which will be noticed hereafter.

k Pacius and Waitz consider πτῶσις and θέσις to be synonymous.

expressed; but it seems probable that he regarded the *formal cause* only as available for the purpose of Definition. For a material cause, properly speaking, has no place in attributes, but only in physical substances[1]; and that which in the former is most nearly analogous to matter, viz. the necessary condition out of which the effect arises, may in such cases be identified with the formal cause. This Aristotle allows in the chapter in question, when he states that the material cause there instanced as a middle term is in fact the same as the formal[m]. The efficient and final causes seem to be excluded, as not being contemporaneous with their effects, so that from the existence of the one we cannot certainly infer that of the other[n]. Whereas the formal cause is expressly distinguished as τὸ τί ἦν εἶναι[o]; and the examples given of it in Anal. Post. ii. 12. 1. correspond exactly to those previously given as Definitions. The other causes only accidentally serve the same purpose, in those instances in which they coincide with the formal[p].

---

[1] Metaph. vii. 4. 6. Περὶ μὲν οὖν τὰς φυσικὰς οὐσίας καὶ γεννητὰς ἀνάγκη οὕτω μετιέναι, εἴ τις μέτεισιν ὀρθῶς, εἴπερ ἄρα αἴτιά τε ταῦτα καὶ τοσαῦτα, καὶ δεῖ τὰ αἴτια γνωρίζειν. Ἐπὶ δὲ τῶν φυσικῶν μὲν ἀϊδίων δὲ οὐσιῶν ἄλλος λόγος. Ἴσως γὰρ ἔνια οὐκ ἔχει ὕλην, ἢ οὐ τοιαύτην ἀλλὰ μόνον κατὰ τόπον κινητήν. Οὐδ' ὅσα δὴ φύσει μὲν μή, οὐσίᾳ δέ, [sc. ὑπάρχει] οὐκ ἔστι τούτοις ὕλη ἀλλὰ τὸ ὑποκείμενον ἡ οὐσία. Οἷον τί αἴτιον ἐκλείψεως, τίς ὕλη; οὐ γὰρ ἔστιν, ἀλλ' ἡ σελήνη, τὸ πάσχον.

[m] See Anal. Post. ii. 11. 3.

[n] See Anal. Post. ii. 12. 3, 4. and Waitz, Org. vol. ii. p. 411.

[o] Anal. Pr. ii. 11. 1. Metaph. i. 3. 1.

[p] See Rassow, "Aristotelis de Notionis Definitione Doctrina," p. 16. A very different view has been taken by some Logicians. Crakanthorpe, for example, maintains that Demonstration can only be, "a causa efficiente per emanationem, vel a causa efficiente per externam actionem, vel a causa finali;" and he devotes a chapter to shewing that neither the Material nor the Formal cause can be a middle term in Demonstration, though the efficient cause of the Attribute may be the formal cause of the Subject. A similar view is maintained by Sanderson, lib. iii. cap. 15.

We have next to consider the Definitions of Substances. Here too the investigation of Cause is the root of the whole inquiry; but the manner in which it is conducted is not at first sight so obvious as in the former case. To ask the cause of an attribute, is to ask why the subject is so affected. Why, for example, is the moon eclipsed? But what is meant by the *cause* of a man, and in what form will the question be proposed? To ask why man exists, is in fact to ask why there are such beings in the world,—a question admitting only of Grangousier's solution[q],—and, when so solved, contributing nothing towards the Definition. To ask why a man is a man, is, as Aristotle himself observes, futile[r]. The only form in which the question can be put is, Why is this or that individual a man? What are the essential constituents of the notion Man, the possession of which entitles Socrates to be reckoned in the class? Here too the formal cause determines the Definition.

These Definitions form the first of the three kinds distinguished in Anal. Post. ii. 10. 4. Ἔστιν ἄρα ὁρισμὸς εἷς μὲν λόγος τοῦ τί ἐστιν ἀναπόδεικτος. These Definitions are assumed prior to all demonstration[s], and are real, inasmuch as the existence of the objects is assumed with them. The ground of the assumption will vary according to the nature of the object to be defined[t].

With regard to the third class of Definitions, described as τῆς τοῦ τί ἐστιν ἀποδείξεως συμπέρασμα, Commentators

---

But to support this interpretation requires considerable straining of Aristotle's language.

q Tristram Shandy, vol. iii. ch. 41. see also Rabelais, liv. 1. ch. 40.

r Metaph. vi. 17. 2. τὸ μὲν οὖν διὰ τί αὐτό ἐστιν αὐτό, οὐθέν ἐστι ζητεῖν.

s Anal. Post. ii. 9. 1. ὥστε δῆλον ὅτι καὶ τῶν τί ἐστι τὰ μὲν ἄμεσα καὶ ἀρχαί εἰσιν, ἃ καὶ εἶναι καὶ τί ἐστιν ὑποθέσθαι δεῖ ἢ ἄλλον τρόπον φανερὰ ποιῆσαι.

t Metaph. x. 7. 2. Λαμβάνουσι δὲ τὸ τί ἐστιν αἱ μὲν [ἐπιστῆμαι] διὰ τῆς αἰσθήσεως αἱ δ' ὑποτιθέμεναι· διὸ καὶ δῆλον ἐκ τῆς τοιαύτης ἐπαγωγῆς ὅτι τῆς οὐσίας καὶ τοῦ τί ἐστιν οὐκ ἔστιν ἀπόδειξις.

are at issue, whether they are to be regarded as nominal, or as imperfect real definitions^u. The question is of the less importance, inasmuch as Aristotle elsewhere condemns the use of such definitions altogether^x. The weight of authority is perhaps with the latter interpretation. But, judging merely from the text of Aristotle, the former seems far simpler and more natural^y.

From the above statement it would appear that Nominal Definition, according to Aristotle, is one in which there is no evidence of the existence of objects to which the definition is applicable. In form it need not necessarily differ from a Real Definition. There may be a quasi-genus and a quasi-difference, as if we defined a centaur, " an animal with the upper parts of a man and the lower parts of a horse;" but, until we have ascertained the existence of creatures possessing these characteristics, the definition is only one of the signification of a name^z.

^u Of the former opinion are Averroes and Zabarella, who are followed by M. St. Hilaire in his Translation of the Organon. The latter is maintained by the Greek Commentators, by Pacius, and in the recent Essays by Rassow and Kühn.

^x See De Anima, ii. 2. 2.

^y The decision partly depends on the interpretation of a doubtful passage, Anal. Post. ii. 8. 4. τὸ δ᾽ εἰ ἔστιν ὅτὲ μὲν κατὰ συμβεβηκὸς ἔχομεν, ὅτὲ δ᾽ ἔχοντές τι αὐτοῦ τοῦ πράγματος. The instances which follow may refer either to the one or to the other.

^z It may be questioned whether the *name* Nominal Definition is sanctioned by Aristotle. Trendelenburg indeed (Elementa, §. 55.) so renders the λόγος ὀνοματώδης of An. Post. ii. 10. 1. and the interpretation, if correct, would seem to shew that Nominal, as well as Real Definitions must be *sentences;* but the context, λόγος τοῦ τί σημαίνει τὸ ὄνομα ἢ λόγος ἕτερος ὀνοματώδης, seems rather to mean, " a sentence explanatory of the signification of a name, or of another sentence having the force of a name." On the other interpretation, the word ἕτερος is superfluous, and the example, οἷον τὸ τί σημαίνει τί ἐστιν ἢ τρίγωνον, unintelligible. By λόγος ὀνοματώδης is therefore meant a sentence whose signification, like that of a single noun, is *one.* Such are all real Definitions, of which the example is a specimen. See De Int. 5. 2. Metaph. vi. 4. 16. vi. 12. 2. vii. 6. 2. Alex. Schol. p. 743. a. 31. In the Greek Commentators, on the other hand, λόγος ὀνοματώδης is clearly used for Nominal Definition. See Philop. Schol. p. 244. b. 31.

There is also no warrant in Aristotle for limiting the means by which Nominal Definition may be effected; as is done by those Logicians who specify synonyms and etymologies. The latter method indeed seems to have trespassed on the domain of Logic from that of Rhetoric. Nor has it the slightest connection with the former, save by an ambiguity of language. The etymology will in nine cases out of ten declare, not the present meaning of the word, but either one that has become obsolete, or some secondary notion, which may account for the imposition of the name, but which at no time formed, strictly speaking, any part of its signification. This holds equally of real objects and imaginary. It is only by an equivocation that "bull-piercer" can be assigned as the *meaning* of "centaur," or the notions of a swine and a quickset fence be combined into that of "hedgehog."

Definition by synonym, on the other hand, may be one of the means of explaining the signification of a name; though relatively only, and from the accidental circumstance of one word being more familiar to the hearer than another; in which respect all translations from one language into another are equally nominal definitions. It is not, however, specially mentioned by Aristotle[a]. As a real definition it is obviously inadmissible, as it neither assigns the cause of a phenomenon nor developes the contents of a notion.

The above data will also furnish us with an answer to a question, which, latterly at least, has been a sore puzzle to the tiro in Logic. What are the limits of Definition? If all real Definition must be by Genus and Differentia,

---

[a] Synonyms are expressly denied to be real Definitions in the proper sense by Aristotle, Top. I. 5. 1. though admitted to be ὁρικά. As Nominal Definitions, they are allowed by Alexander on Metaph. vi. 4. p. 442. ed. Bonitz; but the genuineness of this portion of the Commentary has been questioned.

the object defined must in every case be a *Species*. Summa Genera and Individuals are in that case alone indefinable. And for this limitation, the authority of Aristotle may be cited. On the other hand, Locke[b] assures us that this restriction is erroneous, and that *Simple Ideas* alone are incapable of Definition[c]. The dispute may be reduced to a mere verbal question. For Aristotle does not maintain that all Definitions must be by Genus and Differentia, but only those of Substances. In the passages which seem to extend this rule, Definition is used in the narrow sense which has been previously mentioned[d]. For it is obvious, to take the instances adduced above, that " quenching" cannot be called the genus of " thunder," or " interception" of " eclipse," in the same

[b] Essay, b. iii. 4. 7. But Locke has in this matter been anticipated by Descartes, Princip. i. 10. Sir W. Hamilton (Reid's Works, p. 220.) maintains that Aristotle has said the same thing. It is dangerous to dispute any thing which a man of Sir William's learning professes to have discovered in so wide a field as Aristotle, especially as he gives no references; but if the passage alluded to be Metaph. vi. 17. 7. one might be tempted to hazard a different interpretation. Τὰ ἁπλᾶ seem rather to be the elements, (ἁπλᾶ σώματα, Met. vii. 1. 2.) which have not, like compound substances, received a definite form, and thus are not definable. Cf. Plato, Theæt. p. 205. c. But the words are not sufficiently decisive to furnish much ground for any theory. A more remarkable passage occurs in Occam's Logic, Pt. i. ch. 23. " Ex prædictis sequitur quod nulla intentio quæ est præcise communis rebus simplicibus carentibus compositione ex materia et forma habet differentias essentiales; quia non habet partes, quamvis possit habere multas differentias accidentales. Ex illo sequitur ulterius quod nulla species quæ est præcise simplicium est definibilis definitione proprie dicta, sive sit in genere substantiæ sive in quocunque alio prædicamento." This, coupled with Occam's Conceptualist theory of Universals, is not very different from Locke's position concerning Simple Ideas.

[c] By Simple Ideas, Locke meant all ideas derived immediately from sensation or reflection. In the formation of these the mind is wholly passive, whereas in the formation from them of Complex Ideas, it is active. Among Simple Ideas derived from sensation, he enumerates solidity, space, figure, rest, and motion; from reflection, perception and volition; from both, pleasure and pain.

[d] As, for example, Topics, i. 8. 3. Compare Metaph. vi. 4. 12, 16. vi. 5. 5. and Alex. in Metaph. p. 442. 30. ed. Bonitz.

sense as " animal" is of "man." Whereas Locke's simple
ideas are exclusively ideas of attributes. By reference
then to Aristotle's account of the latter, it will plainly
appear that he and Locke mean two very different things
by Definition. With the former, it is an investigation
of the objective cause of a phenomenon; with the latter,
an analysis of the subjective impression which that
phenomenon produces in the mind. The *idea* of an
interception of light is not part of the *idea* eclipse, but
the one phenomenon is the physical antecedent and
cause of the other. Inquiries of this kind are still
classed among the most important problems of Physical
Science. What, for example, is light? Is it a succession
of material particles, or the undulations of an elastic
medium? The solution of this question would not be
a Definition in Locke's sense of the word; i. e. it would
not be an analysis of the idea of light produced in the
mind by sensation. The same may be said of colour.
The mental sensation of whiteness or redness is altogether
unaffected by the researches of Optics. The external
cause of colour, regarded as a quality of bodies, falls
directly within the province of the Science°. The determination of such problems will be, in Aristotle's sense
of the term, Definition.

This may be further illustrated by reference to a discussion of Aristotle's which few probably have perused
for the first time, without considering it as singularly
vague and unsatisfactory. I mean the dissertation on
Pleasure, in the tenth Book of the Nicomachean Ethics.
We are struck with the absence of any thing like a
Definition or Analysis of the emotion; and a reader who
commences the study of the book with some previous
knowledge of Locke's theory of Simple Ideas, will
probably be disposed to regard it as an attempt to define

° Compare on this subject, Reid, Inquiry, ch. vi. sect. 5.

that which is incapable of definition, and which in consequence necessarily involves its own failure. The same may be said of the principal opinion which Aristotle controverts. Whether we regard Pleasure, with Plato, as consisting in a motion towards a natural state of harmony, or with Aristotle, in the perfect exercise of a power; neither of these can be termed an explanation of the feeling itself, but only of the cause by which it is produced. Pleasure itself remains an indefinite something, consequent on the one or the other. Yet examined according to Aristotle's own view of the definition of attributes, we see that pleasure is as fairly defined by the perfection of the exercise of power, as an eclipse by the interception of light[f].

There are, however, conditions and limits to the definitions of Attributes, though they are not the same as those of Substances. Every Substance to be definable must be a *Species*. Every Attribute must be a *Property*, i. e. must be capable of demonstration by its cause. Accidents then, as merely contingent attributes, are incapable of definition. This limitation, however, is merely relative to the degree of our knowledge of the matter. The advance of Science may transform Accidents into Properties, and thus furnish the requisite means of definition.

Before concluding the subject, it will be necessary to say a few words on two other points connected with Aristotle's doctrine of Definition.

---

[f] Leibnitz adopts the same view as Aristotle, observing that pleasure admits of a *causal*, though not of a *nominal* definition. *Nouveaux Essais*, ii. 21. §. 46. In another point of view, simple ideas admit of a definition by logical analysis; viz. when they are considered, not as phenomena presented to the sense, to be resolved into simpler sensible phenomena, but as concepts, or general notions, representative of objects of thought, to be resolved into simpler concepts. On this distinction I have remarked elsewhere. See *Prolegomena Logica*, p. 45. (2nd ed. p. 53.)

The first of these is his method of investigating, or, as he terms it, *hunting for*, the Definition. This may be effected in two ways, commonly called the methods of Division and Induction. The first of these consists in taking a wide Genus, under which the object to be defined is evidently included, and contracting it by the addition of successive differentiæ, till we obtain a complex notion coextensive with that of which the Definition is sought. Of the notion thus obtained, each separate part is more extensive than that which is to be defined, though the whole is not so[g]. A good example of this method is given by Cicero: "Sic igitur veteres præcipiunt: cum sumseris ea, quæ sint ei rei, quam definire velis, cum aliis communia, usque eo persequi, dum proprium efficiatur, quod nullam in aliam rem transferri possit. Ut hoc, Hereditas est pecunia. Commune adhuc: multa enim genera sunt pecuniæ. Adde quod sequitur: quæ morte alicujus ad quempiam pervenit. Nondum est definitio: multis enim modis sine hereditate teneri mortuorum pecuniæ possunt. Unum adde verbum, jure: jam a communitate res disjuncta videbitur, ut sit explicata definitio sic: Hereditas est pecunia, quæ morte alicujus ad quempiam pervenit jure. Nondum est satis; adde, nec ea aut legata testamento, aut possessione retenta: confectum est[b]."

---

[g] Anal. Post. ii. 13. 3. Τὰ δὴ τοιαῦτα ληπτέον μέχρι τούτου, ἕως τοσαῦτα ληφθῇ πρῶτον, ὧν ἕκαστον μὲν ἐπὶ πλεῖον ὑπάρξει, ἅπαντα δὲ μὴ ἐπὶ πλέον· ταύτην γὰρ ἀνάγκη οὐσίαν εἶναι τοῦ πράγματος. Yet in the Metaphysics (vi. 12.) he seems to maintain that the last differentia must be coextensive with the subject; a view generally adopted by the Scholastic Logicians, though manifestly inconsistent, not only with the passage above quoted, but with the example appended, τὸ δὲ τελευταῖον καὶ τῇ δυάδι. In the Metaphysics however he seems to be speaking, not of the specific difference *per se*, but of the difference regarded as dividing the genus. But this is in fact equivalent only to saying that the whole must be coextensive; which no one would think of denying.

[b] *Topica*, c. 6. Cf. Clem. Alex. *Strom.* l. viii. c. 6.

This method was a favourite with Plato: it was rejected as useless by Speusippus[1]. Aristotle adopts an intermediate course, limiting, however, its utility chiefly to two points,—the right arrangement of the several parts of the Definition, and the security that nothing essential is omitted. It would thus seem to be useful, not so much for *discovering* Definitions as for *testing* them[j]; and even in this respect will be applicable only to one class of Definitions, that of Substances by genus and differentiæ.

For discovery, the second method is employed. This is commonly called the Inductive Method; a name, however, not sanctioned by Aristotle himself[k]. It consists in examining the several individuals of which the term to be defined is predicable, and observing what they have in common. If we can obtain one common notion, this is the Definition sought; if not, the object of inquiry is not one but many. This method is equally applicable to Substances and to Attributes, though Aristotle only gives an example of the latter,—the definition of magnanimity, gained by examining into the actions of different magnanimous persons.

Another important remark of Aristotle's is, that although, as we have already seen, demonstration, in certain cases, must always precede definition, yet no definition, as such, can be proved. This he maintains at some length (against Xenocrates[l]), in Anal. Post. i. 4. and shews that

---

[1] See Scholia, p. 179. b. 40. 248. a. 11.

[j] This is perhaps marked by Aristotle's own language. In reference to the one method, he uses κατασκευάζειν; to the other, ζητεῖν.

[k] Aristotle does not give any name to the process: by his Commentators it has been variously denominated the method of Resolution, of Composition, of Induction. See Sir W. Hamilton, *Discussions*, p.178. Zabarella, Logic, p. 1212. Pacius on Anal. Post. ii. 13. 21.

[l] Scholia, p. 242. b. 35. Trendelenburg, in Arist. de An. p. 273. Kühn, de Notionis Definitione, p. 11.

every attempt at such demonstration necessarily involves a *petitio principii*. The reason is obvious: since a definition can be predicated essentially (ἐν τῷ τί ἐστι) of nothing but that of which it is a definition; and since, to prove a conclusion concerning the essence, the premises must be of the same character; the middle term assumed must be identical with the minor, and the major premise with the conclusion.

Such is Aristotle's theory of Definition. Its fundamental principle may still, *mutatis mutandis*, be retained, notwithstanding that the speculations of modern philosophy have considerably modified his distinction of Substances and Attributes. Properly speaking, indeed, all Definition is an inquiry into *Attributes*. Our complex notions of Substances can only be resolved into various Attributes, with the addition of an unknown *substratum* :—a something to which we are compelled to regard these Attributes as belonging[m]. *Man*, for example, is analysed into Animality, Rationality, and the something which exhibits these phenomena. Pursue the analysis, and the result is the same. We have a something corporeal, animated, sensible, rational. An unknown constant must always be added to complete the integration; unfortunately we have no means of determining its value. Still, this does not affect the basis of the Aristotelian distinction. For some phenomena can be accounted for by other phenomenal causes: in others, we must acquiesce in the conviction that they are so, merely because they are. It is clearly impossible for the mere hypothesis of an unknown substratum to explain the reason of all the variety of attributes which different objects exhibit.

One further question remains. How far Definition properly belongs to the province of Logic, was, as we

[m] Cf. Locke, Essay, book ii. ch. 23.

have seen, an early point of dispute among the School-men[n]. On this question the authority of Aristotle is of little avail for either side. That his treatment of the subject has far more of a material than a formal character is undeniable. And to those who maintain that the Organon of Aristotle is designed as a systematic treatise on a single subject called Logic, such testimony must be decisive as regards both the material character of much of the Science, and its inclusion of Definition. But then it remains, and probably will continue to remain, a problem, to frame a conception of Logic adequate to the province thus assigned to it. This question has been already treated of in the Introduction, and need not be repeated here. It is sufficient to say that, as far as any evidence is furnished, either by the writings of Aristotle himself or by external testimony as to their original connexion, it is no more a departure from the authority of the Stagirite to assign a field to Logic incom-mensurate with that of the Organon, than it is to write a moral treatise on the basis of the Ethics, without including the Politics. Leaving then the question of authority, we may fairly assert that Logic as a formal Science can take no cognisance of the following points.

I. It has nothing to do with determining the physical existence of attributes in their subjects; which is in fact an inquiry into the *material truth* of the propositions in which such attributes are predicated. It is true that such propositions are by Aristotle considered as the con-clusions of Syllogism, and so far their truth is merely formal. But it must be remembered, that no attribute can be syllogistically demonstrated of one subject, with-out being in the premise asserted of another; and it is upon the material truth of the latter proposition that the

[n] See p. 40, note o.

certainty of the former, and the demonstrative character of the whole reasoning, ultimately depends.

II. Logic has nothing to do with testing the material *correctness* of a definition, i. e. ascertaining how far the notions developed in our analysis of a given concept correspond to the principal phenomena exhibited by the objects usually included under that concept; nor even with the inquiry, whether our usage of terms corresponds with the ordinary language of others.

III. Still less does it lie within the province of Logic to perform the functions either of a Dictionary or of an Index to Physical Science; to convey, that is, information from without, whether concerning the meaning of words or the nature of things, into a mind previously ignorant. Whereas, from the statements of some Logicians, one might almost imagine that they regarded their Science as furnishing, as it were, Logarithmic Tables of things in general; Catalogues of Genera and Differentiæ, to which we have only to refer any given object, to obtain full information concerning it°.

These being excluded, the only office that remains for Logic to perform, is to contribute to the *distinctness* of a given concept, by an analysis and separate exposition of the different parts contained within it. This operation is

---

° Thus Melanchthon, *Erotemata Dialectices*, p. 109. ed. 1568. " Cum quærimus definitionem inspiciuntur tabulæ prædicamentorum. Unde disces an res, de qua dicturus es, sit substantia an accidens. Et si est accidens, in qua parte sit, in corpore an in anima, &c." And so Keckermann, *Syst. Log. Min.* lib. i. cap. 17. " In hunc enim usum istæ rerum tabulæ et delineationes præcipue illic adumbrantur, ut definitum quæratur, simulque animo lustretur, quid ex parte superiori proxime definito adjaceat: id enim erit ejus Genus: e. g. cupio conficere definitionem Hominis: cogito ergo primum in quo . prædicamento sit. Homo, et deprehendo ex notis Substantiæ, esse in prædicamento Substantiæ: quocirca tabulam hujus prædicamenti perlustrans animo, deprehendo hominem proxime collocari sub animali: hinc concludo hoc esse proximum ejus genus. Sic in aliis proceditur definitis per singula prædicamenta."

analogous to that of drawing formal inferences, *virtually* contained in their premises, though not explicitly developed[p]. It is a process of self-examination, not dissimilar to the Platonic application of Dialectic, though widely differing as regards the objective truth of its results. For the Logical process furnishes only a subjective criterion: it enables us to represent more distinctly to the mind, the notions previously existing there in more or less confusion: its rules direct us to compare concepts one with another, and furnish some security for our own consistency in employing them; but they do not enable us to ascertain their accordance with external objects, or to add the deficient parts, where they are inadequate representatives of the latter. The mind, like the sky, has its nebulæ, which the telescope of Logic may resolve into their component stars. But here the parallel ceases. The Logical instrument discovers no luminary whose rays have not previously entered the eye; it tells us nothing of their relative distances, of the velocity with which their light travels; of any thing, in short, which did not form a confused portion of the sensuous representation[q]. This may seem but beggarly service to be performed by the Art of Arts and Science of Sciences. Inferior certainly it is to the gigantic purposes which more than one Logical Titan has essayed to accomplish with the same instrument. But let not its legitimate uses be contemned, because it has abated somewhat of the "vaulting ambition which o'erleaps itself." It furnishes the mould by which the ever-accumulating matter of consciousness is reduced to form and consistency: it were ungrateful to despise it, because it does not also dig the metal itself from the mine.

[p] Cf. Anal. Post. i. 24. 11.   [q] Cf. Kant, Logik, Einleitung. V.

Note D.

ON MATERIAL AND FORMAL CONSEQUENCE.

A MATERIAL CONSEQUENCE is defined by Aldrich to be one in which the conclusion follows from the premises solely by the force of the terms. This in fact means, from some understood Proposition or Propositions, connecting the terms, by the addition of which the mind is enabled to reduce the Consequence to logical form. This is easily seen, both in Aldrich's example, " Homo est animal, Ergo est vivens," and in the rather more complicated instance given by Sanderson, " Socrates est risibilis, ergo, Aliquis homo est rationalis." The latter, when the necessary conditions are supplied, is expanded into two syllogisms.

> Omne risibile est rationale ;
> Socrates est risibilis,
> Ergo, Socrates est rationalis.
> Socrates est homo,
> Ergo, Aliquis homo est rationalis.

The failure therefore of a Material Consequence takes place when no such connexion exists between the terms as will warrant us in supplying the premises required : i. e. when one or more of the premises so supplied would be *false*. But to determine this point is obviously beyond the province of the Logician. For this reason, Material Consequence is rightly excluded from Logic.

Moreover, even where true premises can be added, and the Consequence legitimately deduced, we cannot, except from knowledge of the matter, determine into what form the reasoning will naturally fall. In some cases, as in the example above quoted from Sanderson, the proof may be given in categorical syllogisms. In others, it is far more naturally exhibited in the hypothetical form. A hypothetical premise is sometimes the only materially allowable assumption in cases where the given antecedent and consequent have both terms distinct. E. g. A is B, therefore C is D. We may supply, If A is B, C is D; but to determine the truth of the assumed proposition, whether it be hypothetical or categorical, does not fall within the province of the Logician. It may be questioned, however, whether the mere assumption of a hypothetical premise can make a material consequence formal. See below, Note I.

Among these material, and therefore extralogical, Consequences, are to be classed those which Reid adduces as cases for which Logic does not provide; e. g. "Alexander was the son of Philip, therefore Philip was the father of Alexander;" "A is greater than B, therefore B is less than A." In both these it is our material knowledge of the relations "father and son," "greater and less," that enables us to make the inference.

Another of Reid's examples is the following: "A is equal to B, and B is equal to C, therefore A is equal to C." This reasoning is elliptical, and therefore, *as it stands*, material; though, owing to the suppressed premise being self-evident, its deficiency is apt to be overlooked. Stated in logical form, the syllogism runs thus:

Things that are equal to the same are equal to each other;
A and C are equal to the same,
Therefore A and C are equal to each other*.

Another example of the same kind is that sometimes called reasoning *a fortiori*. E. g. "A is greater than B,

* Hamilton on Reid, p. 702.

and B is greater than C, therefore *a fortiori* A is greater than C." The logical form is,

> Whatever is greater than a greater than C is greater than C ;
> A is greater than a greater than C,
> Therefore A is greater than C.

Or if it be required that the *a fortiori* nature of the reasoning appear in the conclusion, we must state the major, " Whatever is greater than a greater than C is greater than C *by a greater difference*."

Of the same kind is the reasoning " A is equal to B, therefore twice A is equal to twice B." The logical form is,

> The doubles of equal things are equal ;
> Twice A and twice B are doubles of equal things,
> Therefore they are equal.

The major premise might be stated more generally, " Equimultiples of equal things are equal."

NOTE E.

IS THE SYLLOGISM A PETITIO PRINCIPII[a]?

The eagle of the Libyan fable was killed by an arrow feathered from his own wing. The armoury of the Logician has been fondly imagined to contain the fatal weapon of his own destruction. But the champion destined to wield it, if such there be, is somewhat tardy in his forthcoming. More than one Sir Kay has essayed the adventure of the sword; the Arthur destined to achieve it remains in all the mysterious dignity of a Coming Man. In other words, many writers have succeeded in shewing their own ignorance of the nature of the fallacy called Petitio Principii[b]: they have not been equally successful in proving the invalidity of the Syllogistic process.

Let us first endeavour to ascertain what the Petitio Principii really is. The name is a blundering translation of the Aristotelian τὸ ἐν ἀρχῇ (or τὸ ἰξ ἀρχῆς) αἰτεῖσθαι: i. e. the assumption, not of the *principle* properly so called[c], but, in some form or other, of the *question originally* proposed for proof. And it is remarkable, that

---

[a] This charge against the syllogism may be traced back as far as Sextus Empiricus. See *Pyrrh. Hyp.* II. 195.

[b] Of the numerous absurdities gravely propounded by Logicians in relation to this fallacy, perhaps the happiest is the exquisite etymology of Du Marsais, *Logique*, p. 81. " Ce mot s'appelle *pétition de principe*, du mot grec πέτομαι, qui signifie *voler vers quelque chose*, et du mot latin *principium*, qui veut dire *commencement;* ainsi faire une *pétition de principe*, c'est recourir en d'autres termes à la même chose que ce qui a d'abord été mis en question."

[c] " Without entering on the various meanings of the term Principle, which Aristotle defines, in general, *that from which any thing exists, is produced, or is known*, it is sufficient to say, that it is always used for that on which something else depends ; and thus both for an original *law*, and for an original *element*." Sir W. Hamilton, Reid's Works, p. 761. Cf. Arist. Metaph. IV. 1. 3.

among the five modes of this fallacy enumerated by Aristotle, one is in form not distinguishable from the legitimate Syllogism[d]. Selecting this variety, as that by which most of all the objection is to be sustained, we will proceed to examine its peculiarities.

In the first place, it is manifestly necessary to a *Petitio Quæsiti*[e], as the fallacy may more correctly be called, that there should be a question proposed for *proof*. And hence it was long ago acutely remarked by Petrus Hispanus, that such a fallacy cannot be committed in a Syllogism of *inference*[f]. If, that is, the truth of the premises is known beforehand, and the only question is, what may we infer *from them?* there is no necessity for *begging* or *assumption* of any kind. It is clear then, that not the Syllogism in general, but at most only one particular application of it, can beg the question.

But it may be answered, that the truth of such premises never can be ascertained, but by a previous induction embracing all particular cases, and that Syllogistic inference is therefore at least futile, since the conclusion drawn must be presumed to be already known. But this answer itself assumes what has never yet been satisfactorily proved, the dependence of all knowledge of Universals on Induction. If axiomatic principles can be acquired in any other way, one class of Syllogisms is at least exempt from the charge[g].

---

[d] Top. viii. 13. 2. Δεύτερον δὲ ὅταν κατὰ μέρος δέον ἀποδεῖξαι καθόλου τις αἰτῇσῃ, οἷον ἐπιχειρῶν ὅτι τῶν ἐναντίων μία ἐπιστήμη, ὅλως τῶν ἀντικειμένων ἀξιώσειε μίαν εἶναι.

[e] Pacius in Anal. Prior. ii. 16.

[f] "Sciendum quod hæc fallacia non impedit syllogismum inferentem, sed probantem, *et ita fallacia petitionis peccat contra syllogismum dialecticum in quantum dialecticus est.*" Summ. Log. Tract. vi.

[g] Kant's criterion of necessity as the sure characteristic of a cognition *a priori*, has not yet been refuted by those who refer all principles to Induction.

And even with respect to principles allowed to be inductive, the actual previous assumption of every possible instance is not necessarily implied. And it is here that an able defender of the Syllogism, Mr. Mill, has taken a low and inadequate ground, a ground too, inconsistent with his own subsequent analysis of the process of Induction. His defence in fact amounts to an abandoning of all formal reasoning. All reasoning, he tells us, is really from particulars to particulars. But in that case, all inference must depend upon the matter, and cannot be reduced to any general type. If, for example, I conclude that a man now living is mortal, solely from the premises, " A, B, and C, who are dead, were mortal, and this man resembles them in certain other attributes of humanity ;" I may, by an argument of precisely the same *form,* prove any given man to be six feet high, because A, B, and C, whom he resembles in the common attributes of humanity, were all of that stature.

This portion of the question resolves itself into the following. What do we mean when we assert that all men are mortal? Is it merely a concise mode of stating that Socrates and Plato possess this attribute, in common with a number of other individuals, *quos nunc perscribere longum est?* If so, to argue, " Socrates is one of the individuals above mentioned, therefore he is mortal," is, if not a *begging* of the question, at least a needless repetition of a previous statement.

But, in fact, the Universal Proposition means no such thing. It means that, by virtue of a certain established law, certain attributes, or groups of attributes, are always so united, that in whatever individuals we find the one, we may look upon them as an infallible mark of the other. A conviction of this kind however, as it can never be gained by any mere observation of particulars, so it need not presuppose a complete enumeration of them [b].

> " For, when one's proofs are aptly chosen,
> Four are as valid as four dozen."

To determine under what conditions such a conviction can be obtained, is a question requiring an analysis of the whole process of Induction. Such an analysis, in many respects most ably performed [i], will be found in the third book of Mr. Mill's Logic; but few I think can compare that part of the work with his earlier defence of the Syllogism, without admitting that the two presuppose different and inconsistent theories of the import of

---

[b] " Hinc jam patet, inductionem per se nihil producere, ne certitudinem quidem moralem, sine adminiculo propositionum non ab inductione, sed ratione universali pendentium; nam si essent et adminicula ab inductione, indigerent novis adminiculis nec haberetur certitudo moralis in infinitum. Sed certitudo perfecta ab inductione sperari plane non potest, additis quibuscunque adminiculis, et propositionem hanc : totum majus esse sua parte, sola inductione nunquam perfecte sciemus. Mox enim prodibit, qui negabit ob peculiarem quandam rationem in aliis nondum tentatis veram esse." Leibnitz, de Stylo Nizolii.

Mr. Mill's *adminicula* to Induction are certain canons stating the principles of the Method of Agreement, of Difference, &c. which, together with the whole law of universal causation, he makes dependent upon a *weaker* evidence than philosophical induction; *the inductio per enumerationem simplicem*. At the same time he enters his protest against " adducing, as evidence of the truth of a fact in external nature, any necessity which the human mind may be conceived to be under of believing it." His words, strictly taken, would on his own shewing destroy the evidence of our senses; for, according to the theory of perception adopted by himself and his favourite authority, Brown, sensations can only be regarded as states of mind, and the only reason we have for referring our internal consciousness to an external cause is, that by the constitution of our minds we are necessitated to do so. The admonition of Hooker is not quite obsolete even amid the lights of modern philosophy. " The main principles of Reason are in themselves apparent. For to make nothing evident of itself to man's understanding were to take away all possibility of knowing any thing. And herein that of Theophrastus is true, ' They that seek a reason of all things do utterly overthrow Reason.' " Eccl. Pol. i. 8. 5.

[i] His theory of Causation must however be excepted.

Universal Propositions. It will be sufficient, however, for my present purpose to observe that, unless the establishment of an Universal Proposition requires an explicit and conscious examination of every existing and also of every possible particular instance, no charge of Petitio Principii, or even of vain repetition, can be maintained against the Syllogism. Those who maintain the antecedent, abandon themselves to an absolute scepticism[k]; and against such, no defence of any source of human knowledge can or need be attempted.

With regard to the syllogism of *proof*, we may examine the question a little more closely. The Petitio Principii is a *material*, not a *formal* fallacy, and consists in assuming, in demonstration, a non-axiomatic principle as axiomatic, or in dialectic disputation, a non-probable principle as probable[1]. It does not affect the form of the reasoning; but depends on the selection of premises, when the syllogism is employed for the particular purpose of *proof*, demonstrative or dialectic. Those are guilty of it who do not adopt such premises as the laws of the two processes require; in the one case, propositions axiomatic or deducible from axioms; in the other, probable statements, sanctioned by the general opinion of mankind or the authority of eminent persons.

In reading Aristotle's account of this fallacy, it is evident that the whole point of the matter lies in the word αἰτεῖσθαι, or λαμβάνειν; and that the question to be asked is, not whether the premises virtually contain the con-

---

[k] Sed ea ratione prorsus evertuntur scientiæ, et Sceptici vicere. Nam nunquam constitui possunt ea ratione propositiones perfecte universales; quia inductione nunquam certus es, omnia individua a te tentata esse; sed semper intra hanc propositionem subsistes, omnia illa, quæ expertus sum, sunt talia; quum vera non possit esse ulla ratio universalis, semper manebit possibile, innumera, quæ tu non sis expertus, esse diversa." Leibnitz, de Stylo Nizolii.

[1] See Anal. Pr. ii. 16. Top. viii. 13.

clusion^m, but whether such premises can properly be said to be *begged,* or *assumed*ⁿ. It is clear then that *Petitio Principii* is not the fault with which the Syllogism is chargeable, unless it can be shewn that every statement of an Universal Proposition must be, in this sense of the term, *begging* or *assuming.* If there are any cases in which the assertion of such propositions depends on a warranted conviction, not on a gratuitous assumption, from whatever source that conviction may arise, such cases must be exempt from the charge of *Petitio Principii.*

And if there be any such cases, the opponents of the Syllogism have themselves unwittingly stumbled upon a fallacy cognate to that with which they taunt its

---

^m One class of reasonings are perhaps fairly chargeable with the fallacy. I allude to what are commonly called the *proper syllogisms* of the Ramists, which have two Singular Premises. In the first figure, it is evident that the conclusion is not one out of many inferences contained in the major premise, but the very same proposition stated in different language. The third figure is open to the same objection, but it may be allowed as an *ἔκθεσις* or expository instance—a process not reckoned by Aristotle as syllogistic. Proper syllogisms in the second figure are valid, and frequently serviceable; but when reduced to the first, (which Aristotle regards as a necessary test of validity,) the negative premise must be converted from singular to universal.

Nevertheless, as the Petitio Principii is a material, not a logical, fallacy, this does not furnish grounds for objecting to the convenient arrangement by which singular propositions are considered as in syllogism equivalent to universals. They may be regarded, in common with other cases of the same fallacy, as reasonings valid in form, but unsound from material circumstances.

The Proper Syllogisms, however, though a post-Aristotelian innovation, did not originate with Ramus. Aquinas expressly denies that both premises in a syllogism may be singular, and admits the *ἔκθεσις* as a non-syllogistic process, being an appeal to the senses, not to the reason. See Opusc. xlvii. init. Occam, on the other hand, virtually surrenders the whole principle, when he allows that the major premise in the first figure may be singular. Logic, p. iii. cap. 8.

ⁿ That axiomatic principles are not of this character, may be seen from Anal. Post. i. 10. 6. Οὐκ ἔστι δ᾽ ὑπόθεσις οὐδ᾽ αἴτημα, ὃ ἀνάγκη εἶναι δι᾽ αὐτὸ καὶ δοκεῖν ἀνάγκη.

defenders. For the *Petitio Principii* being in that case a particular misapplication of the syllogistic method, and postulating the latter as a condition of its practicability, they have inverted the relation of prior and posterior, and assumed *Petitio Principii* to be necessary to the existence of Syllogism.

But if, on the other hand, there are no such cases, and the Syllogism is in consequence henceforth to be banished from Philosophy, what do we gain in exchange? We reduce the Laws of Thought from necessary to contingent. We degrade certainty into probability, and can claim for that only a subjective validity. But until this latter hypothesis is proved, the Syllogism, whatever may be its errors or deficiencies, cannot be comprehended under any one of the fallacies *admitted to be such by the Logician.* And this is sufficient as a defence of his own consistency. His method may be an incorrect analysis of the laws of the reasoning process; it may be that there are no such laws at all. But of either of these positions the *onus probandi* lies with the assailants, not with the defenders of the Syllogism°. It is quite enough for the Logician, if he exhibits all that is generally considered valid reasoning in a syllogistic form. If any maintain that a simpler or better type is attainable, he waits with patience till they produce it. If all reasoning is fallacious, he may be contented to behold his theories fall in the general overthrow of all human knowledge. But, pending the decision of this question, he may leave

---

° To the charge of *Petitio Principii* which Campbell makes against the Syllogism, Archbishop Whately replies, that *it lies against all arguments whatever;* the Syllogism not being a distinct kind of argument, but any argument whatever, stated regularly and at full length. And this reply is substantially valid, even if we reject the Archbishop's mode of exhibiting Induction as a Syllogism in Barbara. For the objection of Campbell, if valid at all, lies against all formal reasoning; and logical Induction, in its true analysis, is equally formal with the Syllogism.

his adversaries their choice of one or the other horn of a dilemma.   If there are universal principles of truth not entirely dependent on sensation, the existence of such principles will warrant syllogistic inference.   If there are not, whatever be the value of our individual sensations, all inference from them, by induction, example, analogy, or any method whatever, is, in respect of objective certainty, worthless.

Note F.

ON THE ENTHYMEME.

THE Enthymeme is defined by Aristotle, συλλογισμὸς [ἀτελὴς] ἐξ εἰκότων ἢ σημείων. The word ἀτελὴς is now universally admitted to be spurious; and that upon abundantly sufficient evidence, both external and internal [a]. Externally, it is not countenanced by the best MSS. Internally, it is inconsistent with the ordinary language of Aristotle; with whom the *imperfect syllogism* signifies, not a Syllogism with one portion suppressed, but a Syllogism in the second or third figure, which is not immediately evident by the *dictum de omni et nullo*. The word is an interpolation, and a clumsy one, designed to accommodate Aristotle's definition to subsequent views of the nature of the Enthymeme, and made by a scribe not particularly well versed in Aristotelian phraseology.

The εἰκὸς and σημεῖον themselves are Propositions [b]; the former stating a *general probability*, the latter a *fact*, which is known to be an indication, more or less certain, of the truth of some further statement, whether of a single fact or of a general belief. The former is a proposition nearly, though not quite, *universal;* as, " Most men who

[a] For a full account of the evidence on this point, see Pacius on Anal. Pr. ii. 27. 8. and Sir W. Hamilton, *Discussions*, p. 154.

[b] As is stated, Anal. Pr. ii. 27. 1. and Rhet. i. 3. 7. In a looser sense, however, the terms εἰκός, σημεῖον, τεκμήριον, are often used for the Enthymemes drawn from each. The εἰκὸς is clearly regarded by Aristotle as a *general proposition*, employed as a premise. In the Rhetoric, i. 2. 15. he describes it as having the same relation to its conclusion as an universal to a particular. In another sense, any proposition may be called probable, which can *as a conclusion* be supported upon (morally) reasonable grounds; in which sense Anaximenes, or whoever was the Author of the *Rhetorica ad Alexandrum*, defines the εἰκός. (ch. 8. 4.)

P

envy hate:" the latter is a *singular* Proposition, which however is not regarded as a sign, except relatively to some other Proposition, which it is supposed may be inferred from it. The εἰκός, when employed in an Enthymeme, will form the *major premise* of a Syllogism such as the following:

> Most men who envy hate,
> This man envies,
>
> Therefore, This man (probably) hates.

The reasoning is logically faulty; for, the major premise not being absolutely universal, the middle term is not distributed.

The σημεῖον will form one premise of a Syllogism which may be in any of the three figures, as in the following examples:

Fig. 1.	Fig. 2.
All ambitious men are liberal;	All pregnant women are pale,
Pittacus is ambitious (Σ),	This woman is pale, (Σ),
Therefore, Pittacus is liberal.	Therefore, She is pregnant.

> Fig. 3.
> Pittacus is good (Σ)ᶜ,
> Pittacus is wise,
>
> Therefore, All wise men are good.

ᶜ In the first and second figures, the σημεῖον is clearly the *minor* premise; this alone being singular. In the third, as far as quantity is concerned, we may choose between both premises. It seems more natural however to prefer the major; because, in assigning a reason for our belief in a given proposition, we should naturally state a premise having either the same *predicate* or the same *subject;* not one in which the predicate of the premise is the *subject* of the conclusion. For example: Why do you believe Pittacus to be liberal? Because he is ambitious. Why do you believe wise men to be good? Because Pittacus is good. This is far more natural than to answer, " Because Pittacus is wise." The same consideration will furnish the data for interpreting an obscure passage in Anal. Pr. ii. 26. 5. which however it would exceed my present limits to attempt. The reader will find it rightly explained in a note to St. Hilaire's Translation, vol. ii. p. 341. with the exception that the syllogism may be more clearly stated in Cesare than in Camestres.

The Syllogism in the first figure is alone logically valid. In the second, there is an undistributed middle term : in the third, an illicit process of the minor.

The σημεῖον is defined by Aristotle, πρότασις ἀποδεικτικὴ ἀναγκαία ἢ ἔνδοξος; in which the words *necessary* and *probable* do not relate to the modal character of the Proposition in itself, but to the nature of its connexion with the Conclusion which it is adduced to prove ; i. e. to its *logical* validity when the other premise is added[d]; *without which addition, expressed or understood, there is no Enthymeme at all*[e].

But it may be thought that the above examples do not furnish a sufficient criterion for distinguishing between the two kinds of Enthymeme. If both premises *must be* mentally, and *may be* orally, supplied, before there is any Enthymeme at all, how are we to determine whether any given specimen is an instance of reasoning from a sign, or from a likelihood ? Why, for example, in the

---

[d] Rhet. i. 2. 17. Ἀναγκαῖα μὲν οὖν λέγω ἐξ ὧν γίνεται συλλογισμός. Cf. Anal. Pr. i. 1. 6. Συλλογισμὸς δέ ἐστι λόγος ἐν ᾧ τεθέντων τινῶν ἕτερόν τι τῶν κειμένων ἐξ ἀνάγκης συμβαίνει. Here *syllogism* is used in its strictest sense. From another passage in the Rhetoric (i. 2. 14.) it has sometimes been imagined that all σημεῖα are necessary, at least as *propositions*; and the σημεῖον has even been defined, " a proposition in necessary matter;" as if " necessary matter" were the proper province of Rhetoric. The interpretation however is too inconsistent with Aristotle's subsequent language to be tenable. The words in question, if properly belonging to this place, (the resemblance to Rhet. i. 2. 8. is suspicious,) must be so interpreted as to identify the necessary propositions with one class only of σημεῖα, the τεκμήρια. The reference to the Analytics I conceive to allude, not to the account of modal conclusions deduced from modal premises, but to the *necessary conclusiveness* of premises logically connected, as opposed to the more or less *probable conclusiveness* of illogical combinations. As a special reference, supply Anal. Pr. i. 27. 12.

[e] Anal. Pr. ii. 27. 4. Ἐὰν μὲν οὖν ἡ μία λεχθῇ πρότασις, σημεῖον γίνεται μόνον, ἐὰν δὲ καὶ ἡ ἑτέρα προσληφθῇ, συλλογισμός. The context shews that he is speaking of Syllogism only in the looser sense in which all Enthymemes are included.

instance given above, may we not call the fact that "this man envies," a *sign* that he hates, as well as the general statement a *likelihood?*   Does not the whole distinction depend on the question, which is the *stated,* which the *suppressed,* premise?

To this it may be replied, that Aristotle distinguishes the εἰκός and σημεῖον merely as propositions, and no where says that they may not be combined in the same syllogism. In the instance given, it *so happens* that the minor premise is a singular proposition, and may fairly be considered a *sign* of the conclusion.   But we might obviously employ a minor premise of another kind, such as, " All malignant men are envious;" in which case there is, properly speaking, no *sign* employed in the reasoning.   But this does not affect the distinction between the two *Propositions.*   A likelihood is such, *per se,*—a proposition stating a general truth, which we are at liberty to apply or not to particular cases.   A sign is a sign of something else,—a single fact stated as a proof of something further; which proof may, according to material circumstances, be logically or only *morally* conclusive.

Another question sometimes raised is, " If the Enthymeme has both premises supplied, how is it to be distinguished from the Dialectic Syllogism?"   To which it may be answered, that, taking the word Syllogism in its strictest sense, as a reasoning logically correct, the same argument may in different points of view be considered either as a Syllogism or an Enthymeme.   This is, of course, only the case with the τεκμήριον; the other specimens of the Enthymeme being logically invalid. The argumentation ἐκ τεκμηρίου is in this sense both an Enthymeme and a Syllogism;—an Enthymeme on material grounds, inasmuch as its premise is a *sign* of its conclusion;—a Syllogism on formal grounds, inasmuch as it complies with the conditions of logical reasoning. It is a Dialectic Syllogism, if employed for the purpose of dialectic disputation; and, as it usually relates to those subjects to which dialectic disputation is practically applied[f], it may in general be regarded as, potentially at least, dialectic[g].

In fact, it is not as an Enthymeme, but as a *Rhetorical Syllogism*, that a given specimen of reasoning is distinguished from the Dialectical. The object of the two arts is distinct. That of Dialectic is to convince the Intellect; that of Rhetoric, to persuade the Will. The same instrument may be employed by both, and it is merely the purpose for which it is employed that constitutes the distinction between them[h]. Whether the same means are always available for both purposes; whether the same informality of reasoning is allowed in Dialectic as in Rhetoric, must depend on the conditions by which the disputants in the former choose to bind themselves. The Rhetorician has to influence an audience: if he can effect this, he will not always be scrupulous about

---

[f] This, however, is by no means necessary. Matters not usually discussed either by the Dialectician or Orator may equally be proved by means of τεκμήρια. For example; the falling of the thermometer to 32° is a *sign* of freezing; the obscuration of the moon in eclipse is a *sign* that the earth's shadow is interposed between it and the sun. Such subjects are not *practically* dialectical, at least in Aristotle's view of the art. As far as the mere interrogatory form is concerned, it may be, and was by different Philosophers, applied to all varieties of matter.

[g] This proceeds on the supposition that the Dialectician is bound to logical accuracy in his reasonings; a restriction which Aristotle at least would regard as salutary. See Anal. Post. i. 6. 10. We need not however suppose that all disputants actually conformed to it.

[h] Cf. Crakanthorpe, Logic, lib. v. cap. 1. "Utrique Disciplinæ hoc commune est, quod doceat probabiliter arguere: finem vero diversum uterque sibi proponit. Quoniam ergo eâdem omnino formâ probabiliter arguendi uterque utitur, nos hic quod utrisque commune est tractabimus, unicuique liberum relinquentes, an Dialecticus esse velit, et uti hac formâ probabiliter arguendi *ad verum inveniendum;* an Rhetor, et uti eâdem formâ probabiliter arguendi *ad suadendum aut dissuadendum.*"

the logical accuracy of his reasoning. In Dialectic, two champions are opposed to each other : they may, before engaging, dictate the conditions of the combat.

As regards the account of the Enthymeme in the Prior Analytics, I am not aware that any further explanation is needed[1]. But in the corresponding chapters of the Rhetoric one or two difficulties remain, an elucidation of which, though not strictly within my present province, may perhaps be serviceable to the readers of the latter Treatise.

In Rhet. i. 2, 18. we are told, that when the Enthymeme is in the third figure, the σημεῖον is to its conclusion as a particular to an universal. In the second figure, on the other hand, as an universal to a particular. The relation in the first figure is not mentioned; but the context seems rather to connect it with the former than with the latter.

This passage may be interpreted in two ways. Either we may compare the conclusion of the Enthymeme with the σημεῖον itself, or with the major premise of that Syllogism whose minor is the σημεῖον. In the former interpretation the word σημεῖον is used properly for the *proposition;* in the latter widely, for the reasoning of which such proposition forms a portion.

If the first interpretation be adopted, (which seems preferable,) we must compare the two propositions relatively to that term in which they are unlike; i. e. if they have the same subject, we must compare their

---

[1] Except perhaps that Aristotle, in Anal. Pr. ii. 27., admits a σημεῖον in the second figure, which in the former chapter he condemned. The condemnation seems to be made on logical grounds. The *logical* value of two affirmative premises in the second figure is absolute zero; whereas the σημεῖον in the third figure, though faulty as employed to prove an universal conclusion, is valid for particulars. For rhetorical purposes, however, the second figure is also admissible; an accumulation of Enthymemes, all *logically* worthless, may amount to a *moral* certainty.

predicates; if they have the same predicate, we must compare their subjects.

According to this method, it will be seen, that in the first figure, the predicate of the sign is to that of its conclusion as part to whole, or as species to genus. Hence its logical validity: whatever subject is included under a species is necessarily included under its genus. But in the second figure the relation is that of whole to part, or of genus to species; and this is illogical, the whole genus not being included under one of its species.

But if we adopt the second interpretation, and compare the major premise with the conclusion, we shall be compelled in the first figure to compare together the two *subjects*, since both propositions have the same predicate. In this case the relation will be inverted; the premise being to the conclusion as an universal rule to a single instance. In the second figure, we are at liberty to compare either the quantity of the two propositions as determined by their subjects, or the extent of their respective predicates. In either case, however, the result is the same; the relation remaining that of universal to particular.

The Enthymeme in the third figure presents no difficulty. Whichever interpretation be adopted, the same proposition, " Pittacus is good," is compared with the conclusion, " All wise men are good." In both cases, the comparison lies between the two subjects, and the relation is that of particular to universal.

But perhaps the most difficult passage in this portion of the Rhetoric is that in which Aristotle describes an important, and previously, as he tells us, unnoticed distinction between various classes of Enthymemes. Some of these; he says, belong to Rhetoric, some to other arts and faculties. The same may be said of the connexion of the Syllogism with Dialectic. Dialectical or Rhetorical reasonings are founded on τόποι; the others on the peculiar principles of that Science or Art to which they belong[k].

This passage is generally found puzzling to a beginner on two accounts. Firstly, he is apt to fancy Dialectic synonymous with Logic, and to confound it with the formal Science of that name; an error which the Commentary most likely to fall in his way is not unlikely to confirm. Secondly, having previously seen the Enthymeme defined as the Rhetorical Syllogism; there seems some inconsistency in the subsequent observation, that some Enthymemes are Rhetorical, others not so.

In explanation it may be observed: First, that Dialectic and Rhetoric are not formal Sciences, but material Arts. Their Logic is not a *Logica docens,* treating of the general form of Reasoning, but a *Logica utens,* treating of Reasoning as applied to a particular matter. That matter is furnished by the τόποι. Rhetoric and Dialectic do not merely lay down the form in which their reasonings ought to proceed, but likewise provide certain general principles of probability, from which the matter of their major premises is to be drawn. These τόποι or common-places hold the same position in the Dialectic Syllogism, as the most universal kind of axioms in the Demonstrative. They are not gained by exclusive observation of any one particular class of objects belonging to this or that art or faculty, but are indifferently applicable to all. Such is the example quoted by Aristotle as ὁ τοῦ μᾶλλον καὶ ἧττον τόπος. Of this in the Topics he gives four cases, of which the following may be taken as a specimen. "If the more likely assertion on any subject be untrue, the less likely is probably untrue likewise." A general maxim of this

---

[k] Rhet. i. 2. 20, 21.

kind is obviously available περὶ δικαίων καὶ φυσικῶν καὶ περὶ πολιτικῶν, καὶ περὶ πολλῶν διαφερόντων εἴδει.

Secondly, it may be observed that the Enthymeme is not necessarily confined to the Rhetorical kind of matter. A syllogism from likelihoods or signs, whatever be the object, is an Enthymeme. In like manner, any syllogism in probable matter may become an instrument of Dialectic reasoning; whether it be based on the general probabilities which Dialectic materially furnishes, or on more limited assumptions drawn from special observations. The Physician, for example, within the field of his own experience, may know that in nine cases out of ten where a patient exhibits certain symptoms, the disease terminates fatally. The student of history may learn that in the majority of cases revolution leads to anarchy, and anarchy is suppressed by despotism. Either of these may become the basis of a reasoning process in probable matter; but the Syllogism or Enthymeme is not, properly speaking, Dialectical or Rhetorical, but Medical or Political. And although there is nothing in the Dialectical or Rhetorical Method that prevents its being applied to these or any other special subjects, yet in proportion as any one so applies it, Aristotle regards him as departing from the legitimate *matter* of Dialectic or Rhetoric, and adopting that of some definite Art or Science[1]. For the same reason, when he speaks of the special application of Rhetoric to Political deliberation, he warns us that its object matter must not be considered as that of Rhetoric *per se*, but as primarily and properly belonging to Politics, secondarily only to Rhetoric in one of its practical applications[m].

[1] Rhet. i. 2. 21. Ταῦτα δέ, ὅσῳ τις ἂν βέλτιον ἐκλέγηται τὰς προτάσεις, λήσει ποιήσας ἄλλην ἐπιστήμην τῆς διαλεκτικῆς καὶ ῥητορικῆς· ἂν γὰρ ἐντύχῃ ἀρχαῖς, οὐκέτι διαλεκτικὴ οὐδὲ ῥητορικὴ ἀλλ' ἐκείνη ἔσται ἧς ἔχει τὰς ἀρχάς.

[m] Rhet. i. 4. 4, 5.

A few words in conclusion on the origin of the name
Enthymeme. That its etymology is to be found in ἐν
and θυμὸς, is undeniable; but only in the same degree as
is also true of ἐνθυμεῖσθαι, ἐνθύμιος, and other cognate terms.
But that it has no special reference to a premise *in the
mind,* is evident; first, because θυμὸς in the Aristotelian
phraseology is not "the mind," and has nothing to do
with the expression or suppression of premises: secondly,
because the word ἐνθύμημα occurs in writers earlier than
Aristotle, and before it could have assumed its technical
meaning. To ascertain the true derivation, however, is
not so easy as to refute a palpably absurd one. If,
however, we were compelled to make a suggestion, the
following, though not confidently put forward, has at
least the merit of not being positively ridiculous. According to the analogy of words of the same termination,
such as φιλοσόφημα, ἐπιχείρημα, σόφισμα, &c. ἐνθύμημα will
properly signify the result of an act of reflection[n]. Hence
it is used by Sophocles for a *thought suggested* by a person
or thing[o], and by Xenophon[p], for a *plan designed,* opposed
to ἔργον, *the execution.* The term is thus naturally enough
applicable to the *suggestions* or *persuasive arguments* of
Rhetoric, as distinguished from the *demonstrations* of
Science.

[n] Cf. Melanchthon, *Erotem. Dial.* p. 187. ed. 1568. Enthymema significat
cogitationem seu quiddam cogitatum, ut nos dicimus, *Ein Bedenken.*

[o] *Œd. Col.* 292, 1199.

[p] *Anab.* iii. 5. 12. See also *Œcon.* 20. 24.

Note G.

ON INDUCTION.

Induction, as far as it is a Logical process at all, is equally formal with Syllogism; though proceeding in the inverse order; viz. from the aggregate of individuals to the universal whole constituted by them; instead of from the whole to the several individuals contained under it. It is defined by Aristotle, " proving the major term of the middle by means of the minor[a];" in which definition, the expressions *major*, *middle*, and *minor*, are used relatively to their *extension*, to designate respectively the attribute proved, the constituted species of which it is proved, and the aggregate of individuals by which the species is constituted. The form in which the Inductive Reasoning[b] naturally appears, exhibits an apparent, though not a real, resemblance to the *third* figure of Syllogism. Thus:

X, Y, Z, (minor,) are B (major);
X, Y, Z, are all A (middle); therefore,
All A is B.

The resemblance to the third figure is apparent only; the true distinctions being, 1. That in the minor premise of the Induction, the copula does not represent the subject as *contained under*, but as *constituting*, the predicate. 2. That in consequence of this distinction,

[a] Τὸ διὰ τοῦ ἐτέρου θάτερον ἄκρον τῷ μέσῳ συλλογίσασθαι. Anal. Pr. ii. 23. 2.
[b] In a loose sense, Aristotle calls it ὁ ἐξ ἐπαγωγῆς συλλογισμός, where the word does not denote the Syllogism proper, or reasoning from the universal whole to the contained parts, but is extended to formal reasoning in general. In like manner, in Rhet. ii. 25. 8. he speaks of the Enthymeme as including Example.

an universal conclusion is logically drawn in this form, which is not valid in the third figure of Syllogism.

We see then, that in the Inductive process the Copula is ambiguous, expressing in the major premise and in the conclusion, the relation of a contained part to a containing whole; in the minor premise, that of constituting parts to a constituted whole. This ambiguity has been remarked as a deficiency in technical language [c]; but there is no term sufficiently naturalized in Logic to serve as a substitute to express the latter relation.

On Induction, as exhibited above, it may be remarked,

I. That the distinction between a perfect and an imperfect Induction is extralogical. Logic recognises no inference that is not necessitated by the Laws of Thought: and therefore it must be presumed that the Induction is *perfect*, i. e. that the Individuals mentioned are in reality the whole constituents of the species, before the Inductive Inference can come in any way within the province of the Logician. To inquire what is the warrant for this presumption; to ask what amount of observation will warrant us in assuming X, Y, and Z, to be *all* the members of the class A; is like asking in syllogistic reasoning, how do we know that the premises are true? undoubtedly a most important question, but not to be answered by Logic. So also any compromise with material probability, any statement of the individuals as *samples* or *adequate representatives* of their class [d], is a surrender of the essential principle of Logical Reasoning: the parts *are* absolutely the whole; or the inference is, logically speaking, worthless.

It is manifest, however, that the Induction may be

[c] Edinburgh Review, No. 115. p. 229. (reprinted in Hamilton's *Discussions*, p. 168.) From this admirable Article the greater part of the materials for the present note have been derived.

[d] Whately's Logic, p. 260. (Sixth Edition.)

easily stated in such a form, as to transfer the material difficulty from the minor premise to the major; in which case the question may be satisfactorily answered by that Art or Science to which the Proposition materially belongs. Thus the example given by Aldrich might be stated as follows :

The magnets which I have observed, and also those which I have not observed, attract iron ;

The magnets which I have observed, and those which I have not observed, are all magnets ;

Therefore, All magnets attract iron.

In this mode of stating, the minor premise is undeniably true. The doubtful part of the major, relating to the properties of unobserved objects, must be determined by the analogies of the Science to which the objects belong, and by the *material* inquiry, what kind of samples or specimens will warrant our asserting of others what we have observed in them.

II. It is precisely in the mode of answering this material inquiry, that the whole difference lies between the ancient *Inductio per enumerationem simplicem*, and that Interpretation of Nature insisted upon by Bacon. The disciple of the former method, when asked, How do you know that other specimens of your class possess the same property as these? will reply, Because I have never seen one which does not possess it. The Baconian, on the other hand, will answer, Because I have selected such instances as give evidence of an universal law : I have examined those specimens of the class which have nothing in common, except the possession of the property in question : I have compared them with objects not possessing it, and I find its absence always accompanied by that of one of the essential attributes of this class[e].

[e] Bacon, Nov. Org. lib. ii. Aph. x sqq. xxii sqq.

A recent writer has exhibited the Inductive Method of Socrates as a specimen of that *Inductio per enumerationem simplicem* which the Baconian philosophy has superseded[f]. But it has been before observed that the Socratic reasoning is not properly *Induction,* but *Example.* It is inconclusive, not because it is an Induction by Simple Enumeration, but because it is no Induction at all. The Simple Enumeration, if complete, will form the basis of what, logically speaking, is a valid Induction ; and it is precisely because the Socratic Method does not pretend to completeness, that Logic does not recognise the inference. It is true that in Simple Enumeration this completeness is often difficult, sometimes impossible to attain. And it is the additional security on this point that constitutes the chief merit of the Baconian process. But this is a *material,* not a *logical,* merit. It affects our *ground of confidence* in the truth of certain propositions, not the *nature of the inference* from those propositions assumed to be true. Neither in Induction nor in Syllogism does the Organon of Bacon supersede that of Aristotle. "Each," as Sir W. Hamilton observes, " proposes a different end ; both, in different ways, are useful[g]." The ancient Philosopher considers " the laws under which *the subject* thinks ;" the modern, " those under which *the object* is to be known." The Induction of Bacon, as furnishing more accurate rules for physical investigation, may supersede the Induction of Socrates ; for the latter owes its validity solely to the *matter.* It cannot affect the Induction of Aristotle, of which the validity depends solely on the *form.*

The perversions of the Aristotelian Induction by Aldrich and Archbishop Whately have already been noticed. On this point it will be sufficient to observe, that any attempt

[f] Lewes, Biographical History of Philosophy, vol. i. p. 215.
[g] Reid's Works, p. 712.

to reduce Induction to Syllogism, in the strict sense of the term, must commence by inverting the whole operation; stating as a preliminary assumption that which is really the conclusion of the Inductive process. It moreover leaves us no alternative between converting mere empirical judgments into self-evident axioms, or destroying the whole foundation of reasoning, by commencing with a Syllogism whose premises themselves must be proved by another Syllogism, and so on *ad infinitum*.

The Aristotelian Induction proper has been described as an *analytical*, its counterpart, Syllogism, as a *synthetical* process; and the two have respectively been identified with the λόγοι ἐπὶ τὰς ἀρχὰς and ἀπὸ τῶν ἀρχῶν of Aristotle[b]. And this is in one sense correct, though, according to a various notion of whole and part, the terms Analysis and Synthesis have perpetually been interchanged with each other. According as we look to the *comprehension*, or to the *extension* of the notions, we may regard the Genus as a part of the Species, or the Species as a part of the Genus. Hence the notions of Synthesis and Analysis, of the composition of parts into a whole, and the resolution of a whole into parts, will, as we adopt the one or the other point of view, be inverted. We have previously spoken of Induction as an inference from the constituting parts to the constituted whole. In this respect it is *synthetical*, the parts and whole being viewed in their *logical* or *extensional* relation. In the same point of view, the Platonic method of division is sometimes called analytical[i]. On the other hand, in the ordinary modern use of the terms, Induction is analytical, adopting the *metaphysical* relation

---

[b] See Michelet in Eth. Nic. p. 25.
[i] Diog. Laert. iii. 24. Van Heusde, *Initia*, p. 261. Cousin, *Fragments Philosophiques*, I. p. 275. ed. 1847.

of part and whole as simpler or more complex notions. In this point of view, Division and Definition are respectively the Synthesis and Analysis of notions *as expressed in simple terms.* In the former, we combine Genus and Differentia into Species; in the latter, we resolve Species into Genus and Differentia. A similar relation exists between the processes of uniting Accidents to a Species, in distinguishing its several individuals, and abstracting the Specific notion from the Accidents, in the formation of Universals. Syllogism and Induction in like manner are respectively the Synthesis and Analysis of the same notions *when forming the subjects of a judgment.* For on examination of the first figure, which is the natural form of Syllogism, it will be seen, that it proceeds, by *division* of the middle term, to predicate of the several Species what was previously predicated of the Genus. Induction, on the other hand, in its natural form, proceeds by a process of *abstraction,* from the individuals constituting a Species to their common Species so constituted.

As regards the etymology of the name; both the Greek ἐπαγωγή, and its Latin equivalent *Inductio,* seem to have been originally applied with reference to the Socratic *accumulation* of instances to serve as an antecedent for establishing the required conclusion. The Platonic use of ἐπάγειν will support this view[k]. Such is also clearly the interpretation of Cicero. " Hoc in genere præcipiendum nobis videtur, primum, ut illud quod *inducemus* per similitudinem, ejusmodi sit, ut sit necesse concedi; nam ex quo postulabimus nobis illud quod dubium sit concedi, dubium esse idipsum non oportebit.

[k] Cratyl. p. 420. d. Ταῦτα ἤδη μοι δοκεῖς, ὦ Σώκρατες, πυκνότερον ἐπάγειν. Where Heindorf renders, " Confertius quam priora afferre, ita ut alterum alteri addas, in singulis nihil immorans." The substantive ἐπαγωγή has a very different sense in Plato; e. g. Rep. ii. p. 364. c. Leg. xi. 933. d. Cf. Ruhnken, Timæus.

Deinde illud cujus confirmandi causa fiet *Inductio,* viden-
dum est ut simile iis rebus sit, quas res, quasi non
dubias, ante *induxerimus*[l]." Quintilian, however, applies
the term rather to the *bringing in,* as an inference, of
the question to be proved. " Nam illa, qua plurimum
Socrates est usus, hanc habuit viam ; cum plura inter-
rogasset, quæ fateri adversario necesse esset, novissime
id, de quo quærebatur, *inferebat,* cui simile concessisset ;
id est inductio[m]." Another meaning of the Greek ἐπάγειν
and ἐπαγωγός, as well as of the Latin *inducere* and *inductio,* might seem to point rather to the persuading and
influencing the mind of the hearer[n]. But the first derivation is preferable. The question, however, as far as
Aristotle is concerned, is not of any great consequence.
For, as that Philosopher did not invent the name, but
only modified the usage of a term current among his
predecessors, the etymology will be of little service
towards illustrating the notion which he attached to it.

[l] *De Inventione,* i. 32.
[m] *Inst. Orat.* v. 11.
[n] Rod. Agric. *de Inv. Dial.* ii. 18. Melanchth. *Erot. Dial.* p. 188. Burgerdsd.
Inst. Log. ii. 11.

Note H.

ON EXAMPLE AND ANALOGY.

EXAMPLE is defined by Aristotle, "proving the major term of the middle by a term resembling the minor[a]." This definition is obscure, from being worded so as to contrast with his definition of Induction, in which the major term is proved of the middle by the minor. It does not apply to the singular conclusion ultimately established, but to the universal proposition which forms the conclusion of the inductive portion of the Example. Thus, if we expand Aristotle's instance into its complete form, composed of an imperfect induction and a syllogism, it will run thus:

> The war of the Thebans and Phocians (D) was an evil (A),
> The war of the Thebans and Phocians was a war between neighbours (B),
> ∴. All wars between neighbours are evil.
> A war between the Athenians and Thebans (C) is a war between neighbours.
> ∴. It is an evil.

In this reasoning there are four terms, A the major, B the middle, C the minor, D the ὅμοῖον. The definition applies to the third proposition, in which A is proved of B by means of D. If the final conclusion were taken into account, the Example might be more correctly defined as a reasoning in which the major term is proved of the minor by means of a middle, of which middle the major has been proved by a term resembling the minor.

---

[a] Παράδειγμα δ' ἐστὶν ὅταν τῷ μέσῳ τὸ ἄκρον ὑπάρχον δειχθῇ διὰ τοῦ ὁμοίου τῷ τρίτῳ.   Anal. Pr. ii. 24. 1.

Example differs from Induction in two principal points. 1. Induction enumerates all the individuals in the minor term, so as to constitute the middle: Example selects single instances. 2. Induction stops at the universal conclusion: Example proceeds to infer syllogistically a conclusion concerning another individual[b].

The Example, as thus exhibited, has no *logical* value as an independent reasoning. We are not warranted in assuming, as a necessary law of thought, that two things which resemble each other in *any one given quality* must likewise resemble each other in *any other*[c]. The reasoning may have more or less *material* weight, according to the character of the particular qualities compared, and to what we may empirically know of their connection with each other. It thus comes under the kind of evidence mentioned by Bishop Butler[d] as *probable;* which admits of degrees, and of all variety of them, from the highest moral certainty to the very lowest presumption. But degrees of evidence are inadmissible in Pure Logic. Either the conclusion necessarily follows from the admitted truth of the premises, or it does not. In the former case, all reasonings are in a logical point of view equally necessary; in the latter, all are equally worthless[e]. That the inference in Example is material, not formal, appears the instant we attempt to state it in symbolical form: e. g. A and B are both X, A is also Y, therefore B is Y. This reasoning has no force until we know the *matter*, i. e. what particular objects are signified by A and B, X and Y[f].

---

[b] Anal. Pr. ii. 24. 3.
[c] Cf. Hegel, Werke, vol. v. p. 151.
[d] Introduction to the Analogy.
[e] See Sir William Hamilton, *Discussions*, p. 159.
[f] Kant classes imperfect induction and analogy as *syllogisms of the judgment,* and describes them as furnishing a *logical presumption* of their con-

On the other hand, the Example has a strictly logical value, when it is used, not as an independent reasoning, but as an answer to objections. Thus it does not *logically* follow, because A and B are both X, and A is Y, that B is also Y. But the union of X and Y in the instance of A *logically* proves that X and Y are not incompatible with each other; that one X at least is Y; and therefore that the two attributes may coexist in the same subject. Hence the Example is logically valid against any reasoner who maintains that a thing cannot be Y, *because it is* X. But, in this case, the conclusion is not assertorial, "B *is* Y," but only problematical, "B *may be* Y."

The Example is sometimes loosely called reasoning from *Analogy*[s]. This term, however, properly belongs not to absolute similarity in any given quality, but only to similarity of relations. Thus Aristotle speaks of an *analogy* between sight and intellect, the one being related to the body as the other to the soul[h]. And the argument of Bishop Butler's *Analogy of Religion to the Constitution and Course of Nature* may be put into the same form. The difficulties in Religion, natural and revealed, have the same relation to their respective systems, that the difficulties in the course of nature have to the entire system of nature. If then the latter be admitted to proceed from a Divine Author, the difficulties in the two former are not a valid objection against a like origin. This reasoning from Analogy corresponds to what is sometimes called the Induction of Socrates, and to the παραβολὴ mentioned in Aristotle's Rhetoric[i]. Like the Example proper, it

clusion. But this classification ought to have excluded them from Formal Logic.

[s] See Reid, *Intellectual Powers*, i. 4. Mill, *Logic*, b. iii. ch. 20. Hoffbauer, *Logik*, §. 453. Krug, *Logik*, §. 168.

[h] *Eth. Nic.* i. 4. 12. Cf. Whately's Rhetoric, Appendix, note E.

[i] Παραβολὴ δὲ τὰ Σωκρατικά. *Rhet.* ii. 20. 4. Compare the reasoning of

has no logical value as an independent reasoning; its symbolical form being, A is to B as C to D; A is X, therefore C is X. Here it is evident that the premises may be true and yet the conclusion false. Its material value, like that of Example, may admit of any degree, from zero to moral certainty. Like Example too, it has a logical value as an answer to objections. Thus, in Butler's argument, the difficulties in Religion are not intended logically to prove its divine origin; but to shew, as is admitted by the antagonist in the case of the natural world, that the existence of difficulties does not furnish a logical argument against it.

Socrates, in the *Gorgias*, p. 460. with the criticism of Boethius, *de Syll. Cat.* lib. ii. *Opera*, p. 600.

NOTE I.

ON THE HYPOTHETICAL SYLLOGISM.

THAT the συλλογισμοὶ ἐξ ὑποθέσεως of Aristotle are not identical with those which, since the time of Theophrastus and Eudemus, have been received in Logic as Hypothetical Syllogisms, is now generally admitted[a]. The word *Hypothetical* is never by Aristotle opposed to *Categorical*, but to *Ostensive* (δεικτικός[b]); and he remarks that the *Syllogistic portion* of the reasoning in Hypothetical Syllogisms is ostensive, and requires no reduction; but that the determination of the original question is not effected by Syllogism at all, and cannot be exhibited in Syllogistic form. The meaning of this may be clearly explained by examples.

Of the Hypothetical Syllogism, two principal kinds are mentioned by Aristotle. One is the ἀπαγωγὴ εἰς τὸ ἀδύνατον: the other is a Syllogism of which the conclusiveness depends entirely on agreement between two contending parties, and which is therefore chiefly serviceable in dialectic disputation. The latter may be exhibited as follows.

The original question being to prove that some A is not B; the contending parties agree to the *hypothesis*, that if some A is not C, it is not B. The reasoning proceeds thus:

No X is C;
All X is A;   (συλλογισμὸς ἐξ ὑποθέσεως.)
Therefore, Some A is not C.

---

[a] We must except M. St. Hilaire, who professes to discover the ordinary Hypotheticals in Anal. Prior. i. 44. 1. But the text of Aristotle will hardly warrant the assertion. Cf. Sir W. Hamilton, *Discussions*, p. 152, (2d Ed.) *Lectures on Logic*, ii. p. 387. In the latter place, Sir W. Hamilton notices that Aristotle has himself described the process of reasoning commonly called hypothetical, but denies it to be a syllogism. See *Anal. Pr.* i. 32. 7.

[b] See Anal. Pr. i. 23. 2.

And then, *in consequence of the previous agreement, but not of the Syllogism,* it is allowed that some A is not B. The Syllogism in form is an ordinary Categorical in the third figure ; the Conclusion, however, not being the original question, but the antecedent of a Hypothetical Proposition, of which the question is the consequent[c].

The ἀπαγωγὴ εἰς τὸ ἀδύνατον is also Categorical, so far as it is Syllogistic. In this, the Conclusion syllogistically proved is a falsehood ; the original question being inferred only by Hypothesis, because a falsehood results from the assumption of its contradictory[d]. The *Hypothesis* in this case is, that the contradictory is true[e]. Thus, if it

[c] Ἐν ἅπασι γὰρ ὁ μὲν συλλογισμὸς γίνεται πρὸς τὸ μεταλαμβανόμενον, τὸ δ' ἐξ ἀρχῆς περαίνεται δι' ὁμολογίας ἤ τινος ἄλλης ὑποθέσεως. Anal. Pr. i. 23. 11. Τὸ μεταλαμβανόμενον is explained by Alexander as applying to the conclusion of the syllogism, because it is taken in a different manner from that in which it was originally enunciated ; being at first part of a conditional agreement, and afterwards a categorical conclusion. For this reason, the syllogism is said to be κατὰ μετάληψιν. Anal. Pr. i. 29. 5. Were it not for this authority, it would seem simpler to interpret μετάληψις merely "change of question ;" the disputant turning from the original question to the proof of another on which it is supposed to depend. The other kind of hypo-thetical syllogisms mentioned in the same passage, those κατὰ ποιότητα, seem to have been a kind of argument *a fortiori,* or *ab æquali,* the relation being assumed in the hypothetical premise. Thus Philoponus, in Anal. Pr. f. 74, b. explains : Κατὰ ποιότητα δὲ ἐκεῖνοι λέγονται ὅσοι ἐκ τοῦ μᾶλλον ἐπιχειροῦσιν ἢ ἐκ τοῦ ἧττον ἢ ἐκ τοῦ ὁμοίου .... οἷον ἐκ τοῦ μᾶλλον· εἰ ὑγίεια μᾶλλον ἀγαθὸν ἢ ὁ πλοῦτος, οὐκ ἀγαθὸν δὲ πάντως ἢ ὑγίεια, οὐδὲ ὁ πλοῦτος ἄρα. ἐκ δὲ τοῦ ἧττον· εἰ ἡ ὑγίεια ἧττον ἀγαθὸν δοκοῦσα εἶναι τῆς ἀρετῆς ὅμως ἀγαθόν ἐστι, καὶ ἡ ἀρετὴ ἄρα ἀγαθόν. ἐκ δὲ τοῦ ὁμοίου κατα-σκευάζομεν οὕτως. εἰ ὁμοίως ἡ ἰσχὺς καὶ τὸ κάλλος σώματος εἰσὶν ἀρεταί, ἀγαθὸν δὲ ἡ ἰσχὺς, καὶ τὸ κάλλος ἄρα. A similar explanation is given by Alexander, f. 133, a. b. Cf. Prantl, vol. i. p. 390.

[d] Anal. Pr. i. 23. 8. Πάντες γὰρ οἱ διὰ τοῦ ἀδυνάτου περαίνοντες τὸ μὲν ψεῦδος συλλογίζονται, τὸ δ' ἐξ ἀρχῆς ἐξ ὑποθέσεως δεικνύουσιν ὅταν ἀδύνατόν τι συμβαίνῃ τῆς ἀντιφάσεως τεθείσης. I have substituted a mere symbolical syllogism for the instance given by Aristotle, on account of its intricacy, and the length requisite to expand it. The reader will find it explained by Waitz, vol. i. p. 430.

[e] Anal. Pr. i. 29. 3. Πάλιν εἰ δεικτικῶς συλλελόγισται τὸ Α τῷ Ε μηδενὶ ὑπάρχειν, ὑποθεμένοις ὑπάρχειν τινὶ διὰ τοῦ ἀδυνάτου δειχθήσεται οὐδενὶ ὑπάρχον.

be required to prove that some A is not B, we reason
from the assumption of the contradictory,

> All A is B;⎫
> All C is A; ⎬ (συλλογισμὸς ἐξ ὑποθέσεως.)
> Therefore, All C is B. ⎭

The Conclusion being supposed to be a known falsehood. .

This mode of reasoning, as exhibited by Aristotle,
does not directly appear in the same form as the former.
For in this the hypothesis is a *premise;* the conclusion
being the impossibility which has not been previously
enunciated.   In the former, the premises are both new
assumptions; the conclusion being the antecedent of
the conditional proposition which was agreed upon as
a hypothesis.   Both, however, agree thus far, that the
syllogistic portion of each does not differ in form from
an ordinary Syllogism; and that in neither is the original
question syllogistically proved.

The notices of these Syllogisms in Aristotle are, it
must be confessed, sufficiently scanty.   Thus much,
however, may fairly be gathered.   Firstly, that, as
regards form, they are merely the common Categorical
Syllogisms applied to a particular purpose.   Secondly,
that their conclusiveness, as regards the original
question, is by way of *material,* not of *formal* consequence.   The syllogism by agreement obviously refers
to dialectic disputation, and furnishes the grounds for
a mere *argumentum ad hominem,* in consequence of a
previous admission.   Apart from this special application, which does not appear in the syllogism, the
proof amounts to this:

> No X is C; ⸳
> All X is A;
> Therefore, Some A is not C.
> Therefore, (by material consequence,) Some A is not B.

In the ἀπαγωγὴ εἰς τὸ ἀδύνατον, the proof is of the same character. It has indeed no special reference to Dialectic, and is frequently employed in demonstration[f]; Aristotle's own example being taken from Geometry. But still its connexion with the original question is not formal, but material; for we assume,

All A is B;

All C is A;

Therefore, All C is B.

And this conclusion, from material grounds, we know to be false. We also know (materially again) that the minor premise is true; and all that is logical in the process is the consequent decision that the major must be false, and hence, by the principle of contradiction, that the original question is true.

But one step only is wanting, to convert these material consequences into formal ones. We have in the συλλογισμὸς ἐξ ὁμολογίας clearly the germ of the Conditional Syllogisms of Theophrastus. It needs but to commence with the original hypothesis, not as a mere dialectic convention, but as a proposition having its own independent value, and we have at once a distinct form of argumentation, to which the Aristotelian specimen is related merely as a prosyllogism supporting one of the premises. This done, no great sagacity is required to see that the prosyllogism may in this, as in any other case, be omitted or not, according to the material character of the premise which it supports.

To the ἀπαγωγὴ εἰς τὸ ἀδύνατον may in like manner be traced the origin of the Disjunctive Syllogism. The most natural proceeding in this case is to state the two

[f] For the principle of contradiction may be assumed as self-evident, without any convention between disputants. And in this lies the principal difference between the *deductio ad impossibile* and the syllogism of agreement. See Anal. Pr. i. 44. 3.

contradictory propositions as alternatives, one of them being disproved by a prosyllogism.

> Either Some A is not B, or All A is B ; in which latter case
> All C is A ;
> Therefore, All C is B.

This conclusion being manifestly false, we have no choice but to admit the other alternative. The prosyllogism in this case, as in the former, may be omitted, if the falsehood of the alternative is evident without it. We have thus the Disjunctive Syllogism.

We may agree therefore with M. St. Hilaire thus far, that, though the form of the Hypothetical Syllogism is not explicitly exhibited in the extant writings of Aristotle, we have nevertheless the data from which it needs but one step to develope it. Whether that step was taken by Aristotle himself in a lost work, or supplied by his disciples, is a point of little consequence; though external testimony is decidedly in favour of the latter supposition.

Far more important, in a logical point of view, is the inquiry whether the hypothetical syllogism, by whomsoever analysed, is a legitimate addition to the forms of reasoning acknowledged in Aristotle's Organon; and consequently, whether its omission can fairly be censured as a deficiency in that treatise. On this question, I find myself compelled to hold an opinion different from that of the Logicians whose views have been mainly followed in the present work.

By Kant and his followers, the Hypothetical Proposition is described as representing a form of judgment essentially distinct from the Categorical ; the latter being thoroughly assertorial, the former problematical in its constituent parts, assertorial only as regards the relation between them. Two judgments, each in itself false, may thus be hypothetically combined into a single truth; and this combination cannot be reduced into categorical form[g]. The Hypothetical Syllogism, in like manner, is a form of reasoning distinct from the Categorical and not reducible to it, being based on a different law of thought, namely, the Logical Principle of Sufficient Reason, *a ratione ad rationatum, a negatione rationati ad negationem rationis valet consequentia*[b].

Of this principle, as applied to judgments, I have elsewhere remarked, that it is not a law of thought, but only a statement of the necessity of some law or other[1]. As applied to syllogisms, it has the same character. It states, generally, that whenever a condition, whether material cause of a fact or formal reason of a conclusion, exists, the conditioned fact or conclusion exists also. Thus viewed, it is not the law of any distinct reasoning process, but a statement of the conditions in which laws of nature or of thought are operative. When a material cause exists, its material effect follows, and the phenomenon indicates a law of nature : when a logical premise is given, its logical conclusion follows, and the result indicates a law of thought. *What law*, must in each case be determined by the particular features of the phenomenon or reasoning in question; but a statement of this kind is distinguished from laws of thought, properly so called, by the fact, that it cannot be expressed in a symbolical form: we require the introduction of a definite notion, *Cause, Reason, Condition*, or something of the kind, which is a special object of thought, not the general representative of all objects whatever. The principle in question is thus only a statement of

<hr/>

[g] See Kant, *Logik*, §. 25. Krug, *Logik*, §. 57. Fries, *System der Logik*, §. 32.

[b] Kant, §. 76. Krug, §. 82. Fries, §. 58.

[1] See *Prolegomena Logica*, p. 197, (2nd ed. p. 214.)

the peculiar character of certain matters about which we may think, and not a law of the form of thought in general.

It is obvious that the relation of premises and conclusion in a syllogism may, like any other relation of condition and conditioned, be expressed in the form of a hypothetical proposition: " If all A is B, and all C is A, then all C is B :" and the actual assertion of the truth of these premises will furnish at once a so-called hypothetical syllogism : " But all A is B, and all C is A, therefore all C is B." This was observed by Fries, who hence rightly maintains that analytical hypothetical judgments are formal syllogisms[k]. It is strange that, after this, he should not have gone a step further, and discovered that synthetical hypothetical judgments are assertions of material consequences. The judgment, " If A is B, C is D," asserts the existence of a consequence necessitated by laws other than those of thought, and consequently out of the province of Logic. The addition of a minor premise and conclusion in the so-called hypothetical syllogism, is merely the assertion that this general material consequence is verified in a particular case.

The distinction so much insisted on by the Kantians, of the *problematical* character of the two members of a hypothetical judgment, is, like the whole Kantian doctrine of modality, of no consequence in formal Logic. All formal thinking is, as regards the material character of its objects, problematical only. Formal Conception pronounces that certain objects of thought may possibly exist, leaving their actual existence to be determined by experience. Formal Judgment decides on the possible coexistence of certain concepts ; and Formal Reasoning, on the truth of a conclusion, subject to the hypothesis of the truth of its premises.

[k] *System der Logik*, §. 44.

To state that this hypothesis is in a certain instance true, adds nothing to the *logical* part of the reasoning, but only verifies the empirical preliminaries which the Logician in every case assumes as given. To exhibit a formal consequence hypothetically, is only a needless reassertion of the existence of data which the act of thought presupposes. To exhibit a material consequence hypothetically, is not to make it formal, but only to state that, in a certain given instance, a consequence not cognisable by Logic takes place. The sequence of " C is D," from " A is B," is not one whit more logical than it was before; it is only stated to take place materially in the present case.

The omission of hypothetical syllogisms has frequently been blamed as a defect in Aristotle's Organon; and his French translator takes some fruitless pains to strain his text, in order to make out that he does in fact treat of them[1]. If there is any truth in the preceding observations, it will follow, that Aristotle understood the limits of Logic better than his critics; and that his translator had better have allowed the omission as a merit than have attempted to deny it as a fault. When the hypothetical proposition states a formal consequence, the reasoning grounded upon it may always be reduced to categorical. When it states a material consequence, it states what the Logician, as such, cannot take into account. Aristotle is therefore quite right in saying, that in this case the conclusion is not *proved*, but *conceded*[m]. Syllogism may be employed as a logical proof of the antecedent: the consequent is admitted to follow on grounds which the Logician, as such, does not investigate, but which may

[1] St. Hilaire, *Logique d'Aristote Traduite en Français*, Preface, p. lx.
[m] *Anal. Prior.* i. 23. 11.

be warranted by the principles of this or that material
science.

The true character of hypothetical reasoning is lost
sight of in the examples commonly selected by Logicians,
which have for their subject a *proper name*, and indicate,
not a general relation of reason and consequent between
two notions, but certain accidental circumstances in the
history of an individual.   The adoption of this type has
led to the logical anomaly, that the propositions of a
hypothetical syllogism are generally stated without any
designate quantity; whereas it is obvious that, wherever
concepts are compared together in any form of reasoning,
two distinct conclusions may follow, according to the
quantity assigned.   For example: to the premise, "If men
are wise, they will consult their permanent interests,"
we may supply two minors and conclusions, in the constructive form, according as we affirm the antecedent of
all men or of *some*.   It thus becomes necessary to distinguish between two different kinds of apparent hypothetical syllogisms; those in which the inference is from
a general hypothesis to all or some of its special
instances, and those in which a relation between two
individual facts is assumed as a hypothesis leading to
a singular conclusion.   The former contain a general
relation of determining and determined notion, which
may always be expressed in three terms; the occasional
employment of four being only an accidental variety of
language.   Thus the general assertion, "If any country
is justly governed, the people are happy," is equivalent
to, "If any country is justly governed, it has happy
people."   This we may apply to special instances; *all
countries, some countries*, or *this country*, being asserted
to be justly governed: and this is properly *hypothetical
reasoning*.   The latter denote only a material connection
between two single facts, either of which may, to certain

minds possessed of certain additional knowledge, be an indication of the other; but the true ground of the inference is contained in this additional knowledge, and not in the mere hypothetical coupling of the facts by a conjunction. This is not hypothetical reasoning; i. e. it is not reasoning *from the hypothesis,* but from other circumstances not mentioned in the hypothesis at all[n].

It thus appears, that the only hypothetical judgment which can be employed as the real major premise of a syllogism, may be expressed in the form, " If any A is B, it is C," where A, B, and C represent concepts or general notions. The complete categorical equivalent to this is, " Every A which is B is C, because it is B," which admits of two interpretations, according as B stands for the physical cause of the fact, or for the logical reason of our knowing it. In the latter case, the judgment is analytical, and represents a disguised formal consequence with B as a middle term: e. g.

---

[n] This may be made clearer by an example. The following is cited by Fries, as an instance of a hypothetical proposition, not reducible to categorical form. " If Caius is free from business, he is writing poetry." This may be interpreted to mean either, generally, " whenever Caius is disengaged, he writes poetry;" or, specially, " if he is now disengaged, he is now writing poetry." Under the former interpretation, it is a general hypothesis, which may be applied as a major premise to particular instances: but in this case the true form of the reasoning is, " All times when Caius is disengaged, are times when he writes poetry; and the present is such a time." Under the latter interpretation, it is one of the cases of a material connection of two facts mentioned in the text. Now in this last case, it is obvious that the inference is really made, not from the hypothesis, but from some circumstance known to the reasoner, but not appearing in the proposition. Any man being asked, " Why do you infer that Caius, being now disengaged, is writing poetry?" would reply, " Because he told me he should do so;" or something of the kind. Assuredly he would never dream of replying, " Because *if* he is now disengaged he is writing." In this case then he does not reason *from the hypothesis,* and the expressed propositions do not compose a syllogism.

" Every man who is learned has studied, because he
is learned." Here the notion of study is implied in
that of learning, and the major premise is, " All learned
beings have studied." The hypothetical proposition
thus becomes a complete syllogism, to which the subsequent consequence is related as an episyllogism°. In
the former case, where B stands for a physical cause,
the judgment is synthetical, and indicates a material
consequence, which it requires some additional knowledge of facts to reduce to formal: e. g. " All wax
exposed to the fire melts, because it is exposed." Here,
on material grounds, we know that we cannot supply the
premise, " All bodies exposed to the fire melt;" but
only, " All bodies soluble by heat and exposed to the
fire melt." In this case the consequence is extralogical,
and requires additional data not given in the thought.
But here also, when the judgment in question is employed as the premise of a reasoning, the conclusion
follows categorically; though the premise itself cannot,
as it stands, be proved by a prosyllogism°.

The Disjunctive Judgment is usually described as
representing a whole divided into two or more parts
mutually exclusive of each other; and the Disjunctive

° Thus :

Hypothetical Syllogism.	Categorical Analysis.
If any man is learned, he has studied :	All learned beings have studied :
Some men are learned ;	All learned men are learned beings ;
∴ Some men have studied.	∴ All learned men have studied :
	Some men are learned men ;
	∴ Some men have studied.

ᴘ The analysis in this case may be exhibited thus :

Hypothetical Syllogism.	Categorical Equivalent.
If any wax is exposed to the fire it melts :	All wax exposed to the fire melts (because exposed) :
This wax is exposed to the fire ;	This wax is exposed to the fire ;
∴ This wax melts.	∴ This wax melts.

The parenthesis indicates the material ground of the major premise.

Syllogism is supposed to proceed either from the affirmation of one member to the denial of the rest, or from the denial of all but one to the affirmation of that one, by the Principle of Excluded Middle [q].

This can scarcely be regarded as a correct analysis of the process, unless the two members are *formally stated* as contradictory. The Principle of Excluded Middle asserts that every thing is either A or not A, that of two contradictories, one must exist in every subject; as the Principle of Contradiction asserts that they cannot both exist. But if the two members are not stated as contradictories, if my disjunctive premise is, " All C is either A or B," I make the material assertion that All C which is not A is B. If then I reason, " This C is not A [r], therefore it is B," I employ the Principle of Identity in addition to that of Excluded Middle. Again, if I maintain that No C can be both A and B, I make the material assertion that No C which is A is B; and from hence to reason, " This C is A, therefore it is not B," requires not the Principle of Excluded Middle, but that of Contradiction. In the first case, the Excluded Middle does not lead directly to the conclusion, but only to the contraposition of the minor premise. When we deny this C to be A, this principle enables us to assert that it is not-A, and hence to bring the reasoning under the Principle of Identity. But in the second case, in which one of the opposed members is *affirmed*, the ground on which we deny the other, is not because both cannot be false, but because both cannot be true.

It may be questioned whether this second inference is warranted by the *form* of the disjunctive premise. Boe-

---

[q] Kant, §. 27 sqq. 77, 78. Krug, §. 57, 84, 85. Fries, §. 33, 59.

[r] The indefinite minor, " but *it* is not A," is as objectionable in this syllogism as in the conditional.

thius calls it a *material consequence* [*]; and, in spite of the many eminent authorities on the other side, I am still disposed to think he is right. But let us grant for a moment the opposite-view, and allow that the proposition, "All C is either A or B," implies, as a condition of its truth, "No C can be both [t]." Thus viewed, it is in reality a complex proposition, containing two distinct assertions, each of which may be the ground of two distinct processes of reasoning, governed by two opposite laws. Surely it is essential to all clear thinking, that the two should be separated from each other, and not confounded under one form by assuming the Law of Excluded Middle to be, what it is not, a complex of those of Identity and Contradiction. Thus distinguished, the moods of the disjunctive syllogism are mere verbal variations from the categorical form, and may easily be brought under its laws [*].

---

[*] *De Syll. Hyp.* lib. i. *Opera*, p. 616.

[t] Aquinas, Opusc. xlviii. *De Enunciatione*, c. xiv. Krug, *Logik*, §. 86.

[*] Thus:

Modus tollendo ponens.	*Modus ponendo tollens.*
Every C which is not A is B.	No C which is A is B.
Every ⎫	Every ⎫
Some ⎬ C is a C which is not A.	Some ⎬ C is a C which is a A.
This ⎭	This ⎭
∴ It is B.	∴ It is not B.

The first is governed by the Principle of Identity, and the second by the Principle of Contradiction.

NOTE K.

ON THE DEMONSTRATIVE SYLLOGISM.

SCIENTIFIC knowledge (τὸ ἐπίστασθαι), except when of axiomatic principles[a], requires a conviction of the necessity of the proposition known, and a knowledge of its cause[b]. This is produced by the Demonstrative or Scientific Syllogism, which, according to Aristotle's definition, is ἐξ ἀληθῶν καὶ πρώτων καὶ ἀμέσων καὶ γνωριμωτέρων καὶ προτέρων καὶ αἰτίων τοῦ συμπεράσματος[c]. As the conclusions of this Syllogism are necessary, so must also be the premises; this necessity consists in their being *per se,* in either the first or the second sense of that expression[d]. If any of these conditions are not complied with; e. g. if the premise, though containing

---

[a] In the strict sense of the terms, ἐπίστασθαι is said of necessary truths which we receive by deduction from higher truths; νοεῖν, of those which we receive as evident of themselves. Hence the principal meanings of the corresponding terms, ἐπιστήμη and νοῦς. The latter, however, or rather its result, is sometimes called ἐπιστήμη ἀναπόδεικτος. Cf. Anal. Post. i. 3. 2, 3. i. 33. 1. ii. 19. 7. Eth. Nic. vi. 9. 9. The word ὅροι, in the first and last of these places, does not mean, as Pacius explains, simple terms, but, as M. St. Hilaire renders, " les propositions immédiates," i. e. axioms—the *limits* from which Demonstration commences.

[b] Anal. Post. i. 2. 1.

[c] Anal. Post. i. 2. 2. By *first* and *immediate* are here meant the same thing; i. e. not demonstrable by a middle term from any higher truth; γνωριμώτερα sc. φύσει, not ἡμῖν, i. e. more universal.

[d] Of necessity, three degrees are enumerated, Anal. Post. i. 4. Κατὰ παντός, καθ᾽ αὑτό, and ᾗ αὑτό; usually rendered, *de omni, per se,* and *quatenus ipsum.* Of *per se,* as applied to a proposition, four senses are given. 1. When the predicate is part of the definition of the subject. 2. When the subject is part of the definition of the predicate. 3. When existence is predicated of a substance. 4. When the subject is the external efficient cause of the predicate. Propositions in Demonstration proper must be *per se* either in the first or second meaning. See Anal. Post. i. 6. 1.

the cause of the conclusion, is not the first cause, (in which case the syllogism is not ἐξ ἀμέσων[e],) or if the premise be an effect and not a cause of the conclusion, or if the premise, though immediate, be a remote and not a proximate cause of the conclusion,—under these circumstances, there is no Demonstration, in the proper sense of the term, as we only know the fact, but not the cause[f].

From the above data, the scholastic successors of Aristotle have constructed the following specimen of *demonstratio potissima.*

> *Omne animal rationale est risibile;*
> *Omnis homo est animal rationale:* ergo
> *Omnis homo est risibilis.*

In this syllogism all three propositions are *per se;* the major premise and the conclusion in the second manner; for the subject *homo,* and consequently *animal rationale,* forms part of the definition of the attribute *risibile:* the minor premise is *per se* in the first manner; for *animal rationale,* its predicate, is the definition of *homo.*

In all the propositions of this Demonstration, the predicate and subject are coextensive, and the pro-

---

[e] From this it may fairly be inferred that the *demonstratio propter quid sit per causam non primam,* would not alone be regarded by Aristotle as a Demonstration, though it may form a subordinate portion of a complex Demonstration. The ambiguity of the word ἄμεσος, which has partly led to the discrepancies on this point, has been explained before. See p. 121.

[f] See Anal. Post. i. 13. The distinction between *demonstratio propter quid potissima* and *non potissima* cannot fairly be attributed to Aristotle. The whole of the chapters of the first book of the Posterior Analytics, from the first to the thirteenth inclusive, treat of one kind of Demonstration only. The passages in the *second* book, (ch. 17 and 18.) which seem to favour the distinction, are treating only of the inferior sense of Demonstration, in which it is applicable to τὰ πεφυκότα ὡς ἐπὶ τὸ πολύ. Cf. Anal. Pr. i. 13. 5, 6. An. Post. i. 8. 3. i. 30.

position simply convertible. This is requisite, in order to comply with the condition of *quatenus ipsum*.

This Demonstration is exceedingly satisfactory, if we are only allowed to assume all the conditions on which its validity depends; viz. 1. that risibility does flow as an effect from rationality as a cause; 2. that the major premise, in which this causation is asserted, is an axiomatic principle, cognoscible *a priori*, and, as such, carrying with its cognition, the conviction of necessity; 3. that the conclusion is not a mere repetition, in different words, of the major premise; *homo* and *animal rationale* being identical; 4. that any Demonstration acknowledged to be valid can be resolved into the above form.

But waiving the consideration of these questions, which are more easily asked than answered[g], we may find a simpler way of testing the *demonstratio potissima*, by going back to the original authority. For Aristotle's examples are principally taken, as is natural, from the Mathematics; and it is to a Geometrical theorem that the texts of καθ᾽ αὐτό and ᾗ αὐτό are expressly applied[h]. Can it be believed, then, that Aristotle regarded the following as a correct analysis of Geometrical Demonstration?

Every rectilinear figure of three sides has its angles equal to two right angles;

Every triangle is a rectilinear figure of three sides; therefore Every triangle has its angles equal to two right angles.

---

[g] " Si scrupulosius inquiratur in rem hanc; Num qua sit *essentialis connexio* inter rationalitatem et risibilitatem, quo sit ea *propria causa* hujus, seu *causa per se;* ut Rationalitas, propter ipsam sui *Essentiam*, non possit esse absque Risibilitate; neque hæc absque illa: et quidem *immediata*, absque interventu aliûs considerationis qua connectatur; atque *adæquata*, ut ad omnes rationales extendatur atque ad hos solos: subtilior forsan esset inquisitio quam ut ei facile satisfiat." Wallis, Lóg. lib. 3. cap. 22.

[h] Anal. Post. i. 4. 6. Καὶ τῷ τριγώνῳ ᾗ τρίγωνον δύο ὀρθαί· καὶ γὰρ καθ᾽ αὐτὸ τὸ τρίγωνον δύο ὀρθαῖς ἴσον.

It is not denied that there are passages in Aristotle which may seem to countenance this interpretation; but there are others so palpably inconsistent with it that we are compelled to seek for a new explanation of the former.

In the first place, Aristotle distinctly condemns the assumption of Definitions as a *Petitio Principii*[1], a charge to which the above example is obviously liable; the real question to be proved being, that the three-sided figure has its angles equal to two right angles, whether it is called a triangle or not. In the second place, he says that Demonstration proceeds from *axioms*, and cites as a specimen of the latter, " If equals be taken from equals, the remainders are equal[2]." These axioms, he says, are common to many classes of objects; but, in any single Science, need only be assumed to an extent commensurate with the object-matter of that Science. The above axiom, for example, is true of other things besides Geometrical Magnitudes, but it is sufficient for the Geometer to assume it as true of these only.

Now if an axiom of this kind be the major premise in a Demonstration, it is manifest that its predicate will also be the predicate of the Conclusion; and that the logical form of that Conclusion will be, not " All triangles are figures having their angles equal to two right angles," but, " Triangles and figures having their angles equal to two right angles are equal to each other."

The immediate Syllogism from which this proposition is proved by Euclid, may be logically stated as follows:

---

[1] Top. viii. 13. 2.
[2] Anal. Post. i. 7. 1. i. 10. 2.

" Magnitudes equal to the adjacent exterior and interior
angles of a triangle are equal to each other ;
The three interior angles and two right angles are equal to
the adjacent exterior and interior angles ;
Therefore, they are equal to each other."

The major premise of this Syllogism is an immediate
deduction from the first axiom ; thus :

" Magnitudes which are equal to the same are equal to
each other ;
Magnitudes equal to the adjacent exterior and interior
angles are equal to the same ;
Therefore, they are equal to each other[1]."

That the true syllogistic analysis of Geometrical Demonstrations will always be in this form, the axioms standing
as major premises, and the constructions in each case
furnishing the proper minor, is evident.   It only remains
to see whether the text of Aristotle can be accommodated
to this interpretation as well as to the other.

With some passages it evidently tallies much better.
The places in which the axioms are mentioned in
connexion with demonstration have never been satisfactorily explained on the scholastic interpretation[m].
There are others which *prima facie* appear to favour

[1] See Wolf, *Philosophia Rationalis*, §. 492. 551. 552. 798. Mill, *Logic*,
vol. i. p. 285.   Sir W. Hamilton, *Reid's Works*, p. 702.

[m] The difficulty is evaded rather than surmounted by distinguishing
immediate propositions from axioms, and saying that the latter are employed
in demonstration *virtually* but not *actually*.   Aquinas, Opusc. 48. de Syll.
Dem. cap. 6 ; Cf. Zabarella, in I. An. Post. Cont. 57, 58, Crakanthorpe,
Log. lib. iv. cap. 1.   For, in the first place, Aristotle expressly calls the
axioms immediate principles of syllogism, and principles *from which* we
demonstrate.   In the second place, any principle which virtually enters and
confirms the premises of a demonstration must, if the syllogistic theory be
worth any thing, be capable of syllogistic connexion with the premises
which it confirms : and until this connexion is formally exhibited, no
demonstration can be logically complete.

the latter; but, when both interpretations require some straining of Aristotle's language, it is due to the memory of the Father of Logic to give him the benefit of that which does not convict him of flagrant error in the application of his own principles.

Referring back to the Syllogism above given, the major premise may fairly be regarded as *per se;* the subject forming part of the definition of the predicate. For Equality, in the limited sense in which it is employed in Geometry, is a property of Magnitudes; and the latter, as the first and proper subject, will appear in the definition of Geometrical Equality. This definition has been found by some Geometers in the eighth axiom of Euclid; "Magnitudes which coincide are equal;" which, stated in the Aristotelian form, would be, "Equality is the Coincidence of Magnitudes[n]."

The minor premise may also be considered as *per se.* For our definition of a right angle is, that it is half the sum of the two adjacent angles formed by one straight line with another; and our notion of two right angles is that of the sum of the same two adjacent angles. As regards the Conclusion, we need not trouble ourselves with reducing it to the requisite conditions, inasmuch as it is expressly said by Aristotle to comply with them. This compliance does not directly appear in the only form in which the proposition can be syllogistically proved; but in the equipollent statement, that the triangle is a figure of which the interior angles are equal to two right angles. The predicate in this case states a property of the triangle, in the definition of which property, if any be attempted, the proper subject must be included.

A demonstration of this kind certainly falls short, in some respects, of the scholastic model. The predicate

[n] Cf. Stewart, Elements, Part II. ch. iii. Sect. ii. 2.

and subject in each proposition, *as stated,* are not convertible; and the middle term is not a definition of the minor. But of these requisitions, the first seems to be founded on an erroneous interpretation of Aristotle, according to which that Philosopher is supposed to speak of the Propositions as they appear when strictly enunciated in logical form; not (as seems more probable) of the same Propositions as ordinarily stated by the Geometer[o]. With regard to the second condition, the text of Aristotle does not warrant its imposition. He says indeed, that the middle term in demonstration must be a definition of the *major*[p]; and the precept is intelligible enough, if we rightly understand his theory of the Definition of Attributes. As regards the minor term, it would be difficult to produce a single passage where this condition is clearly laid down as a law of Demonstration; and there is more than one with which it would be no easy task to reconcile it.

If it be thought somewhat over-bold to repudiate positions which so many eminent Logicians have regarded as legitimate deductions from the text of Aristotle; it must be remembered that we have other data for interpretation besides the mere weight of authority. Aristotle's theory of demonstration is principally framed with reference to Geometry : the Scholastic examples, on the other hand, are Physical. The mediæval state of Physical science was perhaps such as to justify, or at least to account for, the Logical and Metaphysical fictions connected with it, and to give a seeming validity to the most potent demonstration of Risibility as an emanation from Rationality ; though that emanation

---

[o] In this way we may interpret such passages as Anal. Post. i. 4. 6. i. 5. 6. ii. 17. 3.

[p] Anal. Post. ii. 17. 3. The meaning of this has already been explained. See Note C.

was never dreamed of by Aristotle, and will scarcely claim implicit belief in the present day.   But it is not merely because the revolution effected in this branch of Science has invalidated the individual example, that the interpretation is objected to; but because the words of Aristotle himself expressly direct us to another criterion. The Demonstrations of Geometry are still extant in the same form in which they existed in the days of the Stagirite.   Though Euclid himself, the oldest remaining Geometer, is a few years younger than Aristotle[q], yet, except on the very improbable hypothesis that he was the original inventor of the whole contents of his Elements, that work must be regarded as furnishing a fair specimen of the demonstrations treated of in the Posterior Analytics.   By this touchstone, Aristotle and his interpreters may be tested.   When any modern Herlinus or Dasypodius[r] shall exhibit a single demonstration of Euclid in the form of a scholastic *demonstratio potissima*, we may then recognise this foundling of the Schoolmen as the legitimate offspring of their master[s]. Till that is done, we must continue to believe that Aristotle was sufficiently acquainted with the use of his own instrument, to be able to give a correct Logical Analysis of the Demonstrations of Geometry.

[q] Euclid flourished in the reign of Ptolemy Lagus, B.C. 323—283. This period, however, probably corresponds to the close, not to the commencement, of his life.   This would make him partly contemporary with, though about thirty years junior to, Aristotle.

[r] Of the remarkable work of these two " zealous but thick-headed Logicians," as Sir W. Hamilton calls them, a specimen will be found in the next note.

[s] See on this point the criticisms of Ramus, *Scholæ Mathematicæ*, 1. iii. and of Wolf, *Phil. Rat.* §. 498.   Both, however, treat the scholastic form as Aristotelian.

NOTE L.

ON THE LOGIC OF GEOMETRY.

THE Propositions which have been regarded by different writers as constituting the foundation of geometrical demonstration, may be classified as follows.

I. Definitions, analysing the complex notions of the several magnitudes or figures.

II. Postulates, assuming the existence of the objects defined.

III. Axioms proper to Geometry, or synthetical judgments, stating self-evident properties of certain magnitudes.

IV. General axioms*, or analytical judgments, logically involving the notions of equality or inequality.

Some one or more of these, under various names, (for the language of the several writers has been by no means uniform,) have been selected at different times as the fundamental assumptions or premises from which the conclusions of Geometry may be demonstrated. A brief examination of each may perhaps help to clear the question.

I. According to Stewart, the properties of geometrical figures follow from the *Definitions* of those figures; the general axioms being mere barren truisms, and the axioms proper, (such as the 10th, 11th, and 12th of Euclid,) being theorems requiring demonstration. In this theory,

---

* I have retained the language of the modern editions of Euclid, as that most familiar to the majority of readers. At the same time it may be observed, that this language departs widely from the original text of Euclid himself. In that text the general axioms are called *common notions* (κοιναὶ ἔννοιαι), while the axioms proper are included among the *postulates* (αἰτήματα).

mathematical necessity becomes identified with logical, being only the result of the harmony of a process of thought with its original assumption. This consequence is accepted by Stewart himself, as well as by Archbishop Whately, who speaks of the denial of geometrical propositions as *self-contradictory* [b].

This view may be refuted either directly or by a *reductio ad absurdum;* for, firstly, it rests on an untenable assertion; secondly, it leads to an inadmissible consequence.

Firstly. If the properties of a figure follow from the definition of that figure, it must either be because they are implied in *some one attribute* of that definition, or because they are implied in *the whole*. A triangle e. g. will have its angles equal to two right angles, either because it is a rectilinear figure, or because it is of three sides, or because it is both. The two first suppositions are manifestly false: the third begs the question; for why the notion of a triangle, regarded as a complex whole, has this property, is the very point at issue.

Hence it appears that the Definitions of Geometry, so far as they are employed in demonstration, are merely nominal. From the analysis of the complex notion no conclusion is derived. The Definition only serves to connect the notion as a whole with the name *triangle* [c].

[b] This view is also adopted by M. Cousin in his Lectures on Kant, apparently as an exposition of the opinion of Kant himself, to which however it is diametrically opposed.

[c] This view is supported by the authority of one equally eminent as a philosopher and a mathematician. Pascal (*Pensées*, P. I. Art. II. vol. i. p. 126. ed. Faugère) observes, " On ne reconnaît en géométrie que les seules définitions que les logiciens appellent *définitions de nom*, c'est-à-dire, que les seules impositions de nom aux choses qu'on a clairement désignées en termes parfaitement connus ; et je ne parle que de celles-là seulement. Leur utilité et leur usage est d'éclaircir et d'abréger le discours, en exprimant par le seul nom qu'on impose ce qui ne pourrait se dire qu'en plusieurs termes ; en sorte néanmoins que le nom imposé demeure dénué

The question, why a rectilinear figure of three sides, be it called triangle or not, has its angles equal to two right angles, remains unanswered.

Secondly. If geometrical reasoning is merely " the logical filiation of consequences which follow from an assumed hypothesis," there is no reason why its conclusions should be more important than those of any other analysis of imaginary notions, such as (to use Mr. Mill's illustration) a deduction of the physiological properties of an imaginary animal, or the political history of an imaginary commonwealth. The whole character and history of mathematical science militates against the admission of this consequence.

II. Mr. Mill, while agreeing with Stewart that mathematical necessity is merely hypothetical and consequential, saw clearly that Stewart's doctrine concerning Definitions was untenable. This led him to adopt the second theory, according to which geometrical inferences depend on *Postulates* assuming the existence of the objects defined. Thus a triangle has its angles equal to two right angles, because there may really exist a rectilinear figure having three sides ; and this existence is implied, though not verbally expressed, in the definition.

This theory derives some apparent support from the use of the principle of superposition. When, for instance, the demonstration of the fourth proposition of Euclid supposes the triangle A B C to be applied to the triangle D E F, it clearly assumes the existence of both triangles, not merely as general notions, which are identical in thought, but as distinct individual magnitudes, occupying space, and capable of being transferred from one position in space to another. One non-entity cannot be

de tout autre sens, s'il en a, pour n'avoir plus que celui auquel on le destine uniquement."

applied to another. Thus far Mr. Mill's position is unquestionably true; but I think it may be shewn to be not itself the fundamental assumption of Geometry, but a consequence derivable from a higher assumption.

The existence is clearly only that which is implied in the possible construction of the figure. The actual or possible existence in nature of a body so figured is not once appealed to in the demonstration, and might be denied without affecting its validity. The Postulate, therefore, implies the possible construction of a figure, such as is contemplated in the proposition.

But this construction is mental, not manual. The figure as drawn upon paper is only a representative of the figure as imagined by the mind, and might be dispensed with altogether if the latter could be kept before us with sufficient steadiness. This brings us to Kant's principle of the possibility of mathematical science, viz. the power of *constructing* the objects of its concepts; i. e. of presenting them *a priori* in a pure intuition.

But how is this construction itself possible, and what conditions is it required to fulfil? Mr. Mill regards it as only possible *a posteriori,* and as subject to the same conditions as an object of sense. He says, " the points, lines, circles, and squares, which any one has in his mind, are simply copies of the points, lines, circles, and squares which he has known in his experience. ' We can reason about a line as if it had no breadth; but we cannot *conceive* a line without breadth[d]." This is true; but the author is mistaken in supposing such a conception to be necessary to establish the *a priori* character of Mathematics. The true Postulate is not that of the possible existence of an object corresponding to the *definition,* but of one fulfilling the conditions of the *proper axiom.* We are not required to conceive a

[d] Logic, b. ii. ch. v.

straight line as length without breadth : we are required to conceive it as such that two straight lines cannot enclose a space. The definition itself is but an imperfect attempt to describe in general terms what is known much more clearly by the image. It may serve to lead the thoughts of the learner to the proper image; but it was itself founded on a previous image in the mind of the teacher; and if the definition and the image differ, the former is in fault, not the latter.

III. This brings us to our third theory, which is that maintained by Kant. According to this theory, the fundamental assumptions of Geometry are *Proper Axioms,* or synthetical judgments *a priori;* and the possibility of forming such judgments depends on the power of constructing the objects to which they refer in a pure intuition, i. e. in an intuition containing no adventitious element external to the mind itself. The images of geometrical figures differ from all others in being, not represented modifications of body, but presented modifications of space; and the universal validity of the synthetical judgments is a consequence of the universal presence of space as the form of every possible perception of body.

Three of these synthetical judgments are given in the 10th, 11th, and 12th axioms of Euclid; and either these or other axioms analogous to these must be assumed as evident by intuition, before any of the properties of more complex figures can be made known by demonstration. I do not say that Euclid has given the best and simplest forms of these axioms, but that in some form or other they are indispensable. To regard all such axioms as possibly demonstrable theorems is to be ignorant of the logical conditions under which demonstration is possible; for a synthetical judgment is demonstrable only on the condition that another synthetical judgment may be assumed. Οἱ γὰρ ἁπάντων ζητοῦντες λόγον ἀναιροῦσι λόγον.

It may be true that the image which gives rise to the intuitive perception of the axiom, is not consciously contemplated as more perfect than the corresponding figure as seen in a body; but this does not prove that the axiom is really generalized from the latter[e]. The inadequacy of sensible magnitudes for mathematical certainty does not arise from that of which we are immediately conscious, but from that of which we are not. The straight line as perceived is a quality of body; the straight line as imagined is a modification of space. The portions of the two actually presented at any time may not apparently differ from each other; but our empirical knowledge or ignorance of body may suggest actual or possible variations not perceived in the intuition; for the qualities of body have an objective existence independently of our perception, and therefore may or may not be adequately perceived at any one time. We see, for example, that a line running along the earth's surface is apparently straight; but we know that it is in reality an arc of the earth's curvature, and might be seen to be so in another position or with more acute organs. But the straight line in space exists only as imagined, and is imagined only as mathematically exact. The intuition, therefore, is adequate and valid for any extent of space, and in any portion. The apparent straightness of the visible line is the result of an imperfection in our bodily organs; and with more acute senses we might perceive its deviation. The presented straightness of the imaginary line results from the exactness of our constructive power; and a superior

---

[e] See St. Augustine, *Confess.* x. c. 12. "Vidi lineas fabrorum, vel etiam tenuissimas, sicut filum araneæ; sed illæ aliæ sunt, non sunt imagines earum quas mihi nuntiavit carnis oculus."

excellence in this would only enable us to extend the same image to a greater length, or to retain it more steadily before the mind.

IV. The Synthetical Axioms are thus the ground of all that is properly geometrical in our fundamental assumptions; but the *Analytical Axioms* are employed also, as expressing general conceptions of equality and inequality under which geometrical magnitudes may be brought. Stewart was led into his erroneous view of definitions by his contempt for the syllogism, which he would not allow to be under any circumstances the type of demonstrative reasoning. In this contempt Mr. Mill does not participate, and he has accordingly exhibited the fifth proposition of Euclid demonstrated in syllogistic form. In this demonstration we see both analytical and synthetical axioms employed as major premises; the former as general formulæ, founded on the conception of *equality;* the latter as the means of applying this general conception to geometrical magnitudes, in which the test of equality is *coincidence.* One or the other will be employed in different syllogisms, according as the major term to be proved is *equality* or *coincidence.* The minor premises are furnished by the conditions, given or constructed, of the particular figure.

Against the form of the geometrical syllogism as exhibited by Mr. Mill the logician will have no objections to allege; though the metaphysician will not be disposed to acquiesce in his statement that the axioms of both kinds are gained by induction. And it is not strictly accurate to represent the first three axioms of Euclid as capable of proof by an imaginary superposition. To the axioms in their general form this principle is inapplicable; for coincidence is not the test of equality in general, but only of equality in superficial magnitudes. To the axioms as employed in Geometry

s

the principle of superposition may be applied : but even here it adds nothing to their evidence. Magnitudes given as the sums of equal magnitudes are *ipso facto* thought as equal ; and to have recourse to superposition tends to confound the evidence of logical necessity resting on the laws of thought with that of geometrical necessity resting on the conditions of intuition.

Much error and confusion on this subject might have been avoided, had modern philosophers observed Aristotle's distinction between ἀϱχαὶ ἐξ ὧν, or assumptions from which we reason, and ἀϱχαὶ πεϱὶ ὅ, or assumptions about the objects of our reasoning. In the former class he rightly places the axioms ; in the latter, the definitions. But the true distinction between the axioms proper and the definitions, as synthetical and analytical judgments, has not, I think, been as yet accurately carried out in reference to Geometry.

––––––––––

The above remarks were written as an appendix to a pamphlet of mine on the Limits of Demonstrative Science, published in 1853. In the remainder of this note, I propose to resume a question which was then only partially considered, and to point out what appears to be the chief deficiency in the logical arrangement of geometrical principles.

Plato asserted that mathematical demonstration was founded on *hypotheses*[f]. Aristotle in like manner enumerates *hypotheses*, along with definitions, among the proper principles of science[g]. By this term both philosophers appear to have meant the same thing ; namely, that the real existence of the objects of demonstration is not *proved*, but *supposed*. If there exist any where

[f] Rep. vi. p. 510. C.   [g] Anal. Post. i. 2. 7.

two perfect straight lines, those lines cannot enclose a space; and if there exists any where a figure formed by three such lines, it has its angles equal to two right angles. But this supposed existence of the objects cannot be verified by any process of mathematical reasoning. To bridge over the chasm which separates thoughts from things; to determine how far a subjective necessity of thinking indicates a corresponding objective necessity of existence, is the office, not of Mathematics, but of a Science of Being, of Metaphysics, or, as Plato would say, of Dialectic.

But though objective existence is beyond the province of the mathematician, there is a further condition of subjective existence, which he is bound to verify for himself, by an appeal to *pure intuition;* i. e. by constructing in his mind an image corresponding to each assumed conception. As far as mere nomenclature is concerned, we might employ the term *biangle* to denote a rectilinear figure of *two* sides, or the term *bicentrical circle* to denote a figure in which all straight lines drawn from *two* interior points to the circumference are equal to each other. There is no logical contradiction in such definitions; and those who maintain that all mathematical certainty depends on experience, are bound in consistency to admit that these conceptions are no more absurd than those of a centaur or a hippogryph; representing objects no otherwise inconceivable than that experience has shewn them to have no real existence.

Hence it follows, that no expression in Geometry which combines together a plurality of attributes can be regarded as a pure definition. For the assumption that such attributes can coexist in an image or figure is either demonstrable or indemonstrable. In the former case the definition is coupled with a theorem, in the latter

s 2

with an axiom. Thus, for example, to define a triangle as a rectilinear figure of three sides involves the assumption that three straight lines can enclose a space, which is quite as much an axiom as the assumption that two cannot. Again, to define an acute angled triangle as one that has three acute angles involves the assumption that three straight lines inclined at acute angles to each other will enclose a space. Accordingly we find in the ordinary editions of Euclid many of the definitions accompanied by figures, which furnish an evidence of the possibility of the conception by a direct appeal to the intuition. So also the definition, that " a circle is a figure contained by one line which is called the circumference, and is such that all straight lines drawn from a certain point within the figure to the circumference are equal to one another," involves the assumption that a line so drawn as to be always equally distant from a given point will return into itself or be one line including a space;—an assumption which might be more properly classed as an axiom than as a definition [h].

From this we may conclude that the numerous attempts of Geometers to diminish or get rid of their axioms have been steps in a wrong direction [i]. The number of axioms, instead of being diminished, should be very considerably increased; and the errors that have hitherto prevailed on the nature and foundation of Geometrical reasoning have been mainly owing to the manner in which many indispensable assumptions have been either omitted altogether, or concealed among the definitions.

[h] See Whewell, *Philosophy of the Inductive Science*, vol. i. p. 108. ed. 1847.

[i] An account of thirty methods at different times proposed, in order to avoid the assumption of the twelfth axiom of Euclid, is given in the Appendix to General Thompson's *Geometry without Axioms*.

Some valuable hints on this point may be gathered from a very able and interesting paper by Professor De Morgan, printed in the *Companion to the Almanac for* 1849. The following extracts indicate a principle which might be pursued to further results.

"Book I. *Definitions.* Of these, iii, vi, xiii, are obvious statements, but not definitions of words; viii, xxvi, xxxi to xxxiv, are never subsequently used; xviii, if semicircle have its etymological meaning, as seems the intention, is a theorem, which ought to be iii. 1. The remaining definitions are of two kinds: first, those which do not explain their terms, but demand a notion already existing in the student's mind; they are i, ii, iv, v, vii, ix: secondly, purely verbal definitions; they are x, xi, xii, xiv to xvii, xix to xxx, and xxxv. Insist on angle as a *magnitude:* on the comparison of angles as to greater, equal, or less, by superposition; on the rights of angles equal to and greater than two right angles. The angle made by a straight line with its own continuation is a definite angular magnitude; and its half is the best definition of a right angle. It is to be regretted that there is no single phrase for " two right angles."

" *Postulate* and *axioms:* In Euclid, *postulates* and *common notions.* All Geometrical demands are *postulates* in Euclid; *his* axioms or common notions are in every instance notions common to all kinds of magnitude as well as space magnitudes. Restore this: that is, let the postulates be, Simson's postulates, and axioms, x, xi, xii; but instead of xi, substitute " if two right lines coincide in two points, they coincide when produced," as more self-evident. From this it is seen that the doubles of all right angles are equal, and thence that all right angles are equal ; and this should come between I. 12. and I. 13. as a proof of the theorem, " all right angles are equal." For xii. substitute " two lines which

out one another are not *both* parallel to any third line,"
from which, after I. 28. prove Simson's axiom xii as a
theorem.   Remark that the distinction of postulate
and axiom, as *problem* and *theorem*, could not have been
Euclid's notion, for he does not recognise the last
distinction; both are with him simply propositions.
The expressed six postulates of Euclid are not the
only ones which occur; others are tacitly adopted, as
will presently appear.   Nothing should be tacitly assumed
by those who will not assume without express statement,
that " two straight lines cannot inclose a space."

" I. 1. The following postulates are demanded : " if
two figures which have one or more points in common
have each a point which is not in the other, the boundaries of those figures must cut," and " every point is
without or within a circle, according as its distance
from the centre is more or less than the radius."   With
less, the intersection of the circles cannot be proved.
I. 4. This postulate is assumed, " any figure may be
removed from place to place without alteration of form,
and a plane figure may be turned round on the plane."
But for this right to turn, I. 4. would not prove I. 5."

In the general principles of Professor De Morgan's
criticism I fully concur, though slightly differing from
one or two of his details.   Definitions iii. and vi. are synthetical judgments, not developing the conceptions of
the point and straight line, but affirming a property of
each.   These then should be classed among the *axioms,*
or, as Mr. De Morgan more properly terms them, the
postulates.   Definitions i, ii, iv, v, vii, viii, ix, are not
really employed as conceptions, but only serve to refer us
to the corresponding intuition; which in every case is
the basis of one or more axioms, implied, if not expressly
stated.   Among such axioms must be classed the following assumptions.   " Two lines can meet each other, and

the place where they meet is always a single point."
" Two lines can intersect each other, and the place
where they intersect is always a single point."
(These are properties of the point, and assumptions of
the possibility of angles.) " A straight line may lie in
and form part of a superficies." Definitions xiii, xiv,
xvi, are the only purely verbal ones; for Definitions x,
xi, xii, and xvii, assume that straight lines can be drawn
to comply with certain specified conditions; and the
others, being definitions of figures, assume that lines
under specified conditions can enclose a space.

The above remarks will sufficiently shew in what
respects the attempts of Geometers to dispense with
axioms have failed. They have not been aware that
every synthetical judgment assumed without demonstration is a axiom. They have attempted to deal, not
very successfully, with the *expressed* axioms of Euclid;
but they have neglected, and in their own attempts have
assumed, principles equally axiomatic, though only
understood; and they have not been aware that an
assumption resting on an appeal to the senses or to
the imagination is as much an *unproved assumption* as
one which appeals to the thought; for of the one we
can only say that we are so constituted that we cannot
but *perceive* it, and of the other, that we are so constituted that we cannot but *think* it.

An ingenious and instructive but unsuccessful attempt
of this kind is made in General Thompson's " Geometry
without Axioms." The author every where identifies
intelligible magnitudes with sensible; and this identifi-
cation gives rise to a multitude of subordinate assumptions, inadmissible in strict demonstration, but which, if
admissible, would be as much axioms as any thing in
Euclid. By identifying intelligible magnitudes with
sensible, it is implied that all the perfections which are

conceived to exist in magnitudes regarded as modifications of space may also be *perceived* to exist in similar magnitudes regarded as portions of bodies. The perfect straight line and the perfect triangle and the perfect circle are not merely imaginable forms, but tangible substances. But it is further assumed by the author, that the sensible properties of bodies, whose very existence can only be proved by the testimony of experience, may exist, along with the Geometrical qualities, in a manner in which experience has never presented them. Thus " figures of all kinds, lines and points," are " always considered as exhibited on a hard body of some kind, which causes the position of the several parts or points to be fixed with relation to one another; and will, on occasion, be supposed to be turned about an assigned point or points, in any manner that can be shewn to be practicable with the hard body on which they are understood to be represented. Nevertheless, the application of one object to another will, when required, be imagined to take place without bar of corporeal substance;—that is to say, without impediment from the existence of other parts than those it is desired to compare." In other words, the surface of a solid and the linear boundary of a surface may be considered *ad libitum* as in or out of connection with the bodies of which they form part, retaining in both cases the attributes of body, such as hardness. Surely such assumptions as these, be they legitimate or illegitimate, are to be treated as postulates or axioms. At any rate they are not definitions.

But further: a Body is defined to be " any thing that can be made the object of touch;" and a hard body is " a body which resists all change of form." But bodies which resist all change of form are assumed at the same time not to resist all change of size; for the genesis of the straight line and the proof of the axiom of parallels are made to depend on a supposed inflation of the sphere. Here is another implied postulate or axiom. " A hard body may be increased or diminished in size to any extent without losing its hardness." Empirically, this is untrue. A body which resists all change of form cannot in practice be expanded or contracted *ad libitum*. To assume it as imaginably true is to assume an axiom, not a definition.

Again: the author attempts to prove the majority of the axioms of Euclid by superposition; laying down beforehand these two definitions; " Things which occupy the same place, are said to coincide ;" and " Magnitudes which, if their boundaries were applied to one another, would coincide, or might be made capable of doing so by a different arrangement of parts, are called *equal*." In the latter definition again there is an assumed postulate : " The parts of a body may be arranged in any way, without affecting the magnitude of the body." Otherwise the two meanings of the term *equal* are a mere equivocation ; and the demonstration of the equality of any two given bodies is a mere play upon words. A is equal to B because it actually coincides with it. C is equal to B because it may be made to coincide with it. But how do I know that it is the *same* C before and after the change in the arrangement of its parts ? If I may assert that the two bodies are *now equal*, because a different arrangement of parts may make them so, why may I not assert that they are *now equal*, because by taking away a part of one of them they may become so ?

But even after this assumption is made, it may be questioned whether the principle of superposition can be legitimately applied to magnitudes considered as exhibited on a hard body. Magnitudes in space can be constructed *a priori* in a pure intuition, and in any one part of space, as readily as in any other. Hence they may be transported by the same intuition from one position in space to another, and all their constituent attributes with them; for they contain no attribute which is not presented in the image. ·But the empirical qualities of a hard body cannot be constructed *a priori* in a pure intuition; and tangibility, which the author adopts as the test of corporeity, cannot be conveyed into the mental image by the construction, nor conceived to exist, so long as it is transferred from one place to another solely by the imagination. If I draw two triangles upon paper, I can only shew their coincidence *as bodies* by cutting one out and placing it on the other. Thus the statements of Geometry are reduced to empirical truths dependent on actual measurement; a method quite as applicable to theorems as to axioms, and which, consistently carried out, would dispense with demonstration altogether. For if I may prove by measurement that magnitudes which are equal to the same are equal to each other, I may apply the same test with equal directness to shew that the angles of a triangle are equal to two right angles.

Another work, nominally of a similar character to that of General Thompson, but differing considerably in its method and actual results, was published in 1856, by Mr. Hensleigh Wedgwood, under the title of " the Geometry of the three first Books of Euclid by direct proof from Definitions alone." The opposition, however, between the principles of Mr. Wedgwood's treatise and those maintained in the preceding remarks is more verbal than real. According to the view of Kant, which has been adopted in the preceding remarks, the science of Geometry is founded on the successive synthesis of the productive imagination in the generation of forms or magnitudes in space; and its axioms express those conditions of the sensible intuition *a priori,* under which alone the scheme answering to a given notion can be formed[k]. Mr. Wedgwood transfers these "conditions of the sensible intuition" to the definitions of his elementary magnitudes, the straight line and the plane, which he defines, not by a description of the appearance which they present to the eye or the imagination, as magnitudes already existing, but by a statement of the manner in which they may be supposed to be generated by motion from a given point. Such statements contain considerably more than a mere analysis of the attributes indispensable to the conception of the magnitudes in question: they contain the assertion that a magnitude which our intuition, whether pure or empirical, presents to us as having a certain form, and which is already conceived or known by that form, possesses also a certain property or properties in respect of its distance and direction with regard to a given point. Assertions of this kind, as being synthetical and not analytical judgments, would be classed by Kant as Axioms, not as Definitions.

As an appropriate conclusion to this note, I subjoin a specimen of Euclid reduced to syllogisms, extracted from the very curious and rare *Analyses Geometricæ* of Herlinus and Dasypodius. I have selected the fifth proposition of the first book, as that which has also been analysed by Mr. Mill[1]. To the curious in such subjects it may be interesting to compare the two demonstrations.

[k] See *Kritik der reinen Vernunft*, p. 143, ed. Rosenkranz.
[1] Logic, b. ii. chap. iv.

Propositio V.

Theorema.

Τῶν ἰσοσκελῶν τριγώνων αἱ πρὸς τῇ βάσει γωνίαι ἴσαι ἀλλήλαις εἰσί· καὶ προσεκβληθεισῶν τῶν ἴσων εὐθειῶν, αἱ ὑπὸ τὴν βάσιν γωνίαι ἴσαι ἀλλήλαις ἔσονται.

Triangulorum qui duo æqualia habent latera, anguli ad basin sunt æquales. Et productis æqualibus illis rectis, etiam qui sub basi sunt anguli, inter se erunt æquales.

ἡ ἔκθεσις.

Sit triangulis æquicrurus $\overline{\alpha\beta\gamma}$, habens latus $\overline{\alpha\beta}$ æquale lateri $\overline{\alpha\gamma}$, et ducantur lineis $\overline{\alpha\beta}$, $\overline{\alpha\gamma}$, ἐπ' εὐθείας lineæ $\overline{\beta\delta}$, $\overline{\gamma\epsilon}$. ὁ διορισμός. Dico quod angulus $\overline{\alpha\beta\gamma}$ est æqualis angulo $\overline{\alpha\gamma\beta}$. Et quod angulus $\overline{\gamma\beta\delta}$ est æqualis angulo $\overline{\beta\gamma\epsilon}$. ἡ κατασκευή. Sumatur in linea $\overline{\beta\delta}$ punctum quodvis ζ. Tollatur a majore linea $\overline{\alpha\epsilon}$, minori $\overline{\alpha\zeta}$ æqualis linea $\overline{\alpha\eta}$, per propositionem tertiam. Ducantur rectæ $\overline{\zeta\gamma}$, $\overline{\eta\beta}$.

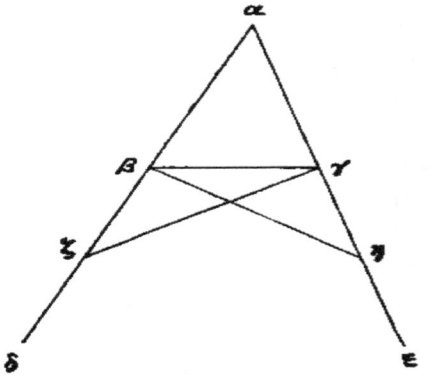

ἡ ἀπόδειξις.

Syllogismi quatuor.

Primus. Quicunque duo trianguli habent duo latera duobus lateribus æqualia, alterum alteri, et angulum angulo æqualem, qui æqualibus lineis continetur, etiam basin basi habebunt æqualem, et reliquos angulos reliquis angulis æquales, alterum alteri, quos æqualia latera subtendunt. Trianguli $\overline{\beta\alpha\eta}$, $\overline{\gamma\alpha\zeta}$ habent duo latera $\overline{\beta\alpha}$, $\overline{\alpha\eta}$, æqualia duobus lateribus $\overline{\gamma\alpha}$, $\overline{\alpha\zeta}$, alterum alteri, latus $\overline{\beta\alpha}$ lateri $\overline{\gamma\alpha}$, et latus $\overline{\alpha\eta}$ lateri $\overline{\alpha\zeta}$. Et habent angulum $\overline{\beta\alpha\eta}$ communem. *Ergo.* Trianguli $\overline{\beta\alpha\eta}$, $\overline{\gamma\alpha\zeta}$, habent basin $\overline{\beta\eta}$ æqualem basi $\overline{\gamma\zeta}$, et angulum $\overline{\alpha\beta\eta}$ æqualem angulo $\overline{\alpha\gamma\zeta}$, et angulum $\overline{\alpha\eta\beta}$ æqualem angulo $\alpha\zeta\gamma$. *Explicatio.* Major est propositio quarta. Minoris pars prima est ὑπόθεσις. Secunda est nota ἐκ τῆς κατασκευῆς. Tertia est nota per se. *Secundus.* Si ab æqualibus tollantur æqualia, quæ relinquuntur sunt æqualia. A lineis æqualibus $\overline{\alpha\zeta}$, $\overline{\alpha\eta}$, tolle lineas æquales $\overline{\alpha\beta}$, $\overline{\alpha\gamma}$. *Ergo.* Manet recta $\overline{\beta\zeta}$, æqualis rectæ $\overline{\gamma\eta}$. *Explicatio.* Major est κοινὴ ἔννοια. Minoris pars prior est nota ἐκ τῆς κατασκευῆς. Posterior est ὑπόθεσις. *Tertius.* Quicunque duo trianguli habent &c. ut syllog. pri. Trianguli $\overline{\beta\eta\gamma}$, $\overline{\gamma\zeta\beta}$, habent duo latera $\overline{\beta\eta}$, $\overline{\eta\gamma}$, æqualia duobus lateribus $\overline{\gamma\zeta}$, $\overline{\zeta\beta}$, alterum alteri, latus $\overline{\beta\eta}$ lateri $\overline{\gamma\zeta}$, et latus $\overline{\eta\gamma}$ lateri $\overline{\zeta\beta}$, et habent angulum $\overline{\beta\eta\gamma}$ æqualem angulo $\overline{\gamma\zeta\beta}$. *Ergo.* Trianguli $\overline{\beta\eta\gamma}$, $\overline{\gamma\zeta\beta}$, habent angulum $\overline{\beta\gamma\eta}$ æqualem angulo $\overline{\gamma\beta\zeta}$, et angulum $\gamma\beta\eta$ æqualem angulo $\overline{\beta\gamma\zeta}$. *Explicatio.* Major est propositio quarta. Minoris pars prima et tertia est conclusio syllog. primi. Secunda est conclusio syll. secundi. *Quartus.* Si ab æqualibus tollantur æqualia, quæ relinquuntur sunt æqualia. Ab æqualibus angulis $\overline{\alpha\beta\eta}$, $\overline{\alpha\gamma\zeta}$, tolle æquales angulos $\overline{\gamma\beta\eta}$, $\overline{\beta\gamma\zeta}$. *Ergo.* Manet angulus $\overline{\alpha\beta\gamma}$, æqualis angulo $\alpha\gamma\beta$. *Explicatio.* Major est κοινὴ ἔννοια. Minoris pars prior est conclusio syll. primi. Posterior est conclusio syll. tertii. τὸ συμπέρασμα. Ex conclusione syll. quarti liquet trianguli $\overline{\alpha\beta\gamma}$, angulos $\overline{\alpha\beta\gamma}$, $\overline{\alpha\gamma\beta}$, qui sunt ad basin esse æquales. Et ex conclusione syll. tertii-liquet angulos $\overline{\beta\gamma\eta}$, $\overline{\gamma\beta\zeta}$, qui sunt sub basi esse æquales. Triangulorum igitur qui duo habent æqualia latera, &c. ὅπερ ἔδει δεῖξαι.

Note M.

ON THE CLASSIFICATION OF FALLACIES.

It has been before observed[*], that Aristotle's Treatise περὶ σοφιστικῶν ἐλέγχων has properly only a historical value; that it is important as an account of modes of reasoning in use at the period to which it refers; but that it is not, and does not profess to be, a classification based on any logical principle. Its divisions, however, have been followed without question by the majority of subsequent logicians, centuries after the circumstances which gave it its chief value had ceased to exist; and its language has become in a manner classical, though not always restricted to the sense originally intended by its author. *Petitio Principii* and *Ignoratio Elenchi* still hold their place as recognised forms of fallacy; and the continued use of the Aristotelian nomenclature, at different times and under different circumstances, has given in some respects a permanent value to that which originally was designed only for a temporary purpose. It is not therefore intended in the present note to propose an entirely different classification and nomenclature, but only to point out certain principles, according to which, if Logic is regarded as the Science of the Laws of Thought, an arrangement of Fallacies may be attempted on properly logical grounds, and some of the deficiencies of the received enumeration supplied.

The Aristotelian list is confined to Fallacies connected with Reasoning. But if Logic is the Science, not of the Laws of Reasoning only, but of those of Thought in general, it will follow that the spurious forms of Conception and Judgment are equally entitled to a place among Logical Fallacies. And if all the processes of Thought, so far

* See above, p. 181, note a.

as they come within the province of Logic, are governed by the same laws, we may naturally expect to find some resemblance between the illegitimate forms of each. The resemblance, as will be seen hereafter, is by no means perfect; but the same general principles of classification will be found applicable to the various processes of Thought, whether we are examining their legitimate or their illegitimate results.

The first and most obvious principle of division is into Formal and Material Fallacies, according as the source of the deception lies in the act of thought itself, or in the object upon which, or the circumstances under which, it is exercised. Strictly speaking, Formal Fallacies alone come under the cognisance of the *Logica docens*, or Logic properly so called; as being apparent but not real thoughts, or at least not the kind of thoughts which they profess to be. Material Fallacies, where the thought is legitimate, but the relation to things inaccurate, belong properly to the province of the *Logica utens*, and can only be adequately guarded against by that branch of knowledge which takes cognisance of the things. A minute division of Material Fallacies may thus be carried on to an indefinite extent; for any object about which we think may be represented in thought inaccurately or untruly. The Logician must content himself with indicating the most general principles of such a division; and that not strictly as a portion of the theory of his science, but as a hint for its application to practice. To these two classes of Fallacies, which are those which suggest themselves *a priori*, as implied in the idea of any possible exercise of thought, it becomes necessary in practice to add a third class, comprising those which arise from the ambiguities of language. Words, whether written, or spoken, or exhibited in some other system of signs, are proved by experience to be universally necessary in practice, both to the formation and to the communication of thought; and any defect in this indispensable instrument is communicated to the operations which it performs. This was clearly seen by Aristotle and his followers, who have assigned a prominent, indeed too prominent, a place to language in their classification, by dividing Fallacies, in the first instance, into those *in dictione* and those *extra dictionem;* according as the deception does or does not depend upon the particular words in which the reasoning is conveyed[b]. Looking to the actual position of language in relation to thought, it will be better to adopt a threefold division of Fallacies; those in the Thought, those in the Matter, and those in the Language; the last corresponding to the *fallaciæ in dictione* of Aristotle; the two former representing a still more important though often neglected distinction, which is lost sight of in the vague negation of *extra dictionem.*

In the application of this principle of division to the several operations of Thought, as exhibited in the following Table, some slight differences will be observed, which in some instances will explain themselves, while in others a few preliminary words of explanation may be desirable. Fallacies of Language, it is obvious, will become more numerous as the process of thought becomes more complicated. While a Concept can be misapprehended only in the term (whether expressed by one word or more) in which it is conveyed, a Judgment may be ambiguous, either in the meaning of one of its terms, or in its entire construction; and a Reasoning admits of still further ambiguity, from the repetition of a term or sentence in different senses. Hence a different enumeration of Fallacies *in dictione* will be required in different parts of the Table.

[b] For some further remarks on this division, see p. 133, note b.

As regards Formal or Logical Fallacies, a fuller explanation may be needed. The ultimate test of the logical validity of any thought is *conceivability*. This test may be applied to judgments and reasonings, as well as to concepts. A concept is logically real if it is conceivable; that is to say, if its constituent parts can be combined with each other in an unity of representation. If it complies with this criterion, it is real as a thought: whether its supposed object be real as a thing, is a question with which Logic has no concern. A judgment, again, is logically true or necessary, (for Logic recognises no truth short of necessity,) if its contradictory is inconceivable: it is logically false or impossible, if it is itself inconceivable; but if two contradictory assertions are both equally conceivable, it does not lie within the province of Logic to determine their truth or falsehood. A reasoning, in like manner, is logically necessary, if the contradictory of the conclusion cannot be conceived as true, consistently with the assumed truth of the premises: it is logically impossible, if the conclusion itself cannot be so conceived. If, however, the conclusion and its contradictory are equally conceivable along with the assumed truth of the premises, the conclusion may or may not have a material value, but it is one which cannot be recognised by Logic.

But though the test of conceivability is thus applicable to judgments and reasonings, as well as to concepts, it is applicable in a different manner. A given combination of attributes may be inconceivable, either because it contains too little, or because it contains too much. That is to say, it may either be defective in the conditions under which alone attributes can be united in representation, or it may contain such attributes as mutually exclude one another. Thus, inasmuch as unity of representation is only possible under the condition

T

of limitation by difference, because the thing represented must be known as an actual object, and not as the universe of all possible objects, it follows that the indefinite ideas corresponding to the terms Thing, Existence, Being in general, are not conceivable, as having no distinctive characteristic. They may be elements of the conceivable; that is to say, they may become conceivable when combined with and determined by other attributes; but so long as they are given as isolated, and therefore as unconditioned, they are inconceivable. The logical rule here violated is the Law of Identity, which requires that every object should be conceived as itself, and as distinguished from every thing else. Here the supposed Concept contains too little. On the other hand, if the given attributes are incompatible with each other, the rule violated is the Law of Contradiction, which requires that two contradictory attributes should not be united in the same object. Here the supposed Concept contains too much. The third law of thought, that of Excluded Middle, may also be violated in relation to the same process, if we attempt to conceive an object of which neither of two contradictory attributes is predicable. Here again, the supposed Concept contains too little.

But it is obvious that these three laws cannot all be equally violated in a pretended act of Judgment or of Reasoning. In Judgment, the concepts are already given; and nothing remains to be done, but to connect them together by an affirmative or negative copula. Here there is no room for a deficiency of attributes; which would affect the conceivability of the terms themselves, not the possibility of their union in a judgment. The only logical fallacy possible must consist in uniting notions which are essentially distinct, or in separating such as are essentially the same. In Reasoning, again, the truth of the premises and the conceivability of the terms, are not examined, but assumed; and the only possible logical fault must consist in drawing a conclusion incompatible with the premises themselves, or with something which they imply. In these two cases, the only possible instances of inconceivability must arise from a direct or indirect Contradiction.

A Fallacy, according to Aristotle, is a reasoning which, either in matter or form or both, appears to be that which it is not[c]. Extending this definition from the process of reasoning to that of thought in general, we may regard any thought as fallacious, which, in form or matter, has an apparent but not a real validity; and a Logical or Formal Fallacy is one which exhibits an apparent but not a real conformity to the Laws of Thought. An apparent thought may thus be formally fallacious in two ways; either generally, because it is not a thought at all ; or specially, because it is not the kind of thought which it professes to be. For the elements of a judgment may be perfectly legitimate as objects of conception, but self-destructive when united together as parts of a judgment; and the premises and conclusion of a syllogism may be valid, even all together, as independent judgments, yet involve a concealed contradiction when placed in the relation of antecedents and consequent in an act of reasoning. Thus, if it be argued " All A is B, C is not A, therefore C is not B," it is obvious that the three statements, viewed merely as judgments, may be all true together. But when we view them as parts of a syllogism, we assert that C is not B, *because it is not A;* in other words, that nothing can be B which is not A, or that every B must be A: Whereas the premise, in stating that all A is B, leaves it open as at least a pos-

[c] *Topics,* i. 1. 3. 'Εριστικὸs δ' ἐστὶ συλλογισμὸs ὁ ἐκ φαινομένων ἐνδόξων, μὴ ὄντων δέ, καὶ ὁ ἐξ ἐνδόξων ἢ φαινομένων ἐνδόξων φαινόμενος. See also *Soph. Elench.* c. 2.

sible truth that some B is not A. Hence the same belief is regarded as possible and impossible at the same time; and thus the conclusion, though not directly at variance with what the premise *asserts*, cannot be drawn consistently with what it *permits*. Hence these and cognate forms of reasoning are classed in the Table as violating the Law of Contradiction *indirectly;* and the conclusion is noted as formally invalid, though materially it may be either true or false. Thus the whole process may be valid as a series of judgments, but not as a reasoning; and the thought, therefore, is not the kind of thought which it professes to be. On the other hand, if a conclusion is drawn opposed to that which the laws of thought require, the conclusion is neither materially nor formally possible; and the supposed reasoning is in reality no thought at all. Thus we may, verbally at least, argue, " All A is B, C is A, therefore C is not B ;" which requires us to conceive C as being at the same time B and not B. Here the Law of Contradiction is violated *directly*. The relation of logical fallacies to this law will be seen much more clearly, if, in accordance with the system of Sir William Hamilton, we assign to the predicate as well as to the subject of every proposition an expressed mark of quantity.

To attempt a complete enumeration of Material Fallacies would be an endless as well as a profitless task. Under the head of Reasoning, it has been thought sufficient to arrange in their proper places the members of the usually received list. The arrangement has been made according to the instances given by Aldrich and other modern Logicians, as being most familiar to the majority of readers. These, however, occasionally differ in points of detail from those which are found in the original text of Aristotle. The discrepancy is of little consequence; as the notes to the corresponding portion

of Aldrich's text will in most instances enable the reader
to compare and classify Aristotle's examples for himself.
Indeed, Aristotle himself confesses that the arrangement
is in some degree arbitrary, and that the same Fallacy
will admit of being classed under different heads.

As regards Material Fallacies of Conception and Judgment, I have contented myself with indicating, in the most
general way, the sources of Obscurity and Indistinctness
in Concepts, and of Falsity in Judgments. A concept is
obscure, when it cannot be distinguished as a whole from
certain others : it is *indistinct*, when its several component parts cannot be distinguished from each other[d].
The obscurity or indistinctness of a concept may obviously arise, either from accidental circumstances, such
as the want of a sufficient observation of the object on
the part of this or that individual thinker, or from
circumstances essential to the concept itself, such as the
want of those conditions which experience shews us to
be indispensable to all clear or distinct thinking. Under
this head may be classed the notions, so familiar to all
students of Logic, of *summum genus* and *infima species*.
Both of these terms represent limits to which we may
indefinitely approximate in thought, but which we never
actually attain. Neither of them can be regarded as
logically inconceivable ; for, under different conditions
of the matter of our thought, both might be practically
apprehended. But, in actual thinking, it becomes manifest
that our several concepts present in all cases such an
affinity or homogeneity one with another, that it is impossible, on the one hand, to fix on two cognate genera
which possess no common element to form a higher
genus, (until we arrive at abstractions too empty to be

---

[d] This distinction is due to Leibnitz. See his *Meditationes de Cognitione,
Veritate et Ideis. Opera*, ed. Erdmann, p. 79.

conceived at all,) or, on the other hand, to arrest the process of subdivision at any limited number of attributes, as the greatest number that can possibly be united in one concept*.

Thus the notion of a logical highest genus, that is, of a concept so simple as to be incapable of further analysis, is essentially obscure; for, in actual thought, we find that, so long as there is limitation and difference, there is also community, and, therefore, a possibility of further analysis'. Again, the notion of a logical lowest

---

* The Highest Genus and Lowest Species of Logic must not be confounded with the same terms as applicable to this or that branch of natural science. The Highest Genus in any special science is the general class, comprehending all the objects whose properties that science investigates: the different Lowest Species are the classes at which that special investigation terminates. In Geometry, for example, under the *summum genus* of magnitudes in space, we find three coordinate *infimæ species* of triangles, the equilateral, the isosceles, and the scalene. The Geometrical properties of the figures are not affected by further subdivision. But the Logician, as such, knows nothing of Geometrical limitations. To him the highest genus and lowest species are limits of the possibility of thought; the former denoting a notion so simple as to admit of no further subtraction, the latter, a notion so complex as to admit of no further addition. In thought, the notion of an equilateral triangle whose sides are three feet long is a subordinate species to that of an equilateral triangle in general.

' It is not easy to draw the line between the materially and the formally inconceivable. Being in general (*Ens*), and such like abstractions, may be regarded as formally inconceivable, as having no contents. But these abstractions are not necessarily identical with the notion of a highest genus;—indeed, the majority of Logicians have placed the *summa genera* in the Categories, of which *Ens* and the other transcendents were regarded as predicable *equivocally*, or *analogously*, but not *univocally*. But the Categories, again, are practically inconceivable *per se*; for a substance is only known by its attributes, and an attribute as existing in a substance. But it is at least supposable that, under other conditions of experience, we might arrive at notions sufficiently definite to be conceivable, yet so diverse as not to admit of classification under a higher genus; and this is virtually admitted by Kant, who, notwithstanding, regards the laws of homogeneity, specification, and continuity as logical principles of the reason. I prefer to consider them as empirical, though perhaps indicating psychological conditions of experience. Thus viewed, they are not, properly

species, or a combination of all conceivable compatible attributes, is essentially indistinct; for the number of such attributes is indefinite, and, to go through them in thought, enumerating and distinguishing one from another, would require an infinite grasp of mind, and an infinite length of time, for its accomplishment.

Another class of notions may be specified as materially inconceivable; those, namely, which, though presenting no logical contradiction, contain attributes materially heterogeneous, and thus incompatible with each other. Such combinations of attributes as *circular virtue*, or *coloured thought*, are of this character. "Black spirits and white, red spirits and grey," are only conceivable by investing the spirits with a body for the occasion, and not by connecting the idea of colour with that of spirituality. To the same class belong all combinations of attributes inconsistent with the *a priori* conditions of intuition; such as a *bilinear figure;* which, though not logically contradictory, are mathematically inconceivable. These must be carefully distinguished from those notions which, though empirically known to be unreal, are yet perfectly consistent as thoughts; such as the conception of a centaur, or of a golden mountain. In respect of these last, Logic recognises no distinction between the real and the unreal. An opposite class of notions materially inconceivable, are those which are defective, as separating attributes whose union is testified by experience to be indispensable to conception. Thus, inasmuch as we know by experience, that no surface can be conceived, without being of some colour, and that no colour can be conceived, except on some surface, the conceptions of an uncoloured surface or an unextended colour, though they present no logical contradiction,

speaking, laws of thought; and thus, as far as Logic is concerned, they belong to the matter of thought, not to the form.

must be classed as essentially, though materially, inconceivable [s].

As regards the truth or falsehood of Judgments, Logic
properly takes cognisance of Formal Truth or Falsehood
only, which depends on the agreement or disagreement
of a thought with its own laws. Material Truth, which
is sometimes defined as consisting in the agreement of
the thought with its object, might be more correctly
explained as consisting in the agreement of the object
as represented in thought with the object as presented
in intuition; for the object exists, relatively to us,
only as given in some form of intuition. But, however
it may be defined, it is manifest that no general law
or criterion of material truth and falsehood can be
given; for the essence of such truth consists in its
adapting itself in every case to the diversities of this or
that special presentation [h]. To enumerate in detail all
the various sources of material falsehood would be
impossible; I have contented myself with referring to
the three general heads of Mathematical, Metaphysical,
and Physical Judgments; which appear to possess essentially different degrees of certainty or impossibility.
These propositions will admit of a different classification,
according to the theories held by different writers as to
their origin. By some, mathematical judgments will be
classed with physical, as due solely to experience: by
others, they will be merged in logical truth or falsehood,
as owing their evidence to laws of thought. Metaphysical
judgments, again, will be considered by some as purely
empirical: while by others they will be referred to

[s] The error of those philosophers who maintain that colour can be
conceived without extension is exposed by Sir W. Hamilton, *Reid's Works*,
p. 143.

[h] That a general criterion of material truth is not only impossible but
self-contradictory, is shewn by Kant, *Logik, Einleitung*, VII.

certain fundamental laws of human belief, originating in the constitution of the mind itself. Into the various controversies connected with these questions it would be irrelevant now to enter. The reasons for the classification which I have adopted will be found given at length in a separate work, to which for the present I must content myself with referring[1].

[1] See *Prolegomena Logica*, chap. iv. and v.

:IES.

Of Reasoning.

In the Matter.

In the Language.
(Fallaciæ in Dictione.)

s)

Conception given as
unconditioned. (Law
of Identity,) e. g.
Being in general.

Of a Term.

Of a Proposition.
(Amphibolia.)

irectly.
iction logi-
dmissible, as
Direcicting what
(by Statnise permits.
e. g. a surfonsequeuce
white and n materially
but is not
Concepnally.)
in

In itself.
(Æquivocatio,
Accentus,
Figura
Dictionis.)

In its relation.
(Compositio,
Divisio.)

Undistributed
Middle.

Attributes heterogeneous
e. g. circular virtue,
or bilinear figure.

se false.
uding
ausa pro
usa,
rium
ationum.)

Premise doubtful.
(including
Petitio Principii.)

Conclusion irrelevant.
(Ignoratio Elenchi.)

Ju

In the Language.
Judgments ambiguous.

Directl
Contradiction
e. g. black is n

In a single Term.
(Æquivocatio.)

In the whole
Proposition.
(Amphibolia.)

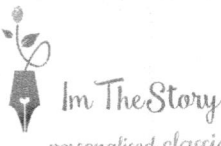

CPSIA information can be obtained
at www.ICGtesting.com
Printed in the USA
BVHW081819220819
556561BV00020B/4446/P